Birth
Childhood
Adolescence
Manhood
. . . AND THEN

A Strawberry Hill Book

SCENCE

The Dangerous Years

Fred McMorrow

Published with Quadrangle / The New York Times Book Co.

A Strawberry Hill Book
Published with Quadrangle/The New York Times Book Co.

Inquiries may be directed to Strawberry Hill Publishing Co., Inc.,
230 Park Avenue, New York, N.Y. 10017, or to Quadrangle/The
New York Times Book Co., 10 East 53rd Street, New York, N.Y. 10022

Library of Congress Cataloging in Publication Data

McMorrow, Fred, 1925–
        Midolescence: the dangerous years.

        "A Strawberry Hill book."
1. Men—Psychology.   2. Middle age—Psychological
aspects.   3. Climacteric.   I. Title.
BF692.5.M32   155.6   74-78999
ISBN 0-8129-0481-8

For R
his A
and
my own E

Acknowledgments

The Clarendon Press, Oxford for permission to quote from Book I "The Republic" from *The Dialogues of Plato* trans. by Benjamin Jowett, 84th ed. 1953, Vol, II;

Doubleday & Company, Inc. for permission to quote from *A Stillness At Appomattox* by Bruce Catton. Copyright 1953 by Bruce Catton, and for permission to quote from *The Moon and Sixpence* by W. Somerset Maugham. Copyright 1919 by W. Somerset Maugham;

Farrar, Straus & Giroux, Inc. for permission to quote from *The Revolt of the Middle-Aged Man* by Dr. Edmund Bergler, a Hill & Wang title, (c) 1954 by Edmund Bergler;

Barbara Fried, the author, and her agent, James Brown Associates, Inc. for permission to quote from *The Middle-Age Crisis,* (c) 1967 by Barbara Fried;

Harcourt Brace Jovanovich, Inc. for permission to quote from Babbitt by Sinclair Lewis.

Harvard University Press for permission to use a quotation from Ben Shahn that appears in *The Shape of Content* (c) 1957 by Harvard University Press;

Herald Press for permission to quote from *Middle Age: A Test of Time* by Chester Raber, (c) 1966 by Herald Press;

Holt, Rinehart and Winston, Inc. for permission to quote from *Steppenwolf* by Hermann Hesse, translated by Basil Creighton. Copyright 1929 (c) 1957 by Holt, Rinehart and Winston, Inc.;

Liveright Publishing Corp. for permission to quote from The Broken Tower, which appears in *The Collected Poems and Selected Letters and Prose of Hart Crane* by Hart Crane. Copyright (c) 1933, 1958, 1966 by Liveright Publishing Corp.;

McGraw-Hill Book Company and Catherine J. Jackson for permission to quote from *The Years After Fifty* by Dr. Wingate M. Johnson, (c) 1947 by McGraw-Hill Book Company;

New American Library, Inc. for permission to quote from Mark Schorer's afterward to NAL's edition of Babbitt.

Random House, Inc., for permission to quote from The Random House Dictionary of the English Language, (c) 1966 by Random House, Inc., and for permission to use the poem "It Will Soon Be Too Late," translated by Francis Wrangham, from the *Complete Works of Horace,* edited by Casper J. Kraemer, Jr.

Charles Scribner's Sons and Jonathan Cape, Ltd., and the executors of the Hemingway estate for permission to quote from "The Snows of Kilimanjaro," by Ernest Hemingway, which appears in *The Fifth Column* and *The First Forty-Nine Stories,* (c) 1938 by Ernest Hemingway.

Simon & Schuster, Inc. for permission to quote from *Sex and the Mature Man* by Louise P. Saxe, M.D., and Noel Gerson, copyright 1964 by Simon & Schuster, Inc.;

The New York Times for permission to quote from Merle Miller's article "What It Means to Be a Homosexual," (c) 1971 by The New York Times Co., and from an article by Joan Cook that appeared on April 5, 1971, (c) 1971 by The New York Times Co.;

The Viking Press, Inc. for permission to quote from *Herzog* by Saul Bellow, copyright (c) 1961, 1963, 1964 by Saul Bellow.

Contents

Publisher's Preface

This book is not a sociological or psychoanalytical study. It makes no pretensions. There is nothing scientific about it in conception or execution. You will find no verifiable theories or concepts in the pages that follow, no surveys or statistics to back up such theories or concepts. The author did not interview four thousand men and women, or four hundred, or even forty; nor did he select subjects at random or try to come up with what statisticians and poll-takers might call a significant or random sampling. He spoke to a small number of men and women—people he knew or whose names had been suggested to him because their lives seemed to illustrate an idea.

That idea—that the middle years of men's lives are always troublesome, often turbulent and sometimes tumultuous—was born, not out of a spirit of detached scientific inquiry, but out of the very personal observations of an editor. Among those he knew or knew about, and in news stories, plays and novels, there was more than a sprinkling of men whose lives changed abruptly with the coming of middle age; there was a deluge of them. Men with histories of long and outwardly stable and happy marriages who were divorced or separated; men with histories of long and apparently satisfying careers who were no longer producing, who were in trouble on the job, or who had struck off in new directions; men whose lives had changed so drastically that they seemed hardly recognizable.

To translate the idea into a book, the editor did not turn to an author with scientific credentials or to someone trained to do research, accumulate mountains of data and abstract from those data a cohesive and intellectually satisfying thesis. He turned, rather, to a writer, to a man trained to observe, and finely tuned in to, the nuances of human words and actions. He turned to a man who would fly in the face of formal methodology: who would start with living, feeling men and women—and end with them, as well. The abstract man, the average man, Mr. Everyman (or, in this case, Mr. Midolescence) makes only a brief appearance at the start of the book. Then he disappears, and his place is taken by real people.

The publishers, the editor and the author can be accused of starting with a premise and then selecting cases to fit that premise, conveniently ignoring those that did not fit, We concede that there is justification in such a charge. But this is not, as we said, a scientific, objective book; it is, as we said, a book based on personal observations. And if, within the limited world of two people—an editor and an author—there are so many men whose lives seem to fit a pattern, then surely in the far wider world there are that many more. It is too mind-stretching to ascribe it to coincidence.

You will find, as the author did, much that is depressing in the lives, or the portions of lives, that are sketched in these pages, a great dollop of what could dramatically be called tragedy. But you will also find, again as he did, that the picture is not all black. Out of some of the ruined and nearly ruined marriages and careers arose new marriages and new careers. New lives. And some of those who changed directions in the middle years did so virtually without trauma, rounding the curve of life gently rather than skidding wildly.

Midolescence is a coined word, but a very real problem. If this book helps, in whatever small way, to help make men and women aware of that problem, if it helps them to deal with it, if it does no more than make a man realize he is not alone in this troubled time of life, it will have served its purpose.

Author's Preface

A human being's time is one of the more precious things he can give to another human being. For busy men and women, time is money. How does it go? If you want something done in a hurry, go to a busy man? Well, I went to several very busy men and women for insights into the male middle-age crisis, and they gave me their time for nothing. For those gifts of valuable time, my thanks to Dr. Joseph Wortis, Dr. Paul Metzger, Dr. Ernest van den Haag, Edmund L. Van Deusen, Dr. Lawrence J. Hatterer, Merle Miller and Dr. William Lee Curry; thanks, too, to the (anonymous) labor-relations lawyer and the (anonymous) executive and business consultant I interviewed, and to the judge who, while I have not used his interview, shed so much light for me on how middle age affects men in professions like his.

Special thanks to Mr. Van Deusen, the six other (anonymous) men and the seven (anonymous) women who opened their private lives for my inspection in the chapters that are the heart of this book, "The Men Speak" and "The Women Speak." A word about the transcripts of those tape-recorded interviews with The Men and The Women: They run long. All have been editorially pruned somewhat; if they ran to their original lengths, "Midolescence: The Dangerous Years" would resemble "Manhattan: Yellow Pages."

xiii

There is essence to each of those interviews, and each could still be trimmed. But then what would we have? A man had affairs with two women and lost his job; a man had a peculiar non-sexual relationship with a woman and it nearly capsized his marriage and did direct him into a new career; an opera singer gave up the stage for the world of business; a clinical psychologist became an actor; a young woman living with an older man has a marriage that is more a marriage than most that are protected by licenses. See what I mean? Facts, yes, but just that, facts without flesh.

That these people did these things (and many other things, as you will see) is not what is most important about them. The most important aspects of their lives are not the *who, what, where, when,* but the *how* and the *why*; to develop and resolve those issues takes a little time. And space.

There are some marvelously warm and witty people in those two chapters ("Er," says a girl to a man who has just slipped a bill into her bodice, "I only do it for nothing"), and there are some rather unpleasant creatures too, whose quotes should be read in context, in fairness to them.

I prefer to think of these interviews not so much as interviews but as conversations. Normal conversation touching on deeply personal subjects does not get to the heart of the matter one, two, three, because humans are not like that. They have to talk things out to arrive at conclusions, or truths. That is the spirit of those interviews and indeed the spirit of this whole book. You may find some of these conversations even tedious; I certainly hope you do not. Give them a chance and you may find that in looking into those fourteen lives, as I did, the book was well worth the candle.

Fred McMorrow
Baldwin, N.Y.
Aug. 29, 1974

Midolescence:
The Dangerous Years

I.

Introduction

The Man in the Mirror

It is 7:55 A.M. The buzz of the alarm clock invades George's dream and as at the touch of a match his dream world goes up in a puff of reality. It is time to face another day. George's eyelids flutter and open. He rolls over to shut off the persistent buzzing. He swings his legs over the edge of the bed and sits up. His glasses are on the night table. He puts them on, blinks, takes stock of things. Outside the bedroom window the leaves of the big maple are dancing a solemn minuet in a slow spring breeze. On the 11 o'clock news the night before, the forecast had been for possible showers, but now the sky is clear. George will take a chance and go to the city without his raincoat or umbrella.

The house is still, save for the radio playing softly downstairs. Norma is in the kitchen dawdling over coffee and a cigarette and the morning paper and listening to an early-morning disc jockey. Norma always arises an hour before her husband does, to get the two boys up and pack them off to school.

George gets to his feet and shuffles into the bathroom where a familiar sight greets him. The boys have left the bathroom in a bit of a mess. They always do; they always have; they always will. It's not a federal case, but it is the kind of little thing that has lately been

3

irritating George. "God damn it," he announces to the world as he picks up after his sons, "I like a little order in my life!"

"What's that, dear?" Norma calls.

What, indeed. A trifle. A nothing. "Nothing," George calls back. He cleans the sink and turns the faucets on and waits for it to fill. Kids. Christ! Wait till they grow up and become parents, have businesses to go to, become responsible for others; then they'll know—he has looked up and seen the man in the mirror. In the early morning this is always a bit of a shock, because every day that man seems to look a bit older, a bit more worn, than he did the morning before. The ghost of a sour smile lifts the corners of George's mouth. Wait till his sons grow up? How does he know he's going to live that long?

He cleans his razor, which the older boy has just used, and changes the blade. A memory stirs: Last year, his oldest, their daughter, would shave her legs with her father's razor and leave it on the floor near the bathtub; she would also take the deodorant out of the bathroom and squirrel it away in her room. This doesn't happen any more, because the girl has run off to California with a boy and her family has had no word from her for months; for all they know, she is living in a tree. The thought of her almost makes George cry. Forget it! There are things to do, responsibilities to face. George lathers his face. The mentholated cream is soothing. Shaving is one of the last private rituals left to man.

He completes the shave, rinses his face, picks up the razor once more to trim the fringe of his modish sideburns, which he grew only recently (and which came in gray; after all, George is 46 years old). The man in the mirror, the drugged look of sleep gone, looks a little better now, but not much. My friend, George says, I have been looking at you in mirrors for four long decades, and what have you got to show me? Obeying the latest of a series of wild, out-of-character, outrageous impulses, he touches his throat with the razor, presses the blade, speculatively, against the gently throbbing lifeline. The impulse, like a wisp of wind, passes as quickly as it came. George cleans the razor and puts it away, uses the deodorant, brushes his teeth for more than a full minute, rinses his mouth with a strong but pleasant-tasting, pleasant-smelling astringent. There are people in his life whom he does not want to offend. Yes, George has a girl.

In the bedroom, dressing, George tries to exorcise the vague sense of unease, uncertainty, the hint of dread that he felt looking at himself in the bathroom mirror. All right: Maybe he is not a young man but, dammit, he certainly isn't an old one yet. Not yet. He has a good home here. His wife has been a good mother. His children are probably a lot healthier than he was at their age and, who knows? In adult life they may turn out a lot brighter and more successful than their father. This should be a comforting thought but, as it always does, it gives him a tiny twinge of—yes, it has no other name. Jealousy. And yet he loves his children.

George loves his wife, too. No matter what happens, he will never stop loving her. George knows that, his wife knows that, and the girl in the office who has been his mistress for the last eight months knows that, too, because George has told her. As for work itself, George has a good, responsible job, not at the top of his profession, but by no means at the bottom, either. George is a middle-management man. All right, he's not at the top, but at his age how many men are? If he isn't doing what he really wanted to do in life or he hasn't achieved all he *thought* he was going to achieve in life, how many men have? George marches these thoughts through his head. This is what he calls positive thinking. It helps, a bit.

As he sits on the bed and pulls on his socks, his eye catches his attaché case, opened slightly, with a sheaf of office papers between its black jaws. All it needs is eyes and it would be the square head of some monstrous dog and the papers would be a stick the brute wants him to throw, over and over and over in some kind of hellish game. The papers are not play. They are work, homework George should have done overnight. No time now, and there won't be enough time on the train. Now he'll have to take care of it on the job, and it will add to the tedium of the day. Hell and damnation.

There was a time when George loved that job, when it seemed to be its own reward, when he was doing it for something more than money. Now that job seems to be going stale, insipid, like a drink left in the sun, turning dull, even exasperating, where it was once challenging and exciting. Little chores, like the homework he has neglected, now seem more like ordeals than matters you take care of with your left hand, as he once did. They annoy him all out of proportion to their real dimensions, their real importance, just as other things, like the mess the boys leave in the bathroom, annoy him.

Nothing at George's place of work has changed very much in the long years of his tenure there, but George is beginning to see the office in a different and disturbing light. He has been looking at the young men there, many of whom he trained and brought up in the business, not with a sense of pride in their accomplishments but with a sense of dread that they will some day take his job away from him. He has been looking at the young women in the office not simply as fellow workers but more as women, desirable women, and has, indeed, taken one as a mistress. Once that office was a second home; somehow, God knows how, the permanence of it, his identification with it, his feeling of safety there—all these things seem to be fading. He answers these misgivings with more positive thinking: They've kept him in that job all these years, haven't they? If they didn't like the way he did the job, they'd tell him so, wouldn't they? Thus he tries to down his deadliest fear: Some day they will tell him that.

All right. Let's go. George selects a tie for the day, a Countess Mara tie. He didn't buy it or pick it out, but he told his wife he did when she asked. She was mildly curious about it. Norma has lately been mildly curious about a lot of things. About George's new, stylish sport jackets, his butt-hugging bell-bottomed trousers, his whole new, youthful wardrobe. "Honey," George tells Norma, "it's a young world, whether we like it or not."

Has he forgotten anything? Oh, God, yes. The valium. Six years ago, at work, George received from out of nowhere a stunning blow in the chest; his heart thumped, seemed to stall, then began to race. They took him to a hospital. He spent ten days there undergoing tests before he was told that it wasn't a heart attack, that he was just carrying too much tissue and had to lose about fifteen pounds. He did so, and his internist prescribed three five-grain pills of valium a day, to keep his motor quiet. "Take more if you need them, take less if possible; use them as a brake," the doctor said. There have been no subsequent attacks, and George has unerringly gained back most of the poundage, but he never goes anywhere without the pills. He has never forgotten the terror of that moment at the office. He puts the vial in his shirt pocket, snaps the attaché case shut, squares his shoulders and goes downstairs.

"I can fix you some eggs if you've got time," Norma says.

"Just coffee," George says. "One egg has . . ."

"Yes, I know, seventy calories," Norma says. She pours him a cup of coffee, black. "Will you be late again tonight?"

"I don't know. I'll call you." George drinks slowly.

"I really wish you would, if you're going to be late," Norma says.

No answer. She has something difficult to say; she is groping for the right words. There aren't any. "I don't . . ." she trails off.

George drains the cup and puts it on the sink. "You don't what?"

There is a freshet of tears; the voice is trembling; "I don't *see* you any more, that's all!" Quickly, George takes her in his arms. He is almost frightened by how tightly she holds him. How much does she know? Does she suspect?

She has regained control of herself and she is looking straight at him. "George, you haven't got another girl, have you?" she says. "Have you?"

"Come *on*," George says. "Whatever gave you that idea?"

"Well, last night I was in bed ready for you and you just went to sleep."

"Oh, honey," he says, "hell, I'll make that up to you tonight. Why didn't you say something?"

"God damn it, do I have to *say* something?"

All this is a bit of a challenge, but George handles it. By the time he is ready to leave Norma is smiling. He'll be home on time, and when the children are asleep, they'll make love. It's a date. He kisses Norma goodbye and goes to his car. They have two.

On the way to the station, he congratulates himself for having been able to lie. He never thought he could. And he begins casting about in his mind for ways to explain to his mistress why he will not be able to see her that evening, and the absurdity of this comes to him in a double take. He has nothing to *explain* to the mistress; all he has to do is break their date. And he really has to do that; if he has sex with her and is then unable to perform with his wife, her suspicions will approach certainty.

George cannot explain to his wife that it is a fear of impotence on his part that eroded their sex life and sent him to another woman's bed, because George does not know that. Neither does he know that in having an affair, he is 1) trying to relive, recapture his youth, which has gone glimmering into his past 2) prove that he is still a man and can still satisfy a woman. George does know, however, that he is doing *something* wrong, and it bothers him. In the car, he seeks a distraction. He turns the radio on and gets the same disc jockey that Norma is listening to at home.

"And now, an Oldie," the disc jockey says. "Remember this?" It is Peggy Lee, singing "Is That All There Is?" George has stopped for a red light. He glances at the man in the next car as he listens to the touching melody and lyrics, so evocative of a circus parade fading into the distance, into the past. The man in the next car has gray sideburns and is wearing a tie that looks much like George's. George has the momentary illusion that he is looking at himself, in that other car. A feeling of deepest sadness sweeps over him. Is that —is *this* all there is to him? Is *this* as far as he goes in life? And isn't there anything he can do about it?

No such thoughts, no such fears, no such dread, no such despair ever afflicted one man all at once, but few men pass through middle age without encountering some of these things. There is no such person as George; he is a compositite of only some of the problems and challenges facing a man in this bridging, uncertain time of life. He is a midolescent, and he is suffering from midolescence. You will not find that word in your dictionary. Other writers on this subject call it middlescence; my coinage contains the O because the behavior, the boat-rocking impulses, the aberrations, the inward-turning, unreasoning and apparently unreasonable things that middle-aged men do are so much like what adolescents do when they seek to cope with their problems. In some cases in this book you will find midolescent men virtually trying to repeat their adolescence, whether that earlier stage of life was happy or miserable.

Adolescence and midolescence are both periods of physical and psychological transition. A boy is moving into the long stretch of young manhood; a mature man is in the seventh-inning stretch of his life, an often-troubled pause before he moves from the ascendant time of life to the long plateau of middle age. Midolescence is the middle-age crisis, that time when a man recognizes and/or rejects the truth about himself, that for better or worse, he has reached the point at which he has achieved, if not all he thought he *would* achieve in life, just about all he ever *will*. For decades he has been conditioned to living in a steady ascent; every day led to a tomorrow, every year to a Happy New Year, let's *make* it this time, let's do *better*. Now he has reached a leveling-off, the end of youth, which some mistake for the beginning of old age and the approach to death.

Who is middle-aged? What is middle age? It is all things to all men. Different cultures and, in our own culture, different sectors of our society have different ideas about when "middle age" starts. In terms of work, it begins when physical decline becomes apparent, when job-performance begins to slacken, when an employer who has for decades let George do it begins to doubt that George can do it any longer. Then there are the extremely specialized fields for which definitions of middle age offer no parallels with other fields. When an athlete reaches his late twenties his muscle tone slackens, his wind gets shorter and his reaction-time longer. He is then faced with a change of career, but it has virtually nothing to do with midolescence.

An unskilled laborer may not experience a decline in physical power until his fifties or sixties; on the New York docks there is a longshoreman called Fast Harry who can still sling a hook with the best of them at seventy-seven. A member of the white-collar, middle or upper middle class, who works with his head, may face the middle-age crisis anywhere between his late thirties and mid-fifties.

It has been said that the middle-age crisis has very little effect on the very rich or the very poor, who do not rise above or all fall below their environments because neither has anything to gain or anything to lose. This book is about the man in the middle of society. He has no great inheritance, like the very rich; his assets are what he has acquired by himself. He does have ambitions, which the very poor, the very limited, do not dream of. His success, his survival in our society, are measured by its sternest standard. His next achievement had better be at least as good as his last.

The middle-aged men in this study have kicked over traces, have risked everything they have accomplished in abrupt changes of career, have lost jobs, have deserted their wives' beds temporarily or permanently for those of other women (not as a rule, but to a heavy degree, younger women) who seemed to fulfill needs long ago forgotten; have gone as far in their inverted, unsolaced despair as to consider suicide. And this report will cover some who *did* kill themselves. The crisis, or the victims' uncounseled response to it, has destroyed some and is destroying others at its leisure right now. In the live, taped interviews in this book, you will find the survivors and those who are trying to survive. In those interviews you will also find creatures of apparent perfect equilibrium, whose surface calm runs deep, people who will seem to have suffered no great crisis at all, but who did make changes in their lives—and for the better.

The damaging effects of midolescence go beyond the individual. A man cannot feel fear unless he has something to lose; these men, in most cases, are persons not only of some achievement but of some position in society and business. Their aberrations as heads of families sunder the bonds of family; their aberrations as men in management positions threaten the stability of their businesses and the professional, workaday morale of the people they work with and the people who work under them.

The midolescent is not necessarily less capable at his work. "Rarely," says a participant in this study whose business is finding new roles in business for men who feel they are at dead ends, "is a man in trouble on his job because he doesn't have the *ability* to handle it." But it is at this stage of life when inner problems overcome inhibitions and affect a man's work, make him short-tempered with subordinates and sometimes even insubordinate to superiors, make him turn inward, make him neglect the homework he should be doing to keep up with the pace of technological advancement in an age in which we have gone from the horse collar to the moon in less than 100 years. "The job hadn't changed," says Barbara Fried in her book, *The Middle-Age Crisis,* speaking of an individual midolescent's problems; "He had."

The implications for a man's career are obvious. His company is not a charitable institution. When his employer is faced with the choice of keeping George, who can no longer do it, and a younger man to whom the most modern techniques are the A.B.C's of his recent education, that employer's decision will be dictated by economics, not humanity. That more knowledgeable younger man can be hired for $10,000 a year and it is costing the company $25,000 a year to keep George in groceries. The second chapter of this book examines the way midolescents react to this greatest of challenges to their survival and the way business reacts to them.

The Youth-Exploitation Explosion
This is the time, says a doctor interviewed in the next chapter, when a man's son is telling him he's "full of shit," when his daughter is "marrying the black drummer"; whatever such pressures have been earlier in life, there are more of them in the forty-to-fifty-five bracket. For an American middle-aged man, this is a time of confrontation with a society that adores, exalts and exploits youth. The message is everywhere. Only the dead cannot receive it. Whoever thought up "the Pepsi Generation" did not have to say it was a younger generation. In one quite literal sense, a middle-aged man may find that he no longer fits into the scheme of things; if he has put on his perma-

nent weight and he is over two hundred pounds he finds it difficult and expensive to buy clothing or shirts, because most wearing apparel comes in slim, tight sizes, for slim, youthful, agile bodies. If a play, a book, a movie, a television show is about a middle-aged man, it is almost always a tragedy, or the aging protagonist is a buffoon. "The Odd Couple" are not boys. "Last Tango in Paris" is not about Paris in the spring of a lifetime. *Herzog* is an odyssey through the most forbidding country of middle age.

There is also the confrontation—indeed, the collision—of the midolescent's standards, traditions and ideals with what to him seem the non-standards, non-traditions, anti-ideals of the young. Maybe the midolescent didn't totally agree with the values imposed on him by his parents, but he bought them nevertheless. His children do not buy *his* values. Marriage is no longer a desirable state; what he might consider Free Love is no longer a dishonorable state. Whereas, twenty or thirty years ago, when you heard a friend who was living with a girl remark, "I've got all of the conveniences of marriage with none of the inconveniences," you remarked, "Famous last words," and you were right: Sooner or later those two married. When the young make such declarations today, they are quite serious. It is heartbreaking, alienating for a middle-aged man to see his son or daughter casually reject the institution once so mandatory, once so compellingly permanent, once the only decent thing to do when you loved someone. (There is also, and often, more than just a touch of envy at work here.)

Midolescence and Menopause

There is a generous supply in any library of reading material on what happens to women in middle age, in menopause. This is a definite, physical, operative change of life. A woman gradually stops producing the hormones necessary to create new life. There is no doubt about this and no debate about it in medical circles. But the question of whether there is indeed a *male* climacteric (Greek, "round of the ladder") is a matter of lively and sometimes angry medical controversy. Some behavioral therapists, for instance, reject the concept as "demonology," in that it gives a name to something that does not exist, in that it lumps, groups, generalizes the mass of middle-aged men, each of whom is the product of individual dynamics.

What happens to a woman in menopause is something happening mostly in her body, while what happens to a man in midolescence is something happening almost exclusively in his head. "Medically speaking," says the late Dr. Edmund Bergler in *The Revolt of the Middle-Aged Man*, a study done in 1953, *"not a shred of proof has been offered that there is a biological basis for man's middle-age revolt."* The italics are Dr. Bergler's.

Dr. Edgar F. Berman, a retired Maryland surgeon who stirred a women's lib hornet's nest in 1970 by implying that women are unfit for such roles as the Presidency because of their instabilities during menstruation and menopause, has this to say in an article in the New York Times: "I, personally, from my own experience, don't think that there is a male climacteric. Both sexes go through the same emotional stage of aging, but over and beyond that, women have hormonal changes that precede another emotional state. Give a woman estrogen [the birth hormone] and the 'hot flashes' clear up; no amount of testosterone [the maleness hormone] produces a similar effect on men."

But then, in that same article: "These hormones," Clifford B. Hicks, the science writer, asserted in "Generation in the Middle," a study he did for Blue Cross, "affect not only the energy level but also the sleep patterns, weight, hair growth, coloration and reproductive capacity of an individual. A person in the throes of the climacteric does not even know that something is happening inside *his* [these italics are mine] body, a physical change that is affecting *his* emotions. Yet *he* is plagued with indecision, restlessness, boredom, a 'what's-the-use' outlook and a feeling of being fenced in."

Farther on, you will find medical experts taking all kinds of positions on midolescence. Even those who insist that there is no such thing in the general sense speak of individual cases that seem to form a pattern. George, the Man in the Mirror, has a mistress and he thinks he knows why: he finds her youthful body more erotic, more exciting than his wife's familiar contours. But he is only vaguely aware, if he is aware at all, of the deeper reasons.

Middle-aged men "whose lives are oriented to work," says Dr. Willard Gaylin, a New York-area psychiatrist, in that Times article, "sometimes turn to sexual activity for reassurance. Having gone as high as they can go, they try to find in sex what they can no longer find at the marketplace and, at the same time, blind themselves to the idea of encroaching age."

Women stop producing children after menopause, but they do not stop enjoying sex. There is no medical evidence that a man cannot lead a procreative sex life until he is dead. Yes, it's true, his body gradually produces less and less testosterone, but the supply never totally gives out; yes, the count of live sperm cells in his semen gradually decreases until, at about age seventy, it is approximately a third what it was at thirty-five; yes, as he grows older, it does take him longer to achieve erection and then to ejaculate. But, given a woman whose reproductive system is still in business, even an elderly man's semen is still viable. A South African called Henry Potts and a Pole named Kasper Raynold became fathers at the age of 105. It's said that a Frenchman, Pierre Deformel, fathered children in three centuries, the birth dates being 1699, 1738 and 1801. The virility and sexual longevity of aged men in Georgia is among the Soviet Union's proudest natural resources.

Men's responses to middle age are as varied as the experiences their years have stored up. Some men of thirty behave as though old age were pressing in on them; some men in their sixties seem to retain an aura of youth. Some seem to sail calmly through the seas of time; others run into squalls that threaten to swamp them.

The men whose lives are examined in depth in this book are in their late thirties, their forties, their early fifties, and—in general—midolescence seems to afflict men in that age bracket. There is one exception in the pages that follow, a man of sixty-five, whose midolescent behavior is referred to briefly in an interview with a young woman who is having an affair with him. No question: there *are* exceptions. But it can generally be said that almost all men encounter the crisis of middle age in some form and in some degree. Some of those who turn to sex find themselves on a sure road to the divorce courts; others find that the extra-marital experience makes the marital experience newly exciting; they return to their wives with revived interest and, the wives discover, heightened performance.

Here are summaries of two cases you'll encounter later on in which sex played a leading role in the middle-age crisis.

Mr. A.

He had been married nearly twenty years. He had a good, responsible and demanding job, near the top of his profession. (He is worried, he told me, about being identified professionally. "Shall we say," he says in his interview, "that it's the—'communications field?' ") At home, Mr. and Mrs. A had always led a vigorous and satisfying sex life. When Mr. A entered the danger years of midolescence, in his early forties, there was an unfortunately coincidental event: His wife had been an active, successful business person herself when they met and then, with the children nearly grown, she had just gone back to business, opening a fabrics shop in the suburban community where they lived. She and Mr. A still had sex, but not as often as they once had. She was not a young woman; she would plead exhaustion and tell him she had been on her feet all day and just did not feel like it. Mr. A felt that she was devoting so much time and interest to her new business that she was neglecting him.

Mr. A was as ripe for trouble as he could be, and it found him. She was a girl he had once worked with, fifteen years previously; now she was in a business that did business with his firm. They met, talked over old times, had several dinner dates, and Mr. A soon found himself in the lady's bed. The affair—it was the first time he had strayed—lasted for several months, until the confused and guilt-pressured Mr. A confessed everything to his wife. She was shattered. There was a wrenching scene. But he said he had come home to stay, and in a matter of hours he and his wife were re-consummating their union in bed; each resolved to try to patch things up at home. Mrs. A closed her shop.

Two years later, he suffered a relapse. He had reached a kind of dead end at his job. Further, he was facing competition from a young subordinate who took over for him when he was away, on a vacation, a business trip, or ill for the day. Rejected at home, uneasy at work, generally dissatisfied with his life, Mr. A turned for solace to a girl in the office. They were made for each other. He, at forty-two, was a mature, accomplished person in his field; she, at twenty-four, was aggressive, ambitious and had cultivated a taste for seasoned male flesh and the additional grace that a man in middle age can offer a woman. It began at a Christmas party in the office. They spoke; they laughed; they necked. He got quite drunk, awakening the mother in the girl; she kept a clear head and got him on his train to the suburbs. Then, a month later, after avoiding each other at work, their paths crossed at another office party and they took another cab ride, but to her apartment.

It was difficult, of course, to have sex with the girl on any kind of regular basis when Mr. A lived outside the city where he worked and the girl lived in it. And it was dangerous, but he managed. A few times, he spent the night in the girl's bed, having thought up some believable alibi for his wife. Most times, Mr. A and the girl would go straight to her apartment from work, have sex for two or three hours, and then she would put him on the train. If his wife asked why he was late, he would tell her it was business. To his happy surprise, on some of those late homecomings he would find his wife quite ready to make love. She was a blonde; the other girl was a brunette. Two women in one night, a brunette in the city, a blonde at home? A midolescent paradise.

The affair went on for several months. Mr. A was not a man without a conscience. The burden of deception and guilt became heavy. He began, unconsciously, casting about for an excuse to unload that burden. He did not have to wait very long. His mistress told him, sincerely, that she loved him because he reminded her of her father, probably the last thing a graying, paunchy philanderer wants to hear. It made him realize the absurdity of what he was doing. He was old enough to *be* her father. Mr. A took his troubles not to the most sympathetic ear but perhaps to the most logical one, his wife's. Again, he confessed everything, the meetings, the sex, even love notes he and the girl had passed through the office mail. Mrs. A was not quite so understanding this second time around. "You bastard!" she said. "You had to unload your guilt, somewhere, didn't you, and you unloaded it on me. But I haven't done anything to you." She wrung the girl's phone number out of her husband and called the girl, to say:

1) if she wanted Mr. A so badly, she was welcome to him, but she would have to take his children, too; 2) failing that, if this affair went on, Mrs. A would see that the girl lost her job; 3) if she ever met the girl, she would try to kill her. A few hours after the phone call, when the weeping and screaming had subsided and Mr. and Mrs. A had entered the eye of their storm, they found themselves in bed, making love.

The girl was only too willing to back out. Mrs. A's threat to have her fired—and she could have, Mr. A says—frightened the young woman much more than Mrs. A's threat to kill her. Given the choice between Mr. A and her job, the girl chose her job.

About a year later, for reasons also linked to the fence-kicking, desperate behavior of a midolescent, Mr. A had to resign his job. The steady friction with his competitor had built up too much heat for things to go on as they were. Mr. A came to work drunk one day, and spent that day abusing fellow workers, talking back to superiors and generally throwing the office out of gear. His embarrassed employer offered to put him in a lesser position, with no loss of pay, but Mr. A preferred to leave, and was awarded part of his severance pay. He did not change his career, but he changed his venue, moving several states away. He and his wife are still married, he is beginning to move up, in another company and another town, and now, he says, "Maybe I'm trying to grow up. It's about time."

Mr. B

He was an impressively educated man, in the formal and the self-made sense. He was an academic, a professor at a prestigious urban university; life there was rewarding, peaceful and serene, and the approach of midolescence, like summer storm clouds across a quiet, sunny bay, did not make itself felt at once, but when the storm arrived, it was a cloudburst.

At age forty-three, Mr. B was not your ivory-tower, bigdome type; he kept up his ties to the world outside Academia, moonlighting, as he called it, by working part-time for newspapers, writing magazine articles, popular books; he was the kind of writer a publisher could lean on, turning out in four or five weeks a respectable piece of work 50,000 or 60,000 words in length, something that might take another writer a year. And he could be assigned to almost any area; if he became interested in a subject, he made it his business to learn all there was to learn about it; if he liked a book in English translation he might learn the author's language to savor the work in its natural tongue.

He had been married for eighteen years. He had a devoted wife and three children. Except for a brief, one-night aberration in the third year of his marriage, he had never strayed. And then, when he was forty-three, a sleek, twentyish advertising woman was assigned to work with him on the campaign for his newest book. As she entered his life, the midolescent storm broke. Brilliant of mind, foul of mouth far beyond the liberal-intellectual bent for spicing heavy thoughts with gutter adjectives and adverbs, she met with Mr. B often in the best restaurants and drinking places, and she always insisted on picking up the tab. They were, ostensibly, professional conferences. There was a great deal of drinking; the conferences took up more and more time, and lasted farther and farther into the night. At the outset, hearing all these vulgarities issuing from so lovely a mouth —he had never met anyone like her—Mr. B thought of the girl as "nothing but a flaky broad"; after two weeks of this with her he was hopelessly, bewilderedly in love with her. If, concluding a confer-ence, she would say, "Well, so long—I've got to go meet my steady fuck," he was not repelled but only more attracted. He discovered to his alarm that he had an appetite for torture.

Whatever she wanted of him, apart from what she could gain professionally from the advertising campaign, she had his number. Something in her perverse nature responded to, recognized his torture-impulse. She would kiss him hello and kiss him goodbye every time they met and every time they parted; finally, when a conference that ended at 3:30 in the morning led to her bed, both of them falling-down drunk, they slept together, but that was all they did. Before dawn he did make an effort.

"I did put my hands in her pants," he says in his interview. "Her bikini pants—she wasn't wearing a top, just the panties, and she said in a drunken, sleepy voice, 'Get your fuckin' hands outta my pants.' And even if she had been willing, it would have been no go because I couldn't get it up. Several times during the night, wondering whether she'd be willing, several times I tried to get an erection. I tried masturbating—and I couldn't get it up! At all! So there I was in bed with this Venus and I spent the night racked with guilt, thinking about my wife—obviously so emotionally drained that my body wouldn't work."

He had never stayed out all night under such circumstances, and without calling home. He told his wife the next day that he had fallen in with a drinking party and that everyone had collapsed at a private home where he woke up. Later, gradually, the truth began to emerge; the truth of what had happened that night, and of what was happen-ing to Mr. B. The picture took form, bit by bit, as though events were pieces of a jigsaw puzzle, and finally Mrs. B knew what was really going on.

Mrs. B did not react with anger, or threats to kill the other woman, as Mrs. A had to her confrontation; she reacted with tears. Her husband, in all midolescent/adolescent-like candor, tried to make a case for his attraction to the girl, praising her brilliant, piercing mind, rhapsodizing about her body. Mrs. A's reaction, in the mid-night of her soul, was not so much that her husband was doing something wrong as that he—and they—needed help. She took the initiative; her husband would come home frighteningly depressed, would speak of suicide; Mrs. B chose sex as a way out, making the advances herself, and gradually he began to respond; their sex life, never very active, in the ten years leading up to his midolescence practically an untended, weedy garden, flowered as it never had. At the same time, Mr. A, doggedly insisting that he was innocent of any technical adultery—as he was—continued to see the advertising woman at the conferences, and, whenever he could get away from the university, took to hanging around her office. So he had sex at home and non-sex with the girl.

While he had no sex with the young woman, his association with her changed not only his domestic sex life but his professional life. He was as much taken with the world she inhabited as he was with her. The pace, the quicksand-like uncertainty, the challenge and glamor of advertising seemed to him a brilliant contrast with what had become the dull and frustrating life of a professor, a dead end. Through her, he entered the advertising field himself, surrendering the security and what he took for the unbearable tedium of Academia.

And because of her, he also threw out all the baggy suits his students were so accustomed to seeing and replaced them with dramatically bright sports jackets, turtle-neck shirts and sweaters and stylish, tight-hipped, bell-bottomed trousers. There were physical changes for Mrs. B, too. Plunged into depression—"for the first time in my life," she says, "I just forgot to eat"—her weight declined precipitously. Mrs. B began to dress her new body differently. "I saw her at a party about that time," says a woman friend of theirs, "and she was wearing a black jersey tie-wrap blouse, open practically to the navel, something meant for somebody about fourteen years old. She looked—silly, that's the only word."

Mr. A and Mr. B may not be completely over midolescence, but in both households the immediate trouble is past. The storms are over, but both men and both wives are keeping an eye on the weather. Some comparisons between the two couples:

Mr. A is his wife's second husband. He had had many sexual encounters before they met; she had had casual sex with men before and during her previous marriage. But she remained totally faithful to Mr. A, as he was to her, until his midolescence. When a rival presented herself, Mrs. A, stunned, then outraged, dealt with the problem simply and directly: Leave him alone or I'll kill you.

Mr. and Mrs. B were by comparison each other's first loves. Mrs. B came to the marriage bed a virgin; Mr. B had had one serious, long-term affair before his marriage, and a scattering of dalliances.

Asked to total the sex experiences of his life, Mr. B pondered for a moment and came up with, "Five." Asked the same question, Mr. A did not have to take time to think. From his interview:

Q. You speak of "catting around" before you met your wife. How many women have you had sex with, if you can count them?

A. About thirty-five. Why? Is that a lot?

Q. Well, the fact that you can answer so promptly . . .

A. I thought you'd ask, so I counted in advance.

Each man now knows that the sexual dangers of midolescence are quite real. Each realizes that having done this kind of thing once, he might be tempted to do it again. But now each knows what it costs, now each might hesitate. Neither man is a prig or a moralist, and neither am I; there are those who can play this game and not hurt anybody, and I have no quarrel with them or what they do; the point here is that there are men, like Mr. A and Mr. B, who *cannot* play this game. These men paid a terrible price for their pleasure in terms of pain for themselves as well as for their wives and in terms of the erosion of relationships founded on mutual trust. For such men these things are expensive, and they are both still paying the bills.

So much, at this point, for sex in midolescence. But there is much more to midolescence than sex; when you read the cases of Mr. A and Mr. B in full you will discover that while sex does rear its head, midolescence is more a hydra than a serpent; it has many, many heads. In some of the other cases it plays only an incidental role and in at least one, virtually no role. As in all inner disturbances, what is on the surface may only be one expression of the complexities within. The pressures of work, of social confrontation, for instance, are some of the other heads.

In later chapters, a singer tells why he gave up the operatic stage for the theater of business; a clinical psychologist tells of quitting his field for an actor's life; a university professor (not Mr. B) tells of what he calls "the fountain of youth," an ever-replenished flow of young people into his classroom, which keeps his mind young in his fifties. Still-married women like Mrs. A and Mrs. B discuss the awful challenges presented by *all* the things that troubled their husbands in midolescence, and they tell how their marriages survived. A divorced woman recounts a frightening process of general deterioration in which her husband gradually let all his responsibilities slip from his hands, finally allowing his marriage to fall into ruin. Because sex does play a role in this, I have also interviewed young, single women who tell why they entered into liaisons with middle-aged men and why they preferred these men to younger men. Midolescence allows no exemptions for homosexuals; there is a chapter in which the problem is examined from the male homosexual point of view.

I have drawn heavily upon what literature there is that deals with the middle-age crisis, for guidance, and I have taken these findings —most of them couched in language accessible only to specialists— into the world of real people to test them. But I made no attempt to conduct a scientific experiment whose results could be verified independently. This book reflects, rather, what could be called an *un*controlled experiment: The people interviewed in the succeeding pages, men and women, medical authorities on midolescence and the midolescents themselves, are all real. The identities of those who might suffer public embarrassment have been cloaked; dates, facts, names and, sometimes, details of circumstances, have been altered. Names have been changed or deleted. Where this was done, I tried to find as close an equivalent as possible to actual dates, facts and details. In no case was the *emotional* content tampered with. The words, like the people, are real.

"If," says the artist Ben Shahn in "The Biography of a Painting," "we were to attempt to construct an 'average American,' we would necessarily put together an effigy which would have the common qualities of all Americans, but would have the eccentricities, peculiarities, and unique qualities of no American. It would, like the sociologist's statistical high-school student, approximate everyone and resemble no one."

The only approximation in this book is our friend George. He makes his brief appearance at the beginning and then disappears to let the real people, with their "eccentricities, peculiarities and unique qualities," take the stage.

II.
The Experts Speak

How can a man cope with midolescence? What kinds of men suffer most? What kinds suffer least? How large a role is played by sex? What are the danger signs in marriages and in careers? And is there, indeed, any sure course to follow through this uncertain, unmarked country called middle age?

In this chapter you will find, if not answers, some rather educated opinions on those and other questions. Doctors examine the physical and psychological aspects of the middle years. A lawyer who deals in labor-management cases for big corporations, an industrial medical director and an executive "head hunter" discuss the attitudes of middle-aged men toward business and the attitudes of business toward middle-aged men. Here and there, you will find the very concept of midolescence challenged, even rejected. But almost all those interviewed speak of something like midolescence happening to somebody they knew at some time.

The doctors speak of early conditioning planting seeds that lie dormant until middle age, then spring to flower. One speaks of the psychological conditioning of the World War II generation, now midolescent: Dividing the world of women into Nice Girls and Bad Girls. The lawyer speaks of the hangover in values of that generation: When you were growing up in the 1930's and the early 1940's the big

21

thing in life was to have a job, any job, to make money, and those who are still in those any-jobs are losing them to machines that do not require pay checks or hospitalization benefits. The head-hunter tells of submitting clients to psychological testing, of sometimes advising a client to stay where he is.

"I have long had a conviction," writes Dr. Wingate M. Johnson in his 1947 book, *The Years After Fifty,* "that Freud was wrong in teaching that sexual maladjustment is responsible for all the mental and most of the physical ills that flesh is heir to. Where sex has wrecked its thousands of homes, financial worry has destroyed its tens of thousands."

Here, speaking in 1974, is a former student of Freud's, Dr. Joseph Wortis. Until 1950, when he published "Fragments of an Analysis by Freud," Dr. Wortis was a practicing psychoanalyst; he now teaches and lectures and has affiliations with several hospitals, including Central Islip State Hospital, Long Island, where this interview was conducted. This interview is more a lecture; Dr. Wortis, at sixty-seven a handsome, commanding man, preferred to give his views directly, without being asked questions, and without a tape recorder.

Dr. Joseph Wortis

Human behavior at any one point in life is a resultant of the physiological condition of the organism, the accumulated experiences of the past, and the realities of the present situation. Every stage in a life differs, and the social situation also differs. A woman goes through the endocrine changes of the climacterium, or menopause; there is nothing comparable for a man. Also, her social role changes, in that her child-bearing period ends. So, on two counts, the woman experiences changes that the man does not.

Your question—who suffers in middle age and who does not? An executive who clips coupons and has a secure income has no transition trouble. Indeed, he may have increased stabilization. On the other hand, his head salesman's professional power in this age period is steadily waning. For the executive, there is a comfortable continuity in life; but for the head salesman, who's going to be fired eventually, there is discontinuity ahead.

Accumulated experience, physical condition and present situation may impinge on a man approaching middle age. He declines in vigor and efficiency. All sports records are held by younger men, in every field; they indicate the efficiency of the organism. For such people, the decline sets in in the mid-twenties.

The middle-aged man declines in physical and in mental vigor. This is compensated for, in part, by experience and authority; he may have more skill, compensating for the physical lack.

In some cases, as experience increases, efficiency decreases. If a man is a day laborer, his increased experience is of no help to him. His growing lack of vigor will hamper him. On the other hand, increase in experience does help the non-manual worker.

There is, yes, a reduction in sexual vigor, but I think the importance of sex in our society is grossly exaggerated; I think the public is sex-crazy.

The decline in physical and mental vigor is coupled with the threatened change in one's social or professional situation and with a decrease in earning, or financial power. Add illness, and you may have an abrupt change. All illnesses occur with increasing frequency in later years. You've heard the expression, I'm sure—"old age is an accumulation of illnesses."

If we have illness, loss of employment and disruption of the family, then crises ensue. They occur in middle age; in old age they're much worse. Human discontent increases enormously with increasing years. It needn't be so, but it is. The old should have roles to follow, but those who are not specially privileged have none.

The following dialogue is between me and a behavioral therapist who declined to participate in this project but who did not decline to try to brief me on his position. It is a transcript of a telephone conversation between us.

Behavioral Psychiatrist

Q. Doctor, one of the main things I'd like you to fill me in on is this "demonology" concept that you mentioned, the last time we spoke. And you got the material I sent you? [The outline and a draft of the first chapter.]

A. Yes, I did. Let me say this, first of all. I read your material you sent me with, er, with interest and carefully. I thought about it, quite a bit. I think that it's a good idea, and I think it may well be a very good seller and a popular book. In my judgment, I think you're going to be faced with the priority of making it sell better with sensational material on the one hand . . .

Q. Yes, that's a great danger, there's no doubt about that.

A. Being, you know, accurate, what not, on the other, and for that reason I don't want to be part of it.

Q. I see.

A. And the other thing is that I'm just not really interested in that subject. That's partly a matter of the way I look at things, which I was alluding to before and partly a matter of—it's just not my sphere of interest. Period.

Q. Your sphere of interest being the family, the . . .

A. Right.

Q. Well, see, most of these guys *do* have families!

A. Well, everybody has a family. And "family" involves everything. But as a family therapist, I don't look for problems inside people; I look for patterns of behavior in sequences, among and between people. You're talking about a problem which resides inside people. I don't look at things that way.

Q. Well, I mean—who could exist in society without having relations with somebody? When you spoke of demonology, were you referring—I immediately thought of the Inquisition, I immediately thought of exorcism, I immediately thought of—far back in time . . .

A. By demonology, I mean exactly what I'm saying, what I just said, which is that there's something *bad* that resides inside a container known as a person, which has to be gotten rid of. The germs theory is another example, and all medical models are based on that.

Q. Yes—but my . . .

A. "Midolescence" is another kind of demon germ.

Q. Hm. But my, my—in speaking to other medical men about this, I've been told that middle age is probably a misnomer in this, that the men might act no differently at twenty-five or thirty-five. Right? And because of the—all the extra attendant pressures of society—the youth-oriented culture, his fear of losing his job, perhaps his baldness—things like that—the aberrant behavior can then be more pronounced. And, if that is demonology, I don't know where I've gone wrong.

A. Well, see, we're not really talking the same language.

Q. I guess not.

A. I don't say you've gone wrong. I just say I don't look at things that way. I'm interested in what goes on between people; I'm interested in things like distance and closeness and systems and what affects one. I wouldn't look for the etiology of things on the basis of age at all. I would say, for instance, that a lot of things happen when the kids go off to school. When the mother has nothing to do, and she starts going out and getting a job. When Mother goes out and gets a job, then Father's going to be having to do something else. I would be looking for interaction among people. I wouldn't be looking for such factors as you're looking for. I wouldn't be thinking about it in the same terms.

Q. All right. I suppose that's the difference between your education and mine, yours is something much more specialized . . .

A. No, it's nothing to *do* with education except in the *broader* sense! Most people don't look at it—I mean most professional people don't look at it the way I look at it at all. I'm a minority.

Q. All right, good enough, Doctor, thank you very much for talking to me.

Dr. Paul Metzger offers a refreshing, sometimes biting, always deeply humanist view of the midolescent male. He is a gynecologist whose opinions on men's problems are partly derived from reflection from his dealings with his women patients. When he goes to the heart of the matter, he occasionally shifts from medical terminology to the earthy language of the streets, if it is pertinent. This taped interview was conducted in his office in Manhattan.

Dr. Paul Metzger

Q. There is a debate about the very existence of a male climacteric; what is your position?

A. When we use the word menopause in gynecology, we are referring to a specific decrease in the hormone level of the woman's ovaries. This results in only one phenomenon, the inability to have children any further. The ancillary symptoms that come about through a lowered hormone level are easily relieved by replacing the hormone; or, if it's not replaced the body adjusts in time and the symptoms pretty much disappear.

In the woman there seems to be almost no correlation whatsoever between this hormone level and libido. Sex drive. Now: With that as a starting point, from a gynecologist's point of view, there is no such thing as a male menopause because the male's hormone levels do not go through any alteration at a specific age of life; indeed there are viable sperm, as you probably well know, in the testicles of men in their nineties. The delivery system may change at ninety, but not the sperm, so much. A forty-five year-old woman is very often faced with her son going into the service, her daughter running off with the musician, maybe of a different race or religion, the rebellion of her children in their teens or early twenties. And her husband may be trying to prove he still has it; he may be running around with his secretary. It may be very difficult to disassociate the woman's symptoms from these sociological phenomena occuring at this time, when she's been married twenty, twenty-five years.

Q. "Disassociate?"

A. She says—"I feel more tense lately; I feel more nervous; I think I'm getting a rapid pulse occasionally; I get more upset more easily." When she was thirty, her thirty-five-year-old husband wasn't going through any problems in business, problems of thinking he was getting older, problems of starting to think about death. At that earlier time, she had two or three children dependent on her; she was the center of the universe; they weren't going off on their own; they weren't going into the service, et cetera. It would be nice if we could take this now forty-five-year-old woman who's starting to have a lowered estrogen level, and put her back to the time when her husband was thirty-five and virile; put her back here and see what her symptoms were at *that* time.

Now we take the man in this period. And again, we must look back first. When a twenty-year-old male tries to have intercourse a second time within an hour, there may be things on his mind that prevent him. "I've got to get up for reveille tomorrow." "I've got an exam tomorrow." "I've got a track meet tomorrow." Or just "really, I've got to get my sleep because tomorrow I have to be sharp for this, for that—" if he doesn't succeed, he just goes to sleep. A thirty-one-year old has this happen; it's still not a catastrophe. But a forty-one-year-old or fifty-one-year-old encounters this, and it plays on the mind. The fifty-one-year-old may go to the bathroom and look at himself in the mirror and say, "This is it!" And he's forgotten that this same thing happened when he was in his twenties and it didn't bother him!

I was in the Air Force. We had an old cliché. The bumblebee, when you measure its weight and its wingspan and its aeronautical dynamics, obviously cannot support itself in flight. But the bumblebee doesn't know that, so it just goes ahead and flies! Long ago, before all these medical articles about the male and female, decades of young women grew up knowing that their Aunt Tillie went crazy when she had her menopause, when she suffered her Change of Life —and that's a hideous phrase. At seventeen, thanks to the whispered conversation among the women of the family, a girl was programed to expect that there'd be trouble in the menopause, and that sex after the menopause was unthinkable. For men today, say, for young men in army barracks, there is another kind of programing—"Everybody *knows* you can't get it up later on in life!" So we're programed. And as in the bumblebee's case, if we didn't know there was supposed to be trouble ahead, we would just go on flying! I would like to omit from this any discussion of physical health. Obviously, a man who's a cardiac case, a man who's a severe diabetic, a man who has rheumatoid arthritis—any physical impairment affects physical activity of any kind and, indirectly, a man's attitude. I think we should also leave out of this discussion men who have had sexual difficulties in earlier years. In menopause, a woman who was always a neurotic will be more a neurotic. A woman who has had a poor orientation to sex, a woman who's always finding excuses not to indulge . . .

Q. What is a poor orientation to sex?

A. Good question. She was brought up to believe that really, "this is not for my pleasure; I'm lying down as a chore, to have children and to satisfy the insatiable lust of the male animal." That's a rather poor orientation to sex. This is changing, of course. There is now open discussion about the female orgasm and of the fact that women may enjoy sex far more than men and for more years, or have the potential to enjoy it far more than men. But through the Victorian era—still a great influence on our present era—women were ideally "respectable," "nice women," not lustful women. And the kids today have good reason to lampoon the World War II crowd, with the Nice Girls and the Bad Girls. To lampoon the programing. "Daddy was supposed to get all his experience before he got married, but he wasn't supposed to get have it with Nice Girls." Who knows? Perhaps in 1910 a very prim and proper wife in New York was a hellion in her bedroom. Perhaps the courtesan of that society could do that, but the wife was supposed to do her duty, very little more. Women —"nice," "respectable" women—were sacrosanct. They were not in man's world. They weren't exposed to insults. They were courted. Today, of course, they've come a long way, baby. Someone recently said that women have rasied themselves down to our equals.

A. From what I've learned thus far in my research, the male climacteric, or menopause, or whatever, seems to be a cause-effect thing. A man's hair goes gray or falls out. It's more difficult for him to climb stairs. He undergoes other aging pains, like growing pains, and they affect his attitude and behavior. He thinks they are signs of mortality. They bring on his compulsive efforts to prove manhood through sex activity; they choose mistresses young enough to be their daughters. How valid is this thinking, that there is a cause and there is an effect?

A. Basically, I agree. But without trying to play the devil's advocate, let me say that there are many very, very stable men who have no compunctions; who understand very well, instinctively, without any books or lectures, that from about thirty on they begin to prefer quality to quantity. They haven't anything to prove. They have no questions about their libido or their masculinity. They enjoy sex; they may or may not stray, if they're married. If they do it, it may not cause them to wallow in guilt. They adore their wives. Without their women by their sides they could not function normally. I don't believe that's too idealistic a portrait. I think many men fit that category.

Q. That's a portrait of a pretty healthy animal.

A. Many men fit this comfortable category, and when these things you mentioned happen to them in middle age, they find surcease, or solace, if those are the words, in other activities—hobbies. Gardening. Farming. Travel. Golf. They thus sublimate, rather than expose themselves to (A) guilt, (B) exposure to their children of infidelity, and (C) economic penalties, which could be suffered on the job, or in the divorce court. So there are many men who do not break out, so to speak, and act foolishly. We must also bring in the fact that there is a normal boredom after fifteen or twenty years with the same partner. It can be felt by women as well as men. It must not be mistaken as a sign of a bad marriage. When a boy marries at twenty-two, for the next ten or eleven years that boy is a youngster, especially in the young Catholic groups, Italian, Irish. That boy plays; he has his bowling nights, his barroom nights, he may even screw around. But no one notices it. The only people who mention it are aunts or in-laws who say, "Why can't Larry be nicer to our daughter? Why does he have to do those things?" For the most part it's harmless. Let the same damn things happen twenty years later and it's labeled male menopause. I've often thought, if I may digress a bit, that later marriages are much better for the simple reason that there's a fighting chance of not getting too bored too early. Now that I've made all these qualifications, let's consider this group of individuals who seem to be acting in a fashion that we question.

Q. People in their forties, people in middle age?

A. Yes. Extra-marital relations. Now I submit that unless we find that there is suddenly an increase of this activity from age forty on, as contrasted with the thirty-to-forty period, for the sake of argument, we don't have anything to discuss.

Q. I don't follow.

A. If, between thirty and forty, among our married men, there is a great deal of extra-marital activity, or amount, and there's only X amount or X plus a little bit more from forty to fifty or even fifty to fifty-five, then I really think that what we're dealing with is a myth. But let us put another qualification in here—that from thirty to forty a man may not be as financially able to support certain extra-marital activities. And he may break out later when he can afford it. Is this then not something that was brewing for many, many years, and finally comes to fruition? In the average healthy heterosexual male there is a constant, never-ending libido that may require varied and many individuals for satisfaction—not necessarily at one time. The marital state may not be totally satisfying. Psychiatrists talk a great deal about healthy adultery. And they talk about adultery being something not necessarily committed with the penis; that if a man is working with a woman bookeeper for twenty years, they may have a very close relationship, though they have never touched. She may have far more involvement in his life than his wife has, but the wife is not disturbed by that. And then, ten minutes with a waitress in San Antonio, Texas, during a convention, in which the penis touches the vagina—*that* will disturb the wife, even though there is no emotion or thinking involved, on her husband's part. At any rate, this—wandering of the male, the proving of himself: At seventeen, eighteen and nineteen, it's considered quite normal for a young male to prove himself. No one questions the fact that this boy has three or four dates on a weekend, or many girls in his life. At twenty-five, they call it virility; at sixty-five, they call it lechery. I'm merely trying to say a good word for the male libido, that it really doesn't change all that much over the years; it only may seek expression. Marriage is a difficult way for humans to live, but it still seems to be the best situation we've developed sociologically for the upbringing of children, the sociological unit.

Q. Is there any other?

A. Well, there's been a lot of experimentation in recent years and it hasn't gone anywhere.

Q. The commune culture, for instance?

A. Yes. The human being, no matter how they try to change him, follows the old pattern. In those communes, they still mate off, one to one. No matter how we try to argue the point, there seems to be some biological truth involved here, in millions of years of evolution. No matter how much women try to prove certain equality economically, there is a biological aspect here in terms of the male orgasm and the male drive and the female sexual apparatus, the female psyche sexually. Maternity, no matter how much women may not want children, is involved somewhere. And in this context of yours we also have to consider change. We are living in a time when change in six months' time is unbelievable. A hundred years ago, a grandfather, a father and a son could all communicate readily together, because none of them knew anything but candlelight, none of them knew anything but horseback riding, and so on; the town they lived in had not changed much in a century. There was a sense of being able to communicate, generation to generation. This is totally changed now. A girl of twenty-five talks to me about "the young kids today." Hilarious! A twenty-three-year-old says, "My kid sister's group—I don't understand them." And the kid sister's group is seventeen! Then the twenty-three-year-old talks about her older, married sister, who's all of twenty-eight, and in another world! As a result, for the middle-aged man, there's a lot of feeling of, "I want to try to relate to the young." Or, "I don't feel I'm over the hill yet; stop pushing me!" Or, "What do you mean I'm old?" The man saying those things may have had disappointments; financial success may have escaped the guy; his wife may be a bit of a shrew; there may not have been a true marriage of minds, as well as bodies; they may be staying together only on a habit basis until the kids grow up.

Q. How great a role does physiology play for a middle-aged man? Hormonal or other bodily changes? How great a role is played by such forces as the job the man suddenly becomes bored with, the routine that becomes intolerable, the decisions that can't be made? And by seeing young men catching up to him, perhaps getting ahead of him in business, his field, in life in general? The pressure of a society focused as it is on youth and the exaltation of youth?

A. A tremendous role. In comparison with other countries, America is at the bottom of the heap in making arrangements for people to age gracefully, males in particular. When we start out in working life, we find there is a tremendous premium put on experience. When one is young, he is faced with job application forms that ask "What is your experience, what is your background?" And yet —except in politics, where a gentleman seventy-four years of age with a coronary and an intestinal operation can become President— except there, we dump. We dump our generals—some of them deserve it, of course—in their prime, in their mid-fifties, when they've reached the point at which you'd suppose all the money we've paid them could begin to pay off. We dump our corporation presidents, generally, at sixty. We dump, dump, dump! As a result, a guy who's been amassing experience all his working life suddenly gets to a point where all that experience doesn't matter any more. Unless he's one of the very few at the top of a very fine funnel, he's had it. At thirty-eight, he might have said to himself, "Oh, the hell with it, I'll get another job." If there is a possibility that he'll lose his job. But at forty-eight, it's "Jesus Christ! I'd better not lose this job; where am I going to go?" The aerospace industry has recently dumped a lot of Ph.D's. At the moment Ph.D's are a glut on the American job market. Not the young Ph.D's, but the man with kids in college, with mortgage payments, facing the prospect of having to go on relief, or collect unemployment checks. He looks for another job and he's told,

"You're highly trained; you used to earn too much money; we can't use you; it's too late to start with us." Hell, they can get a younger Ph.D at half the price! In our society, money is an extension of the penis. Money is sex. Power is sex. Women seem to be attracted to men with political and economic power. The choice tends to be toward such men. A girl is told by her mother, "I know you love him, sweetheart, but look ahead—how's he going to support you?" A boy is told, "You've got to make a buck before you marry." The boy may rebel; he may say, "Oh, how stupid they are! I hope I don't become that materialistic!" The girl may rebel. But eventually they all disappear into the economic grinder. You asked about youth, the exaltation of youth in our culture. Yes, it's true, in advertising, in movies, everywhere. Of course Madison Avenue could, overnight, make experience, age, gray temples attractive. They do just that, with certain fields. To advertise Preparation H, they show a mature gentleman who's apparently a physician; they don't say he is one, but that's the implication. In the movies, when they want a President, they use Fredric March; when they want a wise old sheriff, it's Duke Wayne. Okay. I am given to understand by my patients that for some strange reason, whether it's father-figure, economics, money or just plain maturity and experience, love-making-wise, women seem to be attracted to older men. This is obviously a two-way street.

Q. In that men may choose older women?

A. No, in that the older men know how the women feel. A certain attractiveness may have come upon these men, which they didn't have in their youth. A certain experience in social life. A certain smoothness with romance. A certain sense of confidence, which perhaps eluded them as they were climbing the ladder. And the girls are available. Some men stray, others do not. About those who do not, I don't mean to be the least bit critical or cynical when I say that those men are not goody-goodies, or super-moralists; they have simply found their lives quite comfortable, their sexual needs satisfied. But for the sake of this discussion let us consider those men who do have a little something on the side. As Dr. Brothers blurted out on TV about five years ago, fortunately escaping a bullet in the head, the wife who's being well taken care of at home, rather than think she's safe and does not have a straying husband, may be the beneficiary in her own bed of what he's doing elsewhere. His libido at home may be raised by having a little something elsewhere, once a week or so. This is well known to men, that the more you might get the more you might want; variety arouses you. But the need for variety can be fed harmlessly. When a man comes home from a party at which he has been stimulated by someone else, he performs better with his wife. And the wife may in turn have been aroused. Oh, she doesn't necessarily want to lay every guy at the party, but the flattery, the social attention she received—she comes home aroused, too, and does a better job in the bedroom. So it goes. It's normal social and sexual behavior.

Q. What about men who may be driven to other women because their sexual advances are rejected by their wives who are physically distressed because of menopause, and just don't feel like reciprocating?

A. Rejection is a very definite thing all through a man's life. That can give him the excuse to go elsewhere. They can have an argument about money, and then he suddenly wants to make love, but no, no —she's not ready. They've just had an argument. We men can certainly turn directly from an argument to love-making. Women seem not to be able to. Or they use it as a weapon: "Oh, no, you're not going to get anything tonight, not after what you called me at the dinner table!"

Q. Are women's sexual urges dulled as a result of menopause, or during menopause? Perhaps "appetites" might be a better word?

A. The answer to that generally is no. There is no change in whatever their sexual habits were before menopause. There is little discontinuity. The woman who has always been a good wife, a loyal wife, stays that way. If she has always felt that fellatio and cunnilingus were vulgar and dirty, she will still feel that way. And if she always thought sex was distasteful and tended to avoid it except as a chore, menopause gives her a monumental excuse to avoid it, just as she previously used her period as an excuse. If the marriage is not doing well, it shows in the sexual activity; I don't think it's the other way around. This is apart from the normal boredom that I mentioned earlier. Sex is an expression. If the woman is not enjoying the marriage, if there's always been hardship and aggravation and she's felt there is no financial support, the menopause just makes matters all that much worse, as far as her sexual drive is concerned. But this, too, is a two-way street. If the husband is looking for a reason to justify unfaithfulness, if he feels guilt and has to justify it, he is then like the alcoholic who will find some way of turning the relationship into a situation in which he can feel sorry for himself. He'll go off in a huff, and say "I'll show her!" On the other hand, there are many perfectly happy men who, as I said earlier in my Dr. Brothers remark, are playing around yet happy at home. They would be crushed if their wives ever found out what they were doing, and left them. They don't want anything to upset their lovely marital situation, even though it is *not* sufficient for their sexual appetites! I don't think this is irrational behavior, though society says it is. These men, who have been straying continually for twenty to twenty-five years—in their fifties, their pattern is no different from what it was when they were thirty-five and going off on sales trips.

Q. Which, of course, goes against the entire concept of a male Change of Life, menopause, or midolescence?

A. Which is what I've been trying to lead up to, not too eloquently, all these minutes.

Q. You don't think there really is such a thing?

A. I think there are some of us who suddenly say, "What the hell have I been saving myself for? Why the hell didn't I screw that woman ten years ago? Why didn't I take advantage of Dorothy when she was working for me and she said, 'when we go away on a business trip' . . . why was I so proper and moral? Why, why, why? The kid is telling me I'm full of shit; the wife is tired, having her own problems; she's no sex figure to me. Why?" And that man may be the one we're talking about.

Q. That *is* the man I'm talking about.

A. Yeah, fine, but I'm simply saying that if we were able to view a thousand-room motel on a Saturday night and there were one thousand forty-five- to fifty-five-year-old male behinds going up and down on females other than their wives, we could not say, "that's a homogenous group." Every individual makes his own adjustment through the aging process.

Q. Your way of thinking and of constructing your arguments leaves me either confused or convinced, I'm not sure which. Do you agree with me that there is such a thing as a male climacteric? You keep bringing up people in that age group.

A. I feel there's a great deal to be said about that age bracket without using the word climacteric. We have to consider the unfortunate confluence of circumstances such as the wife's distress about her own medical problems, her reaction to her menopause; there's a possibility, yes, of a feedback. The wife's menopause can make a man feel a bit older. When I deliver a girl of eighteen, I come out when it's over to her parents, a very lovely young couple. He's forty-three and she's thirty-eight, and they have just become grandparents. They will joke: He will say, "I don't mind being a grandfather, but being married to a *grandmother??!!*" And she will laugh, and he will laugh, but I'm not so sure that this is very funny humor.

A. An expression of fear?

Q. I'm afraid that it has its effect, programing-wise, to be married to a grandmother. Now, mind you, a man could marry a woman of thirty-eight when he is forty-three. But when they've been married twenty years—maybe, if this is a beautiful marriage, nothing will happen. But assuming your normal trials and tribulations, this could be psychologically affecting. There are problems through life, but in the forty-to-fifty-five bracket there can be *more* pressures of life, *more* teenage problems, *more* exposure to parental death—ah! This is something I forgot to mention. That that is the age when a middle-aged person's parents most often die, when the teenager is running off to Vietnam, the daughter is marrying the black drummer. This is also the age when the middle-aged man's wife has a coronary and drops dead. These things come into play as life goes on.

And it's all that that sets him off, rather than the specific age bracket, plus America's cultural programing, and the boys in the barracks or the barroom telling, "Jesus, you can't get it up so much later on." And the feeling that he's lived longer than he was expected to live, on an actuarial basis. He knows that from his insurance man, who is not the least bit loath to remind him that on his next birthday the premium goes up. And who tries to cover over that unpleasant news by saying, "It's tough getting older, but that's better than the alternative, hah-hah-hah!" And you think, "How did I ever pick that son of a bitch as an insurance man?" It's all this confluence of factors that, in my opinion, makes up the syndrome which for want of a better word we call the male menopause.

Dr. Ernest van den Haag is a veteran of public discussion of psychiatric and sociological matters. He is outgoing in manner, quick to respond to any question, never at a loss for the right word or words. It must be said that he is also considered a reactionary by some of his colleagues and peers. I found him genial and possessed of a certain Old World charm. From the tape, taken in his home and office in Manhattan:

Dr. Ernest van den Haag

Q. Dr. Van Den Haag, professionally you are a . . .

A. Psychoanalyst. And I am also a sociologist.

Q. Dr. Van Den Haag, have you found that most, if not at all, men suffer some sort of conflict in middle age?

A. Conflict is with us throughout our life. And I think there is a recrudescence, in the peculiar form it tends to take, at middle age. Up to middle age, people think of life as really an infinite progress. They are, of course, aware that life has an end, but they don't really believe in it psychologically. When they reach middle age, they realize that there's not much time left. They realize that instead of steadily increasing their powers, their status, there is a slow decline setting in. At least there is this *impression* they have. Some ailments, instead of being passing, become chronic, and the doctor tells them, "You just have to live with it," instead of telling them, "This will pass." They gain a certain weight, and it's not temporary; that's the weight that they are stuck with. Their hair becomes gray, and so on. Now: We live in a society in which youth is very highly regarded, and in which being youthful, or appearing youthful, is at a very high premium. In most other societies, as physical powers decline, status and prestige increase. The aged are honored. There were some societies that were literally gerontocracies, that were run by the aged. Old China is one example. But even societies in which that wasn't the case honored the aged. And power—and therefore authority, too—was always in the aged. If you take, for instance, nineteenth-century Europe, you find that in the upper and middle classes, the older generation had an enormous power—the power, simply, to *disinherit the young.* Disinherited, the young would be totally lost.

Q. Culturally?

A. No, in fact economically. Financially. If you look at nineteenth-century literature there are novels, operas, even, such as "La Traviata." The power of the older man over his son was very simply:

"If you don't obey me, if you don't uphold family tradition, which means, basically, doing what I tell you, then you you will be disinherited." Disinheritance at that time meant really to be totally lost, because the son could not hope to make it on his own. Whereas, you see, we live *now* in a society in which it might be very nice to get an inheritance but if you have some education—even if you don't—you can make it without this.

Q. You mean the United States society, or the whole Western world?

A. In the United States. It's becoming so in all of Western society, but it's true in the United States more than in any other. It's relatively easy to make a quite decent living if you have acquired some sort of skill in your education. Very few people—one family in a thousand, I think—derive the major part of their income from inheritance. That means, in effect, that the authority of parents over their children is very small, and *that* means, in turn, that their *prestige* is very low—basically, the prestige of the middle-aged or older people. My thesis is very simply this: When the middle-age person sees a decline in his powers, not compensated for by an increase in prestige, he is basically, in most cases, quite realistic, and knows that that *is* the situation; he is not imagining anything.

Q. But there are imaginary situations?

A. Yes. I'm going to come to them.

Q. Then you could answer this: Is there a true male climacteric, in this form? It is not, certainly, parallel to the menopause.

A. I don't know of any physical, direct crisis. But there is a psychological crisis, quite similar to adolescence, a passage from one state to another state. Given some of the social reasons which intensify or aggravate it, there are also psychological reasons. Here you are. You realize—very suddenly, in many cases—that you don't have that much time left: that life is not infinite; that it is limited. And you also realize that you are unlikely to achieve what you have *not* achieved up to then. Now, most people have fantasies about their futures, sometimes articulate, sometimes not, sometimes conscious, sometimes not. The fantasies usually are that the future is infinite, that some day, they'll become king of the universe, or millionaires, or first-rate baseball players, or great actors, singers, poets, writers —whatever the particular fantasy is. Or even just great lovers. Now you've reached middle age, and you realize that you will not achieve anything of the sort. You'll end up living in a suburb, having a reasonable income, perhaps a reasonable job, but not becoming chief, not becoming the boss, not becoming President, not getting the Pulitzer Prize. In the past, you see, you could always avoid this. Until middle age, you could always postpone it. You could say, "I'm young and that's the reason I haven't gone that far yet, the reason I haven't written that great novel."

Q. But this isn't really *postponing* anything, is it? I mean there's nothing *being* postponed?

A. Of course not! But you think there is; you think you are doing that. When you reach middle age, if you are reasonably realistic, you realize that the great novel that you have not written until now, you are not likely to write. If you are a physicist, you realize that most physicists accomplish their major work in their twenties and thirties, and you are now forty, so you'll remain professor of physics in some small school, but you will not get the Nobel Prize!

Q. Is this a *mistake* on the part of the middle-aged man?

A. No. It's perfectly realistic. The crisis consists in the clash between your fantasies and reality. You begin to have a more realistic conception of yourself. I think we mentioned before that there's a crisis in adolescence. But in adolescence you are again, you clash, of course, with some of your childish fantasies, but you replace them with different fantasies which you are permitted to have. Say, for instance, that you are a student. You have not entered what is sometimes called real life. The life of a student is real, too, but still you have not tested, in competition beyond the classroom, your abilities to achieve something. In a sense, the situation of the student is an artifical one, keeping you *in,* entirely, *in dependence.* Or, if you are a junior executive, you still feel that you are being tested—who knows? You may be the one selected to become president of General Motors! and so on. After all, people start as junior executives, and then do become presidents. But when you have reached middle age, if you are realistic, you see the limitations of your career. And that is something that is for most people rather difficult to take. I have so far spoken of a layer of consciousness as fairly much on the surface. But go a little deeper, and then you will realize that we all have unconscious fantasies, in effect, of omnipotence. All girls—I'm speaking from the male viewpoint—*ultimately,* if they come to know us, just are smitten with us! All men ultimately recognize our total superiority! and so on. This, of course, is unconscious. But again, by the time you reach middle age, reality has too strong a bite for you to keep even *that* unconscious fantasy. Hence, the crisis of middle age is simply the recognition of the limitations (A) of life in general (B) of your own life, your own abilities and your own talent, your own vigor, your own physical and psychological potential.

Q. Fine, fine. We recognize this. But where is the *crisis?*

A. The crisis consists in recognizing it.

Q. Or of not recognizing it?

A. Well, some people refuse to. Yes, some people try to run away with the babysitter or whatever it is, if they find a babysitter willing, and babysitters, for reasons of their own, their own transferred realization of the father, might want to run away with you. But of course if you do run away, at fifty, or what not, you sooner or later realize that the babysitter is eighteen, and you are fifty. And that you don't really want the same things; it makes life a little hard. In other words, when you are fifty, you might want to *return* to your adolescence, but that's only part of you. The rest of you wants comfort and slippers, in effect. And also—you're not *able.* You no longer can run a mile at the same rate as before, and so on. And for that matter, it's rather unbecoming when you are fifty to act as though you are twenty. But in our society it's very hard to reconcile oneself to being fifty, because age is not really honored. In fact, you're encouraged to *deny* it. You are encouraged to pretend that you are twenty. And so one of the crises is the culture in which you are placed. There are various ways of escaping this. Some people in middle age retire into premature old age. They give up altogether. Some rebel against middle age and pretend they are adolescents. And some reconcile themselves to the reality: They are neither old nor young. They're middle-aged.

Q. What cultural or income groups are hit hardest by this? The highest? The middle? The lower? Are there some not affected at all? Are there groups to which this is not important? Does religion, for the more religious lower classes, effectively serve as therapy, whereas, for higher classes, medical therapy would be indicated?

A.–[The income group question] is a very interesting and, in my opinion a legitimate question. But I must admit that not only do I personally not know the answer to it, I do not think anyone has done any serious research on it. I just have to use my imagination. I know this is a very strong feeling in the middle-income group, which is *trapped.* Now, if you're very wealthy, it seems to me that your wealth can serve to help you—I wouldn't say *overcome*—but prevent *aware-*

ness of the crisis. If you are fifty and you are very very wealthy, you probably can use your wealth to surround yourself with very young people, and pretend you are one of them. I've known, in fact, more than one millionaire who simply uses his money to get his environment to help him deny that he is no longer young, or attractive. So, if you're very wealthy, you can use your money to influence your mind. If you're middle-class, you cannot. You don't have enough money for this.

Q. This running off with the babysitter . . .

A. —isn't because of a fear of impotence. That's because of a fear of no longer being young, of being trapped with one's wife.

Q. It is not a fear of impotence?

A. No, I don't think so. If you are really afraid of being impotent, you *won't* run away with the babysitter! You'll be *afraid!* [both laugh] She might not find you very satisfactory. No, I think that if you run away with the babysitter, you really feel you are still young, and here you are trapped with this old woman, and you don't *want* to be trapped with her.

Q. Religion.

A. Again—I have to plead ignorance. Theoretically, if people really believe that there is a life to come, they should fear death less, they should fear age less. But I'm not sure how much people believe in this. However, my experience is—first with women, religion tends to be quite important. But you're interested in men. Second, the Roman Catholic man, it can still play a major role. I'm not so sure about Protestants.

Q. I was told once, when I was still in college, that the priest was the working man's psychiatrist.

A. Certainly true. The priest was everybody's psychiatrist until psychiatrists came on the scene. The psychoanalyst *serves* where the priest is no longer effective.

Q. I've come across reports of psychiatrists saying there is such a thing as "healthy adultery." Or even prescribing it. Now this is by extension; she did not prescribe it, but Dr. Brothers says that many wives benefit in their home sex lives because of their husbands' extra-marital activity and experience. Is this true? And is there such a thing as "healthy adultery?"

A. Adultery is neither healthy nor unhealthy, it's just adultery. You could just as well ask, "Is there such a thing as *sick* adultery?"

Q. Well, no. I mean as against the social form, the social norm.

A. Let me put it this way. *Acts* such as adultery are neither healthy nor unhealthy; only *people* are healthy or unhealthy. You might just as well ask, "Is there healthy or unhealthy faithfulness?" It depends upon *why* you are faithful. And adultery also—the evaluation in terms of health depends on why you engage in adultery. Now, as for benefit or harm: Clearly, it depends on the persons and on the motives. There are circumstances where, I should think, a relation with a third person does not damage a marriage, and could even help it. There are other circumstances where a relation with a third person could damage the marriage, and so on. It depends on why it is done, in the context of all it means to the persons. But let me add that the idea of *prescribing* any sort of behavior such as adultery strikes me as utterly strange, and highly unprofessional. The purpose of psychoanalysis is to help people understand why they are doing what they are doing, not to *tell* them what to do! To tell them what to do is something that a moralist can do, a philosopher, perhaps, but *not* a psychoanalyst!

Q. On the job, in America, and probably in many Western countries, there is a policy of *dumping* people. It's illegal in this state to discriminate in hiring because of age, but it doesn't seem illegal to *dismiss* because of age. In the professions, like yours, like teaching, like the law, there seems to be a gentler, phasing-out policy, as contrasted with the *dumping* done in general business activity. Is this dumping policy a waste of experienced manpower? Should there be a legal protection against it?

A. The trouble with the problem is this—incidentally, in teaching, too, there is usually an age limit, at sixty, or sixty-five. But the trouble is this. The reasonable thing would of course be to evaluate each individual case. There are people who can make major contributions at seventy, and there are those who can't at twenty. Any general rule is likely to be unjust and wasteful. On the other hand, though, if a dean had to evaluate each professor, and to tell those who are getting too old for their job to retire, and to keep the others, he would be in a terribly difficult position. You see, the general rule serves as a protection, as it were, for the dean, who can say, "Well, I'm sorry; I think you're great, you're the best teacher we've ever had, but unfortunately, we have that rule." And that makes it unnecessary for him to say that "You're getting old, you're repeating yourself, you're not saying anything new, you're boring your classes to tears." And so on. Which is hard to say to an elderly gentleman. So there are two sides to it. But in industry it seems to me that such a rule is probably doing more harm than good. And in particular, we have to consider the fact that people do live longer now, and they are certainly useful for a longer time. To come back to the crisis of middle age: Now, that is undoubtedly one of the fears that people have, that they are going to be put on the heap of the discarded, and "I won't know what to do with myself." Many people gain an identity through the work they do. If that identity is lost, if they live on the little money they have saved, or on Social Security, they don't know what to do with themselves, they certainly will decline very fast. I think that we simply ought to realize that people can contribute if they're in half-way good health, to work, literally until they die. I see no reason to exclude even a person of eighty from working. He may not be able to do what he could have done at forty, but he can still do something. And *he* is better off if he is allowed to do something and the firm can use his contribution; he can do *something*.

Q. Would a man's feeling of tedium and boredom at work coincide with such physical symptoms as lack of energy, lack of physical ability, fear of impotency, gastric and cardiac disturbances, real or imagined?

A. You have led a life which, whatever its satisfactions, involved a number of frustrations. Which you have bottled up; which you have, for various reasons, not been able to face, discharge, and find a remedy for. So, in effect, these frustrations, or dissatisfactions, or blockages tend to manifest themselves in such things as gastric disturbances, circulatory disturbances, and so on. One way is to say that they are the results of your being dissatisfied and bored with your life. But boredom itself, you see, is the result of having blocked, or having been compelled to block, satisfaction of your original impulses. You're bored when what you do doesn't satisfy you, because it isn't what you really, at least unconsciously, wanted to do. That may manifest itself in a variety of physical, somatic disturbances, or sometimes just psychic depression. You mentioned lack of energy. Lack of energy, or sleepiness, is simply due to a lack of interest in what you are doing. I find that people can get very energetic if they . . .

Q. If they want to do something, they'll do it?

A. Right. But I, too, feel tired, if I am compelled to do something that I don't want to do; it bores me! So: If a person tends to—begins to be bored with his whole life situation—that includes his family, that includes his job, that includes where he lives, the friends he has, the things he does—if he has not by the time he has reached middle age been able to give a meaning to his life, and at that point is confronted with the fact that his own life appears meaningless to him, is not very interesting—he will have what you call a crisis. It may show itself in physical symptoms, in depression, in "nervous breakdown," whatever that means—the layman's term for something being wrong. You can give it more specific names, but basically it's his realization, very hard to face, that he hasn't done what he thought he could do with himself in his life and that it is getting to be too late. And there are other people who are simply resigned.

Q. Can you think of anything else you'd like to say? Without questions?

A. Well, that crisis comes about in middle age because its basis has been laid much earlier, perhaps in early childhood. If you have slowly directed your life to the wrong ends, then you might realize that, in middle age, you give up your illusions, pursuing something that . . .

Q. You mean what an individual *considers* the wrong ends.

A. You find in middle age that perhaps it wasn't right for you. If you have been lucky enough, or wise enough, or both, to lead the kind of life that is basically satisfactory, I think the so-called crisis in middle age will be very minor. If you have led a life that is unsatisfactory, you may realize *that* in middle age, more than before, and it may amount to a crisis.

Q. And what childhood or adolescent factors are there that might lead to the crisis?

A. That would be terribly hard, again, to describe in general, because some people are happy as big-game hunters, others are happy as novelists. One can even be happy as a stamp collector. I would say that if you are a waiter, not a high, prestige job—if you like your job, if you like the people who come into your restaurant, you like to please them and to serve them well, if you make it a skillful job, I think you can lead a perfectly satisfactory life. On the other hand, if you are a lawyer, and you hate your clients, and you are bored with court procedure, and you feel you are not doing anything, you will have a crisis in middle age.

In their reviews of midolescence, the doctors touched upon the psychological effects of decrease in earning power, perhaps even loss of a high-paying job. This is, in a sense, separate from the other problems. This is the rent-money question, the problem that cannot be resolved through treatment or counseling but only by getting up the money. This next interviewee, who asked to remain anonymous, is a lawyer who specializes in labor relations. He has represented a number of business and municipal organizations at the bargaining table, and some unions as well. His views on middle-aged earning power are not the most positive views, but they are brass-tacks realism, based on hard experience. He speaks first of laws that protect against discrimination in employment because of age.

Labor-Relations Lawyer

Q. What legal protection is there?

A. There is a series of laws on the books relating to discrimination in employment. Certain bases for discrimination are made unlawful. For instance, race, religion, sex, national origin, and age. However, age is somewhat different from the other categories in that only the span between age forty and sixty-five is protected. Employers therefore have the right to discriminate on the basis of age up to age forty and beyond age sixty-five. They can have a policy, for instance, that says, "There shall be mandatory retirement at age sixty-five; everybody must stop; we'll never hire anybody sixty-five or over; everybody who works for us must leave, must retire at that age; that's it." And on the other hand the employers could say, "We will not hire anybody in their twenties, or their thirties," because they're in their twenties, or their thirties.

Q. Why would they ever do such a thing? People in their twenties and thirties are more alert and are worth hiring because they can be hired for less money and can be developed. And by the time they are thirty or thirty-five, they are of real use to the company, whereas a man of forty or forty-five, whom the company must hire, is fairly well set in his ways.

A. This is quite true, and this is why, in effect, the laws were enacted to protect employes only at age forty and above. The typical employer wants to have new blood, and new blood is usually young blood, people in their twenties and thirties. In terms of technical fields, the young men are the men who have recently been in college, or other training schools, not the old men, the forty- and fifty-year-olds. Of what use to a company developing some esoteric aspect of electronic R&D work is a man who has a twenty-year-old degree in electrical engineering? He may be of no use to them whatsoever because the art has advanced to the point where the people working, the engineers working on the projects, have to rely on knowledge that wasn't known to anyone five years previously.

Q. But someone recently a student may have this knowledge?

A. Yes.

Q. Would the company try to salvage some members of its older work force?

A. You see, the twenty-two-year-old guy comes in, and he *knows.* Now companies employing large engineering forces therefore have tuition-refund programs in which they encourage, they pay tuitions for engineers of any age to go back to school and learn the new, advanced fields. That, of course, is an expensive proposition for the company, and a man of fifty is not psychologically suited in many cases to go back to school. He doesn't want that. Maybe he never liked school; all right, he went through it, he endured it, he got his degree, long ago, and it's over with as far as he's concerned. In the technical fields, the question of who should be retained to do the work in a given enterprise may result in the older worker—perhaps the professional worker, the engineer, the chemist—being laid off because he's not as good as the younger man. I had a case two or three years ago involving the layoff of a senior chemist from a large corporation employing a sizable chemistry lab. He complained that he was laid off because he was fifty-three years old. Well, it was true that he was fifty-three years old. But the management of the company denied utterly that he had been selected for layoff because he was fifty-three. They said they selected him because he didn't know what they wanted to have chemists know in order to do the work for the lab. He filed a complaint with the New York State Commission for Human Rights. I, representing the employer, had to amass a great deal of data that showed, on a statistical basis, that the probabilities were that he had not been laid off because of age; the employer had retained two or three chemists older than he and had retained a chemist his age a year before—on the basis of these men's specialities.

Q. Then you could say there was no discrimination because the company had hired peers, contemporaries of this man . . .

A. Yes. That's a perfect defense. If you have filled the job with an older person, you've got a perfect defense. There's no more case.

Q. Do company managements realize the harm they do the middle-aged man by laying him off or phasing him out? Do they take into account the panic and trauma? Do they have any real humanist attitude toward this?

A. Any company may have a certain degree of humanistic, charitable or kindly or just plain reasonable and decent attitude toward people who have been working for it for a number of years. It depends on who's leading the company at a given time. Of course, it also depends on what the actual situation of the company is. If it's in dire straits, it cannot afford to carry people, to be very kind. If it's in good condition, well, maybe it will carry people. But if it's meeting stiff competition and has to trim down, in my experience in the American economy, it will lay off people even if they've been there for many, many years—and rationalize this on the basis of an economic decision, that it was necessary. And they do not have a bad conscience.

Q. It's then the welfare of the group as against that of the individual?

A. The company exists on an economic basis. If that economic basis is not adhered to, the company will cease to exist; it's not a charitable institution.

Q. Are men in their middle, panicking years a definite threat to the economy? Is—in a very broad sense—the middle-age crisis a threat to the economy and must it perhaps be dealt with harshly?

A. The people inhabiting the posts on the higher levels of management have gone through quite a test to get there. In my experience they have always been very strong men, strong-willed and determined men. I'm talking about the vice presidents, and, as well, the managers of the branches and to a lesser extent the higher levels of the middle management of the branch divisions of the company. Of course, there's the Peter Principle, that a man rises until he finds his degree of incompetency, at which point he fails; I've seen that happen quite a few times.

Q. Do you suppose you noticed it because you had heard of the Peter Principle, or the companies had heard of it?

A. No. I'm simply observing that I have seen men who have led large *parts* of a corporation, perhaps embracing 10,000 to 15,000 employes, have to be removed and replaced by other men not because of any failings that developed in them at any particular point in time, but simply because they never did have the ability to lead the 10,000- or 15,000-man unit although they had splendid ability to lead the 2,000-man unit—or, let's say, two or three 2,000-man units.

Q. Well, what is society to do with such people?

A. Get them back to the jobs that they can perform, but that's very difficult.

Q. It doesn't happen, does it?

A. No, because it's a question of pride, the pride that the man had in his relationships with his fellow executives. He has to leave that corporation and fall into the hands of the head hunters, and get slotted in some other place. If he has the sense to. Or he may simply throw in the towel . . .

Q. Head hunters?

A. You might call them "executive talent scouts." They make a great deal of money. And they specialize, of course, in the executive class, down to somewhere in the middle ranks of middle management; there, they lose interest in someone who's paid less than a certain salary. It depends to a large extent, I think, on the profession, the occupation involved. Take engineering. Take medicine. A certain percentage of the men involved in those professions will keep *au courant* in order to do their jobs well; they'll do this instinctively. They'll read their medical papers or their engineering papers on the train, at home, in the bathroom, who knows. And they will *learn,* and they will *keep abreast.* And so they aren't in any particular danger. It's the group of professional individuals who are not sufficiently intellectually stirred by the profession they're in to keep abreast of all the things that are happening in it who stand the best chance of being sidetracked and put off on a spur track.

Q. I find it hard to conceive of an engineer or a medical man who would not be constantly interested in rearming his knowledge. But this is something you've seen.

A. Yes. There are individuals who are not as intellectually stirred by the profession they're in as they are stirred by its practical aspects, by making a living from it. Some guy who's learned to do a job at ABC Corporation very efficiently, and is perhaps being paid handsomely to do it, is dispensed with because that job is dispensed with, through automation or other reasons.

Q. How can someone making $20,000 a year be replaced by automation?

A. It's not that he's *replaced* by automation. It's simply that automation makes him unnecessary, because a computer run by three computer repairmen and a computer operator is doing everything that he used to direct forty people to do. He's no longer needed. He can't go to XYZ Corporation across the street because they never had that procedure; it was just an ABC Corporation procedure; it didn't exist anywhere else. Oh, he may get an XYZ job at $7,000 a year, but that's unlikely. XYZ Corporation will say, "Why should we hire this man, who had that high salary just last month, for one third of what he earned before? Is his morale going to be particularly high? Is he going to be a real addition to our work force? Or is he going to be bitter, and start losing time?"

Q. Of all the problems of middle age that cause grief to employers and personnel managers, which *are* the worst?

A. There are several problems. Most of it is lack of education, or lack of perspective on what they're doing. This age group got jobs at the tail end of the Depression, when to get any job was of vital importance. It didn't matter whether that job involved any talent; the thing was just to get the job, to get the pay check, because the guy next door wasn't getting any; they had to fight the guy next door to get the job. And then came World War II, and there was a great Security Complex. And so they stuck to these jobs, they were very proud to have jobs . . .

Q. You mean they were in the service, or in defense work?

A. They might have been in the service; they wanted to get a job when they came back, and it was hard to get a job. When they got these jobs, they were very jealous of the minor, sometimes silly little duties that composed these jobs. And they got into mental attitudes concerning the jobs. If the work really had no job-content, it was still precious. Their sons will not feel that way. The sons will say, "What's the sense of doing that all the time just to get a pay check? Let me get some kind of a skill that I can market." Some of the young men seem to be objecting to dull, routine jobs. At General Motors —or was it Ford?—there was some strike activity because, it was alleged, jobs were too dull! This strike activity was not led by fifty-five-year-old men, but by twenty-five-year-old men.

Q. There was no money package involved? Working conditions were the only issue?

A. Working conditions, in the *technical* sense. Jobs were too *dull!* The assembly lines dehumanized them, and they wanted to tear the place apart. And it was a very modern plant, in the Midwest. The company could not, through the traditional approaches of labor relations, satisfy these demands. Now, with the fifty-year-olds, their demands about work usually are just about wages. That's all they really care about. They're not concerned that the job that they're holding is not terribly rewarding in terms of non-monetary things, because the whole purpose of having the job is to get the money to buy the family's groceries! That's the only reason they have the jobs.

In June of 1974 a semi-documentary television show, "Male Menopause: The Pause That Perplexes,"* examined midolescence from a variety of perspectives. One of the show's participants, Dr. Jermyn McCahan, chief medical director of AT&T Long Lines, testified to the attitude of the world's biggest communications industry toward the problem:

Dr. Jermyn McCahan

Our company has begun to recognize that there is such a thing as middle-age crisis, which can occur usually between the ages of thirty-five and fifty and usually manifests itself by an individual changing in his style of behavior and in his productivity.

We detect these symptoms in our people when, usually when a supervisor contacts us and indicates that an employe is beginning to slip, and he may tell us that their absence record, or attendance record, is beginning to become a problem, their productivity, either in quality or quantity, is becoming at issue, or, if they supervise other people, that their relationship with their work force has begun to become affected, either

*Male Menopause: The Pause That Perplexes, written by Michael de Guzman and produced by Richard V. Brown for NPACT, the National Public Affairs Center for Television.

by the individual neglecting his job or becoming too critical of his people.

This is not a respecter of position in the company. Anyone from the president to the people that are in the operating department doing craft work and operating can be affected. Usually the family's life is also affected by this, as well as the individual's community relationships. It's an all-pervasive thing and it is a problem that I am sure is common to all of industry. It probably has been with us for a long while.

Undoubtedly, it's on the increase, from my observations, and I think that industry in general must face into the fact that they do have these problems. Something can be done about them and we can save many valuable employes if we can intercede in their crises early and assist them through counseling to recover their stability in dealing with their emotional lives.

Men do some thinking before they take what they really consider the biggest step of their lives, before they change their careers, do something else to make a living, give up one professional life for another. And if the change is not sudden, they shop around, they examine their options; they take a good look at the grass on the other side of the fence to see if it really *is* greener. And, before they make their moves, many sit down with executive and business consultants, less pompously known in the world of business as "head hunters." This business plays a symbiotic role with big business itself; it places dead-ended executives in new businesses and it also finds executives for businesses, on request. Here is one of its practitioners. Like the lawyer, he prefers to be anonymous.

Executive and Business Consultant

Q. This is a taped interview with—and we're not saying with whom, are we? Your position in the company?

A. I'm operations manager.

Q. You've seen the outline for this book. What's your reaction to it?

A. Well—I think there's meat in it—I think it, uh, discusses part of the problem. And I think what's said there in essence is true of a great number of people. I wouldn't use it as a sweeping generalization covering all people, but it seems to be a sensible, fairly accurate appraisal.

Q. Part of the problem?

A. Well, I think it's only discussing a small portion of the effect that it has on middle-aged people. For example, I don't see any real connection between what your outline covers and the thing that we deal with. I was trying to see the connection.

Q. I think career change, career dissatisfaction, is very much a symptom of this kind of problem if you accept as fact that there *is* a second adolescence.

A. Well, I think that middle-aged people are concerned with many things, primarily growing old. I have no opinion of whether midolescence and adolescence are parallel. I just don't know. I don't think adolescents are at all aware of the past or the future. They're aware of the present. You're entitled to your opinion. I just don't buy that particular concept. The reasons for the emotional psychological problems of the middle-aged man are totally different from those of the adolescent.

Q. Do you find evidence of a pattern of frustration or dissatisfaction among men in their middle years?

A. Yes. Bear in mind that the people I see in the course of my professional role are people who are here because they are dissatisfied, frustrated, unhappy.

Q. Do they tend to unburden themselves to you?

A. Yes.

Q. About their job frustrations and their personal problems?

A. Part of every client's association with us involves both a clinical psychologist and a consultant.

Q. Does someone who comes to you have to go to the clinical psychologist?

A. It is the spark of every program. A full psychological evaluation and assessment, prior to meeting with the consultant.

Q. What kind of tests?—what do they measure?

A. Thematic apperception tests, sentence-completion tests, picture-drawing, projection of a person's own concept of his future. A pretty thorough battery of conventional tests.

Q. And do you get all the results from these tests or you only get the information that might be important to their career choices?

A. That portion of what the psychologist has learned that's relevant to the career program that the client is involved in.

Q. Are many of the people in personal turmoil, aside from deciding they're going to change careers?

A. I don't think you can separate them. *You can't separate career from personal life, because there's too great an interplay.* We deal with a person's whole life. His career is part of it. A very important part of it. And so is his personal life.

Q. Do the frustrations and bitterness show up in a lessened ability to cope with the pressures of a job?

A. Of course.

Q. A diminishing ability to get along with colleagues? Resentment of younger men who are catching up with or surpassing them?

A. Sometimes. Do people in their middle years resent younger people moving up? I don't think there is a pattern. I just don't see any generalization.

Q. Are middle-aged men who seek new careers or new jobs stable?

A. I would think so, generally. Again, bear in mind, the people who are coming here are also people who are motivated to make a change and to make a change for the better, and they're willing to pay a price for it. I don't mean in dollars—they're willing to pay a price in effort. These are generally people who are—who have a *past record of achievement.* So when you say are they stable, remember we're dealing in our company with the upper level of the working population, not necessarily in terms of what they've achieved but of what they would like to achieve. These *are* the people who are motivated, these *are* the people who are willing to pay the price in energy and effort and time to get what they want to get. We help them achieve whatever the goals are that are determined at these initial meetings with the psychologist and the consultant.

Q. What do you mean by "help them to achieve"?

A. We direct them, for example, if it's a change in position, an exploration of the marketplace. To find what kinds of positions are available.

Q. Do you know of definite positions that you arrange interviews for?

A. That is not what we do. We help people develop interest in themselves by other companies. *We don't perform the role of an employment agency.*

Q. You help a man evaluate himself and then point him in a direction and he's on his own from there.

A. Nooo, no! Our programs with clients in most cases have an active term of service, a relationship with the client for six months or more and, after that, on a lesser basis, for a period of twelve years.

Q. What is an active relationship?

A. Regularly scheduled meetings. And we work with the client in every step toward achievement of his goal, whatever that goal may be.

Q. If it's a career, then he has to find a place to act out his goal. If . . .

A. And if that is what's needed we will help him find what we will set as a desirable goal for him. In terms of career, but there's also another area in which we work—personal development. How does he change some of his own attitudes and behavior so that he can capitalize better on whatever his abilities are?

Q. "Change," not "mask," his attitudes?

A. Well, what word did I use?

Q. You said "change."

A. And that's exactly what I meant. *Change* his attitudes and behaviors. We all have behaviors that are destructive rather than constructive; we all have abilities on which we don't capitalize to the extent that we can and *rarely is a man in trouble on his job because he doesn't have the ability to handle it.*

Q. You don't believe in the Peter Principle?

A. People problems. The ability to handle a job has a great deal to do with your ability to deal with people. I'm talking about technical ability. How many people do you know who, for one reason or another, retire or are forced to resign, where it came about because of their inability to handle the technical part of the job?

Q. *You* tell *me.*

A. It's because of people problems—not being able to get along with subordinates or superiors, of being out of step with policy.

Q. Well, how do you teach a man to handle these things? It took a lifetime to develop these attitudes. I can't see how it could be ameliorated in a very short time.

A. I can understand your not understanding, but it would take hours and hours to explain how it is done.

Q. I just meant that it would seem to me it would take a long time.

A. No, it takes a relatively short time, if done properly, and if the person involved understands himself, understands what made him what he is.

Q. Do you have a background in psychology?

A. No. I'm not a psychologist; I'm a consultant.

Q. Your personal background—how is it tied in here?

A. I have a very standard business background. In sales and marketing, and general management, as do most of our consultants. But our psychologists are in constant touch with the client and the consultant who arranges the program.

Q. You said you keep in contact with a man intensely for six months and then less frequently for a period of time after that. Do you follow up even if he has changed his career?

A. Oh, yes. For a period of twelve years. During that period the client has the privilege of returning to any of our offices anywhere in the country for periodic evaluation of his situation, discussion of a problem, evaluation of a new job offer.

Q. But he would come to *you;* you don't check on *him.* So, unless a man comes back to you, you wouldn't necessarily know how he's doing and how your assistance has affected him?

A. Well, we have a research program that's done through the home office where we follow up certain clients that have agreed to allow us to do this. But by and large our clients are pretty mature individuals who really seek out the help they need.

Q. I was just wondering if you ever get calls saying everything is beautiful.

A. Not as often as the calls we get when a man has a problem, but we do.

Q. Do most of the clients that you have have a history of job stability?

A. I'd say yes.

Q. They don't necessarily come to you if their pattern has been one of long-term job changing?

A. There are some, but by and large it's not a common thing. We're dealing with a pretty high level of executive and if the people that come to us haven't already achieved their mark or achieved a great deal, they're younger people that are going to and that want to. So that while we occasionally get a job-hopper or someone that's been in constant trouble, this is not in any way a majority. People who come to us are people who for some reason have found themselves with a problem that they themselves don't know how to solve. And not necessarily a repetitive thing. It's only when you get to a certain area where your personality and your character come into more play. We find that some of these people will find their progress either slowing or stopping. Here you have the person who is merged out, a change in management in the company, and the person is let out, or he suddenly runs into somebody with whom he can't get along, or a change in the marketplace creates a problem. This is far more common than the sudden emergence of a problem in a man who's been living with constant trouble for ten or fifteen years.

Q. I'm also thinking of the man who feels he's reached a dead end in his firm or his career . . .

A. A man who works in a given field for ten or fifteen years and wakes up one morning and decides he's had it—he hates what he's doing—Daddy sent him into it or he got into it by chance or that was the first job that came along and he took it for—and he wakes up one morning and says "I don't like what I'm doing, I'll change." That's another kind of problem.

Q. Do you get many people who come with this sort of problem?

A. Sure.

Q. What would "many" be?

A. I don't want to mislead you. I don't know. Remember, there are other offices like this throughout the country and I only know part of what comes through *this* office because I don't know every client's background intimately, or his reasons for being here. And generally when people come in it's not for one reason—it's not easy to categorize.

Q. But, assuming . . .

A. You're dealing with an emotional situation in cases where this client doesn't just have one reason. And we have many people coming here to make a change, feeling at the time they come here that there's one purpose, one way of solving a problem, yet after they become clients they find that really wasn't what was bothering them at all. So, very often, people come to us and don't really understand what the real reason is. They believe the reason they come to us is what they think it is, but very often there are reasons they're not aware of.

Q. What happens in a case like that?

A. They learn as the program unfolds.

Q. Could you explain a little more about what you mean by the "program?"

A. You're talking about after they've decided to become an actual client?

Q. Yes.

A. They first come in for a series of meetings for which there is no charge, mainly to find out whether we can help them, whether they want the kind of service we provide. And if they become clients, there is a series of procedures which start with their filling out the assessment material, psychological material, which are then studied by the psychologist. The client then meets with the psychologist as long as it takes to give this client a good look at himself to find out what are his strengths, what are his limitations, what are the things he wants, his needs, his hopes, his fears, his desires—all the things that go to make up a person. And after this meeting he then meets with the consultant *and* the psychologist—the three of them, and this is all during the first day, to decide what his goals are. And I say, we set two kinds of goals: *career* goals, the type of job, the type of industry, at what level, what kind of company in terms of size, as well as personal development—what are some of the things that he wants to do, to change some of the ways in which he feels it would be of benefit to him to change. We have people that constantly are passed over and it shows in a pattern, because we all do function by pattern. They've managed to pick the same kind of boss in the previous three, four or five jobs over a period of years. It's this same pattern of deterioration from the time he starts with a company to the time he finally leaves, and it has to do with his fear, subordinates, his superiors, and these are the kinds of things that are pointed out and where there's a need to change, we help the client make these changes so that what happened before doesn't happen again. *Y'see, a man can change his job, but unless he changes himself as well, whatever has happened in the past is going to happen in the future.* Good *and* bad. We see this time and time again because we all perform according to certain patterns of behavior and certain patterns of—results. So if a man has had unsatisfactory results to him in the past, changing jobs alone isn't going to help. That's why we are sharply different from job-counseling or job-giving. We try to deal with a man as a human being. You can change jobs; anybody can find another job. But unless you change *you,* all the things that happened before, good or bad, are going to happen again.

Q. I guess it takes a tremendous amount of effort for someone to change.

A. Depends on what the change is. There are very simple changes that you could make in one quick lesson, but there are some changes that are difficult to make in some people. It depends on your motivation, depends on the reward, it depends on the pain you've suffered as a result of whatever attitude or behavior you want to change. It's an individual thing.

Q. It depends upon being aware of what's happening, too.

A. Without awareness, how do you know what to do? You can't solve a problem until you know what the problem is. That's part of what we hope to get the client to understand.

Q. Have you dealt with men who wanted total change? To go into entirely unrelated fields?

A. Yes, many times.

Q. Do many of these changes work out? Did the client, in effect, find a new lease on life as a result of a change in career?

A. Well, I don't like your expression. It's a cliché. Clients have changed careers radically and found themselves thoroughly happy with the change. Clients have changed careers radically and found that the ideal they thought this career represented didn't do this and they've gone back to their old careers or made *another* change. We get all kinds of results.

Q. When someone comes in here to change a field drastically do you sit down with him and discuss his concept of that field?

A. Oh certainly. That's part of what takes place at that first meeting; the psychologist and the consultant will lay out goals, and the goals must have two ingredients: one, they must be desirable to the client, obviously; two, they must be realistic and reasonably attainable. It might develop that your personality would be ideally suited to being an aquanaut, but if you have two pierced ear drums and claustrophobia, that is not a realistic goal; we strike it out.

Q. When someone finds that he's made a drastic mistake, he comes back to you, does he?

A. Our program covers what we call a guarantee of services, which simply says that if within a three-year period or after the decision, the final decision, is made, as to what this client will do in terms of career, that decision proves to have been an erroneous one, for any reasons, the client is covered for a three-year period. Should that happen, he is privileged to come back into the program and start right from scratch for another total exploration of marketability.

Q. Do employers ever come to you for help? In dealing with men? Perhaps trusted executives who seem to have reached a point where they feel at a dead end. What do you do for such employers?

A. We have some corporate clients for whom we do internal

counseling. We did more of it in the past, but this division is not involved in that kind of service, although, as I say, we have done it in the past and are doing some counseling for companies in the Midwest.

Q. Have you ever counseled a man not to make a change?

A. Yes. If that is the best alternative the man has, that's what we recommend.

Q. In terms of his abilities?

A. In terms of the whole man.

Q. Does he become a client then, or does this come out of his initial review?

A. Obviously, it has to be a result of his becoming a client. A man will come to us feeling he's got to get out of his company, he definitely can't grow, there's no room for promotion, he's been bypassed, his boss is a terrible person. But as he begins to *address* himself to himself, as he begins to *change* some of his behavior and attitudes, he becomes instrumental in changing the environment of the company. Suddenly he becomes unblocked, suddenly his relationship with his associates becomes different, his boss looks at him differently and what was a horrible place becomes a desirable place. This is not uncommon. And in nine cases out of ten the clients are extremely happy because there is always a fear of making a change, particularly where a man's been with a company for many years. So we're performing as much and in fact a greater service for such a man as the man we help to relocate. [pause] Does that make sense to you?

Q. Very much so.

A. Okay.

Q. What is the age range of your clients?

A. We've had clients in their low twenties—twenty-one, twenty-two, twenty-three—and *I* have had a client of seventy-two.

Q. What's the general age range?

A. It's hard to say. Of course we have less people in their sixties than people in their thirties and forties. I'd say the concentration is in the thirties and forties, but we do have a substantial number of people in their twenties as well as people in their fifties. The cluster, I'd say, would be the thirty-to-fifty range.

Q. Are any kinds of men hopeless? Men for whom it is impossible to find a career or job? And I think you partially answered that.

A. How did I answer it?

Q. Well, in terms of finding a new career or job—the place where they are and what they're doing is best for their abilities . . .

A. There are people who are in a position that for any number of reasons is wrong, where no change on their part can change it, where there are realistic barriers to their satisfaction [in performing]. These people have to change, but we continue to work with them, which is also part of the guarantee, until he agrees that he has made career progress or career advancement in his own company or elsewhere. The specific answer to your question: the only people that we cannot help, that we cannot work with, are those people who are so emotionally or psychologically upset that they cannot profit from our method or from what we do. In that case we tell them so and we recommend psychotherapy. Because we cannot work with a client that is really not in a position to be able to function within quote normal unquote limits.

Q. There's a law prohibiting discrimination on the basis of age. Is this law often flouted? When a company dumps someone because of age?

A. I can't answer professionally the question about age. It eliminates a man from consideration but it's never spoken, so there's just no way of being able to prove it. It's a kind of subtle thing that you can't pin down.

Q. Do clients try to change their statistics? Do some pretend they're five, ten years younger?

A. If they do, we don't know about it because they're not going to tell us about it. And we accept clients on the basis of the way they present themselves. We're not here to criticize or question; we accept people as they come to us, on the basis on which they come to us. I'm sure there are people who, not knowing what we do initially, might give a younger age, for example, or have a degree which perhaps they don't have. But if that's the way they present themselves and that's the only knowledge we have, we certainly aren't going to check into it or explore it. Now: If we see something that doesn't make sense, I would ask this person and accept whatever answer the client gives. We also counsel clients to level with prospective employers and to present themselves as they are. We like clients to feel adequate and to have the kind of self-acceptance that a person should have, regardless of age. This is one of the changes in attitude that we help develop, so that by the time the client is through the program, he is walking a little more proudly.

Q. We didn't discuss whether you felt there really was a middle-aged crisis or not. And this question: Is there anything an employer can do to help a man get through his middle-age crisis intact?

A. I don't necessarily buy that concept that there is a middle-age crisis any more than I buy the concept that there has to be the adolescent crisis. I think it depends on a man's environment, I think it depends on his own make-up, I think it depends on his relationships at home and I, uh—I don't recognize it; I don't necessarily disagree with it but I just don't recognize the commonality of this "middle-age crisis." So it's difficult for me to comment. If you have self-love, you receive love and are capable of giving it; if you have basic inner confidence, people will have confidence in you and you are able to have confidence in others.

Q. You don't feel that there is a middle-age crisis.

A. There are many factors involved other than the fact that chronologically a man is now at a given age. A lot of the changes have to do with changes in social morés, have to do with changes in financial situation, changes in their levels of knowledge and awareness, of understanding, of—well, that's why I can't comment on it. That's what I'm saying about this book on middle-age crisis. I'll tell you what my opinion is, that it's just as big a crock as the so-called adolescent crisis. I went through adolescence and there was no adolescent "syndrome" at all.

Q. No churning, no emotional problems, no rebellion against parental values?

A. Well, not the latter. Yes, during adolescence when the hormones are beginning to flow, where you're concerned about your acceptance by somebody of the opposite sex, yeah. But not in the sense that they're talking about today. The rebellion in values is nonsense. The world is changed. And at the time that I was an adolescent my values were identical with my parents'; and you know something? As a Depression baby, an adolescent, I really didn't have time to worry, nor the affluence, to worry about the so-called adolescent syndrome. I had an object, and that was to prepare myself to earn a decent living so that I could have the things I wanted, and as time went on, marry, raise a family. That was the objective and it was surprising how, with a goal, that all these things that are written about ad nauseam didn't even exist. We live in a different world and our kids don't have the values that we have because they haven't been brought up to the same values and our kids *don't know what their goal is.* Now when you don't have a direction, you cast around. You see, that's the beginning of the so-called adolescent problem. It's the same thing with a middle-aged man. There was a time when a middle-aged man accepted his increasing years and was still working, still providing for his family, and there weren't as many avenues, there weren't jet flights, there wasn't TV, you know all these millions of stimuli. He had no choices to make. He lived in his neighborhood, one out of ten people had a car and he had limited choices, he accepted the choices he had. Some people were happier than others. But all this nonsense about, y'know, the deteriorating, the aging process, hormones, glands—we're living in radically changing times. You know the changes in ten years are changes that would have taken a century to produce. It's the world that's in a state of turmoil. Everything. The world is speeded up. And, you know, while people still make money, I still think that you can't attribute it to a—you know it's a real catchy name, midolescence—but, uh, I would have spelled it, you know, "el" but—oh, well, I see you're trying to convey middle-something. It's a catchy phrase, but I don't buy it.

Q. Men have a renewed, a revived interest in sex at a certain age.

A. Really?

Q. Yes. I'm asking *you.* This is a question.

A. Oh. Well—it's so easy to generalize and, you know, this may very well be true, but a man can only speak from his own experience. I don't really notice any change in my interest in the opposite sex from what it was from the time I became aware that there were women. There are cases like those where you battle with your teen-age son at the same time that you're trying to get into the pants of a teenage girl his age and I'm sure it exists, but as far as this thing as a pattern, as the outline says, why, I don't buy it. What I'm saying is there is a constant revision of value as you go through life and here you pin it to a period of years, and what *I'm* saying is that the changes in behavior that take place take place from the teens to the twenties, in the twenties and thirties, in the thirties and the forties.

Q. You feel it's ongoing.

A. Right. Anyway, I don't thoroughly accept the basic premise.

III.
The
Men
Speak

The "Male Menopause" TV show spent an hour of prime time examining midolescence, in rap sessions between middle-aged men and women, in brief interviews with medical authorities, and in dramatizations—a despairing woman talking about her husband on the phone, a midolescent confronting himself in the mirror while shaving (much like George in Chapter I), a man dictating a memo of grievances to his boss. "The monotonous tone throughout," John J. O'Connor, the television critic of the New York Times, wrote of the show, "is one of self-pity."

Somewhere along the way between the onset of their crises and their acceptance of their situations, the men you are about to encounter in this chapter suffered, too, from self-pity. It is an important part of midolescence. Practically no midolescent escapes it. But, as these interviews will show, self-pity is the beginning of a long process that leads through the crisis to recognition of a man's real situation—that he is what he is and must learn to live with himself as he is, not as what he dreamed he would be.

This chapter deals mostly with what midolescence does to marriages. Only one of the interviewees here is a lifelong bachelor. Of the others, two are still married to their first wives; four have been or are about to be divorced; of those four, one has arrived at a unique arrangement with a woman in which he pays her for her services, and each of the partners to this contract, when he or she wishes, can take advantage of a thirty-day escape clause. The wives of the two men who are still married are interviewed in the next chapter.

In the previous chapter doctors spoke of the middle-age crisis as professionals. The first man interviewed here is a doctor who is able to do that and one thing more—to look at the problem as it affected his own life. In middle age, he divorced a woman to whom he had been married nearly thirty years and chose as a second wife a woman younger than most of his children.

Dr. A

Q. Doctor, you're what age, fifty-one?

A. Fifty-two.

Q. And, you've been married twice?

A. Yes.

Q. Your first wife, with whom you had six children, is about your age, and your second is—thirty years younger?

A. That's right. And we have a child, a girl, now two.

Q. What do you want out of life now, as opposed to when you were starting your career? What were your goals then and what are they now?

A. I don't think I had any particular goals twenty or thirty years ago, except to become a doctor. Now? I feel that I want satisfaction in my work more than I have. My work has largely become drudgery, dictating so many reports on accidents, looking at busted heads. I'm making a lot of money, but I don't think I've ever been interested in that for itself, making money. I'm satisfied that I'm in neurosurgery, but at my age I'd like to add something new; I'd like to look at a lot more tumors, for instance, than busted heads. I could wish, I think, that my practice had more of the classical type of neurosurgery than so many malingerers who are involved in litigation concerning injuries that do not exist! But this seems to be indigenous to the practice of neurosurgery. I do look forward to having a whole new family, with more children, and we're working on that.

Q. What regrets do you have about the conclusion of your earlier marriage?

A. The only regret I have is that my first marriage was not terminated earlier. I think we were bad for each other from the start, but like so many married couples we did not separate because of the children. It was unfortunate that we didn't split up shortly after we were married. Oh, I suppose, with some form of help, support, advice and therapy, something could have been done, but it has been my experience that it's very difficult to change people. The time to abandon ship was many years ago when it became apparent at the start that we did not enjoy each other's company and really did not do much for each other.

Q. How did you meet your new wife? Were you still married then?

A. Yes, I was still married, but it was almost all the way to hell. She was a secretary at a hospital I'm associated with. We had nothing in common, at first. Then I flirted with her, I guess, and we went out together, and after the first night we realized that there was something between us. Er, she liked older men; I was fearful of the age difference, but I found myself fascinated by the prospect. I'd like to say that there were many factors about her that were attractive to me apart from her physical attributes, and these were her apparent genuine love and sincerity and loyalty and mentality. You haven't asked me how I like my new life.

Q. Well, I thought you'd get to it without being asked, Doctor.

A. I will. I am a different man today. I have much more peace within myself. I live in an environment that has virtually no stress; we argue very little. Of course, I have a new baby, and I enjoy this immensely.

Q. The differences between them, Wife No. 1 and Wife No. 2?

A. Well—those differences are obvious, my second wife is that much younger, my first didn't have parallel interests with me, she fooled with other men, young men, at the end. You have to realize that I did not seek out a younger wife. It just happened. What's most interesting, I think, is that since I've been with her I have never had the slightest interest in anyone else, whereas, with the first wife, I always had interest in someone else.

Q. What do you feel, what do you think when you look in a mirror?

A. Nothing much. I feel that I have very little concern, or sensitivity, about getting older. But I'm always disappointed when I see a recent photograph of myself because, in my mind's eye, I don't see myself as I really am. But my wrinkles and my aging face don't really bother me. Not in the mirror. In photos, perhaps; fortunately, I don't have to see photographs of myself very often.

Q. Of those people with whom you and your wife associate, are most in your age group? Hers? Does either of you feel like a stranger among people of the other person's age group?

A. Probably most of our contacts are with people in my age group, though there are two or three couples in hers, and I think I thoroughly enjoy them. I don't feel like a stranger with her group and while I'm not sure how she feels about mine, I doubt that there's any problem there. We have quite an active social life. More, for me, than ever.

Q. Does your wife possibly have any difficulties adapting to relatives who are your age? And most of your blood relatives would be your age. Er—if you didn't seek out a younger wife, might she possibly have sought you out to escape the challenges of associating with the younger people of her peer group?

A. When I met her she already had a lot of relatives much older than herself, and she got along with them splendidly. Yes, I think she does prefer older people. Seek me out to escape such challenges? I know of no evidence.

Q. What did your first wife do to damage her marriage to you? What did she accuse you of doing? You said there were young men in the picture at the end . . .

A. Yes, there was. One young man, anyhow.

Q. What were the real differences between you, you and your first wife? Who was this young man, how did he get into the picture, and was your second wife a contributing factor?

A. First of all, I met my second wife after my first wife and I had been separated and our final divorce was imminent, so I don't think the younger girl had anything to do with it. I believe that my first wife became intellectually arrested in high school; I don't think she was ever of any value to me professionally; she was always embarrassing and humiliating me in public with her behavior. I don't think we ever had what you could call a conversation. She was a tremendous financial burden. She had no concept of financial reservation and frugality. She was a pathological liar; never learned or acquired the value of truth and objective analysis. Finally, she started to drink too much and the young man came on the scene at the age of eighteen. To this day, I don't know what the ultimate relationship between the two was. It may have been a mother-son relationship, but there is some evidence that it was more than that during the late 1960's and early 1970's, as my children lived in constant fear of my coming home and finding him in this house—and he was here often when I was absent. You know, this is all something I think I'd rather drop, right here.

Q. Of course. Doctor, what is the stronger stimulus in a man's life, work or sex?

A. I think work is, but I think also that that's applicable only when the work is of some interest. I don't know if you've ever done anything that was completely interesting and absorbing, in work, but I did. It was during the Korean War, when I worked in a body-armor project for the army. It was so exciting for me that I had no interest in anything else. I think the only people who experience this extreme satisfaction, this complete absorption in their work, are people like Henry Kissinger; what he does is extremely fascinating, productive and self-satisfying. In my field, something comparable now might be when I am involved in surgery in something that is unusual, and I am capable of correcting a person so that he or she is normal forever, rather than dying or being crippled by the condition that I am correcting. I think the vast majority of humans are in a trap, not doing what they really like, and for them, then, sex then becomes more of a drive than work.

Q. You do agree with me that there is a middle-age crisis?

A. Oh, yes. Oh, yes. I'm sure that was what happened to me, and I'm not sure I'm out of it. I'm not sure I'll be out of it for five years.

Q. Have you taken notice of its effect on your colleagues?

A. Doctors aren't immune from ailments. I've noticed it in many of my colleagues and contemporaries. And about a year or so ago, I read several professional articles about it. I'm sorry to say this, but I believe that very few contemporaries of mine are happy with what they're doing, and really enjoying themselves.

Q. Forgetting the professions, like yours, like the law, teaching, which the practitioners stay in—is there any kind of solution, or preventive measure, that might . . .

A. I think that somehow, an individual should program himself for two or three careers, so that he can change his emphasis when he is in his forties. Yes, that's impossible for me, though I would like to do different things within my field. I'm going to a seminar on neurosurgery in Europe this spring.

Q. Taking your wife?

A. And child.

Q. And what is your prognosis of your own midolescence, doctor?

A. All right. I think that state of mind, that crisis state of mind, awareness that something was wrong, something could be wrong again—I think that it will be with me the rest of my life. And I think that's good, because it will motivate me to strive always to do something better, and different.

You met him in Chapter One. He is a creature of appetites and strong emotions, which proclivities have gotten him into trouble and also have earned him what achievements he has scored in life: flip over a man's faults and you sometimes find his virtues. He speaks graphically, often in street language, about his sex life, to the degree that here and there it will seem that he is telling a better story than what actually happened. He will also seem to shape the events of his life to suit him; in the next chapter, his wife, to whom he is still married, gives her side.

Mr. A

A. Wait, wait, hold it a second before you ask me anything. You're going to give people fictional names or something?

Q. Not exactly names. I'm doing it like—you see, you'll be Mr. A, the next case will be Mr. B, and so on down the line.

A. Sounds fine. Go ahead.

Q. Okay. You're what, forty-nine? Fifty?

A. Please! [laughter] Forty-eight.

Q. Forty-eight. Okay. And you're married, and you have four children?

A. Four children. You could say six. My wife had two children when we got married and they lived with us. Two boys.

Q. How do you feel about where you are now?

A. Where we're living?

Q. I mean in business, in family life, professional life, sex life, social life.

A. Oh. Kind of a big order. Let's see. How do I feel about where I am now? I have few complaints, I suppose. Kind of like . . .

Q. But there are complaints?

A. I was going to say, yesterday I was in a bar watching the 100th running of the Kentucky Derby and there was this great big field of twenty-three horses, and the bar had a pool, and I'd drawn Confederate . . .

Q. Gamble, do you?

A. —General. No. That's the one vice I don't have. There was this pool, and I drew Confederate General, thirty to one. That kind of thing. Cost me all of a dollar. Anyway, I was watching all those horses, more like a cavalry charge than a race. Well, you know what happened. Cannonade won it. I really didn't expect anything else. You can't dope a Derby. The horses haven't got any records. Anyway, about three-quarters of the way through, I heard the announcer say something about Confederate General, and, you know, I sat up and took notice? All right, maybe he wasn't in the lead, and maybe he didn't even place or show but he was *in* the race and before it was over, he was *heard* from. And he had pretty stiff competition, and he was thirty to one, but he was in there. Well, I was thinking about this interview today, and I kind of thought I'd mention that. *I haven't made it all the way I'd like to, but at least, er . . .*

Q. At least you were in there.

A. Yeah. Probably a lousy analogy.

Q. Not too bad.

A. I don't think much about being a star any longer. I don't know that that's too important.

Q. But if you suddenly became a star, you wouldn't mind?

A. Oh, hell, no. But if that doesn't happen, it won't kill me.

Q. I understand you're not unwilling to talk about your sex life.

A. Well, I think what happened to me has a lot to do with what you're doing, what you're trying to find out, about middle-aged guys.

Q. Then you don't mind if we get to that first. All right, Mr. A, how's your sex life?

A. Today? Well, maybe not all I'd like it to be, but you settle for what you've got.

Q. I don't understand. You mean as a rule?

A. No, I mean in the light of what happened to me. My sex life today—let's say it's not what it was, once. There was a time when we'd do it six, seven times a day. And of course we were both a lot younger then.

Q. You mean when you were first married.

A. Yes, and before. This was in the early fifties.

Q. "And before." There was a long, er, courtship?

A. For about a year, yes. I don't think there were—there was a day we didn't do it at least twice.

Q. At your home?

A. At my home?

Q. Well, you spoke of two children from an earlier marriage, I assume she was married when you met her, I assume it was difficult for you to . . .

A. You assumed wrong. She was just divorced, we did it at her place. I was living there.

Q. And it was a year before you and she were married?

A. It was a California divorce, there was an interlocutory thing.

Q. I see. And she had the children.

A. Right.

Q. How old were these children when you entered the picture?

A. Seven and four. They're both married now. We used to do things like take baths with them—a real father-mother-family kind of thing.

Q. This practice of communal nudity—

A. Oh, I don't think you can call it that. It wasn't conscious.

Q. All right, family nudity—was that a reflection of your own upbringing, or did it contradict your own upbringing?

A. Contradict would be a hell of a lot more like it. The word around our house when I was a kid was, "A boy should not see his parents' naked bodies." But in another way, maybe it was a—what was the word you used?

Q. Reflection.

A. Yeah. I spent a lot of time alone when I was a kid. My brother —there were two kids in our family, he was older—was always off at school, my parents were very social, my mother had clubs to attend and stuff, and in the afternoons I'd find myself alone in the house. And I'd take off all my clothes and look at myself naked in the mirrors. A "reflection," all right.

Q. In your adolescence?

A. In my childhood, about seven to ten, eleven years old. And I'd get an erection, before I knew what it was for. Sometimes a boy and his sister, who lived next door, would come over and we'd have naked-parties together. Not doing anything, just looking, and giggling. Kids do that.

Q. Were you ever caught doing this?

A. Not as a group, but I was. A governess of mine caught me looking at an illustrated book about nudists; this was in the mid-thirties and the nudist movement was getting a lot of publicity then. And I was naked and looking at these pictures, the men and women naked together, everything hanging out—and the governess walked in. She grabbed the book away. "That's a sickness," she said, meaning my erection. She said, "if that happens again we'll have to take you to a doctor!"

Q. To—a *doctor?*

A. You've got to remember when this was. People weren't too enlighted about this stuff then. And when she mentioned a doctor—that was all she had to tell me. I was scared shitless of doctors. I'd been a pretty sick kid as a younger kid and the medical treatments of the thirties weren't quite as painless as they are today. And this modern talk about how masturbation is normal, and harmless—my Christ, at that time my parents, and the governess, and everybody —they would have considered that something like saying rape, or murder, are normal.

Q. When did you have your first real sex experience?

A. The first orgasm?

Q. No, the first time with a girl.

Q. Oh. Yeah. I was about fourteen, fifteen. Some guys I knew, they knew this little girl who must have been about eleven, and one day she went down on the three of us. I remember her saying she liked me best because I was the biggest. Bless her dirty little heart!

Q. This became a steady thing for you and your friends? And the little girl?

A. *Christ,* no! A kid, he may like to jerk off, but he's always real gut-scared he's going to get caught doing it. He may like to get blown —doesn't everybody?—but when it's over with, what if it's found out? I used to walk the other *way* if I ever saw her coming down the street.

Q. And your first real, mature—

A. Whatever that means. My first "real, mature" experience with a woman, where I laid her, was when I was in the army and blind drunk and about to go overseas, in 1945. And then there were whores, and one-night stands, and all that. Just getting my rocks off. What *I'd* call my first "real, mature" experience with a woman came in '46, when I'd just gotten out of the army. We lived in a small town and that summer she was renting a house there. She was an artist, she painted, did illustrations. She was also a little older and a lot more experienced than I was. She'd been married. The—what is it, the verdict of history, is that how it goes?—might tell you how good an artist she was; nobody's ever heard of her. But she did a lot for me. She taught me how a lot of taboos are really a lot of horse-shit . . .

Q. Like what happened with the little girl?

A. Yeah. I've been grateful to her ever since, to steal a quotation from Mr. W.C. Fields, rest his soul. But in lots of other ways this artist girl was bad news, other ways being other guys. This thing didn't end very happily.

Q. Was there an objective, operative factor in the ending?

A. Yeh, the summer ended and I left town to go to college. I, er, I think one of the problems, looking back on all this from the wisé-guy position of—Jesus, almost thirty years?—later, was that I never once spent the night with her. Women like you to do that. I didn't know that then.

Q. Why wouldn't you stay with her? What was stopping you?

A. My parents. I was living at home that summer.

Q. I don't understand. You were grown up. You were—what, twenty-one?

A. Twenty.

Q. And you'd been in the army, you'd been overseas.

A. Right.

Q. And still you had to go home every night?

A. See, I guess I was still tied to the silver cord. Oh, I might stay out all night, very seldom, but when I did it would make me feel more guilty than anything I *did* while I was out, the fact that I hadn't told my parents, that I was worrying them. And you better believe, when I'd come home, I'd get a lecture: "We were ready to call the *police.*" Which they never did.

Q. Did you ever grow out of this? I assume something happened to make your parents accept the fact that you were an adult and could take care of yourself.

A. Well, it was gradual, I suppose. One, I was away from home for long periods of the year when I was in college. So they kind of got used to it, more than they had when I was in the army—hell, everybody's kid was in the service in the mid-'40's, and *because* of that, their parents still thought of them as kids; because it was true of *every* family. But, er—all right. In 1949, I got out of college—I did four years in three, incidentally, by going to summer sessions—and in '49 I went to work. And I met this girl, who was also working, and we dated, and before too long, it happened.

Q. What, the cutting of the silver cord?

A. Yes. Don't get ahead of me. About the second week I knew her I called for her to take her to a movie or something, and she was all dressed, and somehow we started to neck. In her apartment; she lived alone. And—we suddenly decided we'd rather fuck. That was the first time I laid her. It was great. Now—she didn't have a phone. There was a phone out in the hallway, but the first time you're laying a great new girl, who the hell's going out in the hall to call home and say, "Mama, I won't be home tonight!" So we balled the whole night. Getting to know each other, you know. Marvelous. And in the morning, I did put on my coat and go out to call my parents. Same old shit! "We were ready to call the *police!*" I came back inside and told the girl about this and I think her reaction was what cut that silver cord once and for all. She said, "Honey, you're a grown-up man; you're twenty-four years *old!*"

Q. Mr. A, how many women have you had sex with, if you can count them?

A. About thirty-five. Why? Is that a lot?

Q. Well, the fact that you can answer so promptly . . .

A. I thought you'd ask, so I counted in advance. [Laughter].

Q. —indicates the value, the importance you put on that. You didn't marry this girl?

A. No. We just kind of went our ways. I . . .

Q. You what?

A. Once she said, "I almost love you." I just happened to think of it. I guess I remember it more than I remember girls saying they did, er, *love* me. I hope she married—I hope she got a good guy, because she was good news.

Q. Before you met your wife, were there any girls you had sex with or didn't have sex with that you thought you were going to marry?

A. None I didn't have sex with. I didn't bother much with women I wasn't going to have sex with. Looking back.

Q. I see.

A. The girls I did have sex with before I met my wife, yes, there were about four I thought I was going to marry. And three of them were girls I went to college with, before this girl I've just talked about, the girl who cut the silver cord.

Q. And why didn't you marry any one? Did you think you were too young to be tied down?

A. That, sure, I guess, underneath. All right. The first of these, the girl was a rebound affair for me. We had some sex and then she knocked it off abruptly and said we ought to save it for marriage. I told her to save it for somebody else. Another girl in college, we had sex like you wouldn't believe, in cars, on the beach at night, once even in a movie theater. And one day, one afternoon, we went to a sorority sister's home, near the campus—I didn't know why—and after a couple of polite minutes over tea the sorority sister got up and handed the girl a box of Kleenex and asked us to be careful of the sheets, and excused herself. And then the girl, about a month later, phoned me to say an old boyfriend had come over to her house, and they'd made it in her living room, and would I please try to understand, and hell, no, I wouldn't. And then the third college girl, a rebound from the second, we did a lot of balling the last year I was in school and then she went off to the South to teach for a year and absence didn't make the heart grow fonder. [pause] Then, a good while after I'd started working, I had a thing with a girl who could do crossword puzzles in her head, and we had sex, too, but it didn't compensate for the fact that I wasn't as intelligent as she was or her family was, and all of us knew it. So. Yeah, I guess I wanted to marry her, but I'm sure that never entered her mind, or her family's.

Q. And then, after that last unhappy thing, you met your wife?

A. Not right away. There was a period of about a—no, not a year, about six, seven months—when I was laying everything I could get my hands on. The rejection of the girl who was smarter than I was probably had a lot to do with this. For about four months I lived with a woman in her forties—by that time, I should add, I *was* living away from home. Well—that, er, palled, or began to pall, after a while, and I began turning to other women, in a kind of crazy acceleration.

Q. Let me interrupt. How old were you then?

A. Mid-twenties.

Q. Go on.

A. And, er, I laid a couple of guy's wives, and I laid a girl from the office where I was working, and I began drinking a lot and partying a lot and that led to more, and more, and by the time I met my wife, the *week* I met her, I'd had—something like three women in five days. And I guess I was getting tired of it; maybe I wanted a home, something steadier, and she provided that. With the built-in family.

Q. Is there an age difference?

A. Between my wife and me? Yeah. Eight years. She's eight years older.

Q. These girls, the one-night stands, whatever. Can you remember what kind of girls they were?

A. Yeah. I guess I've given you the impression I thought I was some kind of God's gift to women, I didn't mean to. A kid that age, if he wants to do that, the girls are there, but you can't be too particular. I mean you couldn't say they were all God's gift to *men!* What kind of girls were they? Well, one was a girl with terrible skin who was almost embarrassingly grateful that I'd fuck her; another was a girl I'd known all my life, nice-looking, quiet girl, a real lady, in fact, and what I remember of her is—I'd rented this summer cottage at a lake with three other guys and one happy 6-in-the-morning she's down on me and the other guys and girls are pounding on our door and saying, "Breakfast, we're going to have breakfast," and I go off and she spits it out and says, "We've had breakfast." And another was a girl who must have weighed a hundred and three sopping wet and she showed me what Noxzema was for, the old back door. And a nut who got her biggest kicks jerking you off under the table in restaurants. And a poor soul who was the village nympho, and everybody knew it, and they'd laugh at you. Hey. Play all this back, will you?

Q. Sure. [brief clicks and whirrs].

A. I seem to have told you about all the comedians. Actually there was probably more to all those girls than that. And I seem to have told you more about me than about them. But we're talking about sex and that's, those are the things. Anyway, I was into all that, and probably getting a little—what's the word? Sated? Satiated? And so when my wife came along I could have all that and a kind of home, too.

Q. It seems to have lasted.

A. Yeah. Work, having more kids, getting ahead in business. And then, in the mid-'60's, when I was really getting there in life, I had two affairs. Two years apart.

Q. The ages of the women?

A. No, the years, two years apart. When these things happened. The affairs.

Q. You don't call them love affairs.

A. The first certainly wasn't a love affair. You could call it a sex affair, a business affair. I'd just been promoted to a big job. She was in a business that did business with us and I could do her some good. She also happened to be a girl I'd worked with on my first job, back in the early '50's, a girl I hadn't laid then, but always wanted to. So, in the mid-'60's, there was this thing with her, and two years later there was another one.

Q. Did either of these women remind you of your wife?

A. I don't know if that applies. Well, you might say the first one did in terms of character; she was an aggressive, think-on-your-feet, get-it-done, survive-kind-of-girl. She knew something not everybody does: How to live by your wits.

Q. You admire that in women?

A. Being able to think on your feet? I admire that in anybody. Hey. Go to a supermarket and take a good look at the dumpy fat-ass housewives with the curlers in their hair! How long would they last in the business world, how could they amount to anything without their husbands? Now, the second girl, she probably reminded me of my wife in a different way, in bed.

Q. She was physically like your wife?

A. The opposite. My wife is big up here and slim down there, this girl was built just the other way around. What I mean is the attitude toward sex. There was a lot of give-and-take with the second girl, you felt relaxed with her, you didn't just get your rocks off, sex was kind of fun.

Q. And was there the same similarity, the same parallel with the first girl in the sixties?

A. The girl I'd worked with once?

Q. Yes.

A. No. There were hangups there. Oh, you might sleep with her, but if you did you'd only do it once—wham, bam, thank you ma'am, and for the rest of the night she wanted to sleep. She'd had some trouble in her life in that department. She'd had a long and, I guess, miserable marriage to a guy in South America. And she was, she had an American Catholic background, and she went to live down there, and right off the bat he tells her he's got a mistress. He wasn't ashamed of it, either. He told her it was the custom. And he told her she ought to get herself a lover, or some such. Well, it shook her up so much that I guess she retreated from any such steady arrangement with a man, even as a lover. She didn't get a lover, but she got a girlfriend. A double-gaited girlfriend, they'd do it with each other, with another man, another woman, groups, maybe six or seven in one can of worms. And then finally she got all this up to here and she bugged out of all of it and came back to the States. And also came all the way back, reverted is the word, I think, to—to her background, the American Catholic attitude toward sex.

Q. Which would imply marriage?

A. She didn't revert that far. And her attitude toward nudity, that was funny, too. I mean peculiar, not laughable. Here this girl had been in the orgy-scene for years and—see, you might have been balls naked with her for a whole night, in her apartment, and then the next time you rang the bell downstairs she'd say, "Oh, don't come up *now;* I'm not *dressed!*" This is what that experience south of the border did to her; she got her—she got something inside her head all screwed up. Wouldn't let a man see her in her slip but wouldn't mind being naked with him all night. I—looking back, I guess I'm very sorry for her.

Q. Both this girl and the second one were fifteen, twenty years younger than you?

A. No, no, I told you the first girl was somebody I'd worked with fifteen or so years earlier. She was, oh, maybe two and a half, three years younger; the second one, now, yes, she was seventeen, eighteen years younger than I was. And she was also a much bigger mistake. I suppose you've found out that the worst kind of trouble like this is when a guy starts fooling around with a girl in his office?

Q. It depends on the case, of course, but for the sake of this discussion with you—since you seem to think so—let's say yes.

A. Well, she was a kid in my office. Isn't that where it usually happens? Something to do with your business life, which is the other life you lead, apart from your home life, your, er, community . . .

Q. Often enough to make it a danger area, anyway.

A. Yeah.

Q. These two women must have been somewhat similar. Er—no, let me put it this way. They must have been in some way, perhaps, *different* from your wife and *like* her at the same time?

A. What kind of a question is that?

Q. [laughter] Not sure I really know.

A. Well, number one, they were both brunettes, and my wife is a blonde. Number two, my wife is big up here, as I said, and neither of these girls were much in the upstairs department. And I've told you about their different attitudes toward sex . . .

Q. Yes.

A. All right. Number three, and this is something tying the two of them together with nothing to do with my wife, I wasn't the only guy in the picture. I mean each of them had another guy, in addition to me, guys they'd had something going with for a long time before I came along.

Q. A marriage, in either case? You mentioned the South American . . .

A. No, in neither case. The first girl left the South American in South America. And she was back here about a year and a half before I took up with her. Aren't we sidetracking again? I mean, this is more about these girls than about me . . .

Q. That's all right, that's all right, go on.

A. Yeah. So, the first girl. Once I called her up and I swear to God I thought I had the wrong number. She was talking to me like she was some office receptionist and I was some pest trying to get past her to her boss. I knew about this guy. He was a guy way, way down on his luck. She told me about him right off the bat. I'll give her that much. Sometimes it was the other way around, sometimes he'd call while I was there. He was a sick guy, a jealous guy; she'd make me practically stop *breathing* while she talked to him. And these were very long phone calls. She'd reassure him, she'd tell him he wasn't taking care of himself, not to forget he had to see the doctor—and he'd talk, and I'd sit there holding my breath and listening to this whining little voice coming out of the phone. And then if the tables were turned, if I called and he was there, I got the Goddamn office receptionist. See, she didn't try to hide him from *me,* she tried to hide *me* from *him.*

Q. Was this man a factor in the final break-up between you and the girl?

A. Yeah. I had a date with her. I was going to try to begin breaking it off—how do you break anything off easy?—and I phoned before going over there, and got the office receptionist. Well, that was it. I slammed the phone down and picked it up again and got to my wife, at home, and told her the real reason I'd been coming home so late at night, or not at all. And I went home, and we had our scene, and we both cried, and we kissed, and—went to bed and tried to start all over.

Q. All that was the *result* of an affair. What about the *cause* of the affair?

A. The cause? Here was a girl I'd always wanted to lay offering to lay me, what was I going to do, spit in her eye?

Q. I think you can give me a better answer than that. You've told me you had an active sex life with your wife.

A. Yeah, but years before.

Q. See, that's what I'm getting at. You'd never been unfaithful before?

A. No. Oh, I see—if it was all that great at home why was I going somewhere else?

Q. That's what I mean. Why?

A. Yeah. Sure. Well, at the time of this first one, the kids were, they were old enough not to have to be supervised twenty-four hours a day any more. And my wife had once been an active business-woman. So when that time came, she didn't have to be a mother twenty-five hours a day, and she wanted to go back into business, and she did. She opened a fabrics store in the town where we lived. And it kept her on her feet all day, and it stayed on her mind, and when I'd come home, maybe drunk, and looking for a lay, she'd say she just didn't feel like it. And this happened more than once, more than ten times, and I got a little fed up with it, I felt neglected. So, when what's-her-name walked into my life again, I walked out of my own door, my own bedroom door, for a while.

Q. And after the confession and the renewal of your home sex life, things were all right for a while?

A. For two years. We're talking about causes. Okay, that was cause number one, I thought I was getting shorted at home. Er, I haven't said that my wife made a big sacrifice. Her shop was getting in the way, so she got rid of it. And for two years, about two years, we got pretty close to each other. Hah! I remember, right after the breakup of the thing with the first girl, my wife and I went out in the city for a night and spent it in a hotel where my company has an account. It was terrific. I told a guy in my office about staying there and he says, "You must be the first member of this firm who's ever taken his *wife* to that hotel." Ah, God, that was nice.

Q. For two years.

A. For most of two years. Then—I've got to bring the business into this.

Q. Go ahead.

A. My field is—look, if I say what my field really is, a lot of people are liable to be hurt, it's liable to get right home to a lot of people who haven't got it coming to them.

Q. You don't have to name it.

A. How about—shall we say that it's the "communications field?"

Q. If you say so.

A. Right, I can't even name the city, because that'll spill everything, too. Why don't we say Chicago? I always *hated* Chicago.

Q. [laughter] Fine, fine.

A. I'm in the, er, "communications field" there, and I have this job where I'm in charge of a department; it's tough work, and a lot of it is footwork, and some people are better at that than I am. I was —it was a family kind of a business and I wasn't related to the owners, and I had a good job but it was about as far as I was going to go. If I stayed there, it was as far as I was going to go in *life.* And I had competition, people angling to screw me out of my job, or so I thought. Guys this age tend to go paranoid about those things.

Q. Oh, yes, oh, yes.

A. Okay. Well, there I was, thinking I was up against a dead end. I'd been in the job five years—the position, I mean, I'd been with the company longer than that—and I was working just as hard as I ever did, and getting nowhere. I began boozing. I don't think my sex life fell off at home, exactly—I mean, if I'd been there, I could have had it, but I *wasn't* there, I was out with the guys and the girls all the time. And then there was a Christmas party, and this kid starts schmoozing up to me and telling me how she'd always admired me for what I did on the job, and I got pissy-eyed drunk. And I guess it brought out the mother in her; she saw that I got to the train in a cab, and in the cab we necked and I tried to get my tongue down to her pancreas.

Q. [laughter]

A. Enjoy yourself, then I'll go on.

Q. Sorry. Please do.

A. When I sobered up I knew it hadn't been a very good idea. For about a month, we avoided each other, which is hard to do when you work in the same office. Then there was another party, and another cab ride, and we didn't go to any train, we went to her place. Stoned. Blackout! And where, the next morning, I phoned home and gave my wife some bullshit story about a business meeting and I couldn't get to a phone the night before and I got drunk and I didn't have any money and somehow I'd get right home, and my God, she didn't have to, she had the evidence of the last girl—but she believed me. She believed me! And I did go home, but not really right away. First we tried it sober. And found it was worth trying again.

Q. And this time there was no month of waiting before you—tried it again?

A. Well, there were recriminations again, on both sides. The girl's, and mine. She knew I was married. She told me girlfriends of hers had had bad times with married guys, and she was afraid. I didn't know, but she told me, the second time we—the second time I *screwed* her, why try to think up nice words for this—she told me about this other guy in her life. I've mentioned that.

Q. Yes. In both cases, you said.

A. Yes. Well, this one was a little different kind of relationship, he wasn't a sick guy, like the first girl's guy. Very early in the affair, she told me I reminded her of him. I was then—forty-two, he was about thirty-three, she was, I think, twenty-four. He'd been married, and he'd been divorced, he had a kid. He was a bright young guy; he'd made a good mark in business, quite young; I was older, but I wasn't exactly the village idiot, and I'd accomplished something in life. She went for that, she liked a guy she could look up to.

Q. You two knew about each other? You and the younger man?

A. After awhile, he found out, but there never were any collisions. See, he'd stay with her on weekends, and I'd stay with her maybe one, two nights a week, at best. When I could. So if there were any conflicts, they were all in her head, and mine, and his, maybe. I don't know, I've never met the guy.

Q. You've told me about the other young woman's sexual hang-ups. Did this girl . . .

A. Wait, wait a minute. What do you mean, the other *young* woman?

Q. Did I say something wrong?

A. No, I guess it's my fault for not telling you. See, I read some-where, maybe in one of my wife's half-assed women's magazines, that when a guy does this it's got to be somebody young enough to be his daughter. Well, that's a lot of—why does she have to be *younger?* The first girl, now, she was almost my age, I'd worked with her once. All right, the second was about eighteen years younger, so it worked that time. But, you see, in my case, in these two cases, the first one wasn't all *that* much younger. I just don't want to be lumped in with some—syndrome, or something. What'd you ask me?

Q. Sexual hangups. The second girl.

A. Well—and this is just the way it pops into my head—she was inclined to overweight. You remember me telling you my wife has a big bust and slim hips?

Q. Twice.

A. Okay. This girl was built just the other way around. And she had—she'd been to more than one shrink about overeating. She'd lock herself up in a room and go nuts with a pound of cheese and two boxes of crackers. Through her life she was either ballooning out like a whale or starving herself to death to get the lard off.

Q. What's this got to do with sex? I'm sure it has, but precisely what?

A. Precisely is kind of hard to arrive at six years later, especially when you're trying to think about somebody you did your best to forget. I mean I can't dig way back into her childhood for you because I forget just what she told me about it. But in sex, Christ, yes, this came out in sex. She'd just begun a diet when the two of us starting fucking, and she'd never let you see . . .

Q. I don't understand . . .

A. —when she was standing up, see. Oh, in bed, hell, that was something else. Anything went. But then if she had to get up to go to the can, even if it was pitch-dark, she'd always have a towel handy to hold over her. "Don't look at me! Don't look at me!"

Q. Which somehow evokes the other lady.

A. How?

Q. The business about "Don't come up now, I'm not dressed."

A. Oh. Well, I told you what that was. So girl number two had that fat hangup—which I could care less about, she wasn't ugly, she was just big there. Well, look, all girls are self-conscious about their weight. They're programed that way.

Q. I think so.

A. So maybe that wasn't really a hangup.

Q. Except that the, er, preoccupation with weight was perhaps exaggerated, *inflamed,* in the second girl's case, by whatever she told you about her early background. If she told you. And you've forgotten.

A. Forgotten. Hangups. I think I remember this. She was constantly bullshitting me about how tough it was to *relate* to the other boyfriend, in the sack, now that I was in the act. And she kept bugging me with questions about my home sex life, and how my children were, and she wanted to see pictures of them, and God damn, I'd get that up to here, and I'd say, "Knock it off, leave it alone, it's none of your fuckin' business. I don't ask you about *your* business, don't ask *me* about *mine.* " And she'd look at me with these big dumb eyes and say, "But we must be *honest* with each other or how can *we* relate to each other?" Well. To make a long story longer, this—look. I've given you a picture of myself and it's probably a picture of a—er, promiscuous, got his nose in the gutter all the time. Some kind of an ogre. But take all that away and I think you find a pretty middle-class, moral guy underneath. See, to do this, to do things like screw girls who aren't your wife and get away with it, you've got to lie. You've got to lie, and then you've got to lie to cover the lie, and then you've got to lie to cover the lie that *covers* the lie! And no matter how great it is the first time you sink your fangs into a new girl, if you're a basically middle-class, moral guy underneath, something starts inside you, right then. Guilt. An equity of guilt, with compound interest that builds and builds and builds each time you do it again. You're an amateur at this; you're basically an honest guy, and lying isn't for amateurs, it's for pros. Sure, some guys can screw around all their lives, lie all their lives, maybe never feel bad about it. Well, I can't play that game.

Q. [pause] How long did this affair last?

A. About four months. And by that time that guilt-load . . .

Q. Excuse me. "That guilt-load" must have been there the first time, with the first girl, too?

A. Yeah, sure, sure it was, my wife pointed that out to me.

Q. After both confessions? I mean after *each* confession?

A. More so after the second, I mean I remember the impact of that one much more. Anyway: It's been going on four months, right? I've been lying like a rug for four months, right? Maybe we wouldn't be able to screw all night, maybe we'd just have one go and then the girl'd put me on the train, and maybe when I got home I'd find my wife a little drunk and ready for action, and as the kids say, "like wow," two broads in one night, a brunette, then a blonde?

Q. Did that happen often?

A. [pause] Christ. Not often enough, now that I think of it. Probably only once. If it'd happened more often I probably would never have gone back to that—to the other girl, because my wife is absolutely the best lay in the whole world. [sigh] Mind putting my train of thought back on the, er . . .

Q. Sorry. The buildup of guilt, the steady accumulation of lies . . .

A. Don't be *sorry,* you made me make a good point. So! All this, and then one day she—the girl—she tells me all of a sudden, she comes out with, "Do you know why I love you? I love you because you remind me of my *father.*" Right out of a book, right? Jesus! That's all a fucked-up fortyish philanderer, a paunchy slob who thinks he's Adonis all this time, that's all he has to hear. Well. A thing like that is magic, honey. It activates your escape mechanism. But, see, I didn't know the mechanism was working.

Q. And you told your wife what you'd been doing?

A. No, no. Not right away. All right, I was bugged by what the girl had said, but I was still hot for her. What I did was, I told her best friend—my wife's best friend—about how great it was to lay a young body; I was drunk. And of course it got right to my wife, and I had to lie, to deny, to plead blackout. And then I did tell my wife. I was drunk then, too. I told her I had to *have* this girl, I *loved* her, all that. Er—she's going to be interviewed in this, isn't she?

Q. If it's all right with you—

A. It's fine with me, maybe telling all this trouble will make just one half-ass keep his cock in his pants. So. I told my wife. Now— she may tell you things about our, er, confrontation that I don't remember, but what I *do* remember was this: One, she got the girl's phone number out of her, and called her up. Two, she told her she could have me if she wanted me, but she'd have to take all our kids, too. Three, if she was going to give me up and it ever flared up again my wife would have her fired; and she could have done that. Four, no matter what happened, whatever happened, if my wife *ever saw* her, she was going to kill her. She finally hung up and turned around, and she said, mimicking the kid's mousy little voice, "Oh, *no,* Mrs. A, I *love* my job!"

Q. She was more afraid of being fired than of being killed?

A. Much more. What do you know about possibly dying at twenty-four years old? But losing a job, that kind of death, sure. It wasn't a difficult choice for the kid. Me or the job? She took the job.

Q. And then came the sex?

A. Oh, no. Not right away. My wife's no quick-change artist where feelings are concerned. She's a real woman. They can't do that, they're going to get a few good shots at you, too, you hand them something like this. "You bastard," she says. "You had to unload your guilt somewhere, didn't you? and you unloaded it on me. But I haven't done anything to you!" And I sure had done just that. You've been running to her and crying on her shoulder about all your other problems, why shouldn't you unload this one there, too?

Q. And then came the sex?

A. You're a horny bastard, aren't you? [loud, long laughter] Well. Anyway. She was right. Looking back, I've got to say I wish I'd been man enough to settle it myself without doing that, sticking her with my guilt, and doing something a little worse by telling her everything. Or *anything.*

Q. Something worse?

A. This may sound pompous, but a marriage is, it's, say it's a house on the beach and the foundation it stands on is mutual trust, you do something like that, like spill your guts the way I did, you let the ocean in. Erosion. I mean *I* still trust *her,* I always have, I always will, but I can't ask her to trust me any more. That's the price you pay. It's worse than being into the worst shylock in the business. You never stop paying off.

Q. I don't mean this to be a "horny" question, but do you have an active sex life with her now?

A. I think the last time—see, I have to think!—I think the last time was two weeks ago. Maybe three, give or take a week.

Q. In bed? At night?

A. No, in the bathroom, in the morning. The kids were off to school and I was shaving and my wife was taking a bath, and she said the water was nice and warm, why didn't I get in the tub with her? And when we finished she looked at me and let out a laugh I'm sure the neighbors heard. I asked what was so damn funny, and she touched the shaving soap on my sideburns and said, "You look like the baboon in the water in Life magazine." That's the way it used to be all the time, with us. A lot of sex, and a lot of laughs.

Q. All right, given the opportunity, would you do it again? Go astray again?

A. I can only say I haven't been given the opportunity. No, wait, maybe I have, maybe I have. A girl I went to college with—not one of those I laid—she phoned my office last month and asked if I was the same Mr. A who'd taken Economics 140A with her. I said yes, I was. We had a nice conversation. You know how those things go; you always end up by saying, well, why don't we get together some-time? So I said it, and as I did, I realized I hadn't told the girl I was married. Of course I didn't tell I wasn't married, either. Well, she gave me her office phone number and she gave me her *home* phone number, and she made a point of telling me that that number was unlisted, and a *further* point of telling me what nights a week I could come over. Nights. I'm sure I could have fucked her. As I remember, she liked me in school, and here she'd taken the trouble to look me up. And I said I'd get back to her in a couple of days, and I never did. I don't think—I don't think she ever was married. And too bad. She would have liked it.

Q. [pause] Your professional life, now. We've touched on it, but we, I'd like to hear a little more about it.

A. Yeah, fine. I'd like to say something, and it's got nothing to do with business; we'll get to that.

Q. Certainly.

A. All right. All this time I've been talking about getting my rocks off and I've almost never said I loved anybody. Well—I don't know if you're going to keep this in the tape, but I'd like to say that I love my wife, I always have and whatever happens to me I always will, it's the kind of thing—it's a pretty bum rap for a woman, putting up with a shithead like me, and she does.

Q. I hope you won't take offense. This declaration just now. Are you sure this isn't just conscience talking? That you think that by saying it into this machine that lets you off the hook?

A. I don't care what it sounds like to you, pal, I just wanted to say it. Maybe it does do that for me, clears the air. All right. What about my professional life?

Q. The second affair occurred about the time you were beginning to run into some trouble on your job.

A. Oh, yeah. Toward the end there, in this—"communications field," isn't that what we decided to call it?

Q. Yes.

A. In "Chicago," toward the end there, there wasn't anything but trouble. It was a big job, a responsible job, a tough job, they depended on me, and I finally couldn't hack it. I blew it.

Q. And you'd been doing that particular job for, you said, five years.

A. Right. Five years.

Q. And there was trouble all the way along the line? From the start?

A. Oh, no, at the start it was great, it was a challenge, I did good stuff with it. I think I've told you it was a family business and I wasn't related, I was where I'd be forever.

Q. But if they'd kept you in it for five years you must have known what you were doing?

A. Oh, sure. It was my first executive job. I learned to, er, to *deputize.* I knew a guy in a competing firm, a very bright guy, a bit younger than I was. I let my company take a look at him and they liked him enough to bring him in for more money than he'd been getting. He was my deputy if I was off, on vacation, sick, whatever. He'd step into my job if I wasn't there. We worked damn well together, like two wheels in a Swiss watch. We were close friends, too, had the same kinds of interests—I don't necessarily mean girls —and we'd drink together, and visit each other's homes, the whole route, you know. We had a kind of E.S.P. together. And he had something I didn't have: Shrewdness, cunning, and ambition, the kind of ambition that goes so deep it's sick. And I had something *he* didn't have: My job. So, he set his sights on getting it and screwing me out of it. Want to play this part back for me? I think I've left something out.

Q. Sure. [portion replayed]

A. Yeah. Er, this sounds like whining, a guy pretty sorry for himself. You can talk to him if you want to. The other guy I've mentioned.

Q. What for?

A. Oh, to double-check me.

Q. I'm interested in you, not him. Go ahead.

A. Well. See, when I wasn't there, and he did my job, he made sure he always did it a little differently, not necessarily better, but— er—originally, maybe, with a style of his own, maybe, that made the big bosses sit up and take notice of him. I'm sure you've heard of this before. It's the oldest game in business.

Q. I've had some experience of it myself.

A. So people in the office, they'd say over the bar, "I don't want to say this, but," and they'd tell me this guy was after my job. I think he wanted them to know it, too. That's part of the strategy, to lower the victim's morale: You *know* he's going to hear it. So I sweated and brooded about this, and started forgetting details and being sloppy about stuff I once did with my eyes closed, and I drank more and more, and I fucked the one girl, and I tried to straighten out, and I fucked the second girl, and I started to drink more and more heavily. After the breakup of the second affair, she was still working there, but now she was only another face over a desk. One day I came *in* drunk, I stayed drunk all day and got drunker at lunch, and I fucked up the operation something glorious. If a superior tried to interject a thought when I was talking to somebody else, I'd say, "I wasn't talking to you." At one point I think I shoved somebody, I don't remember exactly. Kind of like a guy carrying a load of dishes and he drops one and it—triggers something, he smashes them all.

Q. And what was the trigger?

A. The who?

Q. In your case? That day?

A. [pause] I've seen other guys go out of their tree like that. It's never any *one* thing. Anyway, that was on a Friday, and on Monday the big boss called me in. He said nobody had talked to him about me but that he'd been noticing things. The *hell* nobody'd talked to him! That had to be bullshit because I'd done just what he was doing with me, I'd had to fire guys and in a lot of those cases *plenty* of people talked to me first. So. He said the job was kicking the shit out of me and I needed a change, and after my vacation, which was coming up in about a week and a half, after that I'd be taken out of that job and put on something else, er—individual duty rather than executive, administrative. And for no loss of money. Well, I took the vacation, but I didn't take that, er, lesser job. You can't do things like that and live with people who used to work under you. I'd put in a good number of years there. I put in for my severance, and there was a little difficulty, but we arrived at a settlement. I took about ten thousand dollars and my pride and left.

Q. And you changed your career.

A. No, *no!* Hey, what is this, a *questionnaire,* or something? For Christ's sake—"height, weight, when'd you have your first screw, when'd you change your career"—do I *have* to change my career to qualify for this, er, great cross-section of humanity of yours?

Q. I wasn't jumping to a conclusion.

A. Good. Don't. People don't really fit questionnaires. Ever *watch* anybody fill one out, a simple job application? Maybe they can't answer a question because it doesn't really *apply* to them, you ever think of that?

Q. All right, all right! Let me put it this way. *Did* you change your career?

A. Not sure I like that much better. Well I—changed the direction of it, maybe, I changed the scene. I moved out of there and moved out of "Chicago" to the coast. But I stayed in my field. Another company, a much bigger company, was glad to have me, and I was glad to take a little less a week. Actually, it didn't hurt much. Only about forty dollars less, to start. Hell, I had the ten thousand.

Q. Would you mind telling me how much of the ten thousand you have left?

A. [laughter] Not at all. Not—a—red—cent!

Q. Are you in an executive position where you are now?

A. They're kind of working me into one, yes. Happens everywhere I go.

Q. Do you think you can handle the job they're "working you into?"

A. Let's say I'm that much older and more experienced to be able to say one, no, I don't know whether I can handle it; two, *that's* what makes it interesting; three, people who go into new jobs wondering if they can do them are psychologically setting themselves up with a Lloyds of London guarantee that they're going to fuck up!

Q. Would you say your working life, your home, your sex life—well, forget that, I seem to know a lot about your sex life by now . . .

A. Probably more than you ever wanted to know. [laughter]

Q. All in all, would you say you're content with where you are today?

A. Um—I'm more determined, I guess, that whatever I did that screwed up my whole family isn't going to happen to them again. And I did screw them up, like it was the sins of the fathers, handed down.

Q. I don't think I follow.

A. When I was a teenager my father was in his fifties. And he was going straight to hell. Drinking, more and more. I don't think he was ever unfaithful to my mother, that wasn't his bag, but he was boozing, and his business, he had a construction business, was slowly falling apart, and finally it all went at once. He had to give it up. We had to sell the house and move into some shithouse railroad flat. And he had to go looking for a job, "with my hat in my hand," as he said, and settle for much less money than he'd been making as the leader of a firm. Which then didn't exist any more. The point of this being, I suppose, that that, er, built up a fear inside me that that's what would happen to me when I got to that point in life. And in a way, it did. But I'm sidetracking again.

Q. Were you going to tell me something about your children?

A. Yes. The oldest of our four—the ones she had by me, by that time the two oldest, by the other man, they were starting college— our first boy suffered a lot from this—middlescence, is that what you call this?

Q. Mid-o-lescence. Coined.

A. Right. At that time he was an adolescent and he needed a stable, supportive, I think is the term, household, and here his father just wasn't there, he was out fucking or if he was home he was drunk and fighting with everybody. The boy was just starting junior high school. He screwed up badly. The guidance counselors had us in there at least once every two, three weeks. I'd be sitting there in their office trying to keep the hangover from blowing my head off and listening to words like "supportive," "stability," all that school-teacher talk. Once the guidance counselor was a girl maybe ten years older than my son and here she is giving me all this, and looking worried and sincere, and here I am staring at her left tit and wondering what it'd be like to bite it. Some father! Well, I got the message, they didn't have to spell it out. The way we lived, drunken half-assed father, bills not paid, almost never any money on hand because I was giving it to bartenders and spending it on cunt, the house a howling mess most of the time. Well. By the time I blew the job and got ready to move the family out of—"Chicago," the boy was in his late teens. He didn't go with us. He went the other way, about six states. He came back, finally.

Q. Your problems only affected *him?*

A. Well, of course they affected all of them. And then, too, kids get to an age, they go off on their own anyway. Just this year one of our children, the girl, she turned 18 and she left to go off and live in a cave or something with a boy friend. And now that's over and she wants to come home and there's a bit of an extra problem because my wife's mother is living with us, she's a lady in her eighties, and we've just got so much room! So I've got all this on my hands now and by Christ I'm going to work it out, somehow. Now, if this happened six, ten years ago, I don't think I could have handled it, I think I'd just crawl into a bottle or a cunt, the way I handled all my problems then. All in all, maybe the difference now is that I'm trying to grow up. I think it's about time.

Q. Do you, then, do you have any "all-in-all" conclusions about men in general in this period of life?

A. I think it's when you finally have to grow up, er, accept what you are and what you've made of yourself, and go on from there. I think that mainly you have to stop feeling sorry for yourself and start doing some real thinking about other people, the people you're responsible for. Taking them into account. You have to stop bitching about what a piece of shit life is and start doing something about it for once. It's when you've got to realize that you haven't got the time to be a horse's ass any more.

Mr. B, whose non-affair affair was summarized in Chapter One, is every bit as emotionally high-keyed as Mr. A, but he is no braggart. He speaks more softly of what happened to him and quite a bit less abrasively of the women in his life. He is much more just, fair, perhaps a more *thoughtful* man than Mr. A. Mr. A says of his earlier life, "I didn't bother with women I wasn't going to have sex with"; Mr. B tells of an association with a young woman with whom he did not have sex. But it was an encounter that disturbed his life as much as Mr. A's active sexual philandering disturbed *his.*

Mr. B's wife offers her perspectives later on.

Mr. B

Q. Your name was suggested to me by someone who sketched in very briefly why he thought you might make a good subject. So I know a little about you—very little—and you know a little about what this book is about.

A. As I understand it, the book is about the problems of middle-aged men—the grasping at fading youth, the personal and professional upheavals that come out of those problems. Am I correct?

Q. Yes. The book tries to deal with . . .

A. Then if my understanding was correct, I think I can contribute a lot. I don't think I have any answers, but I think, judging from what has happened to me in the last couple of years, that I could give you a picture of a man grasping at fading youth, finding his personal and professional life, his home—everything completely changed.

Q. Well, that sounds like a classic case, if there is such a thing as a classic case. But let me ask you this: the thing that precipitated the change, the trigger for it, was an extra-marital affair, was it not?

A. I told you I couldn't supply answers, and that's one of the answers I can't supply. There was an affair involved, very much involved, but to start with, it wasn't an affair the way you would ordinarily think of an affair, and secondly—more importantly—it . . .

Q. What do you mean it wasn't an affair in the ordinary sense?

A. It was a non-affair.

Q. I don't follow you. Was it was or was it not an affair, a sexual adventure?

A. An adventure, by all means. Sexual? Well, there were powerful sexual feelings, but I never had sex with the girl. I mean, very bluntly, we never screwed. The extra-marital affair was more part of a pattern, a symptom, than a trigger. I think that all this would have happened, somehow, even if I hadn't had this affair. And further, if I hadn't had this affair with her, I probably would have had something like it with someone else.

Q. You said "all this would have happened." What's "all this"? What—try to sum up, if you can, what happened to you in the last couple of years. Are you still married?

A. Yes, quite, very—yes, I'm still married. And much more satisfactorily married than before all this happened.

Q. Then you'd say you're through your midolescence? You've survived intact?

A. I'm intact, more or less. But through—I don't know, I really don't know.

Q. And your career—that changed, didn't it?

A. Drastically. Completely.

Q. And are you satisfied?

A. With my career?

Q. With your career, with your life, with everything.

A. I have to take a deep breath on that one. [pause] Yes—yes, I think I can say I'm satisfied. Or, no—let's say I'm more satisfied than I was before all this happened. I don't think anyone can ever really be satisfied in the sense that he's completely happy with the way his life is. That implies to me—the word "satisfied" implies to me—that there's no more reaching, that there are no more goals to chase. I don't feel *that* way at all. I'm still very actively chasing goals, trying to do new things.

Q. Then you don't feel you can sum it up?

A. I didn't say that. I think I can sum up *what* happened, but not the *effect* of what happened. I don't think I . . .

Q. Well, then, try to summarize the "what."

A. [long pause] In brief—in barest outline—I got involved in an exciting project, in a new way of living and even of thinking, I found myself questioning some of my most fundamental values and priorities, I met a young woman and fell in love with her, got into difficulties in my work, went to the very brink of divorce and suicide, managed—no thanks to me, really—to climb out of my depression and save my marriage. I changed my career, and, well—that's it, in barest outline.

Q. Some vital statistics. Where were you born and when?

A. I was born in Brooklyn in 1928.

Q. Forty-five. That beard of yours. Is it dyed?

A. Is that a vital statistic?

Q. If you object to the question . . .

A. [laughter]. No, no. Yes. It is. I dyed it because I couldn't stand the thought of growing old. My beard was going gray, more and more. It made me look even older than I was.

Q. Somebody said this to you?

A. Nobody had to say this to me. It was—during the period of the affair, or non-affair, when —my feelings about youth and age came to a head. I mean, I'd always been extremely conscious of the aging process. Thoughts of growing old and of having to die—those things had always troubled me more or less, but at this point, they became practically unbearable. I would wake up in the middle of the night saying that "in fifteen years, I'm going to be sixty." I had always been obsessed with time, and age, and growing old. I must have read four dozen books on time and its effect on people. Philosophically—physically. I was really obsessed with it. And at this point, it passed from the realm of philosophical inquiry, which it had been all along, into hard reality; I was really growing old! When I was a kid and I read a book that chronicled a man's life, I would find myself weeping as the man was growing old. Now it was happening to *me*.

Q. I see. This seems to be saying something about your family, your life as a boy. Were your parents immigrants? Poor? Educated?

A. My father was born in New York City. I didn't know my paternal grandparents because they died before I was born. My paternal grandfather was a tailor who worked day and night just to keep his eight kids from starving. My mother was born in Russia and came here with her family when she was four. We used to move in with my mother's parents when things got tough. My mother's father was a carpenter and bricklayer.

Q. What did your parents do? Did your mother work—were they educated?

A. My mother went through grade school and my father, I think he said he had two years of high school. But he was a voracious reader and rather well self-educated.

Q. "Was?" He's dead?

A. He's very much alive. Still working, in fact.

Q. What does he do?

A. Well, for the last, I guess, fifteen years, he's been a sales manager for an electronics supply firm. But before that, I mean, when I was growing up, he was a hustler. He lived by his wits.

Q. Doing what? Can you be more specific?

A. He was a salesman, sometimes on his own, sometimes for some company. He sold everything from stocks to cemetery plots. He could sell ice cubes to Eskimos. Never high-pressure or scare tactics or anything like that. He had—he *has*—a quick wit. I think he would've made a hell of a doctor because he has this kind of bedside manner about him. I worshiped him.

Q. And your mother?

A. My mother was a Jill-of-all-trades. Seamstress, dressmaker, secretary.

Q. Other children in the family?

A. A sister, ten years younger.

Q. So in effect you grew up as an only child.

A. Quite.

Q. And your parents. Did you get along well with them?

A. Too well.

Q. Odd answer.

A. I mean I never went through an adolescent rebellion. I looked to my mother and father for advice even when I was older. I didn't get married until I was twenty-five and I was still living at home. I mean, until I got married, I never had my own place, I was never on my own except when I was in the army, and I never wanted a place of my own. I was happy, I was delighted to bring my friends, male and female, back to my parents' apartment. I . . .

Q. When were you in the army, by the way?

A. At the end of World War II and then again in Korea. I'd been stupid enough to sign into the Reserves. Like a lot of people. Let's not get into that, it doesn't mean anything.

Q. Right. Your schooling?

A. I went to school in New York City, including City College. I also attended the Sorbonne for a while. And I took graduate work in English, music, biology and philosophy.

Q. Your interests were very eclectic. And you went into what work?

A. Teaching. I was a professor at [deleted].

Q. You changed careers with the coming of midolescence. What do you do now?

A. I have my own advertising agency.

Q. I'll ask you to detail that switch as part of a chronological narrative. It came about, didn't it, as a result of your midolescent episode?

A. Directly. But let me explain something. I think it would have happened, I think I would have left the university even if I'd never met this girl, because . . .

Q. You've referred a couple of times to "the girl" or "this young woman."

A. I'm sorry. Melina. Melina Prokopolous.

Q. For the record, the name has been changed. Now—you said you think you would have left even if you'd never met "Melina." Why?

A. Because I was frustrated, angry, bitter and absolutely certain that I was at a dead end creatively, professionally, financially. I wasn't getting the recognition I felt I deserved, I was being by-passed for all sorts of honors and promotions, which were going to men who had joined the faculty long after I did, to young men who had been my students.

Q. How long were you at the university?

A. At that one? Fifteen years. I'd taught elsewhere before going there, done some freelance work for a while. And then, after going there, to [deleted] I just found a home, or a rut. It depends on—at the beginning it was a home; at the end, it was a rut.

Q. And so you made a total change, not to another teaching post but to a whole new career. What kept you from making the switch earlier?

A. To begin with, I didn't feel those frustrations, I didn't turn bitter until I'd been there about thirteen years. I'd gotten ahead, I'd been promoted, was well-liked, I had in all senses a good, satisfying job. And then the, er, the problems began.

Q. Why didn't you leave then?

A. Because I just didn't have the balls. I had a high salary, I had tenure. What was I going to do, throw it all over? For what?

Q. Then what gave you the, er, balls? To start a new career in mid-life?

A. It wasn't a question of acquiring balls. I was propelled into the change. The immediate mechanism—what Aristotle calls the efficient cause—was my getting a contract to write the book for [deleted]. That led directly into it because it got me involved not only in writing the book, but in all the advertising and promotion. So I got heavily involved with advertising from the inside out. And then Melina introduced me to this guy who was with an agency and who wanted to start his own and, well, the outcome is obvious: we formed our own agency and there we are.

Q. Did you know anything about advertising? I mean, to go from Academe to the hustling world of advertising is about as abrupt a change as I can think of. How . . .

A. Not as abrupt as you think, perhaps, because I wasn't a complete stranger to advertising.

Q. What experience had you had?

A. Oh, not the business end of it. I mean, I knew just about nothing about the business end, but I was—I had had experience in the "creative" end. I'd done freelancing from time to time, writing copy, working with the art people. On one account I'd been hired for, to do the copy, I'd even been in on the brain sessions; I'd been at conferences with the creative director and the client and so I wasn't a stranger to that part of the business. What's new to me is the hustling, the dealing, all that.

Q. I see. So you didn't just stick professions up on the wall and throw a dart and pick that one.

A. No, not at all.

Q. Well, how did you get started? How did you to get involved in advertising, as a new profession?

A. Through Melina. She worked for the agency handling the publisher's account.

Q. The picture is starting to clear. But let's try to tell this in chronological sequence. The day you got the book contract. Take it from there.

A. Fine. Shortly after I got the contract I was introduced by my editor to the ad people. Specifically, I was introduced to Melina, who was handling the publishing account, and she took a personal, very direct role, in the book, which everyone felt was going to be a best seller.

Q. Was it?

A. Yes, it was on the best-seller list for, oh, six weeks or so.

Q. May I interrupt you again—why did the publisher approach you for this book?

A. No mystery there. The subject was one of my hobbies; I'd even written a book about it once. I'd written oh, maybe, half a dozen books that weren't scholarly or texts. Popular books. And in my time I'd been a stringer, a part-time correspondent for a couple of newspapers, and I'd done some magazine pieces, on all kinds of topics. Plus, you know, the advertising work. So I was more or less known by several publishers. There were enough people around to know I was fast, accurate, thorough and reliable. No, there were no mysterious forces at work. It was all reasonable enough.

Q. Fine, fine. So let's go on. You were introduced to Melina. What were your first impressions, or reactions? Did you suddenly become what you think now you had never been, really—an adolescent? Did you—was it love at first sight?

A. No, not at all. The first thing I thought, I remember it as clearly as if I were, well, thinking it for the first time right now, the first thought to occur to me was not "What a beautiful woman," but "What a flaky broad!" She was beautiful, sexy, slim, very lovely, but the things that impressed themselves on me were her clothes and her speech. The first time I saw her, she was wearing sort of pajama bottoms, almost translucent, and a halter top. And her speech! I'd never heard a woman use language the way she did. She sounded like a longshoreman with a hangover. I mean, she used the grandest collection of obscenities I'd ever heard, from a man or a woman. She sprinkled "fuck" and "cocksucker" around like salt.

Q. And that turned you on?

A. No, that kind of language doesn't turn me on. No—it's just that I really had never heard a woman say "hard-on," or "cunt," or whatever, the *way* she did. That plus her clothes made me feel she was this flaky, way-out broad.

Q. And you then had business dealings with her?

A. We had a number of meetings which were nothing special, aside from my being rather impressed with her sharp mind, her way of analyzing things and cutting through gibberish to get at the heart of a problem. And her fantastic memory. She has something close to total recall. Her mind began to impress me at those meetings. And of course I enjoyed looking at her. But still, there was nothing terribly extraordinary about those meetings.

Q. How, when did you feel yourself falling in love with her?

A. Let me tell you something about the book. It may sound like a digression but it's really very much to the point, and I really will be answering your question. You have to understand that she was not only involved with the advertising but she was almost in a sense the editor of the book. The publisher relied on her to keep all the ends tied up neatly and she really did as much work for him as for the ad agency.

Q. You *still* haven't answered the question! When, how did you fall in love with her?

A. There were a lot of last-minute changes in copy, corrections, promotional material and so on. I was on the phone with her a dozen times a day. It all really started—God, I remember the night as though it were yesterday—it started one night when she called me at the university and asked if I could meet her that evening with some copy. I met her at a bar, a very "in" place, very fashionable, with the copy I'd prepared. We went over it all in a very businesslike way, but all the time drinking. We must've been there four hours and both of us got pretty well lit. Somehow, something about her, vibes, instinct, who knows what, something said to me, "This woman not only likes me, but she's available."

Q. Had you ever had an extra-marital affair? Were you faith . . .

A. That's a tough question to answer. [pause] About three years after I got married, I ran into an old girlfriend, someone I'd had a long liaison with—liaison isn't really the right word because when you're twenty years old you don't have liaisons, you just get laid. Anyhow, this girl, with whom I'd had a very hot and heavy sex thing when I was twenty and she was seventeen, she got in touch with me. I saw her secretly a few times and when my wife was carrying our second child, our daughter, I started seeing the girl again. The night Ellen went to the hospital . . .

Q. Ellen?

A. My wife.

Q. Again for the record, the name is changed. Go on.

A. The night Ellen went to the hospital, I phoned the girl and told her the house was empty. She came to our home. We screwed; she spent the night there. There was nothing beyond that one night; I never saw her again, but I wrote the girl a long letter saying I was still in love with her, and Ellen found the letter.

Q. Intercepted it? You didn't mail it?

A. I mailed it. But I'm a compulsive carbon-copyer; I make duplicates of everything, including, er, love letters.

Q. Do you suppose you—wanted your wife to find the letter?

A. Yes, I guess there's an element of self-destruction there. I don't know. Perhaps I didn't try to hide it, I just put it aside. Anyway, Ellen found it. And it all but destroyed her, devastated her. I'd rather not dwell on this incident. It was a passing thing, though, I guess, in a deeper sense, it really wasn't passing. It was part of a pattern. a symptom, of something much . . .

Q. Part of a pattern? I thought you said you had only this one extra-marital affair. Did you have others?

A. No. I didn't, not in reality. But I did in fantasy. I wasn't aware of it at all. I never realized that I fantasized until it began to come out in therapy and, even more so, after the therapy sessions, in the long, painful discussions my wife and I had during the time of my affair with Melina.

Q. So, then, you never actually had an affair, except for the one with the girl from your youth?

A. No. Though, as I said, I did have them in fantasy; my eyes wandered all the time. I would look at girls and wonder what it would be like to be in love with them, for them to be in love with me. And the thing that made me aware of that fantasizing, the trigger mechanism, was this one-sided, non-affair love affair.

Q. So: You were in the bar with Melina and you realized she liked you and was, you said, "available." Please continue.

A. I had once heard one side of a phone conversation in some guy's office in which he had said "Oh, you can touch." I didn't know who he was talking about, who he was talking to or what the context was, but something instinctual told me he was talking about Melina.

It turned out I was right. He'd had a long affair with her. Apparently someone on the other end of the line had asked if she was "fuckable," and "you can touch" was his reply. I must have been already thinking of having an affair with her.

Q. And that man's remark came back to you when you were with her in the bar?

A. Er, not *consciously.* All this is what I discovered, dug out, later in my self-analysis and in those talk-times with Ellen. I just had a feeling that Melina was available. And she was the first young woman who ever gave me that feeling. I mean the first one since my marriage. Anyhow, that night in the bar with Melina—we left the bar and got into a cab. As I started to get out of the cab at the railroad station she turned and kissed me. Everything surged up in me. And I mean everything. My tongue went into her mouth, my hands went to her breasts—she never wore a bra, incidentally, and her breasts were like a Venus's—round, firm, perfect. She said two things to me: "Why don't you stay at my place tonight?" and then, when I said I had to get home, and was still caressing her, she said "You better cut it out, the cabbie is getting a hard-on." I went home in a total daze. Here was this incredibly beautiful, desirable young woman making herself available to me. I didn't have to look and lust any more. I didn't have to stare at the girls on the street, in the offices, in the classrooms, who might reject me, laugh at me if I took one step out of line. I could have this woman! This woman was not only *not* rejecting me, she was taking the *initiative, kissing* me, inviting me to *sleep* with her.

Q. Why didn't you spend the night with her?

A. I had to go home. I had never spent a night away from home, except for very legitimate, professional, explainable reasons, about which, of course, I felt no guilt. How could I have explained *this?*

Q. Did you resent having to go home?

A. [long pause] I don't know. I mentally kicked myself all over creation the next day, the day after that, for not having gone to her place. I dreamed of another such invitation, tried to think of ways to get one. But I don't know that I resented having to go home— home was warm. But it began to fade from my life that night, and it finally disappeared, for a long time. My family disappeared. I've mentioned how I felt about my father when I was younger?

Q. Yes.

A. Well, that lasted long after boyhood. I still adored him. I know I'm interrupting, cliff-hanging here . . .

Q. If you think it's important . . .

A. I *do*, I think this is *paramount*. Up to the time this—non-affair began, I'd phone my father every day, even if we had nothing to talk about, just hello and so long. And then this started and I forgot that he existed.

Q. You avoided . . .

A. Not the right word: I *forgot*. I never phoned him at *all!* It—smashed his—my mother and sister would call me and say "Why can't you phone your dad? You're killing him, he sits at the phone and waits for you, and nothing happens." Christ! If I *did* think about him, if I *did* think of phoning him, I found myself dialing Melina's number. I couldn't remember his number, and I had known it as well as I know my own name! [pause]

Q. And this—rift, this has been healed now?

A. I think my relationship with my father was improved by all this because I now know how I hurt him. Well, thanks for letting me put this in here. We were talking about . . .

A. You were talking about how—not only this, but the thing with the girl made you forget everything, your whole family. From that night in the bar with her.

A. Yes, that night was the beginning of what might have been the end if my wife—except for her.

Q. I thought you said *you* saved this marriage.

A. No. It was Ellen who saved our marriage. We went to a psychotherapist, who was very helpful, very instrumental in getting us to see things we'd been blind to. And he effected something of a revolution in Ellen's life. But it was Ellen's understanding and her incredible love, really, not the therapist, that kept us intact. [pause] If you like, I'll deal with that when I get to it as part of the chronological narrative. Do you . . .

Q. Yes, I'd like you to continue the story in as straightforward a chronological way as you can. Another invitation from Melina—did you get one? Did you—did Melina invite you to sleep with her again?

A. No. That—there was a lot of talk over the phone, I saw her constantly, but no invitation was offered. Then I thought I saw an opportunity. There was a faculty party one night that I knew my wife couldn't get to. I took Melina to the party, and at the end of it I said to her, "Okay, let's go to your place." And she said, "I've got to see my steady fuck." And I put her in a cab and went home in a blue funk. [pause] When I look back on that night I keep thinking of, "O what a tangled web we weave/When first we practice to deceive."

Q. Alexander Pope.

A. Sir Walter Scott. At any rate, I kept—weaving this web and having to content myself with phone conversations. And then a real opportunity came up. An evening faculty conference had been canceled at the last minute and Ellen didn't know that. I had the evening free; I went to Melina's office; I knew she'd be there; she always worked late. We went to dinner and we began drinking. And went on drinking. And talking; she's a long-distance talker. And I kept wondering what I was going to tell Ellen, thinking I ought to call her, but I couldn't think of anything reasonable to say to her, so I didn't call Ellen at all. About 3:30 in the morning, Melina took me to her place and after a drink there, to her bed. I was there. I was in bed with her at last! But—ah, God!

Q. But what?

A. All the drinking: She passed out within a minute. And I lay there, fondling her, wanting to lay her, and thinking about my wife.

Q. Your wife sexually? Fantasizing that this was . . .

A. Guilt isn't that kind of fantasy. I was torn to pieces by guilt and at the same time I was driven by a desire for this body next to me. I wanted to have Melina and have my marriage too. Melina was asleep, but I couldn't sleep. I wanted to sleep; I couldn't. I wanted to *fuck* her; I couldn't do *that.* All kinds of conflicting thoughts: I hadn't called my wife, what was she going through, not hearing from me? I spent that whole night caressing this—gorgeous body, this *inert* body, staring into the dark, thinking about what I was doing to my wife, what I was doing to myself. I felt absolutely trapped. My God, I lay there and cried. Wept! [pause]

Q. And still you were aroused. And she'd brought you there. At some point, didn't . . .

A. Didn't I have sex with her? No, at no point. For one thing, she was out like a light . . .

Q. But women can be aroused . . .

A. And I suppose I was *still* afraid of rejection, even there in her bed. At one point, I did put my hands in her pants, her bikini pants. She wasn't wearing a top. Just the panties. And she said, in a drunken, sleepy voice, "Get your fuckin' hands outta my pants." And even if she had been willing it would have been no go because I couldn't get it up. Several times during the night, wondering whether she'd be willing, several times I tried to get an erection. I tried masturbating—and I couldn't get it up! At all! So there I was in bed with this Venus and I spent the night racked with guilt, thinking about my wife. I—obviously, I was so *emotionally* drained that my *body* wouldn't work.

Q. In the morning?

A. In the morning we got up, she made breakfast, she stood in front of the mirror totally nude and fixed her hair and would keep asking me questions like "Does it look better this way, or this?" She tried on several pairs of slacks and would ask me which looked better and whether her bikinis showed through too much—they did—and all I could think of was my wife and what I was going to say, and what was happening to me. [long pause] We took a cab back to her office, and she dropped me off on the way, leaning over and kissing me as I got out.

Q. How did you tell your wife? Or did you?

A. Yes and no. I telephoned her about ii that morning to say— I remember trying to make my voice sound guiltless, enthusiastic— I told her "Ellen, I'm changing my career! I'm going into advertising." And then I invented a story about bar-hopping with some advertising people and how we all got bombed together and fell asleep in a heap.

Q. Your wife's reaction?

A. Well, initially, the first thing that happened when she heard my voice was that she burst into tears. She'd called all my friends. She'd called my oldest friend who lives in Vermont, and he drove down to comfort her and, God, he told me later he came down with a black suit in a suitcase thinking I was lying somewhere with my wrists slashed. Holy God, what a web I had woven! Ellen was up all night crying and phoning and picturing me a corpse somewhere. So she burst into tears because she was so relieved to hear my voice.

Q. You said "initially." Did she have subsequent, different, reactions?

A. Of course. Anger—well, not really, because at that time she still hadn't learned how to become angry. Only hurt. She felt hurt and abused and, well, the way she put it was probably the best summary: "My world just came to an end."

Q. You make it sound as though she knew it was more than a drinking spree.

A. She did know, in a way, she—let's say she intuited the truth. Or part of it, enough of it, to know something catastrophic was happening to us.

Q. Mr. B: You said you had always lusted for, yearned for, young women and you had a wandering eye. What stopped you all along from trying to follow through on those longings?

A. Fear of rejection, I—*think*. But another element is in the picture, and that's my wife and my marriage. I am closer to my wife than to anyone else in the world; I love her more than I love anyone else; she's the most perceptive and sensitive person I've ever known. I learned—it took this whole experience to teach me—that she's also the most *sensual* person I've ever known.

Q. Mr. B, may I ask how many women you've known, in the Biblical sense? How many you've had sex with?

A. Umm [he takes about a minute to think]—five, including my wife.

Q. And it's on the basis of this experience that you say your wife is the most sensuous woman you've ever known.

A. Wait. Don't knock my appraisal. One makes some judgments on the basis of experience and some on the basis of a sort of innate knowledge. I know, without having experienced sexual relations with more than five women, that none could come close to my wife for sheer sensuality.

Q. You don't think Melina would, for instance?

A. Melina is probably the worst example you could pick. My point is that sensuality should mean more than lust or sexual or physical contact. It has to involve those things, but it takes in much more. It's a sort of total sensitivity in which the whole body becomes a sexual instrument, in which the senses, all the senses, all the emotions, everything is tuned in so finely that the least little touch, the flick of an eyelid, evokes a tremendous physical, sexual, emotional response. My wife is like that. I'm not. And it's something I regret.

Q. Yet you speak of responding to Melina in such a powerful way. Were you being sensual then or not?

A. Definitely not. Not sensual. Lustful maybe—and it was only later, really much later, in our relationship that I became consciously aware of the lust. No. There was no sensuality involved. Oh—maybe some, but if it was there, it was minimal. And in part because I'm not really so totally sensual. When it comes to sex I'm genital-oriented. Every inch of Ellen's body is involved, is turned on to sex, when she's in that mood. But even when I'm aroused, I'm not that way. I'd love to be, because I'm aware of what I'm missing. I've tried to develop it, and to a limited extent I have, but . . .

Q. Was your wife always this way? Were you?

A. I can't tell you. Ellen and I had virtually no sex life for the first eighteen years of our marriage.

Q. *No* sex life? Your children weren't immaculate conceptions. Your . . .

A. It's really a terribly difficult thing to explain. This is one of the things that came out in the therapy Ellen and I undertook. But the simple fact, the obvious fact, is that we rarely—and I mean rarely, like six, eight, maybe ten times a year—had . . .

Q. A *year??*

A. —sex. Yes, maybe—at the outside—a dozen times a year. I . . .

Q. Could you, could we develop that somehwat?

A. I'd really rather not. It's so involved. Please, just accept it. We had in effect no sex life until Melina came into my life and changed everything.

Q. Well, let me just ask you this and then we'll go back to your chronology. Is your sex life with your wife different now?

A. Totally. We have an active, a marvelous sex life. My greatest regret, and I can't begin to tell you how much I regret this, my greatest regret is that it took this to bring Ellen and me the kind of —I don't—sexual aware—sexual—*rapport,* that we have now and that we should have had twenty years ago. A lot of the anger that Ellen has learned to express recently has to do with her—having had these tremendous, huge—these almost primitive sexual urges, all those years, and not being able to—of having, in effect, to live with a eunuch. [pause]

Q. Did you initiate this change in your sex life?

A. No. It was Ellen. That, too, is incredible—I mean, when I think of it now it seems incredible to me that Ellen could—this was after the therapy was well under way and it had come out in the sessions, the truth had come out—I blurted it out one day—that the night I was away from home was spent not with a bunch of advertising people, but with Melina, and the whole story came out. That I'd slept in the nude with her, that I'd spent most of the night crying or staring off into the darkness and that I'd been absolutely impotent. So Ellen—Ellen my wife, my love, my, God damn it! my friend— she set out to prove to me that I wasn't impotent. And she did it by being the aggressor. Night after night after night she'd take the initiative in bed, using every technique a woman can dream up to help me out of my imagined impotence.

Q. And it worked?

A. It worked beautifully. It got our sex life going. Not rejuvenated, because we'd—as I said we never really had one. It got it started, and the momentum hasn't died down yet and I hope to hell it never does.

Q. Back to chronology. You were—gee. Here, let's replay the tape [tape replayed]. You were saying that Ellen had *intuited* the truth about the night you didn't come home. What did she say, what did she do?

A. I can't really say. There's nothing definite, nothing I can—pin down. My wife had always had trouble with her weight. She's not fat, by any means, but she tends to get a little heavy and she always —always, I want to emphasize that— she always ate heavily when she was unhappy or frustrated or depressed. But this time she stopped eating. She just didn't touch food. She was so utterly depressed—weeping a lot of the time, unable to talk. I—you know, I was that way too. I mean I was—I don't know if I can find the right words to describe the incredible depression I was in. One, one night I remember, one afternoon, really, when Ellen and I were sitting on the couch and she had asked a friend of ours to come over and play four-hand piano music with me. She thought it would help me get out of my depression, and . . .

Q. She asked a neighbor in to help *you?* She was trying to lift *you* out of *your* depression? What about her own?

A. Ellen had lost her identity as a human being, as a separate— identity. Bear in mind that we weren't aware of this at the time; it didn't become clear until later, until Ellen began reaching into herself. Do you know what she did when I started studying Greek?

Q. You started studying Greek? To . . .

A. I started studying Greek so I could talk to Melina in Greek. I wanted to be able to say "I love you" in Greek and—and she was so damned chauvinistic about her Greek heritage. She used to say, "We were philosophers when you fuckers were still swinging through the trees." Anyhow, Ellen, when I started studying Greek —and Ellen knew the real reason I was studying it—she bought me Greek records, and books in Greek. I seem to have sidetracked myself here.

Q. A neighbor came in to play four-handed piano.

A. And it helped, while I was playing. And then when the neighbor left I fell on the floor and put my head in my wife's lap and wept. It swept over me, I cried in bursts and sobs. [Pause] Some days later

Ellen got in touch with this shrink, this—er, she knew a couple who'd had some similar trouble, and so she contacted this man. Apparently, she told him she was afraid I was going to kill myself. And she wanted me to see him, so she made an appointment for me.

Q. For him to see *you?* She didn't make an appointment for husband-wife therapy?

A. No, I think she just wanted him to, to keep me from killing myself.

Q. Did she have any reason to think you might really commit suicide? Did she have reason to think your constant talk of suicide might be more than just talk?

A. When I was twenty-two I slashed my wrist. I nearly cut my hand off. I spent several months in the hospital. Ellen knew all about that.

Q. I see. Meanwhile, you and Melina what? Did you continue to see her? Did you try to break off?

A. I didn't try to end it. Quite the opposite. I pursued it. I pursued it relentlessly. And it was terribly easy to do, because if I didn't call Melina, she would call me.

Q. On business? You still had . . .

A. No, that was all over. The book had come out. It was a tremendous success. The whole campaign, everything, worked well, too well, much too well.

Q. What's "too well?"

A. This had been perhaps the high point of my life, all the excitement, the recognition. The other books I'd written were just—well, mostly work and the money, of course. But this one generated a new life for me. With Melina, with the other advertising people, with publishers, celebrities. I was riding the crest of a wave. Everything went beautifully everywhere. At the university I was a celebrity. People who hadn't known I was alive suddenly were courting me. I was—I seemed to be—moving. And of course the constant phone calls from Melina, with the secretary saying, two, three, four times a day "Prokopolous, for you, Professor."

Q. How was all this too much?

A. The stopping was too much. Once it was over, the excitement died down. There was no more need for meetings. I tried to stir it up, keep it going, by helping Melina with other accounts, and she kept feeding me things, giving me copy to write or ideas to polish, so—we, I tried to keep life at that same *high* pitch. But it wasn't real any more. The sense of letdown was sort of a post-partum thing. It only fed my depression that much more. And I started having trouble at the university.

Q. Coping with the job? Trouble with your colleagues?

A. All kinds of trouble. I became—and this was the first time this ever happened—I became short-tempered and would blow up and, I guess you could almost say I had tantrums. All the good signs disappeared. I was summoned to meetings with the department head, with the Dean of Faculty. They wanted to know what the hell was going on, couldn't I control myself? I was accused of stirring up trouble among the students, among the faculty.

Q. Were you?

A. To be honest with you I don't know. My head was not functioning then. I couldn't give you a real answer. Ellen told me, several times, that I was behaving self-destructively. Some of the faculty wives apparently had spoken to her and—I guess I must have been, in some kind of way, stirring up trouble. And I obviously was making trouble for myself. If I'd ever had a chance to move ahead, really make a name for myself, that all went down the drain in the—month, in the two or three months after the book and the publicity were over.

Q. Let me ask a question that's maybe a bit on the simplistic side, but—just for the record. You were a professor at a big university; you'd written a dozen books; you had a good salary. A loving wife. You were, in almost any sense of the word, a success. What more were you looking for? What did you *want?*

A. [long pause] That's hardly a simplistic question, it's an impossible question, because there's no answer. Everything that was happening—the excitement of the book and the advertising world, the non-affair with Melina, the—everything was connected in some way that I still haven't deciphered with what I wanted. I still don't know what I want. I have a new kind of life now, in advertising, my sex life is totally changed, my appearance is different, I . . .

Q. How is your appearance different?

A. In lots of ways. I—for one thing, I stopped wearing ties and suits. I started wearing turtlenecks and clothes that fit. For the first time, we didn't go up to Nova Scotia for our vacation. We'd been going there for years, you know, to a little cottage we rented, and we'd just sit and watch birds or dig clams and live a nature-kind-of-life in the summers. We haven't done that since the Melina thing.

Q. You no longer want to?

A. No, no. It's not—it's not that I don't want that any more, I do, perhaps as much as ever. It's just that with my own business, now, there's no time. I lead a hectic, mad-paced life now, I take work home with me, I have no time to watch gulls or walk on the beach. I'm sure I still need those things, I still yearn for them, but I, I just have no time for them now.

Q. You can't *make* time for them?

A. Ellen makes that point. She says, and she's so right, that when you choose *one* thing you automatically *don't* choose the *other.* By choosing to work as hard as I do I choose not to make time for other things. Ellen used to make that point when I'd come home at 2 or 3 in the morning after being out with Melina. I loved Ellen. I never, at any time, stopped loving Ellen, which is what made life so difficult. I loved Ellen and I'd tell her so and she'd say I had a choice: If I chose to spend my nights with Melina, I was choosing *not* to spend my nights with *her.* It was a very telling point and there was just no answer for it, to it. I remember coming in one night—the night before my forty-fourth birthday—about 3 o'clock and there was a note pinned to the living-room lamp. From Ellen. It said—er, you've got to understand that my wife is a very gentle person, she used to choke on four-letter words.

Q. Does she still?

A. [laughter] No, she handles them very well now. She—anyhow, there was a note on the lamp that said "FUCK YOU!" and I remember when I came in I thought I saw her go out the side door and I heard the car start and pull out of the driveway. There was a birthday present for me on the piano and . . .

Q. What was the present?

A. A Breughel—a reproduction of one of those miniature Breughels—very beautifully framed. Ellen and I both love Breughel.

Q. Ellen pulled out of the driveway. Where did she go?

A. Just for a drive, it turned out, to let the anger burn down. But I was—this "FUCK YOU," I didn't know if she was leaving me or going out to look for a love affair or what.

Q. Has your wife had an affair?

A. No. I know she was tempted many times. Since this all started. But she's—she's much stronger than I am. Much stronger. She knew an affair on her part would be the final blow, would destroy our marriage.

Q. Do you think so?

A. I don't know. My non-affair, whatever you want to call it, didn't wreck our marriage because Ellen *chose* not to let it. She worked hard to salvage our marriage, our love. I don't know whether I would have been strong enough to do that if she had an affair. Maybe, who knows? Maybe I would have killed myself, maybe that would have been just the one little shove I needed to go off the dock. [Pause]

Q. We've established, haven't we, that you never actually had sex, Biblical sex, with Melina?

A. Yes. [laugh] Or, no.

Q. Yes, meaning no. I'd really like to know why not, if you can help me there.

A. I'd like to know that myself.

Q. Well, try.

A. Well, she slept with—and isn't *that* a commentary on something or other, she slept with me! but—I mean she had sex with half the men I knew in advertising, and several in publishing, and who knows who else.

Q. And not with you.

A. No.

Q. This was a unique arrangement, for her?

A. I was so far gone, I know I felt very strongly at one point in all this that perhaps I didn't really want to have her that way because my—affair, with her, was *unique*. I guess I felt that it would have destroyed the, er, the uniqueness. I felt I was different from, set apart from all the other men, or almost all the other men, she knew.

Q. That you were the only one who didn't do that with her.

A. Yes, meaning I was, I *thought* I was, someone special. Oh, there's no question about my wanting sex with her after we'd known each other some time. I would caress her, fondle her breasts. But even that stopped eventually because, well, one night she asked me flat out, she said "If you just want my friendship why the fuck do you play with my tits?"

Q. Well, what stopped you from forcing the issue, saying, "Look, either we have sex or let's end it here and now?"

A. Because I didn't *want* to end it there and then! For whatever reasons, I enjoyed being with her, even though it hurt. Even though —obviously, as Ellen puts it, I chose her. I chose to *be* with her. And I chose not to force the sex issue because, in a way, I was willing to settle for her without sex.

Q. The psychiatrist that you saw, would you say he was helpful?

A. For Ellen, certainly; for us, I think so; for me, I just don't know.

Q. First you went to him alone, and later you and Ellen saw him together?

A. Yes. Ellen got far more out of it than I did. It opened doors for her. He didn't do any analyzing, because he wasn't a Freudian type; he was, he is, a behaviorist, working on, I suppose you could call it, practical relationships between people. He didn't dig into the recesses of the mind, he just got you to behave, to alter patterns of behavior, consciously. But Ellen reacted to it—tremendously. It changed her whole life, her whole concept of herself. That shrink was for Ellen what Melina was for me. She would—I've told you this already, haven't I?

Q. Told me what?

A. That Ellen would sit, or go off by herself, be alone, deep into herself for days on end, and . . .

Q. Yes.

A. Well, she would come up with insights, incredible insights about herself and about her relationship to me and to other people. And it turned her into a new person. She created a new Ellen. She learned how to become angry, how to become a person again, how to deal with her own feelings. She learned to be someone she hadn't been before.

Q. How did this affect you?

A. I think the new Ellen is better for her, better for me, much better for us.

Q. How old is Melina? How much younger than you?

A. Eighteen years. She was twenty-five, twenty-six when we met.

Q. Have you considererd the possibility that she represented a lost youth—maybe, in your case, specifically, an adolescence that you never really had?

A. Oh, certainly I considered it. At one point I was certain I was going through a belated adolescence. I looked at myself and saw all the behavior patterns of an adolescent. I was rebelling against my parents . . .

Q. You had driven your father out of your mind, you said, even forgotten his phone number.

A. Right. So there was the teenage rebellion on the part of a man in his forties. And the insane pursuit of—this wild, romantic pursuit of a girl. And then the lack of responsibility; I was behaving in an irresponsible way on the job, toward my children, certainly toward my wife and marriage. I even kept a diary, which I hadn't done since I was, maybe fifteen or sixteen.

Q. A diary? With all the events of a day, even little things . . .?

A. Not a daily calendar kind of thing. No. Look, I wanted to cry, to cry out, to scream, to talk, to unload my burdens, my guilts. I wanted, I was trying to clarify things in my mind, to work my way through this, and I couldn't tell—I couldn't talk to Ellen about these things. Well, we did have long talks, late into the night, and I did a lot of *talking* then. But—well, look, I lied to her about some things. I *hid* some things. And some things, I—I just couldn't put them into any clear form. In the diary, I just cried, I scribbled fleeting thoughts, asked questions. I tried to talk to myself, to understand what was happening.

Q. Did it occur to you that this diary was another manifestation of your carbon-copy habit? You seemed to want to be discovered.

A. I suppose I did want. And it did occur to me that Ellen might see it. I wrote a lot of it in Greek, so that if Ellen did find it—and my thoughts would race so fast sometimes that I used a very cryptic kind of shorthand to try to keep up with them. It was virtually indecipherable, or at least I thought so.

Q. You thought so? Did Ellen . . .

A. Yes, she found it and read it, but she didn't say anything to me until much later. That came out in the therapy, that she had read a lot of it and knew more than I thought she knew.

Q. And you consider the diary a symptom, if you will, of adolescence?

A. In my case, yes, because I hadn't done that, I hadn't written to myself that way, since my teens. At one point I was so convinced I was going through adolescence that [laughter] I began to look for acne.

Q. And you concluded . . .

A. I didn't conclude anything. That possibility is still viable. But I don't know. I had so many theories about why I was having this affair. For instance, I thought perhaps I was entranced with the recognition Melina brought me.

Q. Recognition? You mean beyond the project you were mutually involved in?

A. No, I'm trying to explain. [pause] Melina was not someone you could ignore. She was too much a personality, whether real or artificial or whatever. When she walked into a room, people noticed her. Everyone on campus noticed her, and some people thought I was having an affair with her. I let them. I even *encouraged* them to think so. It gave me kind some kind of special status, that this sexy, brilliant, beautiful, foul-mouthed woman was calling me and meeting me.

Q. You've mentioned several possible explanations for your involvement with Melina. Were there others that you considered?

A. I came up with new analyses every fifteen minutes, it seemed, but none satisfied me. Sometimes I even thought, "What the hell! Maybe there *is* no deeper meaning. Maybe I just lusted for this woman because—simply because I wanted to get laid!" And that explanation, I felt, was as inadequate as the others.

Q. How long did your non-affair continue?

A. As a non-affair it's still continuing.

Q. You're still in love with her?

A. No, no. I mean, I still see her from time to time, and we're still friends. No, I'm not in love with her. That part, my *intense* involvement with her, went on for, oh, six or seven months.

Q. Do you think that, at that time, you would have left your wife for Melina?

A. My kneejerk reaction to that is yes. I think, during that time, if Melina had ever expressed any *tenderness,* had ever indicated she *wanted* me as a full-time lover, maybe even a part-time lover, or a husband—if she had ever asked me to move in with her or go away with her, I think I would have.

A. Kneejerk reaction?

A. It's a kneejerk reaction because it never entered the realm of reality. It was safe to think about it, to fantasize about it, because there was no chance for it to happen. If it had happened—if Melina had said "Move in with me, become my steady fuck"—if that had happened, then—I don't know. I don't know if I would actually have left my wife or my home, if I would have left my children. I just don't know. [pause] But as a thoughtful reaction, rather than a kneejerk reaction, I think—I think I would have hesitated. [pause] Home meant too much [trails off] . . .

Q. You said the in-love part of the affair lasted six or seven months. And then what? A conscious effort to bring it to an end?

A. Well, I did make a conscious effort. When we met I would deliberately stay physically away from her. Not touch her. Move away if I detected—if I thought she was going to kiss me. Let me tell you—I think this is illuminating—about the ad agency.

Q. The one you started?

A. Yes. Originally, Melina introduced me to Larry . . .

Q. The man who became your partner?

A. Yes. Larry had once had his own agency and then he'd sold it and gone to work for [*deleted*] and Melina knew he was miserable there and wanted out, to start his own agency again. And she knew how I felt, that I wanted to get into the business, so she brought us together. Anyhow, originally Melina was to be in with us in the new agency. But by that time Ellen had begun to change; she was capable of taking a stand. She said I'd have to choose: the ad agency or our marriage. She couldn't live with the idea of my going in to work every day with, working in the same office every day with Melina. And I made a choice. I told Larry I had to bug out.

Q. Did you tell him why?

A. No, I ducked the real problem. I just told Larry I couldn't go through with it and he was—my God, he went white.

Q. Then how did you wind up with Larry and your own ad agency?

A. About two weeks after I'd told Larry it was no go, he reminded me that I'd made a commitment to finish a project for a client and asked if I'd do him just that favor—finish the job. I said I would and I meant to, and then the conversation drifted around to Melina and Larry said he'd rather not have her in the company, that he'd rather do it all alone, without me and without Melina. He said she alienated too many people with her abrasiveness, her language, her far-out clothing. He said that whatever she could bring to the company would be canceled out by the clients that she'd turn off. So he wanted her out.

Q. And that left the way clear for you to come back in?

A. Yes. But first we had to get Melina out. And Larry couldn't bring himself to say anything to her. So I told her.

Q. How did she take this?

A. I think she realized the truth of it and, besides, she had decided, on her own, to stay with the firm she was with. It worked out very well.

Q. So what you're saying is that your intense involvement with Melina more or less trailed off, in good part because you forced it to trail off, and that you were starting to—I use your own concept here—you were starting to *choose* your wife over Melina and . . .

A. Exactly.

Q. Mr. B, where are you now? Where are you now with respect to your career, your marriage, your life? Where are you—are you still, do you still have adolescent symptoms or urges? Do you still stare hungrily at young women?

A. Threw a lot into that pot, didn't you?

Q. You can take them one at a time. Or tell me to go to hell if you'd rather.

A. No, don't go to hell. I'll take them—I'll try to take you up to the present in whatever order I can. With respect to my new career?

Q. Yes. Do you have any regrets about the shift?

A. Once in a *while,* I think back with a touch of longing, maybe even affection, on the academic life. It was—there's such a vast chasm between campus life and the advertising world. Sometimes I wonder whether it was the right thing. But they're fleeting thoughts, fleeting. No, I don't think I regret it. I enjoy the pace, the hustling, the wheeling and dealing—it's still, really, all so new and still, certainly, exciting in a way that teaching never was. [pause]

Q. And your . . .

A. Maybe the thing that tends to give me greatest pause is projecting.

Q. Projecting?

A. Into the future, I mean. Thinking about the next fifteen years and wondering whether the excitement and the enjoyment will pall and whether I'll really begin to long for the relatively quiet things in life. I wonder, for instance, whether I'm ever going to find time again for clam-digging and just sitting on a rock somewhere watching the gulls wheel overhead. I miss those things now, through the excitement I miss them. So I do really wonder whether the time will come when I'll want to do those things and—. But I try to plan for that. I'd like to putter around the house and go sailing—my sailboat is sitting in the water rotting, for all I know; I haven't been on it in more than a year. I'm pushing as hard as I am because I want to build this agency up from the two-man band that it is now to the point where we can hire full-time staff people to get the pressure off, let us live a little.

Q. Where are you and Ellen now and where do you think you're headed?

A. [pause] Ellen and I are, above everything else perhaps, more aware now. We're not victims of illusion, fantasy. We know, we try to know, what the realities are. Ellen certainly has changed, and very much for the better. And I have, whether for better or not. And all signs seem to indicate that our marriage is much better now. Obviously the sex is. I mean, in the last week alone Ellen and I had more sex than we used to have in a whole year.

Q. What were the illusions and what is the reality?

A. You ask worse questions [laughter] than the shrinks. The illusion, or illusions, was that we were a—we were two people madly in love living in some never-never land somewhere. The reality is that we are real people with real and sometimes gnawing problems and that nothing is eternal. Not love, not marriage. Nothing. We're aware that we have gone through a crisis that almost tore us apart. In a sense, a very real sense, it was a good thing, because the togetherness—that all-but-sexless togetherness—had made a zero, a nonentity out of Ellen and had made me a travesty of a man. We were so close that when we began to move apart the sudden release almost sent us out of sight of each other.

Q. So you can look at your marriage now, your life with Ellen, and say it's much the better for the bitterness.

A. Much. We're willing to meet problems head-on now. We talk a lot more than we used to about things that touch us deeply. We talk out our problems and we get angry with each other and we work hard to make it work well.

Q. And Melina?

A. Melina is peripherally in the picture—which is something Ellen can't understand or abide. She gets angry about it, or depressed sometimes, and I react to her anger or depression with anger or depression of my own. But I've stopped withdrawing, crawling into a cave by myself and pulling the stone up after me. I don't see Melina as any kind of threat any more. And I can see some day that she won't be there even in a peripheral way. She's going to fade out and leave behind nothing but memories and the knowledge that she played a critical role at a critical time in my life.

Q. You still see her?

A. Occasionally. She calls once in a while.

Q. What's "once in a while?"

A. Oh, every six weeks or so. Sometimes we don't have any contact for two, three months. And sometimes she'll call me twice a week.

Q. Why? Is she still . . .

A. She keeps me up to date on her affairs, her love affairs, her problems, her job. She'll meet me for drinks and spend an hour or so unloading all her gripes on me, telling me about her latest adventure, her problems with her landlord, her whatever.

Q. Does she still kiss you when you meet?

A. Sometimes. But it doesn't do anything to me.

Q. Are you *free* of her?

A. Absolutely.

Q. And other women? Do you still feel longings? Are you still receptive to the idea of having an affair?

A. I'm receptive, yes. But I'm realistic enough to know that I can't have an affair without its having an effect on the rest of my life. Sometimes I resent this idea. Sometimes I think—this happens pretty often, I'd say—when, and then I—it's a resentment, really, a kind of anger that I can't be free and easy and a swinger . . .

Q. Anger with yourself.

A. Oh, yes, with myself, and sometimes anger at Ellen, with Ellen, that her, her inability to live on the surface of life, her constant searching into herself, into me, into the, I hate to use a phrase like this, but it's the most appropriate one here, this digging into interpersonal dynamics, her constant search for deeper meanings makes it impossible for me, for her, for us to live in a casual way. And that means—and I'm guilty of the same thing myself—that I can't just go out and have a ball and climb into bed with someone and expect it to be—I can't be just a hedonist.

Q. And *this* means that . . .

A. Wait. Let me tell you—this—here I go again, looking for deeper explanations.

Q. Be my guest.

A. Thanks. When I was a kid, a young man, one reason I had so few sexual—only five girls, was that I always had to be in love. It was all or nothing. I remember one girl I was introduced to and she —in retrospect, this became so *damned* obvious! she was hot to get laid. But when the moment of truth arrived I blurted out: "I love you!" I didn't love her, not at all. I didn't even know the girl, no less love her. But some distorted kind of moral conscience grabbed me and, I suppose, to justify fucking, I had to have a moral basis.

Q. Did you have sex with the girl?

A. No. As soon as I said that she backed off. She didn't want to get into any heavy emotional scene. She just wanted to get laid, but not with someone who was in *love* with her. Smart girl; I wish I could be that way.

Q. And you're not. Uh—are there circumstances or situations where this arises? Where you feel you'd like to have an affair? If so, what are those circumstances?

A. Well, it frequently, I frequently—when, for instance, when I'm having lunch with men who *are* that way, who merrily screw their way through life and who manage not to let it interfere with their marriage, their home life, their—even their emotions. They just jump in the sack, have a ball, get up and go their way. I *envy* them. And I often feel "why shouldn't I try it?" But I don't, because I know myself, I think, well enough to know I can't do it that way. For whatever reasons. My upbringing, my—I don't know why, but there it is and I have to live with it.

Q. You're not willing to gamble that you can do it?

A. No. The risk is too great. [pause] The temptation, the desire, is sometimes all but overwhelming.

Q. When is this?

A. Oh, frequently enough. When I walk along the street at lunch hour, for instance, and all those lovely young things are all over the place. I look at them.

Q. You sound as though you're describing your feelings *before* all this began. You spoke about how you used to pant for the girls on campus and were afraid to step out of your father-mentor role. Are you *still* afraid of rejection? Is *that* stopping you?

A. No. Not at all. I know now—I've been around free-and-easy types now long enough to know there are plenty of fish to fry. I never realized—I never knew, when I was on the faculty, that so many young women were willing and maybe even eager to go to bed with older men. But I know that's true. I know now I would have no trouble at all. Oh, sure, some—maybe even most—might tell me to take my trade elsewhere, but there'd be enough around who would accept me. That doesn't enter the picture now; now it's a question of self-restraint. Of this God-damned morality, of this inability just to get in there and float in a pool of pure hedonistic pleasure.

Q. Well, is the principal consideration here your marriage? That you don't want to jeopardize it?

A. If it's not the *principal* consideration it's certainly *one* of the principal considerations. I mean, there are, whether I like the idea or not, there are heavy psychological forces at work here. But on the surface, at any rate, it's certainly a question of self-preservation, of preserving a marriage that I cherish. Look, that aspect of it is—it's rather like an alcoholic, who's gotten himself close to the brink, who's felt death brush too closely and who knows he can't afford to touch the stuff again, not even one drink, because he knows it might—he'd go up in flames, and maybe death would score. Thanks a lot, but no thanks.

Q. One final question. Do you think you are *through* this midolescent crisis?

A. I don't think so. Ellen and I are still in the process of changing, of adjusting, and I'm not yet fully adjusted to my new way of life. I think perhaps that when I strike a balance between the old, quiet life—the clam-and-birds life—and my new one, then I'll be able to say, I think, that I've left midolescence behind. But I'm still too prone to depressing thoughts about age and aging and death. I don't think, as long as I'm still so aware of growing old, that I can say midolescence is done with. No, I think I'm still in it. I hope I come out of it alive and well and living with Ellen.

Unlike most of these people opening their lives to you, Mr. C is not a man in the middle of his field; he is a man at the top. He is also probably a much clearer, nitty-gritty thinker than Dr. A or Mr. A or Mr. B; almost never, in this interview, does he go off on tangents, rebel at questions, try to sidetrack or derail the interviewer. He is a man driven by two great forces, sex and money. He sprang from the meanest of beginnings; "my father," he says, "never earned a thousand dollars a year in any year of his life." He buys, outright, the finding of the gynecologist in Chapter II of this book that "in our society, money is an extension of the penis . . . money is sex . . . money is power." In Mr. C's life, the sex urge and the success urge seem to be a single force.

Mr. C

Q. Your ethnic background, cultural background?

A. Straight Bronx Jewish. My parents were immigrants.

Q. Were you the first generation here on both sides?

A. Yes.

Q. When did your parents come over?

A. Right after World War I, from Poland.

Q. Schools other than high school? Total schooling, education?

A. Harvard Business School. I was an economics major in college but I was an accountant when I got out.

Q. Where?

A. Wall Street. It's the, I think it's one of the largest public accounting firms in the United States now.

Q. Marital status?

A. Technically, I've been living apart for two and a half years, but there's no legal documentation of any kind.

Q. You're not divorced?

A. [shakes his head]

Q. Children?

A. Four. They go from fourteen to twenty.

Q. And you and your wife are no longer living together. Does she live in New York?

A. She's still in the same house in Jersey.

Q. And you live in the city?

A. Yes.

Q. Does she have the children?

A. Yes.

Q. I see. Do you visit them often?

A. No, they . . .

Q. Do you visit them *regularly?*

A. [response unclear]

Q. Their ages would indicate that it's not necessary.

A. They come in. I never visit them. And it's—getting less often, all the time.

Q. They are all in school, or out of college, are they?

A. Two are in college, two are in high school.

Q. Your earliest ambition? I mean, your earliest *true* ambition. Was it to be what you are now, a businessman?

A. No. I wanted to be a lawyer.

Q. You didn't go to law school, did you?

A. No, but I—when I left Harvard, I had planned to just take a year off and come back, to law school. I'd been admitted, for later admission, but once I had money in my pocket I couldn't quite make it back to school.

Q. For economic or other reasons?

A. Economic. I just enjoyed—for the first time in my life I had money.

Q. Military experience?

A. I was in World War II, in field artillery.

Q. Oh? So was I.

A. Yeah, I was in Fort Bragg.

Q. [laughter] So was I!

A. How about that?

Q. The fart center. [Bragg's address was Field Artillery Replacement Training Center] What, er, speciality?

A. One-oh-fives. Radio.

Q. Oh, you were?

A. This was in nineteen-forty . . .

Q. Four. Right.

Q. Did you go overseas?

A. No, I got hurt in basic training, and left the . . .

Q. Oh? How did that happen?

A. I jumped off that fourteen-foot wall and broke . . .

Q. Oh, yeah. The assault course.

A. I broke my ankle in about seven thousand places.

Q. Well, my God. We were in the same hideous place. We went to Raleigh and drank wine and got sick.

A. Right. Until I got smart, and said, "I'm going to stay on the base and read," and that's what I did.

Q. I didn't know people knew how to read there.

A. There was a very nice library, which I discovered, and no one ever used. I stopped going to town. It was too much of a hassle. I was a virgin then and I was ashamed to go to town and admit it!

Q. How'd you get into this, your own company?

A. One of my friends was starting a record company and he asked me to come in with him, and I'd had enough of working for other people, so I made the switch. And I became an owner. That is, in a *while* I became one of the owners.

Q. How long a while?

A. Five years later.

Q. So here you are. I'd like to establish the pattern of your pre-midolescent life.

A. Yeah, okay.

Q. The events that may have led you to where you are today. Let us start with your wife, the lady, how you met, were your interests parallel, were your—*cultural* levels parallel, and who and what was she? Can you characterize her for me, describe her physically? Start with how you met.

A. We met on a blind date arranged by a friend of mine. She was nineteen and I was twenty-seven. And I had been living alone for the last eight years.

Q. Let me establish quickly—you were only married once?

A. Only once.

Q. Right. Living alone for eight years. Well, when you say "living alone," you mean apart from your family.

A. Yes. I had my own apartment in the Village. I was leading a swinging singles life! I really was. As I look back—and I met this child, right off a farm—and, uh, we got married . . .

Q. A farm? Where?

A. In Connecticut.

Q. And how long until you married?

A. Three months later she got pregnant. And because of all my good medical connections . . .

Q. Medical connections? How did you happen to have . . .

A. A lot of—well, several of my friends, from college, had gone into medicine and we just, you know, kept up the friendships, and . . .

Q. I see.

A. —and I got three letters, and got a legal abortion.

Q. Three letters?

A. Well, in those days you got a legal abortion if you get three letters certifying . . .

Q. Right, certifying that having a baby would imperil the woman's life, et cetera, her health, welfare and so on.

A. Right. About two months later, she got pregnant *again!*

Q. Oh, dear.

A. And we went through the same routine again. And she went into a severe, severe depression, and somehow or other, three months later we got married.

Q. Did you have any kind of a [phone call interrupts; when he hangs up and the taping resumes he is laughing] . . .

Q. What's so funny?

A. Well, they—it's fascinating! Two and a half years and we can't come to an agreement. I've run up $10,000 in legal fees already! He just asked me for a check. [he laughs again] That was my divorce lawyer.

Q. Ah! So this is in the works.

A. Oh, yes, it's been, for two and a half years.

Q. This—matter of abortion: At that time, the '50's, a lot of people thought that was murder. Did you have any mixed emotions about it?

A. Yeah. I'm not Catholic, but I had lots of, yeah, very mixed feelings about it, and I think that after that second abortion I decided, "enough!" So we got married, and within the year we had the first child, and two years later we had a second child. And three years later we had another child. And by the time the fourth child came we were not getting along. At all. I don't know—I think one reason was at that time I'd gotten so totally involved in my job, and I really and truly was working six, seven days a week. We were building a new company and we were being very successful and—and I just started arranging evening meetings, and some . . .

Q. "Evening meetings"—are you speaking humorously or are you talking about business?

A. Business. No, business reasons, and this was not—and I was not screwing around, but there was a lot of tension because I was really away a lot.

Q. Do you think the Job—the capital-J Job—is a tremendous factor in this kind of thing we go through? *I* think it is. The kind of lives we lead?

A. You've got to understand, I was terribly ambitious. I was raised in poverty, and I could see . . .

Q. You *were?* Raised in *poverty?*

A. Yeah. Virtually. We were one step removed from going on welfare. My father never earned over a thousand dollars in any year of his life. He was a garment worker, a sewing-machine operator. And I saw that we were going to be successful here. It was obvious that if we worked like hell we were going to make a lot of money, and I was absolutely driven to make a lot of money.

Q. This would be fourteen years ago, this would be fifteen years ago . . .

A. When I was in my early thirties, yeah. And then, of course, the wife, buying a house in Jersey, and two cars, and . . .

Q. Before the trouble came or during?

A. Both. During, yeah. It was all going together.

Q. Describe your wife physically.

A. Short. Lean, dark-haired. Quite attractive.

Q. Was your wife working herself at anything that meant anything?

A. No. She was doing nothing at the time, excepting raising kids.

Q. No, no, no! *Before* you—when you met her.

A. Oh! She was a—what do you call it?—a laboratory technician. And she was a, she was a *child,* and she was—she had lots of problems about sex.

Q. For instance.

A. She didn't like it [giggling].

Q. Didn't like it? How can you not *like* it? This is ridiculous.

A. It happens.

Q. This, this is—she had been programed—was it programed in her, er . . . ?

Q. It was programed in her by her parents, by childhood.

A. "You shouldn't do this, you should get up at 4 o'clock in the morning and go out and milk the cow"—or whatever, rather than lie in bed and screw?

A. Or collect the eggs. It was a chicken farm. Yeah.

Q. Yeah.

A. And, then I'd come from a rather intensive sex life . . .

Q. You're one of how many children?

A. Two.

Q. You mean your *own* sex life, you don't mean your parents' . . .

A. Seven or eight years, living alone in New York . . .

Q. And yet you were nineteen before you were not a virgin any longer, is that right?

A. I was twenty!

Q. Twenty—ah!

A. Well, I tried making up for lost time.

Q. Yes, of course.

A. And I think I did, at that time. And I kind of accepted this.

It didn't—I was so involved in work that I didn't care. And I started to resent it.

Q. Resent what?

A. Her lack of interest.

Q. And at this time you were in your early thirties.

A. Early thirties, right. About—in my fifth year of marriage, the fifth or sixth year, one of the women in the office came in to see me. It was after 5 and she said, "Why don't we fuck?" And I said, "That sounds like a wonderful idea." We proceeded to do it right then and there, in the office. And I discovered, "This is fine," and that's when it started.

Q. And you started, and this became a pattern of behavior, did it?

A. Yeah. [he falls silent]

Q. Do you know of any long-standing family conflicts between you and your children as a result of the disruption of the marriage? Do you *feel* that there are any conflicts between you and your children, that they side with her, or with you, or do you feel any resentment toward them because they are living with her?

A. There's terrible resentment.

Q. On your part toward them?

A. No, on their part toward me. They have been totally convinced by her that I am a prodigal, that I'm irresponsible, that all I want to do is work, or fuck, on the outside, and that I have absolutely no interest in them.

Q. What did you think was wrong with your marriage while you were married, I mean, as opposed to what you think now? Do you have any regrets, any recriminations, any reappraisals you have made now, at the age of forty-eight? Toward what was happening to you in your thirties, when you were married?

A. I don't think I *resented* my marriage, ever. I was quite content with being totally involved in the job, having at any one time no less than six girlfriends, and often more.

Q. From the age of . . .

A. Thirty-two on. I had a marvelous thing going. I used to leave my home every morning at 6:30 and stop at different girls' apartments, to which I had keys.

Q. On your way *in*?

A. On my way in.

Q. Boy! [laughter]

A. I would fuck between 7 and 8 a.m. because at 8 o'clock the parking rules came on. I'd have my—I'd go—I'd set the alarm for five to 8, get dressed, charge out of bed and go down and get in the car so I didn't get a ticket.

Q. This was in New York?

A. Yeah. I always arranged to have these girls somewhere between Jersey and downtown, so that as I'd drive in, I—I really *did* this for ten years, solidly. I would just arrange them the day before; I'd say, "I'll see you tomorrow morning," and I had the keys. These women would usually be sleeping, and I'd just let myself in, and put the coffee on, and get undressed and get in bed.

Q. Did you—how do I phrase this?—do you think at the time you were doing this because you weren't getting any at home, or . . .

A. No, I don't think that was it.

Q. It was a chore for her, at home? It was unpleasant, at home? The job impelled you more to this, the pressures of what you were doing, and the pleasure you discovered in—"Well, my God, why didn't I start screwing these girls ten years ago?" A doctor told me this. And he says that really the *time* when this behavior starts is not all very important as far as age brackets are concerned, but that sooner or later a man may say, "Well, why the hell didn't I screw her ten *years* ago? What am I wasting my *time* for? That's ridiculous; this makes me feel better. It's pleasant!"

A. Exactly.

Q. You found this, these encounters rewarding, I'm sure, not just for . . .

A. Yeah. It's a great way to start the day!

Q. The divorce or the separation was your idea, or hers?

A. No, it was her idea.

Q. Her idea. What directly led to this? What was the, er, operative cause?

A. Well, there's a history here.

Q. Right. Let's hear it.

A. In about 19—this is '74—in 1965, I did get very involved with a woman, to a point where I wanted to leave home. That all kind of got straightened out, but after that, what we had was an entente. Détente? Détente!

Q. Who?

A. My wife and I.

Q. She knew about it?

A. She knew about it. The woman came and told her, and at that time, the woman came to the house; my wife was pregnant, and *she* was pregnant, and I was busily arranging for two abortions. Within the same week.

Q. Your wife's and the lady's.

A. Yeah. And the other woman came to the house and told her about it.

Q. Right. And what did she want? Did she want you to marry her? Did she want you to decide? Did she want . . .

A. Yeah. Make a choice. The standard soap-opera scene.

Q. Did you confess?

A. No, I did not confess, and not only that, but I was very cautious. You don't get caught in the morning very often. And I used to make sure to get home by 8:30, 9, and so forth, in the evenings, and so it was really—really *safe.*

Q. Were these ladies very much like your wife? Were they polar opposites? Were they different physically?

A. They were—different physically.

Q. Blondes? They were redheads, they were—this is an awfully superficial thing to say; personality has to go with it . . .

A. They were usually—my wife is quiet, soft-spoken; they were usually loud, they were generally slightly on the floozy side—not slightly, but a range from slight to extreme—they were mostly heavy drinkers.

Q. You did not drink?

A. I did not drink at all. I've never drunk.

Q. Is there any physical reason you don't?

A. Yeah. I get sleepy!

Q. You're not a diabetic or anything like that?

A. No. It just puts me to sleep.

Q. Yes, but that's the reason we drink, to put us to sleep.

A. In twenty minutes? [he laughs]

Q. Oh, sometimes with me, sure. Did desire for other women precede the marital trouble or was it the cause of the marital trouble? Both?

A. It's both. You really can't make that separation.

Q. In your case or anybody's case?

A. In anybody's case. There's something else about me. You have to remember that I was always driven to make money. Simply out of insecurity. I was always worried about money. I took the money that I made and put it in the market, and at one time the market was pretty wild, and I made a lot of money. I mean, like, almost a million dollars. And I still kept this quiet pattern of screwing around in the morning, working till 5 in the afternoon, but getting home about 8:30, 9, a late dinner, say, I had to meet a buyer for drinks, you know, kind of thing. And then the market collapsed.

Q. Sixty-two?

A. No—I'm talking about the '67 collapse. At which point I really was worth about a million dollars; damn close.

Q. And the paper money burned up.

A. Yeah. And—I have nothing now. Zero. In the market.

Q. Well, you have this company, it certainly . . .

A. Yeah, but I have no, no cash, no securities, any money I play with now. And at that time, that's when I started to go crazy, I then stopped even being secretive about my dalliances. I was fucking everything I could.

Q. And did you tell her?

A. I never told her. She would tell me that "I sense you're screwing around," and I would deny. Just wholly deny. Interestingly, my wife became much more interesting, sexually. She went to analysis; it seemed to have helped, and I was having a marvelous sex life at home. Often, good, and the better it was at home, the more I was screwing around outside!

Q. They complemented each other and they fed each other.

A. Yes. Beautifully. Anyway, I got to the point where I stopped being secretive. It was denied, but it was—you'd have to be blind not to have seen what was going on. And finally I took a girl on a trip to Europe with me, in 1971.

Q. Had you known her? Wait—am I jumping ahead?

A. No, no. Go ahead.

Q. She worked for you?

A. Yes.

Q. You described your wife and characterized her as dark, soft-spoken, quiet . . .

A. And highly cerebral. My wife is very cerebral.

Q. And this girl, this 1971 girl?

A. Not really. A phony.

Q. Aha!

A. She's a total fraud. She is not smart. She's shrewd, but not smart. There is a type of—cunning, a—man-eatingness about her, but she isn't really smart. She's totally uneducated, totally unintellectual. She's not smart. My wife is quite smart, very bright.

Q. But, anyway, your wife was all the things you have said about her, in character, spiritually and physically, and this person was . . .

A. The total opposite.

Q. And very shrewd.

A. And very cruel.

Q. Very cruel?

A. Yeah.

Q. What happened during your trip to Europe? Was that—did you have a sexual encounter with her at that time?

A. Oh, yes.

Q. You did. Was that the first . . .

A. No, it was—before we left, we had a couple of small dalliances. And there was a certain excitement. She's totally uninterested in sex. Sex is currency for her. She knows . . .

Q. Totally uninterested in *devoting* anything to it, in *giving* anything of herself?

A. No, she'll give of herself, but she gets nothing out of it. She's . . .

Q. No orgasms?

A. Oh, no. That's the *least!* She's just not interested! And, on the other hand, she is technically, mechanically, *unbelievable,* and I can speak from experience. In bed. Unbelievable! She's almost—she has a quality like the Monkey, in the Philip Roth book. I mean, if you ever want a mental image of the Monkey [he trails off into laughter]

Q. Yes, but I . . .

A. My feeling, when I read the book, I thought, "It's *her,*" and finally, when she had me—at any rate, finally, when we got back, she said, "If you want to screw me, you've got to stay overnight. I don't put up with guys going back to the suburbs." And at that point I was really enjoying—I was enjoying, I think, the total depersonalization of sex. It was absolutely a mechanical procedure.

Q. No foreplay, no courting, no . . .

A. No nothing!

Q. Nothing . . . like how animals walk around each other, the ritual dance . . .

A. Nothing. Get in bed and just start to pound. Something about it just excited me. The depersonalization aspect.

Q. What do you think you saw in her? When I say that, it sounds like a stupid question, but let us go beyond all this; did you see anything, did this make up for a lack in your marriage? Was she such a contrast to your wife?

A. I hate to be pseudo-analytic, but I have spent twenty-two years in analysis. With breaks in-between; it wasn't twenty-two years straight [he trails off].

Q. Go ahead.

A. For every—I would say fifty-nine out of every sixty minutes spent with this girl were unpleasant, ranging from totally unpleasant to miserable beyond description, with one minute of pleasure in the sixty. I think somehow or other I wanted that punishment; I don't know why. I know it's, it's, it's *armchair* analysis, but I know that what I'm saying has some basis.

Q. Have you told your shrinks about her?

A. No, because by the time I met her I'd stopped going to analysis. It was never resumed. I stopped four years ago. Three years ago?

Q. Have you seen her lately?

A. Not since she left here. I've talked on the phone a number of times. I haven't seen her. [pause] Well, she's come up to the *office,* you know.

Q. Has she ever asked to come back?

A. No.

Q. Do you want her back?

A. No, God, no!

Q. Do you want her back in your bed?

A. No.

Q. I have been told that the women you go with now, or are seen with, or the lady you are—you are keeping house with a lady, I believe?

A. Yes, yes.

Q. She's like your wife. Dark, more generously made physically, soft-spoken, and loving?

A. Everything's right except the "dark." She's blonde and has freckles.

Q. Who? Your wife or . . .

A. The one I'm living with. But she's soft-spoken, very attentive, very loving, very young.

Q. How young? [He does not reply. I repeat the question.] How young?

A. Oh, twenty-six, twenty-seven. I . . .

Q. Okay. This thing with the other girl, the one you went to Europe with. How did that start?

A. Pretty soon after she came to work here.

Q. Oh? She *worked* here?

A. Yes.

Q. So it started after she joined the company. And what were the circumstances, if I may ask, of your first encounter with her?

A. Well, she came to work in August, and the end of—I should —it leads up—let's go back to that point in time after the incident with this woman who got pregnant and my wife found out about. Up to that point, we had had what I consider a terribly comfortable kind of life.

Q. Your wife and you.

A. Yes. We had similar interests, we both liked playing bridge, we both liked visiting the same places. We had . . .

Q. What places?

A. We loved traveling, anywhere we'd go. We never argued, never disagreed, never had any money problems. I'd put my check in the bank. We had a joint account; both of us spent . . .

Q. Well, she wasn't working?

A. She was not working. But we had—it was just a very comfortable sort of life. [pause] After this incident, she then said she's unhappy, she . . .

Q. The two-pregnant-women incident.

A. Yeah. She'll never forgive me, and she went into a very severe depression.

Q. It came as a severe, immediate, very traumatic jolt?

A. Yes.

Q. All suspicions realized.

A. Yeah.

Q. The worst nightmares come true.

A. Or confirmed. I decided the thing she had to do, the kids—we had full-time help—I said, "You've got to go back to work instead of just sitting here being a housewife."

Q. Being a lab technician?

A. No. She—she happens to be an excellent mathematician. She never graduated from college, but she's got a fantastic mathematical, analytical mind. I said, "Why don't you go back to work, become a statistician in market research, get into that, where they really can use you?" And she got a job, and she was terrific at it. And then a better job.

Q. After the confrontation.

A. After the confrontation. I sort of forced her. I said, "If you don't go to work, I'm going to leave you." I had to literally push her out of the house. And it worked.

Q. You were resolved at this time to save your marriage?

A. Oh, yeah. Remember, this was the time when sex at home was getting much better, and the kids were growing up, and there were no financial pressures. I was, uh, doing my fucking-around. I was quite content. I had money. I keep mentioning money, but I gather it's more important than I realize. This is a recent realization on my part. And she got a job and went to work for some really big consultants, an all-male operation. I mean, they just don't have women among their consultants. And she came up, in no time at all. In no time at all she became an important person there. And that was terribly satisfying to her. She was actually successful at work. And things got very good between us at that point, and I really—I did most of my screwing out of obligation to girls I didn't want to dump. I did not pursue it; it was just that I'd started all these patterns and I was—I was just letting them drift away. But I wasn't cutting them out totally. And that's how we lived, until the next—until the girl I went to Europe with. My wife and I lived a very comfortable life and marriage got better and better, because she didn't—because of her job and her success—she didn't feel dependent on me. She had interests of her own. If I *did* stay late, she didn't mind because she had her own thing going for her.

Q. I'm a bit confused in my chronology. You spoke of the pregnant woman who confronted your wife, and this was *not* this last girl; this was in '65, is that right?

A. That's right. This is not—not the girl on the boat—er, the jet!

Q. She [laughing]—that would make her about two years old! She's what? Twenty-seven, twenty-eight?

A. She was twenty-five when I—as a matter of fact, she was twenty-four because—When I took her to Europe I called my wife from Europe and it was a—I just missed her, you know. And I called, and she said, "How are you doing?" She knows I hate traveling alone. So she was being very solicitous on the phone, you know. "Are you enjoying the trip?" It was a business trip, to France. I *detest* France! And she sort of was being solicitous, and I said, "No, we're having a nice time."

Q. And [laughing] the next question was . . .

A. No, nothing said. I came back from Europe and she said, "Who were you with?" And I of course denied again. And she . . .

Q. What did you tell her, that it was the editorial "we" that "we're having a nice time?"

A. No, I—yes. I said, yes, it was the editorial we, and she said, "No, no, you were with someone, I know." So it was then that she asked me to leave.

Q. In '71.

A. In '71.

Q. The business trip being when?

A. November. The business trip was in November and I left home by Christmas.

Q. Did your wife ever know who the woman was?

A. Yes.

Q. How did she find that out? You told her?

A. No, I didn't tell her.

Q. The grapevine?

A. People we both know knew about it, and we have friends, and, well, she knew. Also, she came into the office once—spotted her—and then said, "I think I know who you were with."

Q. She felt the vibrations.

A. Yeah, the . . .

Q. Anti-vibrations?

A. Yeah. Anti-vibes.

Q. Here comes a pompous question, Mr. C. Have you found any inner peace, now, with the lady you're now living with? Have you found a way out of whatever problem you had? Have you resolved the problems of midolescence at this point?

A. [pause] No. I met this lady I'm living with a year ago this month, at a party. And we started seeing each other.

Q. Give me a date on this. This is after you left home?

A. Well, *right* after I left home, I lived with the girl, the one the marriage broke up over. I lived with her for a year.

Q. Ah.

A. I—I left home in December. I lived with her for a year, off and on.

Q. Her place, or yours?

A. I didn't have a home for a year. I spent one year without an apartment. I lived—either lived with her, or got involved with some woman and moved in on her. I lived in eleven places in my first year and never had my own apartment till exactly a year later, when I finally took an apartment. 'Cause I had always—in my mind that year . . .

Q. Which was now? When?

A. Seventy-one. I always assumed I was going to go back home. And I did not want to spend the money, I did not want to sign a lease, I didn't want any permanent—I even kept my clothes in Jersey. I didn't—I would take my winter clothes in the winter, bring them back and take out my summer clothes. I was convinced that I would be reconciled, and I conducted my life accordingly. And I believe, in retrospect, that one of my reasons for my involvement—there were many reasons, obviously, but one of them was that it was such an *impossible* situation. It was kind of a holding action till I could get back home. I mean, there was no possibility of anything happening there on a permanent basis; that crazy I'm *not*. Well, maybe I am. But it was only a year later that I realized that I probably was not going to reconcile. So I got an apartment, started trying to lead a *life,* so to speak. Bought some furniture. That kind of thing.

Q. We—the question was—the inner peace . . .

A. Yeah. Let's get back to that question. There's a lot of inner peace, but, you know, I believe that there are people in this world who are just restless, who will always be restless. I think I'm one of these people.

Q. Well, if that were true, wouldn't you have changed jobs a few times?

A. Yeah, but . . .

Q. But maybe you're at a level where that wouldn't happen, because you're—you're at the top. This might happen a few levels below . . .

A. It might happen below. I'm sure if I were . . .

Q. So there are these . . .

A. I don't express my restlessness through work. I do it through women, I guess [laughter]. I think I'm as peaceful as I've ever been. I have great—I have *financial* pressures now, with kids in college, and what not, and that takes away a lot of peace. I live very frugally. I've got this nothing apartment, where I had a fourteen-room house, with four bathrooms, and three cars, with a scooter and, you know, I'd lived very well. I've adjusted. Not well, but I've adjusted to it. I find life with this woman pleasing, but I can't say that—I don't know that I can *maintain* it. I have a feeling that, somewhere underneath, that I'm going to run back into—into another situation.

Q. Because of past performance.

A. Yeah. I think one can't discount past performance.

Q. What have your shrinks told you about that? Do they say you have proclivities for this?

A. Well, if you want the analytic interpretation . . .

Q. I think it would help.

A. I'm not necessarily subscribing to this interpretation, but the analytic interpretation goes back to my father. Who was never successful. He never made a thousand dollars a year. It was that I couldn't stand being more successful than my father. This is, remember, not my interpretation. I'm not discounting it, either; I'm just saying that I don't, I haven't, really—and that when I get involved in this—this is one of my analysts' words—"You tend toward the floozies, the obvious floozies, and this is some form of punishment, because you think you've been more successful than your father." Whereas other guys go out and fuck up on their jobs, somehow, I've not been able—I've gotten—I've not done that, but I do it with women.

Q. You do not see other women now, do you?

A. No, I do not. I have not since May of last year.

Q. Do your children know about this present lady? Have they met her?

A. Yes, oh yes. They met her, we go out together when they come in.

Q. How do they feel about her?

A. Well, she's terribly likable . . .

Q. You don't feel any conflicts here.

A. I think there are terrible conflicts, because of her age.

Q. Her age being near theirs.

A. *Too* near theirs, yeah. They never took the girl on the boat— the jet—seriously. That was—she fit into their mother's portrayal of me.

Q. How did they feel toward that girl and she toward them? Did she resent them? Did she ever express hostility toward them?

A. That one? Yeah, but the point—they always thought of her as being part of my insanity. I mean, they didn't treat her seriously. They treat *this* woman seriously, and I think there's tremendous resentment.

Q. When your divorce finally comes through, do you intend to marry the lady you're living with?

A. I'd like to. But I'm not sure she intends to marry me, at this time.

Q. Getting back to what the shrinks told you about your father. Do you think you ever had any conflicts with your father? Do you remember any conflict with your father? Do you remember resenting the fact that he never made a thousand dollars a year?

Q. Yes. Yes. And resenting the fact that he was an immigrant. I remember coming to work for a WASP firm, maybe the ultimate WASP firm, and most of my associates came from families whose fathers were executives, of various companies, and so forth, and I was, I was very, very much out of place there.

Q. And you'd go to their homes.

A. I'd go to their homes . . .

Q. And you couldn't take them to your home.

A. No.

Q. I see. Well. What's with the—the one you keep calling the girl on the boat, when it was a jet?

A. What's that? Escape? That I say that? Well, I think she's doing, I don't think she's doing anything.

Q. This girl, the direct cause, the cause-and-effect cause, of your marital split-up.

A. Yeah. Thinking back—I'm sure you've had this experience. Some woman has left you, split, and you find her next lover is somebody you think is a totally impossible person. You feel some kind of personal humiliation.

Q. Like, "What's that son of a bitch have that I didn't have?"

A. Yeah. My wife, I think, was terribly resentful of her. Thinking she had nothing going for her.

Q. In a woman's eyes.

A. In a woman's eyes. I think one gets a vicarious pleasure in seeing one's ex-lover associating with someone that one likes, or respects, who . . .

Q. Who, exactly, are we talking about?

A. I'm talking about my wife's reaction . . .

Q. Oh.

A. I think it was like the ultimate insult to her that I was involved with an animal like that. And very involved; not just a casual fuck! That's . . .

Q. At the same time, could you not have become involved with the Virgin Mary, and your wife would have taken offense? Could you not have had the sweetest, most charming person in the world, and wouldn't your wife have felt the rivalry, her own animalistic protection of the home, her saving of the marriage . . .?

A. Yeah! But it's a different—you see, for example, when this woman came to the house to say she was pregnant, she was terribly attractive, terribly bright, and my wife, later, when she could calm down, said, "Well, I have to say this: Your taste isn't bad." [laughter]

Q. Do you now think there is any hope for saving your marriage, even at this late date?

A. No.

Q. What is holding up the divorce?

A. Money.

Q. The settlement.

A. Yeah.

Q. You were fairly quick to accept this premise of mine. Do you think midolescence is as big a problem as I make it out to be? [He nods slowly]

A. Every man I know over forty is just terribly depressed and unhappy, and doesn't know why, doesn't know what to do about it.

Q. More so than you?

A. Much more so. I think I've come through fine, I've had my— yeah.

Q. But you don't think it's over? [He shakes his head.] The answer is no.

A. I think I'm heading for a crisis with the woman I'm living with. I'm—there's a point beyond which there's got to be a permanency in a relationship.

Q. That is, the crisis will be, "Put your cards on the table?" She feels that way?

A. Well, the basic issue now—she wants children. I don't.

Q. Why not? You're too old?

A. Too old. I just couldn't *stand* having infants around. The second thing—I didn't want to use the word "love" . . .

Q. Why not?

A. I just don't. But there's a tremendous concern for her. I feel a genuine concern about her. And, where she can't see—at the age of twenty-six, she's not even twenty-seven—I figure my, the most I will live is twenty more years. I come from a family of everyone dying in his early sixties.

Q. But you're a product of different medical and health . . .

A. Yeah, *maybe!* Let's assume I have twenty years to go. That would make her forty-six when I die. That's a *hell* of a time to be a widow. And I've *said* this to her. I said, "I'll be gone, and at forty-six you don't want to be a widow." And I feel terribly selfish about this relationship. It's great now. And while she's willing to concede on the children, she still wants to *have* children. And that's why, somewhere, this thing is going to have to wind up in a crisis.

I think it has to be said once more that this is more a report than an analysis. I have no medical credentials in psychiatry; I am at best an amateur sociologist (isn't everybody?). But as I was putting these cases together it did strike me, as I said in the first chapter, that midolescence is more a hydra than a serpent, a many-headed thing, only one of whose heads is sex. Here are two men for whom, in my non-professional opinion, a change in career was by far the most important event, if not the central crisis, of middle age.

Each was in a highly specialized field, calling for years of training and education and a heavy investment of dedication. Mr. D was an operatic singer, a basso, the specially useful kind of singer who can always find work. Mr. E was a clinical psychologist in federal service. For neither was there any question of financial insecurity. Each had built up an impressive career-equity in experience, accomplishment and recognition. And then, in midolescence, each decided that what he had thought was his life's work, what he had been doing for so many years, just wasn't rewarding any more. Mr. D left the operatic stage to become a travel agent; Mr. E quit science to become an actor. In a sense, their paths crossed.

Mr. D could have gone on singing until his voice failed him, but his company wanted him to continue singing buffoon-roles—Beckmessers, in "Die Meistersinger," for instance—when he wanted to sing the big parts, the Hans Sachses. "I felt that this was a kind of death," Mr. D says at one point in his interview. In another: "I decided that I needed a change . . . I needed to find myself. I had to find a new direction." About the same time, his marriage came to an end, for reasons of incompatibility no longer bearable for either long-term partner; the parting was amicable. He married one of his voice students, a woman half his age. But though that aspect looms large in the three earlier life-stories, it seems to play almost an incidental role with Mr. D.

Mr. E showed me his high school yearbook. Each student had been asked to write, under his photo, what he wanted to do in life. The line under Mr. E's picture reads, "To make a spotlight in show business." But he had been reared by people who respected college credentials and professions. And he had become interested in psychology, an interest stirred, he says, by seeing movies about it. And so he chose clinical psychology as his career, and it led him into federal service. But his interest in the theater never flagged. In his late thirties, two forces began to pull at him.

One, he had been nominated for a top job; two, he had become active in amateur theatricals in the Washington, D.C., area, where he worked, and had been commuting to New York on weekends to train at an actor's studio. Finally, someone else was picked for the big job. "I really breathed a sigh of relief," Mr. E says. "I thought, 'that would have been the final seduction . . . no,' I thought, 'I'm not going to wake up ten years from today and wonder what it would have been like if I'd done it.' " And so he did it—"came here [to New York] with no job, and hardly knowing anyone, took my chances," reached for the spotlight at last.

Sex played no part in Mr. E's decision. He is the only lifetime bachelor among the seven men in this chapter. If sex had anything to do with what happened to Mr. D, it was at best a peripheral factor. The compelling force in these two cases was career. In these two interviews you will find soft-spoken and apparently low-keyed men whose chronicles seem to lack the emotional peaks and valleys of Mr. A or Mr. B or the driven-man feeling that pervades Mr. C's words. Yet you will also find, as I did, that midolescence was, for them, no less a time of crisis.

Mr. D

Q. How old are you?

A. Fifty-six.

Q. Tell me about your singing career, when it began.

A. It began when I was twenty-one, and ended . . .

Q. I'll ask you to speak up, sir.

A. Yeah. [I make some adjustment on the tape.] Fred, I don't have to project as much as you do, because my voice will project anyway.

Q. I'm sure you sang in school, didn't you?

A. The first time I sang in public I was in high school, at a high school graduation, and it was at that time that I met my voice teacher, who later became my mentor and guided me to a rather successful career.

Q. Are you a baritone? Bass?

A. Bass baritone.

Q. What was the age difference between yourself and your wife?

A. Seven months. She was seven months older. We went to college together.

Q. You were married at what age?

A. Twenty-one.

Q. This marriage produced . . .

A. A son and a daughter.

Q. Who are now what ages?

A. My son is now thirty-one, and my daughter will be twenty-five next week.

Q. Has either gone into music?

A. No. My son is an insurance agent and my daughter is a businesswoman. And married.

Q. Isn't insurance "business?"

A. Not quite. It's really a professional service. A service job, the same as the work that I'm doing now.

Q. As a singer, where did you begin your career? Did you work on radio?

A. No. I began my singing career professionally, if you can call it professionally, in a synagogue. And then in quartets. We trouped around the country. Along the way I began to build my career, in the Midwest. In Chicago.

Q. You are from Chicago?

A. Born there, yes. And I graduated into the concert field, into oratorio, and had one opera performance, with the Chicago Opera Company. And then I was drafted and served about two and one half years in the army, in the Second World War.

Q. What branch of the army?

A. I started out in the Signal Corps and finally they put me into Special Service.

Q. And on getting out of the service you resumed your career?

A. On getting out of the service, I went back to Chicago, and I spent about six months trying to get myself organized. I came to New York in about May of 1946. Got myself a job in the civic opera, and then I became a replacement in "Carousel." I was there about eight or ten weeks.

Q. Did you have a speaking part?

A. I had a small speaking part.

Q. And you continued in musical comedy, did you?

A. No, I decided that wasn't for me. I took advantage of my G.I. Bill and studied with the American Theater Wing. I studied with a lot of famous maestri, conductors.

Q. And so when did you get into opera?

A. I made my debut in "Boheme" in 1947. I'd rather not name the company. But it was one of the biggest.

Q. Perfectly all right.

A. I remember a famous tenor was with me, in the cast, or I was with him, rather, and he gave me his pinky diamond ring to wear in my appearance.

Q. This debut: Was it in any way a tryout? Were you established there?

A. No, I'd been signed to a three-year contract.

Q. What other roles were there?

A. The first three years, they were very small. And then, in the fourth year, I began to move up the ladder. During the next seventeen years—I was there for twenty years, all told—I sang roles like the Beckmesser in "Meistersinger," the Alberich in The Ring, the Bartolo in both "The Barber of Seville" and "The Marriage of Figaro," Giovanni, Alcindor in "Boheme."

Q. We have now covered a period from 1947 to . . .

A. Twenty years later.

Q. Some of these questions are going to become rather personal, because I want to find out why two things happened. One, you gave up this career; two, your first marriage ended.

A. Yes, but, er . . .

Q. I hope you don't mind if they do seem personal, or prying.

A. If I do mind, I'll tell you. I have strong feelings about certain things! But I must interject—before I departed as a singer, all those years I was also a cantor in a synagogue and the last seven years, I was also a full professor at a university. This was where I met my present wife, who was a student of mine when I first went there, and is starting her career. When I finally retired from singing, I not only left opera, I resigned from the synagogue, and I resigned from the university.

Q. Was this a troubled time, in any way?

A. Yes, it was.

Q. To the operative question, then: What was it that made you give up your singing career? You were not old, as singers go.

A. No.

Q. How old were you, then?

A. Well, let me see; eight years ago, I was forty-eight years old.

Q. What prompted you to change so drastically? Today, you are a travel agent, are you?

A. Right. I have my own agency.

Q. Was there dissatisfaction with your operatic career? Did you feel you'd gone as far as you could go, that you'd never be a Tucker or a Caruso, or a Chaliapin?

A. Well, obviously I couldn't be a Tucker or a Caruso; they're tenors. But I'd gone as far as I could in that company. I went to Europe, and was offered two theaters there, German houses. They would have let me sing the roles that I wanted to sing, and couldn't sing in the American company. But as a Jew, who felt strong about the Second World War and all the resultant unhappiness, I simply couldn't see spending the rest of my life singing in *Germany!* So I was faced with one of two things: Either coming back and accepting what they had for me here or, at that particular time of my life, making a change. Of course, I was certainly given the impetus by separation from my former wife of almost two years; I think we were separated in '66. Because I remarried in '68.

Q. Do you do any singing now?

A. Not at all.

Q. Not even at home?

A. No. I've never sung at home. For me, singing, while it was always a pleasure, was also work. I never sang in the bathroom.

Q. How many children in your immediate family?

A. I have one brother.

Q. What line of work was your father in?

A. A tool-and-die maker, and then he went into the cleaning business, for a great many years. For the last ten years of his life he owned two restaurants.

Q. Going to the change in careers, which is still very startling to me, I'm not sure I understand it—were there dissatisfactions and frustrations all along in your career?

A. If you know singers, if you know artists, there are always frustrations. You never quite do the things you'd like to do; there were many things I wanted to do at that company that I simply couldn't, because the general manager and I didn't get along. We didn't get along from the first day we *met,* because that day I met him across the negotiating table.

Q. You were an active member of the union?

A. I'm a very active member. American Union of Musical Artists. I have a life membership.

Q. Do you suppose your height, or lack of it, had anything to do with this?

A. I don't think I know what you mean.

Q. How tall are you?

A. Five-seven.

Q. Five-seven; is that tall enough on a stage to command a leading role?

A. Well, for the things I was doing.

Q. Yes, but would they like a taller man, possibly? You're a basso. Could you have been a Mephistopheles?

A. Sure, but never in that company.

Q. Why?

A. Their concept is six feet and over.

Q. And in Europe?

A. In Europe, yes. As a matter of fact, I had signed a contract with a recording company to do six albums—for operas in Spain —and among them was the Mephisto. One of the contents of the contract was that they would put the money in escrow, two weeks before my departure. They never did, and my attorney wouldn't allow me to go. But here they never thought of me as a Mephisto; they thought of me as a "buffo," a Beckmesser, an Alberich. I had a talk with a fellow today who told me about finding an old program, fifteen years old, and here was my name with these stars' names. He said he got such a thrill out of seeing my name. I said, "That and thirty-five cents will get you on the subway!"

Q. Well, if there were dissatisfactions and frustrations, did they reach some sort of climax at the time of the career change?

A. No, no, I think the climactic change that took place within me was my personal business.

Q. It was in 1967 that you decided to give up your singing?

A. Yes. I left opera and went into the travel business.

Q. Which seems a very dramatic change to a much calmer area of life; now, I may be wrong.

A. It's calm in some respects, but at the same time, being a singer is being in a service business of a kind. It's entertainment, that's true, but you're performing a service in that you're giving people some insight in what they want to hear, what they want to feel, want to listen for. And in the travel business, you're performing a comparable service, perhaps. I've found a great deal of satisfaction.

Q. Why specifically that field?

A. I had a friend who was a very successful travel agent. One day, after my last trip to Europe, we had dinner, and we talked, and he knew that I'd already given up all the positions I had.

Q. "Positions" you had?

A. I was at the opera company, at the synagogue and at the university, all at the same time, wearing three hats. And the income I had was rather high, and I felt I just needed another change; I needed another change because my marriage of so many years—I was married in 1939—and for twenty-eight years—well, I decided that I needed a change, I needed to find myself. As I look back in retrospect. I suppose I lost confidence in myself at that point in time.

Q. Yes, that's what can happen at that time.

A. Here I had all these things, you know; I was in opera, I was at the synagogue, I was at the school. I thought I had to find a new direction, and it was very difficult for me. The year before, I'd separated from my wife—in 1966. 1967 was a very difficult year for me, financially, emotionally. In '67, I talked with this friend of mine, and he said he thought this might be a good kind of thing for me. I was gregarious, I liked to talk to people, he said; I had a lot of travel background. So I went into the travel business in September of 1967.

Q. And was your present—your second wife in the picture at that time? While you were still married to your first?

A. Yes. We had been seeing each other on a rather casual basis.

Q. And you were separated from Wife No. 1.

A. Yes. And when Wife No. 1 and I were separated, this girl and

I began to see more of each other, and in 1968, we decided that we would get married.

Q. What was wrong with your relationship with your first wife? Which is a very broad, very sweeping, very general question, and has to be asked.

A. My first wife was an exceptional person. A very nice, very sweet person, and we had just grown apart so terribly. It was more and more difficult to find a common ground. All the years that I was growing up as an artist, I used to spend many, many months away from my home. There would be times when I would be away from home for five to seven months, traveling around the world. Europe, Israel, Mexico, and very seldom was my wife with me. We did make one trip to Mexico. At the same time, finances being what they were, it was rather difficult, and besides, I had two youngsters, who . . .

Q. Here comes the first of these interesting questions: Was there any unfaithfulness on your part or on her part in the sexual, legalistic sense?

A. On my part, yes. There was.

Q. And, was it with your present wife?

A. No.

Q. Ah. Was it with a co-worker, a co-performer?

A. Yes, yes.

Q. And so, the home relationship being as bad as it was, you would naturally drift farther toward your work, in which you had invested a great deal . . .?

A. That's right. I was having—finding—when anyone would say to me, "Does your wife understand you?" I would say, "Yes, I'm *sure* she does!"

Q. [laughter] Was that [the unfaithfulness] at all operative in the divorce, was it a legal part of the divorce?

A. No.

Q. Not item one.

A. No. Our divorce was a completely amicable one.

Q. Amicable. Do you see your first wife at all today?

A. I haven't seen her for three or four years; I haven't talked to her for a couple of years.

Q. And so there were frictions and animosities that never resolved themselves over the twenty years—how many years did you say?

A. Twenty-eight.

Q. You would talk about where you'd been and what you'd done and she had no interest in it?

A. Oh—possibly.

Q. A lot of the men I know say they find themselves talking to the wall in that respect.

A. No—well, there were times, there were times. And then later on, in the latter years, when I was singing professionally, only on rare occasions would my family attend.

Q. Your children would not come and see you sing?

A. Not in my latter years, no. In the early years, yes, but not in the latter years.

Q. Did they enjoy the music, or not?

A. My son played the piano, and I think they were both appreciative, but you know, it must be very difficult for youngsters growing up, with everything centering around the father, and the attention being diverted somewhat from them. We tried to change it, you know, as I got older, my children and I, when they were in high school, and college. We spent a great deal of time. We played golf together. We played tennis.

Q. Are you a grandfather yet?

A. I have two grandchildren. One grandchild is a year and a half younger than my son. I have a son who is two and a half now.

Q. When you were unfaithful, was it because of dissatisfaction with your wife sexually or socially? A need to seek sexual or social fulfillment elsewhere?

A. On the social level, our life was fine; we had a full social life.

Q. You wouldn't consider yourself, in that period, a Don Juan, or a Don Giovanni?

A. No, no.

Q. Did you feel the pressure of aging?

A. Er, I think I went through a trauma, a greater trauma, when I passed forty than I did when I passed fifty. I think I'd more or less accepted things by the time I got to be fifty.

Q. Do you think that in leaving the first wife and seeking the company of other women, or in getting married again, you were seeking—you say your wife here is younger than one of your children?

A. My wife is twenty-nine.

Q. Do you think you were trying to recapture your lost youth? As people do?

A. No.

Q. Can you give me some guidance in what really—maybe pick one subject, one facet of your disagreement or your difficulty with your first wife? Could you trace it to any certain time, was there any certain cause, when this began?

A. I think it was an accumulation of partly built-in resentments. I remember once we went to a marriage counselor.

Q. You did make an active effort to save this marriage?

A. Oh, yes. And we went to the counselor, for perhaps six months or so. And my wife told me that she hadn't even been aware of it, but she was in active competition with me. For instance, here I was an opera singer, and we'd have parties. We always seemed to have parties when the [laughs] money seemed to be low! *Lowest!* Small parties would be ten, twelve people; evening-size parties would be thirty-five.

Q. Good Lord!

A. And we had bashes, you know? And, of course, she was a very good cook, as is my present wife, and we might have twelve or fourteen people for dinner. And we'd have this fabulous dinner, and she would come downstairs looking as if she'd just come out of the beauty parlor. And everyone would exclaim how lovely she looked —she was a very handsome woman—and how marvelous the meal was. Well, this, the counselor said, was her form of competition with me. In this way, she could counterbalance her own feeling of adequacy, and it was very important, and I understood that. But these were things, and barriers.

Q. And almost conscious?

A. I don't think she did it consciously, but it was there.

Q. Close to the surface.

A. Yes. And the little things added up as the years went on, and we finally came to irreconcilable differences.

Q. There weren't political differences, were there?

A. No. Never. We were both politically of the same mind. I like to think of myself as a liberal.

Q. Has your new marriage worked out satisfactorily?

A. Yes. Very.

Q. Do you feel now that you are less prone to seek any interest elsewhere?

A. I am not prone.

Q. You're not prone. You probably weren't then, either.

A. Well! I did.

Q. Yes. Do you see yourself playing a father's role, or the role of a father figure, in any respect, in your life with your present wife?

A. No.

Q. Was that a bad question?

A. No.

Q. I was surprised to hear that you were fifty-six. I would have put you at about my age [forty-eight]. Younger!

A. Well, being a singer, you know, for so many years, you have to be physically fit, and I've always tried to keep myself in shape. I don't do the kind of exercising now that I used to do when I was a singer.

Q. What were those exercises?

A. Just the mere fact of singing. For instance in a performance, when I'd be on the stage perhaps for two or three hours—"Meistersinger" is four and a half hours—I could lose five or six pounds. This is physical work. And the constant performing, the constant rehearsals. And all those years I played tennis, and I still play tennis and I still play golf.

Q. You have never had any illnesses that would go with the peculiar changes of middle age?

A. No.

Q. How do you feel at your age having a two-year-old son? Do you feel at all peculiar? Do you feel at all out of place, or out of time?

A. No. As a matter of fact, it's quite wonderful. When my son was this boy's age, I was in the army; I was away for, two, three years. And when my daughter was my present youngster's age, I was wandering all around the country. So I didn't see them grow up.

Q. And so this is something new for you.

A. This is marvelous for me, you see, because I see this boy every day. We have breakfast in the morning; we have dinner in the evening, if he's not too tired; weekends I spend with him. It's a wonderful experience. Extraordinary, for me.

Q. When I mentioned the father-figure role—were you ever conscious of playing such a role with your students, with young singers or dancers, or with your first wife?

A. With my first wife, no; with my students, yes. A teacher, by the very nature of his work, has to act as a confidant, as a guiding spirit, tell people what's right, what's wrong, where they should go, what they should do. See—this is akin to the kind of thing that I'm doing now, in the travel business.

Q. You have an avuncular role in it? You train people, do you?

A. I do now, over the last two years. I have people coming to me who have just come into the business, and want my advice.

Q. Tell me about singers in general, their lives. Does aging have a particular effect on them?

A. It has an effect on their voices.

Q. More than it would have on me?

A. Yes.

Q. In performance, and in personality and in character?

A. It has an effect on their voices. Their voices are not as fresh. The interesting thing is that as they get older, they become more proficient in their work, and their artistry is more finely honed, but the voice just doesn't have the freshness that it had, say, ten years previously. Which is a rather sad commentary. When the voice is fresh, if you could have all the artistry that goes with it, all the experience, it'd be marvelous. But it just doesn't happen that way. Sometimes, if a person retains the freshness, the beauty of the sound, and doesn't wait too long to *develop* the kind of artistry that one needs to become a first-rate performer, then you have a happy combination. But that's not too usual.

Q. Is there a professional life span?

A. Yes. The higher voices have a shorter span than the lower voices.

Q. It takes more power to produce them, does it?

A. No, I think it's the longevity of the vocal cords. They are not able to take the strain in the higher category. A woman, for instance, who is a coloratura, would have a very short span.

Q. How about your voice now?

A. A bass, for instance, has a very long life. When I retired, I didn't lose my voice. My voice is still there. As a matter of fact, for the past two years, I've been called at the last moment—when I'm talking about the last moment, one day before a performance—to fill in. It was one of my friends, a conductor, who called me, to say "hey, you've got to help me. I can't find anybody!"

Q. I thought you said you had done no singing since . . .

A. Well, with the exception of these two performances in the last two years. That's not really singing. As a singer, I was a full-time singer. That's what I wanted to be. And as a travel agent, a travel counselor, if you want a fancy title . . .

Q. No, thanks. [laughter]

A. I'm a full-time travel agent. I devote all my time and all my thoughts to it.

Q. Singers have to have stamina, immense breath control, tremendous vigor; they must be in best of health. So I guess there is a fear of aging. And I guess there is a tremendous physical punishment, as you said, in one performance.

A. I had a marvelous teacher who taught me extraordinary technique, and I never tired vocally. I tired physically, after a performance, but I was never vocally tired so that I was so hoarse that I couldn't speak. My voice always felt fresh and at my command.

Q. I think I allowed this to get derailed a little. I'm looking for an age bracket of effectiveness for singers; You said coloraturas would go first?

A. Yes, and then right down the line.

Q. About what age?

A. Well, a coloratura should reach the beginning of her pinnacle between twenty-six and twenty-eight.

Q. Just like an athlete!

A. That's right. And then, if she takes care of herself physically, and sings well, she can sing for ten, twelve years. And then it begins to deteriorate. Not knowingly, as far as she's concerned, but the audience can hear it. She'll never know it—or she'll never admit it.

Q. Is the next step down in scale the lyric?

A. Yes, the next is lyric. They have a little longer life. A lyric soprano probably reaches the beginning of her maturity about the same age. But then she has a little longer life. And then, after that, there's the lyric spinto, she's a heavy lyric, such as my wife; my wife right now has a tendency to go toward the lyric spinto, but I'm trying to be very careful with her because I want her to sing the light-lyric thing and I want her to have a long professional life.

Q. Is she in that opera company?

A. No. She used to do musical comedy work, and theater and television. And we've been preparing her for an operatic career in the last four years. She's finishing her work now, with two or three splendid coaches. And I've been her voice teacher. We just recently signed a contract with a very fine management. She's going to Europe in September on an audition trip, for four weeks.

Q. For a certain company?

A. For particular opera companies, which will be arranged by the manager. Who will also be there, by the way; he's not going to be arranging it from here, he's going to make the trip, too. What he will do, of course, will be to set the time and the place and advise her what she should be auditioning at each audition.

Q. Now, would the tenor be somewhat parallel to the coloratura in terms of professional life span?

A. Yes, in various categories. Because, you know, there are light lyric tenors; there's the legero; there's the heavier tenor. Then you have the dramatic tenor; you have the buffo tenor. A tenor like Tucker is a full lyric.

Q. And then the baritone, the bass baritone, their lives are professionally longer; you could have gone on.

A. I could have gone on.

Q. Is it less strenuous to produce a basso tone?

A. Yes, it is, a little bit. The baritone, in order to sing in the head, in the top tones, baritone cords have to approximate very finely in order to get the kind of tone. And you need a certain amount of strength that one doesn't need when he's in the middle register and in the low register. It's a strain. A musical comedy voice is so different from an operatic voice. A musical comedy voice has no connection, to the chest, to the support; it's not a complete instrument. You know, when you play the piano, and you play the lower part of the piano, and the middle part, and the upper part, there's a symmetry there. The symmetry is because of the keyboard, and it's all attuned to that. Well, musical comedy singers, for the most part, and I'm saying "for the most part" because there are always exceptions, *don't* sing this way. It's usually a white sound . . .

Q. A "white sound?" Beautiful! Whatever that means.

A. A white sound is a rather blatant sound. When they go to the top of their voice, they don't keep the same color in, and the sound is spread. And a first-class operatic baritone or bass never changes. The color in the top and the middle and the bottom is all the same. This is the difference. This is why their singing lives are longer. They never harm their voices.

Q. Did the thought that you would some day have to give up professional singing bother you when you were quite young at it? Was it a specter in your mind?

A. Never. It was a horrible thing at the time I *hit* it, though.

Q. Tell me about that. Why was it horrible?

A. Well, I'd been a singer all my life. It was so traumatic for me that when I left the opera company I couldn't physically bring myself to go there for a whole year.

Q. Into the *building?*

A. My stomach would turn.

Q. Were there any complaints from your coaches, or from a director?

A. No, it wasn't that at all. It was a personal crisis in my life. The breakup of my previous marriage; not knowing whether I wanted to go on doing the kinds of things that I'd been doing at the company all those years. I wanted to sing Hans Sachs in "Meistersinger" and they didn't think of me as a Hans Sachs. "Whatever we need you for," was the way the manager put it at our final contract talk. I felt that this was a kind of death for me. I told him, "If I don't grow, if I don't continue to grow, all I'm doing is living from day to day, I perform when I have to, but I'm not getting any real satisfaction out of it and I feel that I'm on a merry-go-round. I'm not getting anywhere." And he said, "Well, that's what we have to offer you," and I said no thank you. This was after twenty years.

Q. Were there not other companies? In the States?

A. No, because, you see, I'd sung with them all.

Q. So that it wasn't that you *thought* there was no place to go, but that literally there *was* no place to go.

A. That's right. Either that or go to Europe, where I would have been the rest of my life.

Q. Well, how about recording, radio, television?

A. No, this is entirely, it's an entirely different field.

Q. To go back to something: Would you mind, or would you not mind, it's entirely up to you, telling me the circumstances of your extra-marital encounter before your second marriage?

A. That was something of rather long duration. It was something that started out—a student of mine, and became an attachment, a very close attachment. And remained a rather close attachment for many years.

Q. Okay. Well, you say your new marriage has worked out satisfactorily, you are content with your life, you don't miss singing, or do you miss it every day?

A. Miss what?

Q. The stage. The theater.

A. I did, at the beginning.

Q. Not any more? You mean, you consider the alternatives?

A. Well, I don't know whether it took me a long time to grow up, whether that's the proper term . . .

Q. I think it is.

A. I came to a realization that it would be better for me to stop while I was at the height of my career, rather than wait for the deterioration that I saw so many of my colleagues going through. As an official of the union, I presided over—well, *welfare* cases. I saw some horrifying things. It was always horrifying to me to see people who had made millions of dollars come to us for financial aid. Points in their lives where they became ill, they had no money, no money to pay their rent, to pay for their utilities, to buy food; it was a horrifying spectacle. And I decided that perhaps this was a good time; this might be a good time.

Q. Do you feel now that you have healed whatever great hole you tore in your life by doing that? Changing your career? It had to bother you in the beginning, giving it up.

A. Yes, of course it did. But I think that portion of my life is almost in a fog-like atmosphere. It's entirely distant. Sometimes, when I'm down here by myself [in his basement study], there'll be a mood; some of the things will begin to come back. But they don't penetrate to such an extent that they hurt me.

Q. And they did for a while.

A. They did. But now, now I'm very much interested in my wife's career. Getting her started. This is important to me.

I asked him, then, to play me a recording of his voice. When the tape started, Mr. D turned and walked to a corner of his basement studio, from which he looked at the machine with an expression I have seen in the faces of dramatic directors who are preparing either to praise or to damn a rehearsal. Mr. D's expression was similarly unreadable, but I felt that while his tape was playing, he was back in a theater.

Mr. E

Q. You're now an actor, and you were a clinical psychologist. Could you give me a definition of clinical psychology?

A. I can define it in terms of what it's not. People confuse it with psychiatry. A psychiatrist is a medical man who goes on to specialize in abnormal problems of the mind; a clinical psychologist is not a medical person, but he is qualified to do psychotherapy, he's qualified to do psychodiagnostics—ink blots—measuring the psyche, so to speak. For instance, I'm qualified to give ink-blot tests and I.Q. tests and what they call projective tests. All this is very often done as a team kind of thing in a hospital setting, which is what I did for many years in a Veterans Administration hospital. And also in Washington with the V. A. mental-hygiene clinic.

Q. Did you ever want to be a medical doctor?

A. It's kind of funny when you think about it. A lot of people say, "Why did you go into theater?" and the answer often is, "Because of the movies," because of seeing actors and actresses perform. But I was interested in psychology because of the movies. Movies like "The Snakepit" and "The Broken Mirror," in the 1940's.

Q. And your new career . . .

A. Yes?

Q. Comparing the two careers, were there any parallels between psychology and acting? Are there now?

A. In my high school yearbook, everybody had to list what they wanted to do. I remember to this day, I said "To make a spotlight in show business." Then I never did anything about it. It was as if I'd shelved all that and forced myself into another kind of mold. And then there were family expectations.

Q. Of what? Of professions, er . . .

A. No. A kind of respect for college, no matter what it leads to. Now I went to high school in Washington, and then I went into the Navy in the latter part of World War II, and then when I got out of the service I used my G.I. Bill and got a master's in psychology, and went into the field. But my Dad didn't . . .

Q. Way ahead of ourselves here, thanks to me. You were born in . . .

A. In Washington. In 1926. I was going to . . .

Q. Yes, please, go ahead.

Q. I was going to say that my Dad never graduated from college. Excuse me; I mean he never graduated from *high* school. My parents were married at fifteen, eloped, lied about their age, got married. And I think that's because they were—*deprived* of an education, they had this tremendous desire to see their sons get degrees. So two of us— there were four boys—did, through the G.I. Bill, after the war. We wanted to fulfill their desires, I guess.

Q. I see. In your—when you were a psychologist, in the late 1940's and '50's, did you ever deal with this problem we're talking about, the middle-age thing? What I call midolescence?

A. We didn't call it that then, of course. But certainly there were incidents of various kinds of depressions for middle-aged people, and there were things career-wise and sexual-wise. And—looking back on those cases now, and considering what you're doing here, I think sometimes things like that are over-determined. I mean there's always more than one factor that has to be considered. I think a crisis like this can precipitate something like a change of career, but I think the stage has to be set ahead of time.

Q. The "one factor" being age-bracketing?

A. Yes.

Q. So I've learned.

A. It's dangerous to generalize about that kind of thing.

Q. And I hope I don't. In your work today, does, er—psychology enter into it in any way?

A. For me, yes. I guess I've always had a, er, sensitivity to people. People will say to me today, "I find myself saying things to you that I wouldn't say to my own friends or my own family." I guess they get certain vibrations, and they trust my, er, respecting their confidence. It happens during shows, with people in the cast. And it does not necessarily come out of the fact that they discover that I came into theater from this other field. I guess it's just a human kind of thing.

Q. Mr. E, why was your earlier field not an ongoing, rewarding field for you? What was wrong with it? What needs, *other* than financial, didn't it fill? What needs *does* acting fulfill for you?

A. I have to answer that partly by saying that I felt ultimately that I was in psychology for the wrong reasons. That is, and I think this is true of many people in psychology, there is a thing about playing God. Doctors can do it, too. Priests, of course. But . . .

Q. They'd better!

A. Well, no, they can't play God. That's the thing of it. I mean in the sense of feeling that they have control over people's lives. And I think that I began to feel a certain kind of thing like that happening within me. And, to me, that wasn't the right reason, plus the whole business of maintaining a certain objectivity about giving the patients —the thing that was not happening was, a feeling of, let's say, creation and self-expression. I knew there was a talent for something in me that I was not able to deal with to get out of myself. And it wasn't until I finally got into some local community theater group in the Washington area, and found what an exciting experience it was to create these kinds of characters and find these various modalities of expression, that I thought . . . You see, what you're doing in theater is you're giving, and you're getting back. It's a two-way thing on stage, because there's the audience out there, and they're responding, and you're responding to their response, and . . .

Q. You don't get that from a patient?

A. Not the same kind of thing, no. With a patient you have to use various . . .

Q. The patient keeps *taking?*

A. Exactly.

Q. Constantly?

A. Yes. Your job is to be there and be a mirror for the patient. But not to really give of yourself. You can't. The point is to keep yourself *out* of it, really, and to keep your own personality reactions and blind spots clear so that you can deal objectively with the problems of the patient. But, see, when I got into this business of community theater, I got into a lot of productions back home, and then decided I was at a point of the blind leading the blind, because there was only so much I could learn. So then I started commuting to New York on weekends to take acting lessons, singing lessons, the whole theater thing—while I kept my job down there, in Washington. I came to New York in December of 1964.

Q. And here you are.

A. Yes. May I fill you in on—I don't want to sound like someone who just jumped from this to that . . .

Q. Please do.

A. Right. For about ten years after I got my degree in psychology, I was working in clinical psychology directly or in some ancillary fields, such as with the District of Columbia parole board. I'd go out to the prisons and test the patients—I say "patients," the actual word is "prisoners"—I would find out their potential and then go back into the city of Washington or Baltimore or whatever and knock on doors; go to an employer and try to persuade him to employ this person. All of that was happening, and ultimately I was doing personnel work, for the Department of Vocational Rehabilitation. It was the last job I had down there.

Q. That's a federal agency?

A. No. District of Columbia. And all of the commuting—to round this out, toward the end there, I began, after the community-theater experience in the Washington area, began commuting to New York to study here, at a studio. I did that for about nine months. With a very, er, well-reputed drama school, with many sections, speech, scene study, musical comedy workshop.

Q. You sing, do you?

A. Yeah. I'm singing in a show now. But I didn't know I could do that until I came to New York. I started singing after I got here, you see.

Q. Had you done any singing as a much younger man?

A. Showers; in bathrooms; that was it.

Q. No requests? [laughter]

A. No requests! [laughter]. You see, I didn't know anything about my singing potential, but I was missing a lot of auditions. I couldn't go to them, for musicals. So I decided I'd better learn how, and then I started. And the results have been very satisfying.

Q. So you had the two—activities, your professional field and your acting. What thing, or what combination of things, finally made you choose the one and give up the other?

A. With all the commuting and the studying and the shows in Washington and the job there, I finally had to decide. Because I couldn't ride two horses any more; I was depleting myself. And I gave notice at my job. I was the executive assistant to the director of the department, so it meant a lot of wrap-up work. It took me about three months before I could close out everything I had to deal in. So I left, and I came here, with no job, and hardly knowing anyone, and, er, took my chances.

Q. And you're not married, so, there were no such family responsibilities stopping you?

A. Lifelong bachelor, I guess. At this stage—what else?

Q. I see.

A. I would have to say that the change was certainly gradual. All my major decisions are made that way. I mean, people kid me about being a Libran, and if they believe in astrology, which I don't, they talk about the fact that Librans are slow in making their minds up. I choose to make what I think of as an informed decision, based on getting all the facts. And at the time when I took that big step, people I worked with, colleagues of mine, had varying reactions, which told more about themselves than it did about me. One, feeling that I was having some kind of a nervous breakdown; another one, feeling that with this kind of irresponsible behavior, I would not be a very desirable employe to have if I were to come back and try to work again in the field; to which I said that with his philosophy, I wouldn't really be interested in working with that kind of atmosphere anyhow. Another one said, "How's he doing in New York?" This was a year or two later. And a friend said that I was quite happy, making commercials and doing shows, and generally enjoying what I was after. His response was, "Uh, that son of a bitch, he's doing the kind of thing that we've always wanted to do and didn't have enough guts to try!"

Q. Right.

A. It's interesting, too, now that I've said that. I remember one of the things that went through my mind when I made this decision. I'd forgotten about this. I was up for a very highly specialized position that would have required Congressional legislation. It was a special job, there. It was to have been the assistant to the first black commissioner in Washington. I had had enough experience in various facets of the city government by that time, and I was right down to the wire, you know, including interviews with Congressmen, and that kind—and with the black commissioner himself.

Q. And your age was then . . .

A. Was then thirty—seven, or eight, right in there. And when the chips were down, the choice was made, and the man who became the assistant was a black man. For whatever, you know, that means.

Q. Political reasons . . .

A. The point is that I didn't get it. Now, that would have meant a sizable promotion and a considerable increase in salary. And when it was over, I really breathed a sigh of relief. I thought to myself, "That would have been the final seduction." If I had gotten that, I might have been just off enough on that tangent that I might never have turned back. And I thought, "No, I'm not going to wake up ten years from today and wonder what it would have been like if I had done it, so I'm going to . . ."

Q. The theater.

A. Right. "—so I'm going to do it." So those were the things that were happening in my life at that time, you see. So the choice, as I say, was made. Because of the nature of my position at the time, it took me three months to get things wrapped up at the office, before I could leave. And then I came to New York in December of '64. I've been here just about nine and a half years.

Q. If you had been married, you wouldn't have been able to take the step?

A. I don't think I would have allowed myself to do this, really, because *I* can deal with the uncertainty for *myself,* but I don't think I would have dealt with it for the rest of them, you know. Especially children. An adult wife, that's a different matter, but children—you're imposing a whole lot of potential problems on them. Financially, I'm talking about. Because, as I say, I come from a family that was raised in the Depression, and we were made very conscious of security. Security was a big thing in our family. My father, for instance, was *dumfounded* when I told him what I was going to do, to give up this job that was paying quite a lot of money, and an apartment with a swimming pool, and a car in the garage, and the full—all of those tangible things.

Q. Mr. E, this is a very handsome apartment you have here.

A. Thank you.

Q. The point being that a very handsome apartment costs a very handsome amount of money. The rent . . .

A. It's a co-op. I bought it.

Q. All the more reason for what I'm going to ask. You're not a —I hope you don't mind my bringing this out but I don't exactly see your name lighting up Shubert Alley at night. Not that it won't, some day!

A. [laughter] That's all right.

Q. The point being that you apparently have a respectable income.

A. I have. From television commercials. It's certainly made the difference. It allows me to do Equity Library shows, and stock. If I didn't have that I couldn't have bought this apartment. Not a lot of actors have been as fortunate as I have.

Q. Yes. When you were ready to make the big move, did you put some money by? Considering, as you say, that you're a Libran, you're slow to make up your mind, you take a look at all the facts . . .

A. Yes, I wanted to have a cushion, because in the time when I was commuting up here, before actually moving to New York, I'd have to rehearse scenes with actors who lived in the city, and that meant going to whatever apartment they lived in, and I walked up many a flight of stairs to these, what they used to call cold-water flats, with roaches in the kitchen, and . . .

Q. Oh, yes.

A. —just really, a tough life. And . . .

Q. "Now imagine you're on a beach," sure.

A. [Laughter] But the thing is, I had a pre-taste of what it could be like, you see. And so with all that in my mind, I made up my mind, that I wanted to be sure to avoid that part of it. In other words, I had certainly gotten used to a certain level of, er, life-style. And I wanted to keep reasonably comfortable. And so I was lucky. I had some money put aside. I came here and *made* some friends, a marvelous lady I met in advertising, who put me on to several agents.

Q. When were you in advertising?

A. *She* was in advertising.

Q. *She* was. I see.

A. Yes. And we still have very close contact with each other. And she put me in touch with agents, and they began sending me out on commercials first, *before* theater, because I'm what they call a commercial *type*. I began getting commercials, and that was—that was the start of it. The theater, then, kind of fell into place along the way, including taking up singing lessons after I got here; finally I had a voice to do it with, and even being told that I should be in opera, you know, all of those things that are . . .

Q. Oh? You have that much power in your voice?

A. It's pretty big, yeah.

Q. To digress somewhat, and now we're going back into a very general area: Your early life ambitions and goals—if you had such things—do you think you have achieved any of them, in either field, and what are your goals today? What do you want out of life today as compared with what you wanted out of life when you were younger?

A. I don't think that my earlier goals were that clearly formulated, really. I know that, for instance, evidence of that would be that when I did go to college I had no idea what I wanted to major in. I almost didn't go to college, as I say, except for the G.I. Bill. There was a turning point in junior high school, where you either went into a business curriculum or a pre-college curriculum. I elected to go into the business curriculum, never expecting that I'd be able to afford college. At that choice point I had already filled out the cards and everything for a business curriculum. The home-room teacher, who was like your mentor through junior high, piled me into her car and drove me home and had a talk with the family. She said, "This boy is college material. He should be." Thank God for her! And I started things like French and all that, that I never would have done, you see. So that when it did come time to be able to go to college, I had that much background. But I went to college not really knowing what I wanted to do, taking a general arts-and-science curriculum and gradually working into this kind of clinical psychology field, but not, you know, not with any clearly defined reason for doing it. [pause] My goals now? I don't know how to answer that. I take each day as it comes. I think the important thing for an actor is to be working, to do the kind of thing that he feels he's trained for, to enjoy doing it. I'm very much turned-on, let's say, by people. I mean dealing with people, the humanity of people, and I think that I can do that through acting and also in—just in the contacts I make in the work that I do and the people I meet as a result, who come to see the shows. Life spreads out that way. *Performing* is really the *goal* of any actor. They say you're only as successful as your most recent show, you know; that's how it is.

Q. And financially, you lean on the money from your commercials.

A. Well, I do this, too. [Mr. E shows me tear-sheets of advertisements in which he appears.] Modeling. You get a good rate. Sixty dollars an hour.

Q. Not bad for a Depression baby.

A. [laughter] Yes. This, and the commercials, they're the main source of income; they pay bills that live theater could never *begin* to pay. You don't make that much money in theater to begin with. Many actors have to take jobs waiting on tables, working in department stores, doing all kinds of part-time work that has nothing to do with what they really want to do.

Q. Did you ever fear, did you expect that that might happen to you, before you took the career-changing step?

A. Well, I truly never *feared* that it would happen; I knew that if it ever did come, I could handle it. I probably type better than the average secretary, just from my own background, in training myself, because I needed it for college—theses, and things like that.

Q. Could you have gone back into your scientific field?

A. Sure. I could have. There's a big demand . . .

Q. Could you do that today?

A. Yeah. Oh, yeah. But, again, you see . . .

Q. Have you ever been approached to?

A. I was, just last summer, as a matter of fact. I was working on

Cape Cod in a production of "South Pacific" and one of the girls in the chorus was dating a fellow who's a psychologist. He was up to visit her, and we got to talking, and he was telling me what a hard time they were having filling a certain slot on their staff, back in New York. And he really was very seriously discussing with me my willingness, you know, to come with him. It was nice of him to say it, but he understood that I was . . .

Q. You didn't feel any twinge of conscience or temptation to do this?

A. None at all. No.

Q. No more commitment?

A. No; you see, if I were in any way dissatisfied with this life, then, of course, temptations would always be popping up. Other kinds of —avenues of work, and income. But I haven't had to worry about that. I've just been, as I've said, very blessed since I got here.

Q. Very good.

A. No regrets.

Q. Do you consider yourself superior—and when I say that, I'm not at all using it in the pejorative sense—do you consider yourself superior or more capable, as an actor, because you have a background and an insight that many fellow actors do *not?* Your *scientific* background?

A. I don't know that that would make it necessarily superior, but it certainly helps *me,* in understanding what the playwright is trying to say in a play, and it certainly helps me to investigate a character that I'm trying to portray. There are specific things. I did the role of a man who supposedly had electro-shock therapy. And because I have actually assisted in administering electro-shock therapy, that character was much more meaningful to me. The things he was saying, I could relate to.

Q. In turning to the stage, and now considering what you wrote in your school yearbook, do you think you were seeking—I hate this question, but I usually get good answers—trying to recapture part of your youth?

A. No. I think coming to New York was going *to* something, not running *away* from something. But I do think I was renouncing a set of standards. The way I was living—I guess what I was doing was saying, "this set of standards is not for me;this way of life is not for me." I got so *bored* with Washington cocktail parties.

Q. Where did you live in New York, when you came here?

A. I used to live down in the Lower East Side, in a much more reasonable apartment. I say "more reasonable"—er, the thing of this is, that I end up better off in the long run once I bought this apartment. Because the maintenance is so reasonable here. And I was lucky enough, with the commercial, life that I had, that I could pay cash for this place when I moved in. I didn't go to the bank and do all that business, you see. So, again I was blessed. I planned, again, before I did this; I saved, with the income that I was making here, and I would say probably, all told, I'm better off now.

So far, all the men in this chapter, because they understandably requested it, have been as anonymous as I could make them. Not this final interviewee. He has, quite literally, a missionary urge *not* to be anonymous. This man is the son of two Presbyterian missionaries who were working in China when he was born there in the 1920's. This man has been married, and is divorced. He did not remarry. While he does not knock the institution of marriage for other people, he absolutely rejects it for himself. Like Mr. D, the singer-turned travel agent, he came to a point in life where he felt he had to find himself. His marriage, too, had become untenable, but not—as Mr. D's had—because he and his wife had drifted farther and farther apart; Mr. Van Deusen and his wife, he says, had grown too close, too together. He had lost his identity, and he had to rediscover (or perhaps discover) it. He came up with an alternative life-style, a kind of anti-marriage. Some of you may find it outrageous; others may find it delightful. Whatever. Introducing . . .

Edmund L. Van Deusen

Q. Thank you, operator. Hello? Mr. Van Deusen?

A. That's right. Mr. McMorrow?

Q. Yes. Let me establish for the record that this interview was recorded off the telephone, New York to California. You're in L.A., right?

A. Well, a suburb.

Q. Okay. Mr. Van Deusen, you've written a book called *Contract Cohabitation,* is that the right title?

A. That's it.

Q. And it represents a life-style that you've been following for some time?

A. By the time the book comes out, this [the fall of '74], it will be just short of two years.

Q. And the book deals with the circumstances, the events, the— whatever led to this new life-style?

A. It's the personal history of my twenty-six-year marriage and why I think it ended, and how it was for the two and a half years in between. The period from the end of the marriage to the start of this. Living with someone, and dating, and doing all the trips, and everything leading back toward marriage. And then the decision to try something dramatically different, because we're living in a different period, and we weren't intended to be these old-style selves.

Q. It took you two and a half years to evolve contract cohabitation?

A. No. I could say I had fifty years of research. Now, C. P. Snow, in an interview in Saturday Review World, he made the point that every culture has to have a taboo, a forbidden subject, and that Americans have done such a thorough job of pulling sex out of the closet that they've had to put money back *into* the closet. And money is our taboo subject right now. The fiery part of Nixon's hassle over his income tax. Agnew, over his, and so forth. The furor of playing games with money. We don't want to admit that money is power, we don't want to admit that money is self-identity? Okay? So you land up—and now I'm coming to the point—my book is all about money.

Q. All about *money?*

A. All about money. My book says you can buy affection. My book says that two people can get together on a purely money basis and live very good, productive, self-identifying lives together by using money as the medium. So here we have a whole culture of men —business-type people, professional people—the middle-class cult who have spent their whole lifetime in a money-oriented environment, they gauge their success, their progress and everything else by that pay check. And now they're cast out on the world either by a divorce or by changing values or whatever, but the one thing they're really familiar with, they're not allowed to use. They've got to go

back and sharpen up those sexual competitive instincts that were
effective at eighteen but are now pretty well dulled, and not use the
thing that they are familiar with, which is where their heads really
are: The use of money and the manipulation of money and getting
what they want with money.

Q. How is this taken away from them?

A. Okay. A guy's got a million dollars in the bank and he's got
to go to a bar and compete with a stud type who's got twenty-five
cents in his pocket.

Q. Oh, you're talking about sex?

A. I'm talking about the sexual *companionship* relationship—
leave sex out of it! My book has almost nothing about sex in it. It
deals entirely with companionship, emotional support, the things
that a human being has to have to function effectively, because we're
a social species. And so, he's prohibited by our morés from using his
strong point and forced to go back to an earlier era of his own life
to compete for companionship and emotional support on a really an
eighteen-year-old level, and this is totally destroying . . .

Q. Competing with people more used to that game than he is.

A. Right. Or more realistic than he is. The women are always
infinitely more realistic. This is why your average period of remar-
riage for men is like a year and a half against three years for women,
why the suicide rate is infinitely higher for men after divorce than
it is for women, something like three and a half or five to one. And
because the women are operating with the weapons they've always
had and used, and the men are prohibited from using the weapons,
the tools, that they're used to using. So anyway I say, "Nonsense!
This is the way we really are. Why don't we just acknowledge it?
We're all basically selfish. We are a money-oriented society; it does
have a huge emotional value. Let's structure a life-style based on
where we are rather than on where society tells us we should be.
The"—I'm giving you strictly the pitch from the man's side. Anyway, my immediate history then is, I was married twenty-six
years . . .

Q. Excuse me, may I lead you through this garden path?

A. Okay.

Q. When and where born?

A. Weishien, China—that's in northern China, near the coast. In
1923.

Q. And your ethnic background?

A. I'm half Dutch and half German. My mother was German, fairly recent German, like three or four generations, and I identify as a German.

Q. Your educational background?

A. I'm a chemical engineer, economics, combination, from Penn State. I worked in the field for two years.

Q. You are not now a chemical engineer?

A. No. I became a writer when I was twenty-eight, twenty-nine.

Q. When were you married?

A. When I was twenty, when I was in the service.

Q. And your wife's ethnic background?

A. She's Anglo-Saxon.

Q. W-A-S-P?

A. Very much so.

Q. Children?

A. Five children—four daughters and one son.

Q. Who are now in their thirties, I guess.

A. They range from twenty-eight to fourteen.

Q. They live with Mama?

A. The two younger ones.

Q. Okay, You were saying . . .

A. Okay, so at twenty-eight I decided to live my life, my kind of life, writing was the one vehicle that made sense other than teaching. I could either teach or write as a life-style, to have the kind of time and space freedom that I needed. And so at that point I'd been a purchasing agent for duPont and a salesman for a company that's now part of W. R. Grace, and both of them, first buying chemicals and then selling chemicals. So I decided to become a writer and got a job with a chemical magazine with McGraw-Hill.

Q. In New York?

A. In New York. In 1951. Then eighteen months later I moved on up and became one of the two science writers—associate editor was my title—at Fortune magazine. And I stayed with that long enough to get a reputation on the West Coast and came out here eighteen years ago. In 1956. And I've been a freelance . . .

Q. Wait. You were born in China. When did you come to the States?

A. I came over in '37, when I was fourteen.

Q. And to the East Coast, is that right?

A. Yes, I went to the Hotchkiss School, up in Connecticut, and then the army and Penn State.

Q. To continue, so you are now at . . .

A. I left Fortune and came on out to California. I'd built a reputation out here.

Q. How did you do that? How did you build that reputation?

A. Well, I wrote, among other things, I wrote the first article on the interconintental ballistic missile that had really hit the popular press and—it was the kind of article where [Nelson] Rockefeller, who was in Washington, tried to get Henry Luce to kill the story, in the national interest. But Henry Luce figured that if I was just reporting what I got with that Fortune calling-card, other people must have it too.

Q. This was in . . .

A. That was '55. And that gave me a kind of hero-status with the aerospace people out here, and so I was able to have a freelancing career. How I make a living now is, I mainly write advertising copy, brochures, articles, publicity, for technically oriented companies. And then—the reason for becoming a writer is that it—I could make a living with a part of my time and then the rest of my time has been devoted to inventing and sculpting. Actually what I am right now, I'm a sculptor, but it's designed not to make money and so therefore I write. I write for other people and I sculpt for me.

Q. Let us get into what might have been wrong with your marriage.

A. All right. So, anyway, everything went along just fine and then, roughly three and a half years ago now, four years ago now . . .

Q. Excuse me. This was when you began to realize you'd outgrown your old way of living.

A. I didn't outgrow it all. I just left. I fell in love and left.

Q. And the lady you fell in love with was someone older, younger?

A. Almost the standard ten years younger. And also standard—it only lasted a couple of months. And, also almost standard, I went back. And I then decided that . . .

Q. Back to your wife?

A. Yeah. And it only took a few days to realize that—that—the other person had been a *catalyst,* not a reason . . .

Q. And even though you say it is standard, would you please fill me in on why you think you fell in love?

Q. Who knows? It was a catalyst, and who can explain a catalyst? I was ready to go. As far as I knew I was just fine, until all of a sudden I popped out and left. And, er . . .

Q. And the other party to your falling in love—was that a co-worker of yours? Someone you knew socially?

A. Yeah, it was more social and partly work, but I'd known her for ten years. The families had been very close. The, then—later, much later—much, much later, I looked back and realized why I'd left. But it certainly wasn't clear at the time.

Q. Now what is clear?

A. And looking back the reason was that I really had—I never really had a—my wife and I had not grown apart, that was not the problem. We had grown together. And we were so together that I actually had zero-identity apart from her. I really didn't know who I was. And it wasn't like she was putting a trip on me. It wasn't that she was putting an arbitrary trip on me and saying "Hey, you gotta do this, you gotta do that." It was just that she stood for certain things that I didn't necessarily stand for if I'd sat down and thought about it, but I just instinctively did it her way because I was part of her and she was part of me. I didn't feel any sense of pressure or apartness from her. I felt too much togetherness. And so I had more a group image than an individual image, and I really had reached the point where I was more than anything else curious who I was. Maybe I wouldn't like the real me, but I needed to find out who he was. Anyway, so I split, and then immediately, in less than a week, I was living with somebody else and lived with her for almost a year and it was an exact duplicate of where I'd been before.

Q. Were there any legal problems? Did your wife make any trouble for you?

A. Oh, no. No, I had a *superb* family, just, y'know . . .

Q. Was this out—was this all open and above-board, so to speak?

A. You have to realize all this happened in California. Nobody does much cover-up here. Anyway I lived with someone else for about a year and realized I was back where I had been. Taking care of kids and . . .

Q. Whose kids?

A. The new person I was with. In other words I absolutely duplicated my life, I hadn't really gained a single . . .

Q. She had three children? Four children?

A. No, she had a couple.

Q. Quite a bit younger than yours?

A. Still the same ten-years pattern. Now, in contract cohabitation, there's heavy emphasis on the woman being the employer.

Q. Eh? Once again?

A. On the woman being the employ-*er*. And I make the point that the women's lib group has absolutely turned on to this concept because they can be the employ-*er* in the relationship. In the contract.

A. Well—both parties to the contract are employ-*ers*, aren't they?

A. Oh, no.

Q. Partnership?

A. No partnership, not at all. No way. It's an employer-employe contract.

Q. In your case who is the employer?

A. I'm the employer. But there's one other couple here where the *woman* is the employer, and it works even better.

Q. I was watching some idiot quiz show and the woman was asked about her husband's occupation and she said he was a *househusband.*

A. Yeah. Okay, well the—right now a woman can work her way up to be a president of a corporation, she's still responsible for seeing that the dishes are washed and if she buys her old man a Cadillac because she's done so well in business it's viewed as a ball-busting thing for *him*. But if *he*'s the employe and *identified* as that, that's his first symbol—not man, but employe—then the Cadillac becomes a bonus just for doing a good job and you can accept it in good grace. It's a compliment.

Q. This is a de facto marriage, right?

A. It's—it takes all the rituals of the daytime marriage and moves them into the home. And even if there is a separation, why, it's generally in good grace and somebody leaves to get a better job, not because they hate the person they're with. It's simply a transfer of all of this thing that we're all accustomed to, from the office to the home. And the only thing you really have to accept is that the thing that makes it work in the office is that one person is paying the other person a salary, money. And this makes up the difference for the fact that the employe isn't having it quite the way he or she wants it, compared to the boss, and the salary is the balancing factor; it has an emotional value.

Q. Can this arrangement—will this arrangement work for very young people, in their twenties? Who want children? Do children figure in this?

A. If you want to go through the legal machinery where people want children and guarantee support, okay. I'm on a thirty-day cancellation basis. You can make it a week or two weeks or whatever you want, but we happen to be at thirty days. You have to be able to part. In other words, if a guy went to work for General Motors, he might be there thirty years and leave with a gold watch and feel good about his life. But if he's told the first *day* that he had to be there thirty *years,* he'd quit that instant. Okay, so you have to have the ability to end it immediately, and therefore you don't have to use it.

Q. By the same token, when the end of the working day comes, what he does is none of General Motors's business, right?

A. That's right. So my employe here has very definite hours that she's on duty, and a night off a week and an annual vacation, and the whole shot.

Q. Would you mind describing briefly the duties?

A. Each person defines their contract themselves.

Q. You were out of marriage, you were into living with a person and that was too much like the old pattern. And you went into this. Was there any—moment of truth, anything like that?

A. At a particularly traumatic moment when I really didn't know where I was headed, I said to myself, "God damn it, I've hired people all my life to help me write, and help me sculpt, and help me do all the other things—why don't I just hire somebody to take care of me? Period? That's a job; a *hell* of a job! And I should be willing to pay for it." So I ran an ad offering room, board and salary. I had upwards of a hundred women responding to the ad.

Q. All Californians?

A. All Californians. I went through a regular interview procedure. I had a very high-caliber response. Women with masters degrees who wanted to start their own consulting firms so this would give them a base to operate from. I had artists, I had writers—it was incredibly high quality. And so out of this mix I selected one person who was familiar with my life-style—the Establishment life-style— I wasn't out to drop out or anything like that. I'd been extremely active in local politics and so forth and I was going to continue on that. And so I selected a person who was familiar with that; she'd been married for ten years, she'd done the whole PTA trip . . .

Q. Both of you were divorced?

A. Yes. I was by now divorced. And at the same time she had lived a counter-culture life for the last five or six years, so she al— she also had the flexibility. She had done the commune trip in northern California and had hitch-hiked and traveled around Mexico and things like that. So she'd lived an alternate life-style. Six years. So, anyway, I selected her on the basis of a two-hour employment interview, hands-off, and by the time the book comes out we'll have been together almost two years. And it's worked just beautifully.

Q. What is your daily life together?

A. Okay. She's on duty at 5 o'clock . . .

Q. P.M.?

A. Yes, because that's when I come off the road from talking to clients and that's when I've really got to talk to somebody and get all the steam out of me.

Q. Clients?

A. Yes, I've been working all day. The loneliest part of the day is right at 5 o'clock. That's when the bars are filled because people are uptight and tense from their working day and they've got to loosen up if they're going to have any kind of an evening. In my case I like to work evenings and I really need somebody at that point. And I—alone in an apartment doesn't work. So she's on duty at 5 for a couple of hours and then she's on duty at midnight. And, so she's taking advantage of her days—to learn a clothing-design profession, she and a partner have built a little company—and then in the evenings, why, she does whatever she wants. Until bedtime.

Q. Until bedtime. Two technical—two questions just to fill me in. Clients, you say? You mean people you write for?

A. Right, uh-huh. I'm paid directly by the technical companies.

Q. Now—bedtime being the balance of the night?

A. That's right. I simply can't sleep alone and gave up trying.

Q. And you pay this lady a salary which amounts to what?

A. I pay her five hundred a month, and room and board is also part of what she gets, so that's almost the equivalent of a thousand a month. The five hundred 1 figure is about a third of what it would cost me to support a middle-class family with a couple of kids. So I'm way ahead of the game and she's way ahead of the game.

Q. Is there anything—and this is my own middle-class background talking: Is there anything technically illegal about this? I guess not.

A. Yes, if the contract put any kind of restraint—sexual restraint or demand on either of us, then it would be illegal.

Q. My first thought, when I heard about this, was "My god, it's white slavery!" We're programed that way.

A. Sure. In a lot of states adultery is still a felony. In our case, we reverse that—it would be illegal to put sexual restraints on an employe. In other words, we are automatically *without* sexual fidelity as a legal requirement.

Q. Is this a contract drawn up by a lawyer?

A. No. It can be, if there's a lot of money involved. So the contract does not mention sex, it does not have any restraints, it doesn't say that you can't sleep with someone else if you want to, it doesn't say you have to sleep with me in order to get a salary. Those would be illegal. What it says is we're going to spend the night together and whatever happens, happens. And I make a joke that I don't deduct from her salary when she enjoys it more than I do and I don't give her a bonus when I enjoy it more than she does. And the sex is a symptom of how well we're working together as two people who are in close contact with each other. The sex doesn't make it a good relationship; a good relationship makes good sex. What'd you say, how'd you put it, after you said, "My God, this is . . . "

Q. [laughter] White slavery.

A. Okay. The whole white-slavery and prostitution idea is on the basis that women don't enjoy sex and the man somehow has to pay for it. And so the women's lib, the press of the women's lib movement is protesting—"God damn it, we enjoy it just as much as you do, and therefore let's have a relationship based on that mutual enjoyment rather than on one person's either forcing, or buying, the other."

Q. Did you have what could be called a normal adolescence? Did you rebel against your parents' values? Fight with them?

A. Oh, yes, I did all that. But my adolescence was a little unusual in that I left home when I was twelve.

Q. Oh, really?

A. For missionary kids that's almost old.

Q. Your parents were *missionaries* in China?

A. They were missionaries. You come out of the mission field either an evangelist yourself, or a total—not even worrying about an atheist.

Q. What church?

A. Presbyterian. And so I did the usual rebellion.

Q. That's before you left China?

A. Yes, I went to school over in Korea. There were only two high schools in China for English-speaking people.

Q. Two kinds of high schools?

A. No, *two high schools.* One, for white kids—one down in Shanghai, which most of the central China and southern China people went to, and one over in Korea, that serviced most of the northern part of China. So I left at the eighth grade to go over there.

Q. What was wrong with your parents' values?

A. Well, they were totally oriented toward the church and religion. I was fourteen before I met a white man who wasn't a preacher, and they were human beings and had all the frailties of human beings and so I just came to the conclusion that, you know, at that age, that no one I saw was practicing what they were preaching and so what they were preaching didn't have much validity.

Q. What is the cliché? I've seen it work many times. The minister's son is always the hellion in the community?

A. I fit under that category.

Q. What kind of early sex life did you have and when did you first have sex?

A. Oh, I was a virgin when I got married.

Q. My goodness.

A. Yes, that much stuck from my folks.

Q. How is your wife living now? Are you still friendly with her?

A. Yeah, she's remarried. In fact very shortly after she was sure I was gone, she ran into a guy who came very close to the kind of image that she and I had maintained. She even found a guy with a crewcut, and that's hard to do in this day and age.

Q. Is your ex-wife a Californian also?

A. No, she's from the East.

Q. She's living out there?

A. Yes, she's very happily married. And that is a big relief to me. We're still good friends, and so I don't have to carry any guilt feelings. The home life of our two children that are home is—you just couldn't find any difference—in spirit, in detail, in tradition, everything. My two youngest children have gone through absolutely zero change.

Q. This has not hurt them?

A. She has re-created exactly the environment that we had. Look, let me make this—what do the politicians say, abundantly clear? I don't knock conventional marriage at all, for certain people, I just reject it for me. And I don't regret one day of that period of twenty-six years; I wouldn't have raised my children in any other kind of environment.

Q. Mr. Van Deusen, are your parents still living?

A. My mother is. [pause] Speaking of her, and my father, you know, I am a missionary in a sense. I really believe that we've stumbled onto something. And even if, say, just one per cent of the American population can use this as a viable alternative, you're still talking about two million people.

IV.
The Women Speak

Except in mirrors and photographs, we never see ourselves as others see us. In Chapter III, seven men expressed their views of what happened to them in midolescence, but these were necessarily one-sided, male-sided views. This chapter is the other side, the woman's side. The wives of Mr. A and Mr. B tell what it was like to live with a man in the middle-age crisis, as do five other women, who have no connection with the men of Chapter III. Four of those five provide insight into why some young women prefer older men.

Miss A, the girl on the first tape among the single women, is what many in her line of work would euphemistically term a cocktail waitress, or a hostess; she calls herself a barmaid. She is given to calling things by what she considers their rightful names. Her choice of words, her vocabulary, reflects her working habitat, that of tired men who throw around four-letter words as they might cases, at the warehouse, or beer barrels, into and out of trucks. For five years, Miss A has been keeping house with a man twenty years her senior, a married man who spends part of his evenings with her. "We live just like any normal person would live that was married," Miss A says. "We go out for dinner once a week; I clean, I do his underwear, do his shirts or take them to the Laundromat." And they make love, but never on Sunday.

175

On weekends and holidays her man goes home to his family and Miss A's illusion of married life dissolves. So does she, some of those days; She says, softly, "It's not a Sunday kind of love."

There are some surface parallels between her and Miss B. Both are quick, both are witty, both pepper their conversation with [expletive]'s, but while Miss A comes across over-all as a touchingly warm, direct and compassionate young woman, you will sense a certain quality of attack in what Miss B has to say, and how she says it. And Miss B does not go in for long, marriage-like alliances. Her "average affair," she says, "is three months." A few ended in disaster as far as the men were concerned. All her men, she says, are married, middle-aged and accomplished; this is important to her. She assesses them as "men who are thinkers, doers, leaders." Her men work, as she does, in offices, with their heads, not their hands. She was a difficult subject. She seemed to be trying to compete with the interviewer, talking in wildly tangential, unrelated sentences that went on sometimes for five minutes, in response to the simplest, yes-or-no questions. And then she would cut off abruptly and ask the bewildered interviewer to repeat the question. Her transcript has been adjusted for the sake of coherence. Actually, she has been interviewed twice. Shortly after the first interview she stole the transcription of it, penciled it full of notations, scratched out some answers and angrily wrote in new answers. These written replies and notations appear with her transcript.

Miss C is a teacher, a careful, polite listener, a thoughtful speaker who weighs and measures her words. Her interview covers territory quite similar to that traveled by Miss A and Miss B, but in Miss C's vocabulary the word is, quaintly, "copulate." She had a heavy association with a man for ten years, which whas never consummated because the man was a homosexual; he died, and his male lover cried into Miss C's ear over the phone. There were several others—"er, we fornicated"—but none capsized a household. "I don't want to break up anyone's marriage," Miss C says.

Miss D's interview gives midolescence some historical perspective. Now in her fifties, Miss D recalls with compelling clarity her youthful days in show business, when one affair with a middle-aged man followed another. But there is no intensity in these reflections of hers, no regret, no bitterness, no blame assigned; "realize," she says, "that this was a time when everyone was broke, when we didn't have any money, when people casually went to bed with each other just out of need, out of friendship."

While Miss D has been married four times, Miss A, Miss B and Miss C either reject the institution or feel it has rejected them. "Big bellies," Miss A says, "dirty laundry, get up in the morning, do the wash, change the baby"—not for her. Miss B considers marriage a matter of indifference: "If I wanted to get married, I *could* get married!" Miss C looks upon marriage as an impossible dream. "It is out of my hands now," she says, "Women are somehow chosen, and I have been found lacking."

There are contrasts among the young women in speech, in what they are in society, in their individual views of morality, but there is also something that ties them together. They all say they chose married, middle-aged men over younger men because—three of the four even use the same word—these men are "safe." Safe in the dangerous game of trespassing on other women's territory? Yes, says one, she is "safe" because she does not have to face the test of candidacy for marriage, and where there is no candidacy there can be no rejection. Yes, says another, she is "safe" because married men leave her free to go about her life and to wait for the right, unmarried, man to come along. Yes, says a third, she is "safe" from harassment because married men have their own lives to lead, apart from her, and they do not tie her up with constant demands for her time. And the fourth (the woman who used other words for the same idea)—finds a double safety in her affair: it offers her not only the financial and emotional stability of a marriage without the drudgery of family life, but certainty—the certainty that it will end "when we both run dry."

Two wives, Mrs. A and Mrs. B, assumed some dimension in the perhaps one-sided, male-sided portraits that Mr. A and Mr. B sketched of them in Chapter I and in the previous chapter. Now, in their own interviews, they flesh out those sketches and add dimensions to Mr. A and Mr. B as well. They are still married to those men; they are trying to survive their men's midolescence.

Mrs. C's marriage did not survive. She is now alone. All the signs were there. Her husband began to neglect a business he had created; he began bar-hopping and partying as the crony of "a very flamboyant, razzle-dazzle kind of guy"; he ultimately took up with a "dumb . . . dumb!" bleached blonde. But Mrs. C—who, incidentally, was unable to bear children and had adopted a little boy—refused to read the weather correctly: "It was unbelievable. You know, you'd think a fairly bright, fairly savvy gal would be able to see this coming, but I—I didn't see, I really didn't see it." Mrs. C, while willing to participate in this study, requested that she be interviewed by a woman; her request was honored. In the tape, Mrs. C sometimes gives way to tears. At one point the interviewer finds herself crying.

Now, let the women speak for themselves.

Mrs. A

Q. Before we get into the difficult part, the heart of this matter, let's get a few easy facts out of the way. When and where were you born, where'd you grow up, what was your schooling?

A. In Chicago in 1918. I was born and spent my early years there. I went to school in the Chicago area.

Q. How much schooling did you have?

A. Two years of college and—here and there other—secretarial school, I went to art classes for two years, A.I.D. courses . . .

Q. A.I.D.?

A. Yes—interior decorators.

Q. Oh, of course. And . . .

A. And things like that.

Q. Well, I don't think we need too much more of that. But let's hear a little about your family—I mean your family now. How long have you been married?

A. Twenty-one years.

Q. And you have how many children?

A. Six. Two from my first marriage and four from this one.

Q. And their ages?

A. The two older ones—two boys—they're twenty-five and twenty-two. The kids now, uh—the youngest is fourteen and the oldest is twenty.

Q. And so to the heart of the matter. What was your reaction when you learned your husband was having an affair with a young woman?

A. Uh—only one: The first one was, uh, complete disbelief.

Q. You didn't believe he was . . .

A. I couldn't believe that this had been going on. I . . .

Q. How did you find out about it?

A. He told me. He called me up and asked if he could come home and I said, "Certainly you can come home." He said, "Well, I've been sleeping with someone else."

Q. How long had he been gone?

A. Oh, I think it ran several months.

Q. He'd been gone—away from home—for several months? And you . . .

A. No, no. The affair had been going on for several months. He —he was sometimes, often, away from home for two, three days at a time. No, he wasn't gone for several months, it was just the affair . . .

Q. Okay.

A. And, uh—he felt it was someone he had always wanted to lay but never had. And she simply wanted to use him, professionally, use him to help her get ahead. And I'm not even sure whether she was good, in her work, or not, but she'd say "Now about this—could you see that this—uh . . ." And as I say, he was, he thought he was in love, and when he realized he was being used he thought, "How the hell did I get into this?" He gets into things because he drinks too much. Now, for instance, he's tried to kill me a few times, physically, a couple of times, because he's been very drunk. Completely gone. Uh—the other girl . . .

Q. What other girl?

A. The second time, the second affair, he . . .

Q. There were *two* affairs?

A. Oh yes. Two, and the second one, he called me up one night and he—they—it was a business thing. She threw herself at him, I think, and they were writing poetry and love letters through the office mail and—he wanted to be found out terribly because he told my closest friend all about it. She told me, more or less, and when he finally admitted it to me, uh, I think I had a mild stroke, because the first one I realized, I mean, he couldn't have been too much in love and she didn't seem too healthy herself, mentally. And when he told me—but the second one he was *in love* with. We discussed several times getting a divorce. I said, "if that's what you want," and he said, "Oh, I must have her. I love her I love her. I can't *bear* it." And I said, "Well, you said you always told me the time would come, marrying an older woman that I would get—you would be too old for me—and you're too old for me, absolutely too old for me." And at that moment I was. I was too old for him [laughing]. Because I felt a hundred and two.

Q. When was this?

A. Sixty-eight. The spring of '68. It started around the holidays.

Q. And how old was he then?

A. Forty-two.

Q. Forty-two. And you are now . . .

A. Fifty-six.

Q. So that you were then . . .

A. I was fifty then. I'm eight years older than my husband.

Q. Ah, yes. Okay. And the girl in question, how old was she?

A. I have no idea. I think maybe twenty-two, twenty-three.

Q. In her early twenties.

A. Yes. He was, uh—she didn't drink, so, uh—I'm sure they—he didn't go on the wagon or anything. He continued to drink, but I'm sure he wanted out of it, or he wouldn't have made such great plans for me finding out about it.

Q. Well, what was the effect on you other than the initial effect? How did it affect your marriage? How did it affect your relationship with your husband? Let me ask you some specific questions and you can answer them one at a time.

A. Okay.

Q. Did it rupture your feeling of trust for him?

A. Absolutely. I will never, never, *never* trust him completely. Because, uh—and believe me it was the only trust I had in him, because when you're married to an alcoholic, I can't *tell* you, I couldn't—it would take me years to list the indignities and the things he's done to me drunk, and the people who have pled with me, "Get rid of him. Divorce him. Why put yourself through this?" But I love him, very much, and I believe in him, and I—he doesn't want to be this way. He can't help himself. What was the specific question you asked?

Q. Had it ruptured your feeling of . . .

A. My trust, yeah. I don't—I told him the first time, I said, "The one thing I didn't believe you would ever do to me is this." And I said, "Now that you have done it once, it won't be so hard to do the second time, or the third." And I have convinced myself it will never surprise me if he comes up with a third any day. I really feel that way.

Q. You feel that that will be the final blow to the marriage? Or it will go on?

A. No, the marriage will go on because, strangely enough, he is very, very moral, and—not that I can't conceive of—I think he loves me. And I don't think he's in a position to meet somebody because, you know, he has a limited area now. If he were more social I'd expect more of it. But he's working too hard right now. He hasn't the opportunity. And as I say, you can stay out of a lot of trouble by not putting yourself in a position to be—that doesn't mean I'm running around saying "I'm vulnerable, so I better stay home." Y'know, I think he could do a lot more work if he would, uh—instead of concentrating—because it will initially be sex, which is not always a good basis for a lasting relationship. I'm sorry. I don't really trust him. I will think I trust him and then — [laughter] like Mrs. Alioto coming home after seventeen days and her husband says, "Well, did you get the cigarettes?"—he will go out to the store and not come back. I don't trust him as a drunk. At all. And emotionally I feel, for the toll it took out of me. I don't consider myself a mean, vicious, bitchy, unkind person. And that's what it made me. Real horrible. And I didn't like that at all.

Q. You hated what it did to you?

A. As a human being. I don't think you should make an ugly person out of another human being. It made me ugly to my children. I think they also, uh—lost a certain innate respect, somehow, for me. People say, "Why do you put up with it?" You know, you *have* to put up with a lot of things. You *can't* walk out on things. You *have* responsibilities.

Q. Did you feel, when you learned about this second affair, did you feel a sense of here he is, free to go have an affair, to indulge his sexual caprices, his emotional irresponsibility, while you were saddled with all the responsibility, not free to do this? Did this add to the hurt and the burden?

A. Not necessarily. I felt—I have no—I have no field to go into to look for anybody or run into anybody. Who am I gonna do? The United Parcel guy, or the mailman? Y'know, I have a very limited —which makes it very hard on a marriage if two people who have any brains at all . . .

Q. Well, that's what I mean. That you weren't free to do this.

A. Did I resent the fact?

Q. Yes. That he was taking advantage of his freedom, knowing that you were locked in.

A. No, I don't think I felt that way about it. I may have said so at the time. I don't remember. But, uh—no, I think I blamed the girl more than I blamed him. I think he's an idiot, emotionally.

Q. By that you mean what? Immature?

A. Yeah, because one day he'll tell me what a drag, how I couldn't turn a trick on the corner if I lay there naked all day, I should go out in the garage and hang myself. The next day he'll say, "Gee, I must've hurt you." I mean he's very erratic. I think sometimes when you're—I don't consider myself very talented, I said before, in any way, and I think when you are creative, as he is, when you're that, these other things—you're not very logical, or good at, like stability, or . . .

Q. Did you have to work hard after that affair to keep your marriage intact?

A. Well, it was taken away from me. We tried, you know, let's not do this, let's not do that, and then he had his heart trouble and that took the whole thing away from me.

Q. He had some heart trouble?

A. Yes. He didn't tell you about that, did he?

Q. No.

A. I didn't think he had. He's the kind of guy—I think he's afraid of mentioning it, maybe he was afraid that telling you that would put him down, in a way. Well—I think a lot of his problems were frustrations on the job.

Q. Do you think he had the affair because of the frustrations of the job, and it was providing an outlet for his frustration?

A. I don't know. I think if the girl came along today, I don't—the same girl he had not known that way before—I don't think he would go for that same girl today. His horizons are different. I also think he should have farther horizons than he does. [pause] All right, now you were going to ask me another specific question. Ask. [pause] As I say, the physical thing of his heart took the whole thing way away.

Q. So that you didn't have to deal with it.

A. Any more. As a—a buildup. Then we had a very careful relationship because he was scared.

Q. If you could draw some sort of graph or line or diagram showing your marriage before the second affair—I use the second affair because that apparently was more . . .

A. That was more important.

Q. If you could draw such a line or do an analysis of your marriage before it and after it, how would you say the marriage differs now? What has happened to your marriage, your relationship to yourself, your children, your husband, your whole life as a result of that affair?

A. I don't think I give as much as I should. Until my children are out on their own, I feel I owe a lot to them, and I ought to hang onto myself. I have a few things I want to do when my children are grown. It doesn't mean divorcing my husband or anything. But I don't feel my age. I want to do some things for *me*.

Q. That you felt you hadn't done?

A. Yeah.

Q. Would you attribute part of this feeling . . .

A. I think so. You know you can be hurt and, in a sense, rejected, just so much. I think we will—I think we have a pretty good marriage. I think so. I don't know how he feels. I am not interested in finding anything else. And when I, *if* I go out into my field again, I don't think I will find anyone. I will not allow myself to get in a situation where I can be vulnerable. I think he's vulnerable all the time because that's his makeup.

Q. Vulnerable to what?

A. Well, I think if someone very attractive and wealthy and he had the time to see her and she threw herself at him. I don't think he would deliberately go out and seek somebody or go after her. But of course I was wrong twice [laughing].

Q. And you could be wrong again.

A. And I can certainly be wrong again.

Q. Well, let me cite one of the other cases we have in the book. The husband had what he calls a non-affair, because there never was any sex, even though he wanted sex, and this changed his wife's life completely. His wife, prior to that affair, was totally wrapped up in him. A completely selfless person, locked into a relationship with her husband not just for her financial security but for the security of her whole life, and her life blew up when this affair happened. As a result of that and—to an extent—as a result of the therapy they took to try to resolve this—she realized that she had no life of her own. She wasn't even a person in her own right. She was a reflection of her husband. And, realizing this for the first time, she tried hard to break out of that, to make a life for herself, to give herself some self-worth, a feeling of existence as a separate, desirable, functioning person.

They both think their marriage has improved because of that, tremendously, and I'm now trying to get from you whether anything parallel happened to you, whether this threw a new light on you, *as* you, whether, realizing that you were either vulnerable or dependent to a larger extent than you should have been, that now you had to break free of that.

A. Well, a parallel [pause]—yes, I think I took stock of me and what I had that was mine and mine alone to, in a sense, mend fences, so I can't be hurt anymore and do what I want to do. My life is still completely wrapped up in my husband. He comes first. My children come secondly. I have found that my children don't need me as much as I thought they do. My husband needs me, perhaps not in a way I want to be needed, but he does need me, until he gets ready to do something else about it. And I'm perfectly willing to take as much as he cares to give me. I realize now he can't give me all of what I want, maybe.

Q. Isn't it sort of a truism, one that a lot of people realize too late, that no one person can fulfill any one other person's . . .

A. All, all of them. Yes, it's not true. There are different growths. I simply—we used to have—first of all, I didn't do all my housework; I had a maid. Then I had a cleaning woman. Then I attempted to do it. Now when you live with a drunk and have him knock over buckets of paint and vomit all over the floor and pee on the wall and put his cigarettes out on your leg or on the floor or the carpet or clear off the shelves in anger and break binoculars and put his fist through windows—I got tired of cleaning up. Now I don't do any housework. I read as much as I can. But, I'm trying to look ahead and fortify myself for, the—the eventuality that this could happen to me again.

Q. And at that time you'll be more prepared?

A. I think so. Whether I'll be prepared emotionally or not I don't know. I hope I won't ever have to go through that emotional upheaval.

Q. Let me ask a question that really has no meaning, but perhaps we can extract something from it. Do you think it's worth working hard to save a marriage that is teetering? Do you want to rescue it? Do you want to save it, or should you throw up your hands and say "It's just not worth the effort?"

A. If it wasn't worth the effort I would say by all means give it up. Because I certainly did that. I gave up security, a beautiful life. I . . .

Q. In what way? What was, or is, your profession, your work?

A. Interior decorating. I—I had a marvelous thing going with artists, fabric designers. I do designing myself—and I had offers, I had an offer to work with a group of people—designers, decorators, artists, craftsmen, people like that—in France, and I threw it all away for somebody I met in a bar, somebody who was . . .

Q. The "somebody" is your present husband?

A. Yes. I threw that away. I threw away those chances for a guy who was making seventy-five bucks a week because he represented more to me than this, uh—this marriage of a person who was cruel to me.

Q. You're speaking here of your first marriage?

A. Yes, the first one. He was cruel, mentally cruel. We never spoke a loud cross word. Never. But there were—there were horrors going on that you could never write down. Mental horrors. And, had I stayed in that marriage, I would have started to have one affair after another. As it was, I was having an affair. The marriage—that marriage—was not worth saving.

Q. But this one is.

A. Oh, by all means! We have an awful lot together when we're together, I think.

Q. So that . . .

A. Right now I think he needs me very much and will continue to need me until we find out what happens to his mother. Now this can happen. If something happens to his mother I may very well become his mother, because he has tremendous ties there he's not even aware of. Extraordinary ties. And then he may need a, another wife—y'know?

Q. So that you will fulfill the mother role and he'll go looking elsewhere for . . .

A. Well, I'll—I—as I say, I don't know how long I could take something like that. But I have a lot more patience than I used to. I have learned to keep my mouth shut. Now this morning or yesterday morning he said I castrated him. I can't do that. It's perfectly impossible. He can't be castrated. He—we're all "a bunch of leeches," we're no damned good, we're all—"you're pulling me down." And the next hour he's something entirely different. He's got more temperament than fifteen actresses.

Q. And that's part of the appeal, isn't it?

A. Not the appeal—that's not appealing to me. It's just something

I live with. Like an idiot child [laughter]. When he's good he's very very good, when he's bad he's horrid. I had to trust him and count on him and he never kept his word. I used to go into the city, call home—he never showed. And this would happen time after time after time. Then I had to decide: should I go home and raise my kids or let 'em just run ragged and loose, kill each other, set fire to the house? Or should I go home and just stay home? And that's what I did. Now I made the choice. In no way let it be thought that I gave up my career for him.

Q. It was your option?

A. I would say so.

Q. And you chose to come home.

A. I chose to stay home.

Q. When your husband had the second affair, is there any—are you aware of—any desire on his part, whether conscious or unconscious, to chase his fading youth, and if you were—did it play a part in your reaction to this affair? Here was a man of forty-two who was . . .

A. You see, I don't think he has any *fading* youth.

Q. You think it's still there?

A. Yeah. But none of us know how we see ourselves.

Q. No, but there are certain realities that you face, you face them in the mirror every day. You face the reality of—you slow down, your body gets a little sluggish. They're all realities you face. You can emotionally . . .

A. He probably felt very thrilled that somebody so young found him very desirable. I have had the experience repeatedly with my daughter, my oldest daughter's boyfriends, and my oldest son's boyfriends. A great attachment. And one boy became very attached and I told him not to come around any more. And I am old enough to be some of my children's grandmother, almost, y'know. So I have never felt an age thing at any time. Maybe this is something a man —I never had that menopause crap. I must look pretty ridiculous to my kids sometimes. We went to a gas station the other day and it was leaking out of the—it was the transmission fluid. I got down on my stomach and looked at it, and my son said, "Oh my god! Get up, come on mother, what are you doing?" I said, "I'm looking at the transmission leak—what do you think I'm doing?" "Well, a woman your age . . ." I said, "Frig my age!" C'mon! [pause] When my husband had his heart attack and went to the hospital that time I farmed all the kids out. When he went to the hospital, I shut the door, cleaned out the icebox, and started to paper and clean the entire house. And then one day he calls and says, "Guess what? I'm coming home." I said, "Oh, my God!" He said, "Aren't you glad?" And I said, "I've got *this* room half done and *that* room half done, and so on." My son comes home from scout camp and he says, "Hey —this is miraculous!" I said, *"What's* miraculous?" "That an old woman like you could hang all this wallpaper." [laughter, long and hard]

Q. I remember when I was fifteen I went out with a girl of fifteen and she showed me a picture of her older sister, who was a model, and she said, "My sister is thirty," and I remember thinking to myself, "God, how could a woman of *thirty* be a model?" When you're fifteen years old, that's a whole other world out there. [pause] Let me ask you: You said that before you married your present husband you had an affair. Was that with a married man?

A. Yes, a married man.

Q. Well, now, when you became the wife of a man who was having an affair, did you recall in any way the other side of the coin —when you were the "other woman," the younger woman who was having an affair with a married man?

A. Yeah.

Q. How did that affect your reaction to your husband's affair?

A. I felt, thank *God* I never allowed it to go to this point! Thank *God* I never—what pain, what horror, what *tragedy* I could have created!

Q. You were moral enough or smart enough or big enough or wise enough or something never to have allowed it to

A. Never to get into that. I don't think this girl wanted it to get into that. Believe me. Because when I called her up and I said, "Look, is this Janet? This is Mrs. A." "Oh yes, Mrs. A. . . ." like I was going to give her a letter or something. I said, "I just want to tell you I have bathed and dressed all my children and I am coming down there and you can have them. You can have my husband and I'm going to your employer. You are going to give up your job as of *right now,* because you are now going to be the mother of four kids. And that is that." "Oh, my God! I can't give it up—oh no— I promise you I'll never see him again. I promise you, I'll never never never." And I said, "Well, it's too late for that now. He told me he wants to marry you and that's the way it is." "Oh, no, no. I will never. Never, never, never!" And I told him. He said, "She gave me up? Just like that?" And we didn't have a car; he got on his bicycle and pedaled down to phone her from outside. And he came home and decided that was the end of that. Six weeks later—it was the night of his son's graduation—he came home drunk. And don't think his son didn't feel this or remember this. He was too drunk to go. And that time I called her and I said, "Look, if you ever see my husband again—I realize you work in the same office—you will never know the day I will walk in there with a gun, a knife or a bottle of acid—so just watch out!" Cause by this time I'd gotten my second wind. I—I was in such bad shape I couldn't eat—my neighbors came over and forcibly fed me, because I just felt this [gesture of horror] awful; I couldn't do anything. I couldn't drink, I couldn't eat. You talk about destroy—blow up. I blew up. *I* was destroyed *totally!* I closed this door.

Q. Destroyed by the fact, or destroyed by the feeling . . .

A. Destroyed by the fact that my marriage was over. He wanted to marry this girl. I thought, "I will never find anything more wonderful than this man, and he no longer wants me—at all."

Q. But you came out of that. You came out of that with a feeling that you were better than—you came out of that *feeling* better than ever that you were someone.

A. Yeah. But . . .

Q. And that the marriage was a good one.

A. I think that was my training from long ago. I had been schooled in rejection so many times. My mother rejected me, I had boyfriends reject me. My first husband got transferred to Manila. He didn't have to go; he asked to be sent away. Now if this isn't rejection all the way down the line—so sooner or later I've got to stand up and take care of myself or just become a slut or a drunk.

Q. Suppose you hadn't taken that stand with that woman. Suppose you had . . .

A. Oh, I think it would've—the heart attack would've ironed something out. I don't think she had any intention of breaking up a marriage and marrying him.

Q. He wanted to marry her but not vice versa?

A. He had to marry—he had to want to marry her to justify why he was doing everything. He couldn't just say, "Well, it was a love affair, I did it and it's over." He had to want to marry the girl. This guy's very, very moral. [pause] He—when he was going with that first girl he'd be out with her all night and come home and lay me.

This somehow fixed it in his head. "Well, I'm still doing it to my wife so I can't be doing, y'know—it isn't too bad." This was to justify himself by whatever means he had. I justified myself when I was going with a married man. He—I suppose he had to justify *him*self in a certain way. I think—you know what he said to me once? I said, "If you ever . . . " I was always afraid I'd have an affair with somebody because I had had a pretty exciting life. I didn't believe I could be faithful to one man. I said, "If you ever get involved with someone, if you ever have an affair, will you tell me about it?" He said, "If I ever did such a thing to you, I promise you, I would walk out and never see you again." But that—it didn't work out that way. When it got right down to [trails off into inaudibility]. Maybe he hasn't had the real one yet. If there is one, maybe when the real one comes along, he will. Then there is the little thing of economics. What would he have done if he'd had all the money in the world? Because it's completely impossible for him and me to separate. To set up two separate living—we can't even [laughter] handle the one we have.

Q. I think if you want desperately enough . . .

A. —you do it. Which is what I did with my first husband. I mean that certainly—that's the other side of the coin, as you said. I left my husband for a younger man. But you have to realize that I did a lot of things from a very male standpoint. I went into everything. I took care of all my own abortions. I supported myself. I took care of the contraception, most of the time. I was very moral. But when, when suddenly—you know, I saw him long before I met him. And I fell in love with him. He was on the walk and I was on the ferryboat. And I saw him walking in the rain and I said, "My God! Why didn't anyone like that ever fall in love with me?" And he didn't have a prayer once I ever spoke to him. But I just don't like to get hurt. Who does?

Mrs. B

Q. Your birth date?

A. March 2, 1935.

Q. Ah, education, interests—how long were you educated? Did you go all the way through college? Did you just go to high school?

A. I went to a woman's college and left after eighty-five credits on a maternity leave, which was mandatory. At the time, if you were pregnant, you had to take a year off. Now I'm back in school, to get a degree.

Q. B.A.? B.S.? What?

A. Bachelor of Arts.

Q. Your major?

A. I'm not quite sure yet; I'm thinking of architecture.

Q. This maternity leave—were you, uh, married at the time?

A. Oh, yes.

Q. Where were you born and reared?

A. In Queens.

Q. When and where did you meet your husband?

A. Met him? In—at a party, in Brooklyn. We had mutual friends.

Q. The date?

A. We first met each other in, in 1952, I guess. We used to say— I used to—we used to say we knew at once, we felt at once, at that party, that it was—we used to use the expression "Across a crowded room . . ."

Q. These mutual friends. Were they family friends? Were they friends in cultural interests?

A. That's hard to say.

Q. Why?

A. I guess in cultural interests.

Q. Like what? Music?

A. For me it was art. For Arthur [the name is fictionalized] it was probably [she laughs lightly] biology. And, uh, it was more *personality* than interests.

Q. Personality? We get a little far afield. Do you mean *his* personality, *your* personality and his? Did they cohere, did they . . .

A. No, the personality between—what it really is that draws people together as friends, sparks each other, or fills needs, and attracts them. Between two people, not—not male and female, but . . .

Q. This is the whole group, or this is yourself and Arthur?

A. Oh, no. I'm talking about his friendship with his friend and my friendship with my friend. We had mutual friends.

Q. I see. Did you have an interest in biology at the time?

A. Well, I was interested in the sciences also at that time.

Q. What sciences?

A. Oh, general.

Q. The oldest—the one we're looking into here—human behavior?

A. General.

Q. Well, you had that in common. And so you courted and you went together—for how long a period—before you were married?

A. A year.

Q. A year. Did you have sex together before you were married?

A. No.

Q. Did it seem important whether you did or not, to either of you?

A. I don't think we verbalized.

Q. Were there—I mean, was it ever suggested?

A. No.

Q. Did you ever have sex with anyone *else* before you were married?

A. No.

Q. You, ah, went to a party last night, you told me earlier, and had some trouble. About—about Arthur projecting toward people, or something?

A. Arthur has had many instances, in the past, through the years, which he denies, that he has anything to do with—them, where people in the advertising or publishing field have invited him to things, in advance, to things like birthday parties, and which don't include us as a couple, but just him, which is fine. But these [invitations] are from people who know me, and who've been to my home, but there isn't a concept of Arthur as a part of a couple.

Q. There was not, last night?

A. Last night, Arthur was, um—invited to sleep with one of the women and . . .

Q. Are you sure about this?

A. Yes.

Q. And is he?

A. Yes, he told me.

Q. He told you about the woman?

A. He didn't really know her. I don't think he said more than three words to her. I think that she was in need of a man.

Q. What was the nature of the invitation?

A. [long silence]

Q. Let me give you an example. It's best if we do it that way. I asked one of the other men interviewed for this book how he got into all this business, this strange sex life he led years ago. And his reply was that one of his women employes came into his office one afternoon after everyone had left and said, "Why don't we fuck?" And he said, "I think that's a marvelous idea." And he went on from there. I thought I was being put on when I heard this. Well, this invitation last night was not tendered in this way, was it?

A. I don't know. I wasn't in the room. She was totally unaware that . . .

Q. How do you know that?

A. Because Arthur, before we left—she came over to say something to me and in the conversation she discovered that Arthur and I were married, which took her greatly by surprise. She had taken it for granted that he was totally unattached by, I feel, by what he projects. And how he projects it. Which is different from flirting with someone, or having the verbal interchange, or fantasy . . .

Q. What was said?

A. Between the two of them? I don't know.

Q. Between the three of you. The three of you, at this time of leaving the place.

A. Oh! Nothing. Just that she came over to me to make a comment . . .

Q. What comment?

A. She came over, and she asked me about myself, and she said I looked very *regal.* And would I be interested in, did I—something about theatricals, she pictures me as a—Greek queen, and—she chose Medea.

Mr. B. offers this version: This broad was stoned out of her skull. I was standing there watching some people playing scrabble, and she came over, grabbed the zipper on my shirt and pulled it down; she then said, "This is very sexy." She was looking at my hairy chest. She said, "I need a place to sleep; would you like to sleep with me?" My wife was sitting no more than eight feet away; this girl had come in bombed and she was drinking her way through this night. I said, "You've got problems, haven't you?" She replied incoherently. I learned later that she propositioned every man at the party. As for my projecting availability, that's how I feel, I can't help that.

Q. She said she was active in this [theatricals]?

A. Said she was *active?*

Q. Yes.

A. She just came over, I assume, for a parting-type conversation; I had been sitting across the room, talking with other people, all evening. And she was totally unaware that Arthur and I had any connection with each other.

Q. And so you got the message that something had gone *on* there, or . . .

A. No, Arthur told me afterwards.

Q. Do you think he told you—in the manner—did you have anything to drink, either of you?

A. I don't know if he did.

Q. You don't know if he did. Well, there are still areas you don't know, in which a man may say, boyishly, "You know, I got *propositioned* by *that* one!"

A. No.

Q. It didn't come that way. Did you ask him about it? Did *you* bring this up? Was it you who found out . . .

A. No, I was, I had been very angry with him. I feel he says one thing and he projects another. And that he is either lying to himself or to me. And if he's lying to himself, then he should perhaps be aware that his actions and his words and his *projections,* er, aren't the same! And he ought to tune in to himself a little more. Because there's just too much consistency in people's reactions to him. It's not a chance thing.

Q. And this reaction was consistent with past performances? This reaction of *hers?*

A. Well, I don't know her; he'd never met her before; this reaction has been consistent with women inviting him to sleep over; either to sleep over because they're interested in him as a person, because they're interested in him sexually, or because he projects the fact that he has no place to go. And he's a wandering soul. I don't know what they see. I really can't remove myself enough to be objective.

Q. He—does he admit this?

A. No.

Q. He does not. Was there any, er . . .

A. I don't even know if he admits it to himself.

Q. Last night, was there any difficulty, any quarrel about it, between you? Was there any scene between you about it? Was this said in the car, was this said . . .

A. This was a conversation. We have a long tendency, a long habit of not—we've *never* fought! And I think part of that is bad, because then you don't air your feelings, or you don't vent your *fury*, or your *anger*, or your *disagreements*, your misunderstandings, you don't really get to know how the other one is feeling.

Q. It's kind of dim in my mind just what did happen.

A. It was a very insignificant incident that was just—symbolic.

Q. Had it happened before, at any time? Had there been any other parties where you'd seen this happen? How could you . . .

A. Lately Arthur had been going to parties in the advertising field, or others, without me.

Q. Where's he get time?

A. [smiling]: He—makes—time. This sort of thing has been going on for the past three years.

Q. What sort of thing?

A. That he has been—socializing.

Q. Well. Let us get right to the heart of the matter, which is this young lady your husband had what he calls a "non-affair" with. Have you ever met the woman?

A. Yes. Once.

Q. Tell me the circumstances.

A. Sh-sh-she, and I, were invited to the same very small dinner party. There were seven people present.

Q. And you were introduced?

A. Yes.

Q. By?

A. The host. And hostess.

Q. And what was her behavior? Toward you? Did she know who you were, did she . . .

A. Yes. She brought me a present. Of a cookbook.

Q. At that time?

A. Yes.

Q. She presented you with a *cookbook?*

A. Yes.

Q. Had she known you'd be there?

A. Obviously.

Q. Uh-huh. How'd you feel about that present?

A. Curiosity—hostility . . .

Q. Do you think it was symbolic?

A. Arthur swears he did not know she'd be there, and I believe him.

Q. How did you take the present of the cookbook? With goodwill, or with some suspicion? Here was this—this free and easy cat, with . . .

A. —with anger.

Q. Then you did take the present of the cookbook as symbolic of you, who were the one who spent her life in the kitchen, the *house-wife* . . .

A. Yes! But I don't think it was necessarily presented that way. I don't think she knows anything about me. I don't think she *knew* anything about me. I think it was just a matter of—this was a new book that was out, and, er—to take something along.

Q. Did she just happen to have it with her, or did she bring it to the party expressly . . .

A. No, she brought it to the party, expressly for me.

Q. What was she wearing? And did you notice what she was wearing?

A. Yes. I'm very conscious of . . .

Q. Yes, well, right, you're a woman, they do that. So what was it?

A. A Danskin top and a wrap skirt.

Q. What is a Danskin top?

A. Stretch-knit.

Q. Uh-huh. And did Arthur speak to her at this party? Did you, the three of you, have any palaver together?

A. Arthur behaved toward her as if she were almost a total stranger.

Q. And did you speak more words to her than just "thank you for the cookbook" or . . .

A. No, we, er—she spent the evening propositioning . . .

Q. Other men?

A. Crudely propositioning [Mrs. B names a well-known and highly respected international figure whom I shall call Brian] to the point where I felt that she was totally insensitive.

Q. And did you hear the way she did this?

A. Yes, I was sitting—Brian was in the middle, on the couch, between her and myself.

Q. What did she say? I'm sorry this has to be District Attorney, but it's a way of . . .

A. She said—she said, "Don't you like . . ."—he was very very, very uncomfortable.

Q. Dignified? Reserved?

A. Reserved, cultured, or at least this is what he likes to present. He was with his peers, and this was very blatant, very loud. She asked him, er . . . "Don't you like" er . . ."

Q. Don't you like what?

A. "Don't you like,"— er—"Don't you like dark nipples? Do you know what a hard-on is?" And—she was making him very uncomfortable! Whether he would have reacted to this privately differently I don't know, but in this public situation he was squirming, and getting upset, and she pursued it.

Q. Did you get the impression that "privately," as you have said, she might not have said it that way?

A. No. I really don't know her. I just know about her by hearsay. I just felt that she was very crude and insensitive to another person. And it was not just a matter of four-letter words; it was a matter of just one person's total insensitivity to how someone else was feeling.

Q. I don't think you can read that as insensitivity; it's perhaps over-sensitivity . . .

A. And a provocation, the desire, the need to provoke.

Q. And this guy finally got up and walked away?

A. No, he wasn't in a position—he was a guest at this person's home and it was a very small group of people, and it was a very awkward situation.

Q. And it was resolved by his removing himself? Or did she press this?

A. I—I don't know. I moved away because I felt uncomfortable for him. And I had spoken with him for about an hour and a half before we got to the party. We had come up together in the car, Arthur and he and myself, and we had come—had all kinds of conversations, and he had showed me, at the party, small sculptures that he had found in New York and had been fascinated by.

Q. Well, let's drop this matter. Tell me, was there—did you notice —was there an upsurge of sexual activity, a fulfilling upsurge between you and Arthur?

A. You mean after, during . . .

Q. When the discovery was made, when he told you, or whatever.

A. Arthur and I had no sex life. *Before* that.

Q. You had *no sex* life? Well, the children were not produced by osmosis, were they?

A. No, but, er, shall I say a very, er . . .

Q. I hope this doesn't, you're not offended about this, because it's quite important, and . . .

A. There was almost no—Sex was very rare.

Q. And afterward?

A. We began to have a sex life.

Q. Mm-hm. Was it any different from what it had been? What it had been twenty years ago?

A. Oh, very much so, very different.

Q. How different? And is that an embarassing question? Different techniques?

A. Umm—Arthur had, er . . .

Q. Go on. Had trouble?

A. No. He had trouble during this period. I didn't know, I had unfortunately not had very much experience before. And I didn't know . . .

Q. Yes. You had—*no* experience before.

A. Right. And didn't know what sex was really supposed to be, or what it could be, er—Arthur had always made me feel that there was something physically wrong with me, and that I was repulsive.

Q. All through marriage?

A. Yes. Very much so.

Q. In what way?

A. Er—he has a very narrow concept of the female form. And he has very specific . . .

Q. Likes and dislikes?

A. Likes and dislikes, in terms of breast shapes, and such. And I'm just wrong.

Q. Your breasts aren't large enough, is that it?

A. Oh, no! He likes, er, very small breasts. And mine are not so small.

Q. Is this part of this bothering—would you rather we forgot it?

A. No. It's all right.

Q. Well. How shall I put this? Did you do things other than the straight, missionary position in sex, which is the man on top, or above?

A. Before . . .?

Q. Afterward.

A. Afterward. I took the initiative. I just . . .

Q. In what way?

A. Er . . . [Long, long silences in this part of the interview]

Q. Orally?

A. No, at this time, Arthur felt that his—during his involvement —he felt that he had become a eunuch. When he slept with her, he . . .

Q. Didn't do anything—

A. Didn't do anything. And—my—transcending myself, to— and, my—I guess it was *martyred* love, for him, made me learn about sex and to try to prove that he wasn't a eunuch. So I became the aggressor.

Q. When you say "learn about sex," do you mean from textbooks, or do you mean making an effort to join into this?

A. From books, from talking to people . . .

Q. What people?

A. I talked to friends of mine who introduced me to, er—women and men, who talked to me about male hangups, about technique, about all kinds of things that I had never known before, or had this sort of discussion before . . .

Q. For instance, what had you never known before? Can you be, if it is painful . . .

A. Almost everything! I had, somehow, remained the child. In sexual terms. With a total unawareness; the women's liberation movement, also, the literature they put out—consciousness ways, discussions about feelings, techniques . . .

Q. Yes. Techniques. Er—techniques that you imagined a woman like *her* would practice? Possibly?

A. I knew really nothing about her.

Q. Right. Well, the incident with Brian might lead you to believe this was someone who was pretty much a swinger, is that right? On the very face of it?

A. Someone very free sexually. Which I was not. Someone who regarded sex as an appetite.

Q. To act out her aggressions against men, or against the whole world.

A. I didn't see this or know this about her, I just knew of Arthur's feelings for her, which at that time, he claimed, were totally non-sexual.

Q. How did he tell you, and what were the circumstances? How did he tell you there was anything going on between them?

A. Arthur was then very depressed. After all the excitement of his book. One night he did not come home, and I was very worried, because he had been so depressed.

Q. He had never previously not come home, is that right?

A. Never previously had not come home, and, certainly, if he had slept anywhere, it was always . . .

Q. He would call you from there, right?

A. No, it was always known in advance. If he was working on some project. And he had always come home to sleep. He did *not* come home [that night]. And I was very worried about him because he had been so depressed. I had no idea of his involvement with any other woman. And I—he had appeared to—and spoken of suicide.

Q. After . . .

A. Before. I envisioned him either somewhere with his wrists slashed, or mugged, somewhere in town.

Q. Now, we have to back-track a little, because the chronology is important in these. He had spoken of suicide before you knew there was another woman?

A. Yes. No, wait—I don't know—I saw his depression. And I don't know if he had spoken of it before that time, but I knew from his past history, and his depression . . .

Q. His past history being the scar on his wrist?

A. Yes. I knew that he had attempted suicide a few years before I had met him. So that this wasn't something out of left field, and at this particular time he had been very depressed, and I was very worried about him.

Q. And so, that day, that day, or the next night, he came home to tell you that indeed he had been spending . . .

A. He had not come home that night, and I called several people to find out, including his friend in Vermont, Allan. He had called here to arrange some kind of meeting, or change some kind of meeting, and when I told Allan that Arthur had not come home, Allan thought in the same way I had, because he knew Arthur was very depressed. And he came down here. Allan is Arthur's long, long-term childhood friend, on the gut-level—a soul brother. Allan came in because his feeling was—he, too, thought that Arthur was depressed enough, from his recent conversations, that he might attempt suicide.

Q. And so Arthur did return home?

A. Yes. He had also not been to work that day.

Q. And there was a confrontation between the two of you? You asked him, or he volunteered?

A. He called later the following day; this was about twenty-four hours later. That he had been discussing an advertising project, for his book, and had gotten drunk and fallen asleep with a group of people. At someone's house.

Q. Did you suspect anything? Did you think that was a lie?

A. No. I trust people. And when they tell me something, perhaps naïvely, I believe them.

Q. So how did you find out the truth of the matter?

A. Not then. I don't remember. [Long silences here] He continued to be very depressed . . . His habits changed. He started drinking heavily. Which had just not been his habit. Six, eight drinks, one after the other.

Q. There was a period of how many days between his staying with her and your finding out?

A. I really don't remember.

Q. A week? A month?

A. I did contact a family therapist. At the time I did, I had no idea that he was emotionally involved with someone else. I was just concerned about his depression.

Q. Do you think that your mind has blanked something out here?

A. It's hard to remember, day by day. He continued to be depressed. I kept trying to get him to talk.

Q. And there was no upsurge in sex activity at this time?

A. Oh, no.

Q. And finally you succeeded in getting him to talk.

A. He just kept saying, every day he just kept saying he was going to commit suicide, he was going to the store to buy a gun, a rifle, to put in his mouth, or he was going to drive the car over the bridge. One night he came home with various information that he said I should have about his insurance, or bills, what kind of bills should be paid when, what the insurance policy numbers were. And he told me he was going to commit suicide that night, but he wanted to be responsible, so he should give me this first. And this—every day was like this. At this time, all I could think about was Arthur, and worrying about him. And I became very depressed also.

Q. You are afraid, are you, about telling me about the actual time, you are afraid of your emotions in telling me about the exact confrontation, when you learned this?

A. The exact confrontation?

Q. Answer true or false! [both laugh long and loud] Answer maybe, "Who the hell do you think you are, Fred?"

A. I don't think—the incredible thing is for me to look back on my actions and reactions at the time.

Q. That's—what I want!

A. There *was* no confrontation! My feelings were overwhelming concern for Arthur: "My poor darling!" There was no confrontation. I had ceased to exist.

Q. There must have been a time when you crossed the Rubicon, when you went over the edge, when there was the knowledge that this woman existed, and he had spent the night with her.

A. I was concerned for him, that he thought himself a eunuch. I was concerned for him that he was so depressed.

Q. I *appreciate* that, I *appreciate* that. But can we not get to the very fact of your . . .

A. There was no confrontation!

Q. Well, did you find this out from other sources?

A. No. Eventually, he told me.

Q. Ah! That's what we're trying to . . .

A. Yes—now, but I did not react in any confronting manner. And this is something that I find, in retrospect, very difficult to understand, other than that I must have ceased to exist.

Q. He told you that here? Was this the night when he banged his head against the floor, or the wall, or said "I'm going to kill myself" because of this?

A. Every day, he was going to kill himself. This was just an added . . .

Q. —starter . . .

A. He was in love with her, he told me. And he expanded on it to say he had spent that night.

A. That came out somewhere along the way. And my feelings about myself were that, er . . .

Q. It must have been a *shock,* a *trauma,* it had to be—"Here I am, how do I—" See, often the reaction to a thing, anything like this, is, "Gee, here I am, my leg's just been cut off, and I don't feel—either not all *that* bad about it, or *worse.*" You have to fit into that somewhere, no?

A. I felt that I was of no value. Perhaps, if he had said, "I was sexually attracted," or he'd found her "irresistible," or whatever— that I could have understood.

Q. But he didn't say that.

A. No.

Q. This was late at night?

A. [Long pause before she replies] We—I tried to talk with him, whatever time we could, either late at night, or before he left for

work, or whatever. I was too much the friend, and not the wife. I
think I reacted more as a friend than as a wife.

Q. Did you have sex at that time?

A. No.

Q. You did not; but you began to, not long afterward?

A. [Long and painful exhalation of breath, the kind of sigh I don't
want to hear too often in my life] Er, long afterwards, I think,
er . . .

Q. Would you say a week? Two weeks? Months?

A. I would say several months.

Q. Several *months?*

A. Mm-hm.

Q. Several months. And then you did begin this more active—in
this interim, you consulted these other people, read the books, talked
to the women and the men who told you about techniques and sexual
interrelations that you were not conscious of?

A. Yes. [pause] Part of Arthur's conversations about her was—
was not what he was aware of, but of what seemed to be a repeated
pattern—was her age, her youth.

Q. You're hardly ancient yourself. You're thirty-nine, right?

A. Thirty-eight.

Q. And she was then . . .

A. Twenty-seven or twenty-six.

Q. All right. Well, twelve years or so. There really isn't all that
much difference.

A. It's all in the viewpoint. I think Arthur had ceased to see me
as . . .

Q. He did tell you, did he not, about "her gorgeous body?"

A. No. Not at that time.

Q. Ah.

A. That had nothing to do with his attraction, as far as he ac-
knowledged to himself.

Q. He began to buy more youthful-looking clothing?

A. Yes. The turtle-neck sweaters, the long hair, the—he let his
hair grow. He became very conscious of clothes where he had never
done that before.

Q. Had he ever, speaking of his hair, ever been the third oar at
Yale?

A. [laughing] Oh, no, never. But he became very conscious of his
appearance, and tried to look more youthful.

Q. Mm-hm. And did you try to do so, in sympathy or empathy?

A. Did I do what?

Q. The same thing.

A. I started to shop for clothing, which I had never done before. Or had rarely done. I always used to make my own clothing. And I found myself trying on things that were the style of the youth movement, and finding myself, also, very *angry* that I was doing this.

Q. And, did you go on a diet of some kind, a crash diet?

A. No. I did lose weight, because [laughs] for the first time in my life, I forgot to eat! Because I was so depressed. [another long silence]

Q. Do you think he's still . . .

A. Yes, he's still in the middle of, whatever were his feelings of the time. I don't know. He *tells* me that she is no longer, er, the important figure of his life. I think that his feelings and his needs are still very much where they were at that time, whether he admits it to himself or not.

Q. This is expressed, is it, in the new job, the advertising venture?

A. This is expressed in his attitudes toward women and sex. And he's still seeking things and putting values on things that he'd always had no value for. He's very conscious of his appearance. Of his clothing. He's just ordered, this week, a pair of glasses with steel rims, strictly for fashion, along with another pair, the same prescription, with horn rims.

Q. Wait a minute! Could that not be quite *necessary* for him, since he's doing a lot of contact work, in his advertising venture, since he's *meeting* a lot of people?

A. That's—*BUNK!*

Q. It's bunk! Very good. Very good. Now: Why is that bunk?

A. [no reply]

Q. I think your husband is, apart from all this palaver, one of the more brilliant people I've ever met. He can digest things, and he can understand something so quickly, go deeply and penetratingly into something—So you feel that he is *insulting* himself by doing this?

A. I think that he is giving himself no value for the very beautiful things that he is, the things that attracted me to him in the beginning; that he is seeking to be things that were not normally part of himself for all the time that I knew him. And seeking values that, I don't really respect. Well, appearance is just a symptom. Appearance to look youthful, appearance to look like a swinger, er—but not *just* appearance. All kinds of other things which to me are very—not of any great depth—the tinsel of life, which he never had had any respect for!

Q. The period of trouble is over, is it not? The real crisis? It's a lot easier now than it was, right? *This* is not two years ago. You are not *now* quite so bewildered about it all.

A. Things are very different. I'm very changed. All my values are now in question. My relationship—and relationships in general—are in question.

Q. Did you ever think, at the time this man-eating bitch—that's not in the sexual sense—came into the picture, did you think, in the midnights of your soul, of embarking on an extra-marital sexual adventure yourself? As a means of revenge, as a means of proving yourself as a woman? Of proving your womanhood, which you might have felt was rejected?

A. I—*kept* myself from it, although I came—pretty close.

Q. So you *did* think about it?

A. No, I *kept* myself from it because I thought it would be the most destructive thing for me, it would distract me from the real issues!

Q. But it did enter your mind.

A. Oh, yes.

Q. It did enter your mind.

A. [She weeps quietly.]

Q. There are people who can, who do this kind of thing all their lives, but they don't hurt anybody. They live their double lives and there it is. They don't care. But this is not something your husband can do. Right? The problem is, for many of us, that we would give too much of our heart. And once that starts, you're in a lot of trouble. If you cannot accept such a thing for the pure masturbatory, orgasmic pleasure, pleasure for its own sake, the hedonistic thing, if you're going to go farther than that, then your marriage is going to shake and it is going to tremble and be shattered, if you have a marriage. And so—you were saying before . . .

A. I think that Arthur is still in . . . [lapse into silence]

Q. Oh, you were saying you think he's going to have another . . .

A. Yes, because I think that his associates, the people—so many of the people in advertising—are a very bad influence on him. And I think that he admires them, and he's in this kind of atmosphere, eight, ten or more hours a day.

Q. You told me, when we were sitting in the kitchen, before the taping began, about some wild meeting that your husband had told you about.

A. Yes, this—whatever it was, meeting or excuse for a meeting or . . .

Q. That a client had phoned and asked him to meet him downtown, in a loft on Broadway at some ungodly hour . . .

A. Eleven o'clock, 11:30 at night.

Q. —and that when he got there the client was screwing some woman in a sleeping loft right above Arthur's head and was carrying on a conversation with Arthur at the same time.

A. Yes, it was—it's that kind of thing that Arthur admires.

Q. He admires? He . . .

A. Arthur came home that night, after that—whatever it was the client—and he came home very angry with me . . .

Q. Angry?

A. Angry that he would like to have participated in what was going on there, and he was unable to.

Q. In what way "participated?"

A. That he, too, would like to be very free sexually and—uh— indulge his appetites. His reaction, when he's exposed to this kind of thing, and the feelings that he would like to participate, but feels unable to because of who he is. He reacts by coming home and being angry with me.

Q. And other men get knocked around on their jobs and come home and take it out on their wives.

A. Yes.

Q. Yeahhhh.—This is the other self, the private self that you know about?

A. He's angry with me that he's not twenty-five. He's angry with me that he's not a swinger.

Q. Well! You are a swinger or you are not; it doesn't matter about your *age.*

A. He's angry with me for the things he's not. His clients, several of them, from what he tells me, do this sort of thing daily. And Arthur is exposed to this daily, and stops to think, What's wrong with *him?* Because he, too, would like to . . .

Q. Would you rather have never met these people? Would you rather you didn't know about this? Would that be a more peaceful life?

A. No, I think that that kind of peace is self-deceptive. I think, as painful as it is, it's perhaps better to be aware of the pressures, the, er, the fantasies. I think it's much more brutal to be in the position that I was in, to have a romantic viewpoint toward life and people and yourself and your mate. That's perhaps very unrealistic. And I think that's when you're really totally shattered, if something should happen that destroys all your, uh . . .

Q. What you thought life was all about. The foundations of your whole being, yes.

A. Yes. I think that's when it's devastating.

Q. Well, let's get back to you. You say that the thought of having such sex yourself did enter your mind. Was there any specific person? [no answer] If so, who? [more silence] I mean, did this come to you as a *gesture* you would make, or would you . . .

A. It was a friend of ten years' standing, a male friend, who didn't know any details of what was going on in our life—that is, in my life—but who had been very supportive to me at this time. He asked me, he said that he would like to have a total relationship with me, completely above board.

Q. And he did not know this was going on?

A. He didn't know any details.

Q. But he knew *something* was going on.

A. Well, he knew that both Arthur and I were very depressed. And he went home, and I—I said "No." And I guess he caught my ambiguity. I was, er—I used to just cry. That this was just, in a sense, a relationship that he had very, very strong feelings about, and he wanted . . .

Q. Sex.

A. —very open.

Q. He wanted you to go to bed with him.

A. More than that.

Q. Marry you.

A. No. I mean he did not, I mean there was no question of leaving his family, it would just be—er, two relationships.

Q. It would just be something that would help you in a period of trouble?

A. No, I don't think that it had to do with helping *me;* I think it had to do with his, er, feelings toward me, which are very warm and of very long standing, and caring. And he would like to include sex in that relationship.

Q. And this was not brought up again?

A. Between him and myself?

Q. Yes.

A. It, er, as I said, I said "No," but apparently he caught an ambiguity, because I was very tempted for the warmth and for someone caring about me. Which he does.

Q. Had your sex life with Arthur had its renascence by that time?

A. I think—I can't really pinpoint time. I don't know.

Q. Well, was this six months after your discovery of the other woman?

A. [silence]

Q. Was it in the summer? In the spring?

A. It's hard to remember.

Q. You feel that a lot of things are blacked out for you because of this?

A. [quickly] I don't know what you mean by "blacked out."

Q. "Blacked out" in that you cannot say days, times . . .

A. No, I've never had a concept of time.

Q. You've never had a concept of time?

A. No.

Q. He—he did not bring this up again, this guy, right?

A. Oh, it was sort of *pursued,* for about a month.

Q. Do you think men have to have something like this in their lives? Do you go along with the psychiatrist who says that this is "demonology," this whole thing we're doing?

A. I'm not sure what "demonology" might mean.

Q. Well, what about the psychiatrist you and Arthur went to? He, too, was, you said, a behaviorist, like the "demonology" man. What do you think of him? Was it worthwhile? Your interviews, your sessions with him?

A. You mean . . .

Q. His therapy.

A. His therapy? Yes. Very much so.

Q. What was the burden, what was the thrust of his therapy?

A. I think the thrust of his therapy was learning to tune in to yourself.

Q. To yourself? Or both of you?

A. To yourself. To *one's* self. And from that, the interaction between people would be affected.

Q. You know, you know what those sound to me like? All those words. Like empty phrases in a textbook. I'm sorry.

A. No, he always was concerned, during the course of family therapy, with not what someone did, but how someone felt. How you felt; how, how did I feel if Arthur would say something to me. When I came to him, Arthur and I, we were both very depressed.

Q. Uh-huh. And how long did you . . .

A. Arthur and I saw him for about a year.

Q. Do you think you have profited more from that therapy than your husband?

A. Yes.

Q. How do you assess yourself, briefly, now, as different from what you were? You said all your values have changed, all your . . .

A. My—my values are in *question.*

Q. In question. What *are* your values; what *were* your values?

A. I had a totally romantic point of view. I feel that I was very selfless, in terms of—I wasn't a person in partnership with someone else; I had sort of *fused,* and me, myself as a separate person, had ceased to exist. I think I was much too self*less.* And my concern always was for Arthur, or for what's good for Arthur.

Q. Now you worry more about what's good for you?

A. Now I'm aware of at least putting myself at equal importance, equal consideration. Or I try to be; it's still a battle, because it's still new.

Q. And you go to school.

A. Yes. And I work.

Q. Where do you work? What do you do?

A. Ceramics. Glazing, finishing, shaping, firing—things like that.

Q. Really!

A. That's new, too.

Q. Yeah, well, very good. [pause] You were quite interested just before we began this taping in one of the other men I'd interviewed, and what he had said.

A. I'm curious. I'm very people-involved. I'm very curious about people. I was wondering if he was—I know a friend of his—I don't know him, but I know one of his friends, one of his childhood friends, who seemed to feel that his marriage was not a bad one, although one never knows from the outside. And this friend felt that he was kind of anti-family now, and the relationship with his friend is very strained now. [pause] I think this has changed in Arthur's life, too. And I don't know where we are or where we're going.

Q. But you're going there together.

A. No, I really question . . .

Q. But you've determined that you're going there together.

A. I would *like* to; Arthur *says* he would like to, but his actions lead me to think differently. I think that his involvement in the advertising field, more and more, by dint of time that he's away, and we have almost no time at all together, or sharing anything—and by the things he's involved with now, and the people he's constantly involved with . . .

Q. You are not *sharing* now, despite the therapy?

A. Well, Arthur doesn't tend to talk, or to share nitty-gritty, and I think that this kind of thing, combined with the fact that you don't *have* very much time together, would have to lead to just separate lives. It comes to the point of, "Where do you touch?"

Q. In your going to school and in your work, if someone caught your fancy, would you take it seriously, would you pursue it, or do you still consider yourself totally dedicated to your husband?

A. I don't know any more.

Q. You don't know any more. Is there a danger there that if someone did, something might happen to you, you might have an affair?

A. It depends what's going on here, and how much I think there is a marriage here. Or caring. Or someone here for me.

Q. Uh-huh. And, er, you don't spend much time together during the week, this . . .

A. I don't see Arthur at *all!*

Q. Do you spend all your time together on weekends?

A. No, one of the days of the weekends he's not here. He's here, but he's not here. He set up an office in the basement and he works there all day Saturday. *All* day. And sometimes he spends evenings in the city, also.

Q. Not that my mind's always in the gutter, but this is a physically important part of this: Do you have an active sex life now?

A. Yes.

Q. After your scene last night, did you have sex last night?

A. Yes. Ironically, sometimes the—it's the only communication we have these days.

Q. That's terrible. It should lead to every other . . .

A. It's one of the main communications we *didn't* have, at first.

Q. And so it's now present in an almost perverse fashion.

A. Yes.

Q. Converse, or contradictory. Do you sometimes find yourself saying, in anger at yourself or at him. "Why did it take *this* to enjoy the sex life we have now?"

A. Yes.

Q. You have orgasms.

A. Oh, yes!

Q. Good. I mean, do you find yourself saying to yourself, "Well, why the hell did it take all this to achieve what we should have had together all our lives?"

A. Yes.

Q. When did your—was your sex life very active early in the marriage?

A. No.

Q. No. Was that because he was doing things like going to school, writing magazine pieces, working part-time for newspapers?

A. No. I don't think that had anything to do with it. I didn't know what the norm was, I didn't know what to expect.

Q. What is the norm?

A. I didn't know, perhaps, what to expect from myself. Or didn't know enough to want something for myself. I had some very idealistic, romantic delusions.

Q. And you did come to your marriage bed a virgin, is that right?

A. Yes.

Q. Was there any difficulty then? The first time?

A. I was frightened.

Q. You were frightened. Was it painful?

A. Er, I think more emotionally than physically.

Q. More emotionally. Was it embarrassing?

A. Yes.

Q. Yes. You have to do things—it's kind of outrageous, isn't it, the act? For the first time. Well, what else?

A. Well, what else do you want to ask?

Q. I don't know. I have no idea.

A. In some ways, I wish I knew then, when Arthur and I first met, what I know now. But, er. . . .

Q. What do you know now? You mean about sex?

A. I mean about sex, I mean about interaction, and all kinds of other things. I wish Arthur were more open with me, and . . .

Q. You mean you wish he had been then, right?

A. Yes, and had he been, I think we would have had a better marriage.

Mrs. C

Q. Let's start with some basics. Like how old are you?

A. Thirty-eight.

Q. And where were you born?

A. In New York City.

Q. And if you had to typify your background, how would you do so?

A. I would say typically middle class.

Q. Where did you grow up?

A. I was raised in Westchester by my aunt and uncle and I lived with them from nine months until the day I was married.

Q. Were your parents . . .

A. When I was very small my mother and father separated and it was decided that the best of all worlds was for me to live with my aunt and uncle, which I did. I mean that *was* my home and my aunt became my mother and my uncle became my father and I had very, very limited recollection of my real parents. *None* of my mother and very, very lightly of my father.

Q. Did they . . .

A. They were both deceased when I was a young child, about nine, tenish, around that age.

Q. Do you remember having any feelings of missing them, feelings of resentment toward them?

A. No. From nine months on I was in a closed, loving family and there was very little visitation. I mean, there was no pulling. I was just there and that was my home and I was sort of fortunate, and my aunt is an extremely extraordinary woman.

Q. How old is she?

A. She's eighty-six now. She was fifty when she took me in, and my uncle was fifty-three. They were delighted—ever since, I can always remember them saying, "What fun it was to have you come." It was a second childhood for them, because their children had grown. When I say my "mother" it technically is my aunt, and when I say . . .

Q. You must have been spoiled rotten.

A. No—I *wasn't!* I don't think I really was. When my dad— probably if anybody spoiled me, he would have, but he really didn't. But I was the apple of his eye. He was a very fine gentleman, and he died when I was a senior in high school. But my mother is still living and she lives in Westchester and I see her when she comes here to visit.

Q. Do you see her often?

A. Oh yeah, I'm on the phone with her, back and forth, and we visit. We're quite close. There was a time period, I think, when all kids go through this teen thing, when I was alienated. I couldn't wait to go away to college and was delighted to be away for four years and whatever, but when I started teaching school when I graduated and I lived at home for a year and—that wasn't—probably that wasn't too pleasant because I had, y'know, grown up and been away from home and whatever and that was a little hairy, I think. But, then I met Bill and I was married the second year I was teaching school and we lived close by—about five miles away.

Q. You had not known him before, but he was in that town?

A. No. It's very strange. I did not know him but we had many mutual friends. Bill went to college in Virginia and we knew people who had gone to those schools and whatever, but never had crossed paths. A mutual friend introduced us.

Q. Bill is how old?

A. He's three years older than I. He's forty-one now and I'm thirty-eight.

Q. When you first got married, I take it, you lived in the same town where you'd been brought up?

A. No, when we were married we bought a darling little house in Connecticut. A lovely little—and we lived there for a year and a half. Bill was an executive with [she names a major consumer-product company] and I was teaching school. And then he had the opportunity to buy his own agency in Pennsylvania. That's how I landed here. I'd never go back. And I taught school when I first came and got into the community real quickly and of course Bill, being a businessman, we were immediately swept into all the activities.

Q. This is a hard question to answer, but you must have done some thinking about it. Do you know why you married Bill? What attracted you to him?

A. What attracted me to Bill. [pause] He was just very special. And I had done a lot of dating. I went to college on a scholarship and I was required to maintain a "B" average to maintain the scholarship, and that's exactly what I did. Not one bit more, because I was busy just flying around and having a grand time. And I did that through most of my college years and when I was first teaching. And so I had had a lot of exposure to socializing and dating and whatever.

Q. Were any of those attachments sexual ones . . .

A. No.

Q. —or was it all sort of 1950's romance?

A. Oh, yeah. Absolutely.

Q. Lots of necking.

A. Yep. The classic. Right.

Q. Technical virgin.

A. Right. Absolutely. And when Bill came along he was very special and we got along beautifully and we did a lot of fun things together. We just seemed to hit of it off very well and we—let's see —we dated for a year, solidly, and then we were engaged for six months.

Q. Were you greatly attracted to him sexually, or you can't separate that from the other aspects?

A. Oh, yeah, I think I was. Very attracted to him, and him to me. I don't think if we weren't we would have married.

Q. But you didn't sleep together before you were married?

A. No, but that was my choice, not Bill's. [laughter] Oh, it's such fun to think back on those days, the 50's.

Q. When did Marc [their son] come?

A. Well, let's see. I was twenty-three when I was married and I wanted to finish teaching school and so we were very careful about me getting pregnant. And then toward the spring the third year that I was teaching . . .

Q. What were you teaching, by the way?

A. Third grade. And, uh, I wanted to complete the requirements for my permanent certificate. I really wanted to do that. And so my menstrual cycle was always cockeyed; nobody could figure it out. Sometimes three times a year, sometimes five times—just no rhyme or reason. But anyway we were very careful and then we decided, well, if anything happened now at least I would get through school but, just by the grace of God, just strangely enough, I had great difficulty and lost the baby. But I did finish school in late September. I lost a baby at six months and then I had two more miscarriages and then I went through a lot of testing—oh, they had just a grand time with my innards, but they never really—it just would not hold and they couldn't figure out why. So after two more miscarriages we decided that it was time to adopt. And which is just—it is just an exciting adventure. It's a very special thing. And I was thirty and Bill was thirty-three when we brought Marc home.

Q. Did you have a choice of a boy or girl?

A. Well, you do. Adoption is very open, with this agency. Bill very much wanted a boy and I was neutral, I didn't really care. And so it was fine with me. I mean anything was fine with me. Bill was pretty firm about that and Bill and I have said over and over if we took all the best genes of each of us put together we would never have come out with anything like Marc. He's just . . .

Q. You look very happy now. You . . .

A. Well, Marc is—if you got to know him, you'd—I think when you adopt a child you can probably feel freer to brag about him because it is a special thing.

Q. I take it, then, that things were going well between you and Bill.

A. Oh, yeah.

Q. Your sex life was going well?

A. Well, you know, I think Bill's and my—I really should go back and tell you a little bit about Bill. Bill, of course by the time we were divorced he was an entirely different person. When we first knew one another, when we were first married, Bill was very loving, very supportive, very sympathetic—uh, very much a homebody, but always full of fun and gaiety and laughs. You know, he was just a fine husband. I mean, just—reliable—the Rock of Gibraltar. If anyone had a problem, it was Bill he went to. Bill will figure it out; he will know what to do. Old reliable Bill. And this was pretty much what you would think of as Bill; just a kind of rock, like. And—but very independent, very ambitious. There is no holding him as far as ambition and ego goes. He—and it just got—it grew and it grew, and the more successful he was, this spread the fire of his ego and it just got to be a bonfire and he couldn't put it out.

Q. How successful *was* he?

A. Very. He's a very bright man as far as business, economics, finance, politics. He's just *good* at that kind of thing. Very quick, very quick to make a dollar, and can easily see this is not the right way to do it but *this* is, let's do it this way and boom! he's got a ten-thousand-dollar profit. Let's buy this piece of property because I know in fourteen days and three hours it's gonna be worth this much more. And you better believe that within an hour he's right! He's got an innate business sense. Unfortunately, he couldn't control it; he just allowed it to take over. Everything.

Q. Do you mean he was spending more and more time and less and less . . .

A. Oh yes, absolutely. It just got—when he left the company they were grooming him for a very big thing out West, at the headquarters. Everybody liked him; he's got a—he's a great guy, a good personality for dealing with people.

Q. When did he leave?

A. Well, we were married a year, so he was twenty-seven, I guess.

Q. And then he went into business on his own?

A. He had this opportunity to buy this agency here. And he left because he was making excellent money, he was making great strides, they were moving him and moving him, but he kept saying, "It really doesn't matter how good I am. If the slot is open. I'm not making that slot open. Somebody else has moved on, somebody else has left the company. I'm there so I'm a convenient piece to move up." And that did not really make him happy. He said, "I want to do it myself." And he did want to make good money. And although I suppose if he stayed with a corporation like that long enough you would make a good salary but he wanted to do it on his own and he wanted to do it quickly. So this little agency, he managed to buy it. We had saved some money and we bought a house when we were first married, we bought the house, and when we were engaged we spent our time fixing it up, refinishing antiques, and we had a reception in the house—it was a darling little house, just adorable old house—and it increased in value as he had predicted and all these things and we had equity on the house and had saved some money and had just enough, came to Pennsylvania and he bought the business and he bought this house, at the same time.

Q. This house?

A. This house. And I was teaching school and he started this business and he just knew that he would make a success of it, and he did. And he made money hand over fist.

Q. Did that leave him much time for you? I did ask how your sex life was during this period.

A. Well, it really didn't leave that much time for us. Some time, yes, but not really the time we had had in the beginning. But Bill was really more interested in building his empire and he was just absolutely uncontrollable as far as being determined that he was going to make this thing successful and make strong money. And he just put his whole self into it. And I mean his whole self. He worked. Well, I think anybody who begins a business has to understand that this is the way it's going to be. And I understood that and that was fine with me. I was teaching school. And Bill was happy doing it. And if Bill was happy I was happy. And I was very supportive, I guess, which looking back now I probably should have screamed a little louder and said, "Bill, you know, don't work this hard." I did, in a soft voice, and you cannot use a soft voice with Bill. It's very difficult to use a loud voice and have him hear you anyway. Bill really does what he wants to do anyway. If he get's a thing going there is nobody or anything that is going to stand in his way. And he bought land and he bought more land and then he built a new agency and the profits grew and grew. It then got very large. He probably had forty employes and he started a credit company that worked out of the same office but was a different corporation and he was a very successful businessman.

Q. Played hard and worked hard?

A. Didn't take much time to play, unfortunately. And you know we would have, we never really took time to go off anywhere until Bill was in a state of collapse. There was no saying, "Bill, you know, let's take a week here, a little care. You know, you're getting tired. Let's go to the shore." No. No. "I've got to do this. I've got the bankers tomorrow. I've got this. I've got this deal going." There was always something going business-wise. He is very business-oriented. Loves his home. Loves the trappings. But doesn't put his self into that. His self is really into the business.

Q. So you and Marc became sort of ornaments to a successful businessman.

A. I would say so.

Q. Not much of passionate intensity left for you after building those empires.

A. No. That's very true.

Q. Were you angry? How did you feel?

A. You know it's a funny thing. I wasn't angry, because Bill was happy. Of course, none of us knew the explosion that was going to take place because Bill along with this is a very strong individual and no one would ever think that—you know he was not a social rebel in any way.

Q. Not flamboyant or . . .

A. Oh, no. Business suits to work, Brooks Brothers and crew cut and very conservative.

Q. Rep striped ties?

A. Oh, yes. Absolutely. Very handsome, good-looking, successful businessman with an attaché case.

Q. At that time did he ever have any feelings against people who didn't conform? In this earlier period?

A. No. Bill just—he really didn't care about anybody else, what they did or what they didn't do. He was really wrapped up in just Bill. Really just Bill is the best way to describe it. You asked if I was angry. I really wasn't angry. I had—this was just fine with me. Because Bill was happy. And I'm very much a homebody and I had my home.

Q. Were you still teaching school? Or did you quit when you got Marc?

A. No, no, I stopped that. About two years before we—I stopped teaching. My days were filled. I never really felt left alone because Bill, although he's very independent and very wrapped up in himself, needs a lot of support and a lot of taking care of to perpetuate this thing. And that was fine with me. Because he was happy. Had Bill been unhappy that would have been a different thing. But he really wasn't. This was his bag and and I was content, you know—they talk about the liberated woman. I've never felt as though I needed to be liberated. I could come and go as I pleased. I could do what I wanted to do. Bill never said to me, "you know, you can't go to Philadelphia or New York, you can't go shopping or you can't go on a trip with so and so or don't do this." Bill was very open and very liberal about what I wanted to do or didn't want to do.

Q. And then, what happened?

A. And then what happened! Let's see. Then the economy—and I can't remember the year; I think it was '68, '69 was—when the economy started to slide. And again I must make a point; Bill is really pivotal to his business success. That is his self-image. And the economy started to shake. And Bill's business had grown so and Bill being a super-egotist his company was quite large and although he delegated responsibility he held the reins very tightly. And he was stretched very thin. And he was continually putting fires out. Which is—if you don't know anything about that business, it is really tough. It's very competitive—which he loved—but it can really get to you. And the economy started to slide and his business was stretched out thin, he was just stretched too thin and everybody, all his friends and I too, said, you know "Bill, you know you really just can't, when you're building a business you can put up with this for a year or two but you can't go on like this year after year I mean it's just— something has to give." And Bill would not listen. "No, no, no, I can do this, I can do this." And the business had its ups and downs and

Bill would have his ups and downs. And it was the down curve of business. And I had gone through this year after year with him, knowing, look, you know he's going to perk up in a little while and you know I could just predict pretty much what his personality and how his reactions are going to be about himself and what's going on in the world. And, uh, that spring we went to Hawaii for a few weeks. We went to Antigua for three weeks. When we went to Antigua he was in a state of collapse. He would say, "I've got to get out of here" and in two days we'd be gone. And I can tell you that if in three days we had not been gone he would have been—I mean, it would get that close. And it would always be his decision. He would never listen to anybody else. It was always that he would go and everybody else would get hysterical and run around the office. We'd be in a madhouse and then—pssht! off he would go. And the first week of vacation he would be a basket case. You would never see him. He would sleep and just, you know, be in our room. The second week he would be sort of coming back and by the end of the second week he'd be kind of normal and by the third week he'd be chomping at the bit and hysterical about what was going on at home and Hup! And that's how it went. So that summer he was kind of cantankerous and edgy and that kind of thing. And I attributed it to business: Here we go again. And then he started running around. Now I never even suspected it because Bill is not the—as I said, he's conservative, he's straight. He just completely slipped. Like you're talking to me, a normal gal, and if I came down that stairs five minutes later a blithering idiot. It just is like it almost happened overnight. It was *unbelievable!* He just—psssht! And he got involved. His business really started to slide. He started to run around. And, uh, he chose a hairdresser. A twenty-one-year-old dumb, *dumb* blonde! A long-haired, bleached-blonde hairdresser. I mean, just a typical tramp. And Bill is a boating enthusiast, and he decided he was going to rent a boat, and he went out and took the boat, and he said: "I have got to get away. I am going out of my mind. I wanna take this fella with whom I've been friendly for a while, and he'd like to get away too." And I thought, "Fine, Bill. If you wanna do that, that's okay." Well, I said, not knowing what was going on, and as it turned out, he went out with this gal, the swinger, and he also got involved with a man in town who's a complete antithesis of Bill except that they were both extremely successful businessmen. This Jack is absolutely a quaky man. He has just been married four times—uh, constant affairs, very flamboyant, throws his money around—a razzle-dazzle kind of a guy. And Bill in his state of mind got swept in with this guy.

Q. Is Jack older or . . .

A. The same age.

Q. They were both about thirty-seven, thirty-eight?

A. Right. But Jack has always been like that, that's the story of Jack's life. He's a real character. But handsome, successful, great-going business, very jazzy, very dapper, flamboyant. Bill went, umm, "This is great!" And he just flipped and went off with Jack. And they just did a lot of numbers together and, uh, I . . .

Q. What kind of things?

A. Oh, well, he'd, you know, come home late at night having been with Jack, and I knew immediately, when he got in with Jack I knew what obviously, what probably, was going on. You could not be with Jack and not get involved with some wild goings-on. And then, I will tell you, I *did* get hysterical. Because it was very—first of all, it was very unlike him, unlike Bill. Plus it isn't my life style. I mean, I just wasn't, you know, comfortable in that kind of thing. And—uh, there was no dealing with him, with Bill. He just began to drink a lot, and it got worse and worse. And finally he came home and decided he couldn't—he just couldn't love me any more. And I was upset. And he said, "I'm going off to live with Jack and I want a divorce." And his business was going badly. Nora, his secretary and bookkeeper, who was a Rock of Gibraltar, a real salt-of-the-earth kind of gal and has worked with Bill since we first came to Pennsylvania, she said, "You know, he's just not himself. He's—I cannot believe what's going on in the office. He was just running around here like another person."

Q. Was he into drugs at all?

A. Oh, no, no. Never. Too conservative. No, just drinking—drinking and girls. Lots and lots.

Q. Of both.

A. Right. Of both. And I'll tell you. When Bill sat down on that porch the first time and said, you know, "I'm going to leave," I was hysterical. I could not *believe* it! It was just like me saying I am going to stab you in the chest—*right now!* You would not be able to believe that I would do that. I just—I looked at him. I was dumfounded, and I said to him that day, I said, "Bill, you are going to be sorry you ever started this. You have some problems and you need help. But you do not need a divorce." "No, no," he said. "I want out. Nothing is right. Everything is wrong. I don't want to live with you any more. You love me more than I love you, and I can't live with this any more."

Q. Was it just that he accused you of, you know, that you loved him more than he loved you?

A. Right. That was it.

Q. He didn't call you a bitch, or a square, or . . .

A. Oh, no. He said, "None of this is your fault. I just am not in love with you."[laughter] I mean, it was *unbelievable!* You know, you think an intelligent, fairly bright, fairly savvy gal would be able to see this coming. But I didn't see. I really didn't see it. I excused it as part of his business ups and downs. Which, unfortunately, you know—it's just that it got to the point it got because it had a disguise. And so he left. I said, you know, "Don't do this. You're making a big mistake." And he said, "No, no. I'm leaving" and packed a few things and off he went. He said, "I'll keep in touch with you, and you know where I am. I'm at the office. But I'm leaving." And he did. Well, I can tell you I was one hysterical number. "What am I going to do with this?" I really didn't know where to turn. So I spoke with the couple across the street, he being a doctor, and they said he's just going through a thing. "Sit tight and see," they said. Well, Bill didn't call for a couple of days and I didn't do anything, but I was very upset. And then he called after a few days and just wanted to know if I was all right and Marc was all right and I said yes and then, after Bill called, Nora came here in the evening and she was the first one to know other than the Thomases . . .

Q. The Thomases?

A. Yes, the people across the street. And Nora said, "He is just completely irrational. He is not thinking straight." She said he is just not, you know, in the office half the time. She said, "I don't know how long this is going to go on, but this business can't stand that because it's not in good shape." The economy was shaky and whatever. And he just got worse and worse, and then he came home and said he wanted a divorce. And I said, "Bill, fine. You can have a divorce any time you want. But you can't have it unless you go and get some help. That's the deal. I'll give you one any time." He said, "No, there's nothing wrong with me. I'm just fine, you know, and you're just a fool and unhappy and upset and I'm fine." And I said, "Well, that's the deal, Bill." And he would not go. And, uh—I cannot remember how long he was away. Maybe two months. And I would see him once in a while.

Q. Was he still seeing the hairdresser during this period?

A. Yes.

Q. How did that make you feel?

A. Oh, well, at that point I didn't know about the hairdresser. I knew that there was—that he must be socializing in a very flamboyant way, having anything to do with Jack. I was sure he was sleeping around and whatever. I did not know specifically about this hairdresser until later, when he told me. Then he got very upset and, uh, decided he would go to a psychiatrist because that was the only way he could get a divorce. The next thing was to find a good shrink. And again my good pal Dr. Thomas said, "There is only one good man in the area that really is going to be able to help you." So I called the psychiatrist, Dr. Dawson, and explained the situation somewhat and he said, "Why don't you come down?" So I went down and I explained pretty much what was going on with Bill—you know, his behavior patterns, and he was a just acting like a lunatic. He was just not like anybody I even knew. And here I lived with this man for X number of years. I just couldn't believe it. And meanwhile Jack Clark comes calling at the house and is making passes at me and thinking he'd like to sack in here a little bit. I mean, the whole thing was so bizarre! I am a fairly straight gal and all these weird things are flying around me. So then we went to Dr. Dawson and I explained the whole thing and then Bill went to him and then Dr. Dawson said, "I'd like to see you together." Well, Bill was very negative. He was willing to go only to get out of his marriage, which was fine with me if this was the way I was going to get him to a doctor.

Well, Bill went because—well, you know you can't get a divorce just like that; you've got to try a little of this and a little separation and so on before you get your little piece of paper. And Bill knew he was going to have to go through something. So he said, "Well, I'll come." I had, in the interim, taken him back. He was then home.

Q. Had he wanted to come back?

A. He came back.

Q. What did he say when he came back?

A. Uh, "Let's try again." Then he took off again. And Dr. Dawson said to me, "You have a choice. You can take him back again." Because by this time I was getting hysterical.. Plus there were two going large companies that were being run by a skeleton of people. The rumors all over town were just rampant. I mean, he was, you know, not discreet in the least.

Q. Like what sort of things did he do?

A. Oh, he was just running around with all these women and having a great . . .

Q. Younger women?

A. No, not often. I think, just anything in a skirt that looked attractive. And I think it was a big sexual thing feeding his ego. Plus he knew his business was going down when he was building his ego by a woman.

Q. What had happened to your sex life while all this was going on?

A. Well, goodbye, Zoop! But, you know, it's a funny thing, when you get that upset you don't think about sex. You really worry, you're concerned, you're not thinking about yourself or about sex. Or at least I wasn't. It's not any great loss at that point because you're—I was not thinking about myself. I was thinking, "my God, what am I going to *do* about this guy? He's gone berserk." Dr. Dawson said, "Look, you have a choice. You can take him back." But Bill was not quite ready to come home. He was living with this Jack Clark that was really bad news. He rented a little house down maybe two miles from here. And I knew the minute he was by himself that that would be it. That he wouldn't even last a week there. And he got really frantic. And he called me that night and said, "Please let me come home." I didn't quite know how I was going to handle this business thing because I am completely the opposite of Bill as far as business. I couldn't even balance a checkbook. All I did was write the figures out. I didn't even know how much was in, how much came out. I didn't know how to run a house. I didn't know anything about the bills. I'm thinking, "My gosh, here's these two businesses going down the drain. I know nothing about it and if Bill is here at least there will be some semblance." And Dr. Dawson said, "You know, I've spoken with you enough to know that you are a very stable individual and I think between the two of us we can handle it. But you've got to know that you're in for a very rough time and this is going to be worse before it gets better." So Bill called that night and he was just hysterical. He was beside himself. He said, "Will you let me come home?" So I said yes. I knew as soon as he got by himself, when he had time to think even for one minute, it would hit him. So he came home and I spent one year with him at home that I will never forget as long as I live. It was as Dr. Dawson had predicted: it was really rough.

I cannot tell you what a nightmare it was. It was just unbelievable. And of course that was upsetting for Bill because he had rejected me, his girl-wife, and now all of a sudden he was wrapped—when we slept at night he was wrapped around me like a snake around a palm tree. I mean, I couldn't breathe. It was just wild. And here was Mr. Independent, Mr. Strong, Mr. Have-All-the-Answers, Mr. Successful, all of a sudden I got this withering man who is just hysterical. I mean—he really did just a complete turn. So we got him through most of that, and the business went down. We got him thinking enough to where he made the decision that the businesses were to be sold. And they were sold at a very healthy profit. Had they been sold in the beginning it would have been twice as healthy a profit. And that was a very shattering blow. And he would go and negotiate and these men would come and they were buying a big company. The credit company. And Bill wasn't really equipped to do it, but he had to do it, and he would go down and fight this thing for an hour and then he would come home and collapse, and I would feed him a good meal and put him to bed, both build up his ego and send him into the next thing. This went on for about three weeks. I can tell you it was a nightmare. And finally the companies were sold and Bill then was pretty much—he was happy to be home and he was not a happy individual, but he was happy that he had somebody to take care of him, and at that point I really *was* taking care of him. I was hardly a wife; I was just nurse and mother and supporter, and he was really very appreciative and very content and very happy and very loving about it. And he continued to see Dr. Dawson, and when he got stronger, then again he was not so happy. He kept blaming the home life and blaming me because he felt that his relationship with me was why his business had failed. [pause] Oh, then it was not me, like I-hate-you kind of thing; he never said that. He always said he felt that the marital thing was the thing that was wrong because that was the easy thing to attack.

Q. In what way did he blame it?

A. In what way did he blame it? He just felt that it—he was unhappy and he didn't know why he was unhappy and he felt it must be the marriage.

Q. Did he think the marriage was limiting him in some way?

A. No, I don't think he felt that it was limiting him. I think he just—he was not willing to admit that he had stretched himself too far businesswise. His ego was such that he was really Bill and the business was Bill and when that failed he was a very upset man and did not want to admit that it was the business end of it. The easiest thing to attack was the marriage. So the stronger he got the more unhappy he got and Dr. Dawson counseled with him. And that was when we got into an encounter thing, which was a wild event. Talk about just bizarre happenings! I thought I could see through everything. Dr. Dawson said, "You know, these encounter things sometimes help you to see yourself through others' eyes," and of course he was not about to accept anything *I* said, so, and he said, "If you want to, you can go along on this thing." So I was not too happy about going, but I was really afraid to let Bill go by himself. Because after, I betcha he's going to come home with all these ideas and reports and I'm having no frame of reference on this thing. I'd better go along and see what this number's all about. Well, it was really just incredible. It was a—just a wild thing. It was a group of maybe nine or ten really sick people, and I found that they all started to gravitate towards me. And I felt like I was the only—listen we've all got problems, but not like *these* gals and men! They were really all hysterical mental cases. They'd all been under psychiatric treatment for years and years. They're all lonely, unhappy, sad, searching, forlorn people. And it was quite an experience. And I figured when I went, I thought let the feathers fly; what's going to happen is going to happen. That's what encounter is all about and I am just going to go along with this and whatever happens, happens. Well, a lot of things happened. As I said, those people were really quite ill. And Bill got into a physical altercation—Bill's not a physical type that would ever get into a fistfight, I mean he just isn't like that. And he got into this physical altercation with this guy where they both pounded each other and rolled around and wrestled. I remember sitting there thinking, "Am I really *seeing* this? I mean, is this *me* sitting watching this wildness?" These people, you know, watching and saying "Yes," "Noooo," "Yes," "That's good," and "He's working this out" and, uh . . .

Q. Can you remember what Bill got into the fistfight about?

A. You know, it's a funny thing. He was groping with someone on the floor. They got to that touching number. You know, everybody touches and gets reborn and that kind of thing. There was a little—they get to be very affectionate and very supportive and very loving to one another. And, uh, this is what happened. And this one thirty-year-old gal was there and she had marital difficulties and had gone back and forth from her husband several times and ended up with Bill on the floor and they were kind of loving it up. Just hugging a lot. And I watched that too.

Q. How did that make you feel?

A. I thought that was a very sick scene. I think that if a wife walks into a room and sees her fairly normal husband having an affair with a woman, that's one thing. Then you're going to be angry and going to be put out. But when you're dealing with a man who really is not himself, whom you have brought through a very bad time and are sort of putting him on his feet, it's a whole different bag. It is not the same thing. You are, uh, much more analytical and supportive. It's very interesting because I'd say more than half of the people in this encounter group really attacked Bill. And called him pompous and who did he think he was. He wasn't an honest individual, he didn't really say what he was thinking—that kind of thing. That, of course, is not Bill's image of himself. I remember he was sitting in a chair, everybody was sitting around in a circle and Bill just happened to land in a chair. And two of the people—now you have to remember these people have been on encounter thing after encounter thing. It's a whole—So, uh, because Bill was sitting in the chair and everybody else was sitting around they felt that he had sat in the chair because he felt he was above everyone. And I personally think that kind of thing is a lot of crap. But this was the kind of thing, was how that group went. I really think Bill just happened to land on the chair, but they chose that particular thing and then they went on from there. And Bill had—I'm trying to think what he was wearing—it was a sort of, maybe a button-down shirt or something casual, but it wasn't a tee shirt.

Q. By the way, did he change his style of dressing when he was living with Jack Clark?

A. No, no.

Q. So he was living a different life-style but he was still hanging on to the surface patterns of the old one.

A. I think so. Right, but living different.

Q. He didn't start going in for purple shirts or tight trousers?

A. Oh, no, no. I'd remember it if he did. [pause] So that was pretty much that field, but it was quite an experience, and when we came home we talked to Dr. Dawson about it and unfortunately Dr. Dawson got an opportunity to head up a huge mental clinic in California and he never really got to—he was really getting Bill on his feet when he left. And it was not good for Bill and me that whole time thereafter. It was rocky. Bill was not working and Dr. Dawson had said that Bill had made a nice bundle a of money and built up a fairly good source of money and had some good income properties, et cetera, and had no financial problems. And wasn't he fortunate that he could elect to do anything he wanted. You know, *anything*. And Bill said no. "I am not going to start at the bottom of the totem pole ever." And an opportunity came along where someone, some businessman, heard about Bill and he said, "Bill, I need you, somebody like you who has run a successful deal, to run my place for me." Offered him a fantastic salary and ten per cent of the overall profit of the company. Which is a lot of money believe me. That company was really going strong. And of course there was the old dollar bill and there was the old ego and "Boy, I'll be boss again and I can run this thing," and I remember sitting down and begging him, "Bill, don't do it. You are going to be in the same kettle of soup you were before." "No I'm not, I am not, if my money isn't tied up in it." "Well, Bill, your money isn't tied up in it but you're going to be tied up in it," and I said it is going to be a disaster. And I said, "good, you're going to be away three nights a week" and he said, "Well, I'm gonna do it. And furthermore I'm buying another boat." We have owned fairly good-sized boats and an airplane and I mean Bill is a toy buyer. He loves things. The things that money can buy he loves. And we owned airplanes, as I say, and boats and most expensive cars, et cetera. And he would have them for a little while and then he'd get bored with them and move on to the next. So now he decides he wants a houseboat. He's going to pull it up on the river and he's going to live on the houseboat. Just two nights a week or three nights a week when he has to work late at night. I know that this is disaster written all over the wall.

Q. How was your marriage going at this point?

A. Pretty neutral. Neutral.

Q. Not much sex, not much anything.

A. No. Pretty neutral.

Q. No fights?

A. No, no. No big fights. Uh, you see, unfortunately you know these things too late. I really made a mistake in thinking that Bill because he was happy in his business, and, as I said, it's a real hassle . . .

Q. Yeah, my father was in the merchandising business for years . . .

A. Oh it's a hassle. I had a fine station in life and I was very happy to do this and, you know, it was great and I was happy. I made a happy nest for Bill. When Bill came home there was a drink waiting for him, his dinner was cooked just the way he liked it, his bed was made, his underwear was . . .

Q. Right.

A. The housewifely goody things. His entertaining was done just the way he wanted to do it. The people he wanted to have were invited. In fact, my whole life really revolved around Bill. But by my choice. I was happy doing that because I thought Bill was happy. And as Dr. Dawson said, "Your problem is that you are a giver and Bill is a taker. And that does not make you good or him bad but together it is disaster." And it's really true. If the problem were to be in a nutshell that would probably be it. And unbeknownst to me I was just feeding this thing by being the kind of person I was.

Q. What do you mean?

A. Well, I was supportive and giving and he was taking and not thinking about giving. He didn't have to think about the give and take because I was always there. You know, with no demands or screaming or yelling or whatever, because I always thought, "Yuuh, he's got enough hassle at the office, you know, that isn't really what this man needs."

Q. Did you ever get to a point where you said to yourself, "I'm sick of giving, you know, how about me?"

A. No. I did not. I really and truly did not. And that is why I wasn't angry. I was just thinking, I was really content. Well, anyway, so Bill goes and buys the houseboat. Well I knew . . .

Q. Let me interrupt you. When you say you were content, you mean during the early . . .

A. Yeah. I'm not content when Bill is hysterical and flying around and acting like a bat out of—no I'm not content. But I'm not angry with him. I'm upset and I am thinking what can I do to make this thing right. Something has got to turn here. And I am continually trying and Bill then is really beginning to think about Bill again. Now I am on to this pattern because I've seen it and I've been through this thing with Dr. Dawson and Bill and Dr. Dawson has explained to me why Bill's reacting this way. You know, "The best thing to get him out of this is to do such and such." So now I am becoming a wizard of a psychiatrist. Well. So, I begged him not to do this thing. "Yes I am doing it. And that's it!" And this was pretty . . .

Q. Did you get angry during these—say the conversation about the houseboat?

A. Yeah, that I was angry about. I said, "Bill, this is wrong. I know I [sic] am wrong. And, you, I am angry because you're not listening to me. You just won't listen." I can't understand it. But he really—that did make him angry. It did not make me angry that he was happy to go back to work, this was too prompt, because he was then ready to do something and he needed to do something. And I was happy to have him do something. I was not happy to have him do that. But he was not willing to, you know, be a learner or start-over kind of a person. He wanted to be a success and making a lot of money and being a boss. As he'd been used to before. And giving the orders rather than taking them. So he went and he took that job. Well, it was not long thereafter that it, you know—if there were seven steps for Bill to get off the deep end he was already on the fourth and it was just the same thing step by step by step, that's all. Forget it! I cannot go through this again.

Q. Jack Clark? Girls? Drinking?

A. Well, that had somewhat . . .

Q. He wasn't seeing the hairdresser?

A. Oh, no. She was impossible. But it was not good between us, because I could see the same identical pattern beginning to evolve. And this time the smart—I mean, I knew what was happening.

Q. What particulartly, how did you see him change again?

A. Well, I could see that he was short-tempered, he was not coming home. He would call me at 8 o'clock and say, "Gee, I've gotta work until 9, I'll sleep on the houseboat tonight." And he wanted to associate with people that I really did not approve of. There was a couple up the hill. Both alcoholics. Both teachers. And bad news. I mean, I just I cannot tell you how ugly alcoholics can be. I mean just falling all over and sick and drunk. That really is not my bag. They ruined probably three really nice dinner parties that I had here, knocking wine glasses over and just hanging all over men. She would be over the men and he would be over the women and that kind of thing and I really just—I have no patience with that kind of thing. That kind of thing made me mad. I thought, you know, this is just not ever going to work. I just can't live like this. I went down all summer long, every weekend I went down, Friday, went down on that houseboat, spent the weekend on that rotten tub. Beautiful boat, but I was not happy on that boat, on that pukey old river, when I could be up at the lake here, the beautiful clear crystal lake, swimming. And you couldn't swim in the river, you couldn't do anything but stay on the boat. And I did that all summer because I figured when this thing blows—and I was pretty sure it was going to blow —I am not going to say to myself, "I didn't do this, I didn't try that, I was a creep about this because I didn't consider that Bill wanted to be on the boat. He needed a rest and whatever." And I really did. I went on that damn boat every weekend. And he would come home once in a while during the week and—and one night he went up to those drunks.

Q. Up on the hill?

A. Right, yes. And I had a shower to go to, and I said, "I'll be back about 9, 9:30," and I came home early and I looked around, and Bill was not there. And he took Marc and had gone off there So I called. And I got the wife on the phone, and I said, "Tell Bill I am home and I want to get Marc to bed," and that was that. And Bill didn't come home. They were drinking and having a good time and Bill rolled in here at 2 in the morning. And Marc was walking sleepily up that winding stone walk with a blanket wrapped around him, you know, kinda groggy and sleepy, and Bill was crocked. And I thought, "I have *had* it! That is *it!*" And I will never forget that picture. When Marc was drawn into it, I mean, I visibly saw a very ugly thing. He was irresponsible as far as Marc had gone, you know, driving down this crazy road at 2 in the morning. Then I was angry. I guess the motherly instincts surfaced. I was furious! There was no dealing with him because how can you deal with somebody who's gassed? I mean, he knew I was mad, but there was no settling or discussing anything. So I really let him have it the next morning. I was really angry. When you say angry, I then was *angry!* And I pretty much limped through the rest of the summer and I began to think there were gals on the boat. There very well might have been. I really—I have done whatever I could do to put this marriage together, to hold it together. I have done—I have run the gamut and there is really nothing left for me, there is nothing left for me to do. And I'm not about to live like this. I don't need this aggravation. And I cannot raise Marc in a situation like this. So I said—Oh, we went to New Hope with some friends who have a beautiful home out there and Bill was obnoxious all weekend. He was drinking most of the weekend. You know, this was part of the pattern. He was disturbed and upset and guilty and all these things and he was working long hours at this place and making good money and . . .

Q. He was guilty about the women on the boat?

A. I think he was very guilty. Yeah, I think he was very unhappy.

Q. A lot of them, or one?

A. Well, I think there were—quite a few. There were more than one, but there was one major one that I later learned about.

Q. What was she like?

A. Hello, tramp! Loved his money, loved his boat. I think she eventually—I think she was very fond of him, and probably loved him, but the thing that really attracted her was his money.

Q. Was she younger?

A. Oh, late twenties, two children, divorced.

Q. But a little classier than the hairdresser.

A. Not much, not really very much. [pause] So we came home from New Hope. I'd really had enough of this weird behavior and it's just going in the same direction and I'd really—I know what my wants are and I can't go through this again. I just can't. I've given all I've got. So we sat down and decided that that was it. And—we pretty much came to the thing together. You know, it wasn't—Bill wasn't saying, "I'm leaving" and I didn't say, "You're getting out." But—it—it was a mutual thing. This is it. And then Bill left. And I was not angry, but I was really—Oh, I was very unhappy. I—it was the end of it, of a very—of what had been a very happy marriage at one time.

Q. Would you like to be married again? If not to Bill?

A. Well, I'll tell you. Everybody I know says, "You can't live the rest of your life by yourself. You're too great to be—you should be somebody's great wife." In the beginning I said I will never be married again. I really have *had* it. I am worn out. I was exhausted. I weighed 103. There was just nothing left of me. And I thought for one solid year I really just—I didn't care about going out, my friends were just frantic. They said, "This isn't normal. You're so bubbly and gregarious." I just couldn't have cared less. I just wanted to be left alone and kind of regroup my forces, and just be quiet and be out of any kind of hassle. Because that divorce was unbelievable. It just went on and on and on and we divided up the property and whatever and first Bill would say yes he wanted a divorce, and then he didn't want it. When it got to the point where it looked like the papers would be signed, I remember my lawyer saying, "You've got to serve

Bill with papers." Well, Bill was not about to stay in the state. His lawyers had said don't do it. And I said, "Well, Bill's not going to come into Pennsylvania," and my lawyers said, "You're going to have to get him to come." And I said, "You know, if he's not going to come, how am I going to get him to?" "Well, you know, tell him Marc is sick or something." You know, it's just not in me to lie, and make up some story to get him into the state. And the lawyer said, "I know that's not what you're like and I know that goes against your grain, but there is nothing else you can do. You have got to serve this man." And that's the ugly part you get involved in.

Q. Has some of that ugliness rubbed off on your feelings toward Bill? Is some of the ugliness now connected with him?

A. No, because if I called Bill tomorrow and said, "Bill, I've got a problem," he'd be here in a minute. No—that was the only time I have ever lied to Bill in my life and I—he, uh, said, "Have you been to a lawyer?" And I said no. I wanted to tell him. That was probably the hardest thing I did. Very [her voice cracks and she begins to cry] upsetting.

Q. I can see you're not the sort of person who . . .

A. No, that really went against my grain. That it was just, uh, there was—I understood that it had to be done, but it wasn't a logical thing. And he said, "I'm coming up to see Marc" and I said, "Fine. When will you be here?" And he said, "Oh, Thursday or Friday." That was about five days, and we set the whole thing up and got the papers going and everything, and you've got to have a sheriff serve the papers. And that's the way it went.

Q. Were you there when the sheriff served the papers? What did Bill say?

A. That really was the hardest because [she sobs, and it gets to me, too]—because—he just looked at me and he—It was just like I had stabbed him. I mean he knew that the divorce was coming and he knew that something had to be done and it had to be worked out. But he never ever thought I'd ever do anything like that. That was really the hardest. Harder than the leaving, the deciding to get the divorce or the Marc thing. No, I won't say that. Just having [her voice breaks again]—just ugly, really ugly. And I have not been involved in too many ugly scenes before this one. Anyway, [pause] anyway, all is now forgiven and everything. I mean, we understand that that's the way it had to be. But I can't [her voice drops almost to inaudibility] forget the expression on his face. He just couldn't believe I had done such a thing. And believe me, I did it. [pause] You know, you asked me if I would want to get married again. And you know, I really did not have any feelings of aggression toward him, or real anger. It was just a very sad, vacant kind of feeling.

Q. Do you still feel that vacancy?

A. Well, when I think about being in a married situation, or being single, I think there probably is a vacancy. I have made a very good adjustment, at least I feel I have, and my friends feel I have, but— oh! You asked would I ever marry again. In the beginning I said I would never marry and I'm not sure I would, because I just would not want to leave myself open for any kind of a situation. Being realistic, it probably would not be that kind of situation ever, you know, not your everyday situation. I know about marriage and I don't think I could go through that kind of thing again. I really don't. And you asked me about Bill. Bill's a lot better now. You know, we have discussed this out and he said, "Everything you said was right. Why wouldn't I listen? Why couldn't I listen?" And I said, "Bill, at that point in your life you couldn't." He just didn't have any sensitivity or any understanding about himself or anything. And now I think he does. And I think he'd like to remarry me. If I could remarry the old Bill, with the knowledge that the old Bill has gained . . .

Q. With the knowledge that the old Bill was going to remain.

A. Right. Not the old Bill, because I'm sure he'd go through the same cockamamie thing again. But I if I could remarry the fun-loving, sweet Bill I once knew, with tolerance and with the understanding and the maturity that he has gained from this disaster, it would be different. You know, as I said, I really love Bill and I think I did the right thing for all of us. We have a good relationship. I won't say I never will remarry him, but if he called me tonight, no. Because he's got a handle on it, but he hasn't turned the handle over. But he's a much better person than he was. He's had to feel a lot of pain. He's had to face himself. He's done a lot of sitting at night by himself thinking about who the hell am I? How have I gotten this way? And many is the night he has called on the telephone very depressed and upset and I talked it out with him and made him do a little thinking, and he will say, "Why didn't I listen?" And I say, "Well, you're listening now, aren't you?"

Miss A

Q. How much education did you have?

A. High school.

Q. Is your education continuing in any way?

A. No, unless you want to call the bar business continuing an education.

Q. Your marital status?

A. Single.

Q. Were you ever married?

A. No.

Q. What did you say your age was?

A. Thirty-two.

Q. All right. Look, if any questions offend, shock or turn you off, please don't hesitate to tell me, and tell me why. Now: What is your ethnic background?

A. Polish.

Q. Size of your immediate family?

A. Oh, there's three boys, my Mom, myself, and my father's passed away.

Q. When did your father die?

A. Daddy died about five years ago this coming August.

Q. Do you remember—and this is probably too early to ask this—any conflicts with any relative or member of the immediate family?

A. Sure. I don't talk to any of my relatives.

Q. Why not?

A. I can't stand them. They didn't put up for my father when he was passing away and they didn't put up for my mother when he *did* pass away. In other words, they didn't help Mom money-wise, and they're quite well to do.

Q. Is there any history of physical or psychological illness in your background?

A. It depends on who you ask. Myself, no. My family, no. But you talk to the headshrinker I was talking to a couple of months ago and he'll tell you I'm definitely sick.

Q. Did you go to this headshrinker for yourself?

A. No, this was because I'd gotten picked up on a drunk driving charge and I was going to that school for—er—what the—for, er, drunk—rehabilitation school. And they were giving me special pref- erence, and the man told me I was in definite need of psychiatric help, that was the only reason I drank. And *his* only problem is women and horses!

Q. How old is your mother?

A. Let's see—Mom is, I think she's fifty-three.

Q. Would you say you were the product of a happy home?

A. I guess . . .

Q. With steady parental support and guidance through your de- veloping years? Your developing years being one to twenty, roughly.

A. I guess it was no different from anybody else that came from a middle-class family. Father was first-generation born here, so I was brought up under strict Polish rule.

Q. What's Polish rule?

A. Sternness.

Q. Sternness. What's your father's line of work?

A. He was like a jack of all trades. He did a little bit of everything for this company—everything from mechanical work to carting around messages. He was—uh, he was there twenty-five years.

Q. He was doing this at the time of his . . .

A. His heart attack, yes.

Q. What work have you done, what kind of jobs have you had?

A. When I got out of school . . .

Q. When was that?

A. I got out of school in 1960. I was a bookkeeper for—God! I think I was there for about three, four, five years.

Q. Where?

A. At this place, it was a home-improvement company. Now I was there when I was twenty—eighteen, nineteen, twenty. At that time I had to leave the job.

Q. Why did you have to leave?

A. I was pregnant.

Q. Uh-huh.

A. Let's see—and then, after the baby . . .

Q. You did have a baby?

A. Oh, yeah.

Q. Where's the baby now?

A. I gave him up for adoption when I got—when—I had the baby when I was twenty-one. So I gave him up for adoption, I guess a couple of years ago.

Q. To a Catholic agency?

A. No, no, no, no—a private adoption. I didn't believe in seeing the baby sitting there. I didn't want any of that crap that's been happening in the papers about all of a sudden somebody claiming the kid back again. It was not for me, no. I know who the people are. I saw my baby until about—I guess it was about six years ago when he started to want to know who I was. And then it would get too complicated.

Q. Uh-huh. So you were a bookeeper and then you . . .

A. And then I went back to bookkeeping again after the baby. I worked in a machine shop. I was a bookkeeper there for, oh, about a year and a half before they made me assistant office manager. And from assistant office manager I went to assistant production—from office management I went to production control and, uh, I stayed there for about six years.

Q. This puts you up to about—what—twenty-eight or something?

A. Uh-huh. And then I worked for about a year in an upholstery shop. I was sort of a purchasing agent. I bought the materials and gave estimates on drapes and upholstery. I had a fight with the owners of the place.

Q. About what?

A. Well, I wanted Good Friday off and he wouldn't give it to me and . . .

Q. Are you a practicing Catholic?

A. No, it's a lie if I say I am. I'm a non-practicing Catholic.

Q. But you figure if for other people . . .

A. He takes off Yom Kippur and Rosh Hashanah and anything else and I wanted one day off. So we had a fight and I quit. I went back to, uh, to tending bar.

Q. You went *back* to tending bar? You haven't told me about tending bar yet.

A. Well, I used to tend bar part-time. I didn't think it was worth mentioning. Yeah, I've been tending bar now off and on, for about —since—Christ! since I'm about twenty-two, twenty-three. I found I could make extra money off the books. So now I'm just tending bar.

Q. How long have you been there?

A. Now it's a year.

Q. Are you happy there? Do you make enough to live on?

A. Extremely—extremely lucrative—believe me.

Q. Do you have interests other than work and all the other things we . . .

A. Oh, I like traveling.

Q. Traveling?

A. Yeah, I like to go places. I enjoy meeting people.

Q. How far from home have you traveled? Oh!—Where were you born?

A. In Queens. While I was in production control for the machine shop, which was mainly their expense, I was to New Mexico, Utah —oh, Christ, where else? Canada, Buffalo. And, uh, West Virginia, Virginia, North Carolina, South Carolina—not too much Midwest, though. Either very very East or—I've been in the Bahamas . . .

Q. What other interests? Do you sew? Play the piano? Do you . . .

A. Truthfully, I—it really isn't too much. I just seem to have so much to do all the time I've never thought about it. Like if we weren't here now I'd be—I'd be over to see Barbara, or . . .

Q. Who's Barbara?

A. A girlfriend of mine.

Q. Uh-huh.

A. And we'd, ah, go out to lunch, go shopping, if you want to call that an interest.

Q. It's an interest.

A. Reading, I think, is a—a lot for me.

Q. What do you read?

A. Anything.

Q. What's anything?

A. Well, all right, I . . .

Q. Mysteries?

A. Mysteries I enjoy because they're short and it doesn't take too much longer and I don't have to concentrate on it.

Q. What books that are not mysteries have you read this year, for instance?

A. Oh, good Lord! *The Exorcist*—did I pronounce that right? Yeah, whatever it is—and I read a lot about Judaism. Don't ask me why. I find it more re—maybe it's because I've had Catholicism shoved down my throat so long and I didn't know enough about Judaism.

Q. You found out there's very little difference, really.

A. Basically, basically there's no difference.

Q. All right. Comes to a rather difficult question. This interview will be used in a chapter called The Women Speak, meaning the women who have had affairs with men older than they are. So many, if not most, of the questions, are going to deal with sex. I hope you don't object to that.

A. No, I don't object to it. I live with it every time I go to work.

Q. Yeah, well, I have to determine before we go any further whether you have had such affairs.

A. I'm going out with a man now that is twenty years my senior. If I can help, fine.

Q. Well, let's start this way: what can a younger woman learn from such a man? You're thirty-two, he's fifty-two, right?

A. He's gonna be fifty-two this month.

Q. Can a younger woman profit spiritually, psychologically or culturally from an affair with an older man? If so, how?

A. Well . . .

Q. Think carefully.

A. Let's see. Socially, we have no social life as far as his friends go, which of course is only natural considering he's married. So most of our social life is based right here rather than in Bayonne [New Jersey].

Q. He lives in Bayonne?

A. Yeah. Other than going out and eating good—and he makes a good buck—we go to the plays, go to nice places. I dress well.

Q. You go to the theater?

A. Well, we haven't been recently. I think the last one we went to see was, my God!—I don't know if it was "Fiddler on the Roof" or whadayacallit—what's the one with, uh, Don Quixote?

Q. "Man of La Mancha."

A. Right. "Man of La Mancha." But, uh, what else can he offer me? He offers me the opportunity to work only twice a week. I'd be a liar if I . . .

Q. He supports you?

A. Oh, yeah. I have a lot more free time on my hands. I have extra money on my hands. And I also know the outcome of our affair.

Q. I'm going to get to a question involving that. Meanwhile, is this place solely yours?

A. Right. In my name, yes.

Q. And I have to ask you this: You and Mr. X meet here?

A. Oh yes, he virtually lives here. He doesn't sleep here at night but he's here every night for his dinner.

Q. He's unhappily married, I assume?

A. I don't know if he's unhappy. Apparently both of them just haven't been getting along, I presume. We've been doing this now for five and a half years.

Q. Pretty steady.

A. I do not imagine his wife is foolish enough to think he's out just working constantly to 3, 4 o'clock in the morning.

Q. Doctors have told me that many women prefer such quote *older* men . . .

A. I don't know why.

Q. —socially.

A. Socially? What for?

Q. Wait a minute. Let me finish the question. I mean this is not necessarily my opinion; this is what I've been told by these other people I've been talking to. That they prefer them socially and even sexually than younger men because the older men are more confident, less awkward, less demanding, sometimes even preferable sexually to younger men, younger men being oriented to the orgasm. To the older man, I've been told, that is not the be-all and end-all of sex; they tend to prolong the act itself, to the greater pleasure of the woman.

A. [Laughing] Did you talk to a female doctor or a male doctor?

Q. Male doctor.

A. Yeah, well, tell 'im he's full of shit. I have news for you. There's—Burt is no different—all right, he's twenty years my senior, and of course, as you can conclude, this is not my first affair. I've been with guys younger than myself that've been better than him. He's just as awkward in bed as a younger guy is. And if anybody thinks so—I don't give a damn if they're twenty or if they're fifty. A man is a man, period. He never outgrows his babyhood.

Q. Is that possibly because the woman abets this—by abet, meaning helps along, expects him to play this role?

A. No. When Burt and I first went to bed we were awkward with each other, just the same as any other affair. The only reason we're compatible at it now is we've been practicing a long time.

Q. Unless—and I've found this to be true—there's a great deal of this catalyst [pointing to her cans of morning-after beer] here.

A. Not particularly. Burt is not a drinker. I drink. In fact, if he came in now and found me having a beer, there'd be all hell to pay. No, we do not need booze to get ourselves sexually oriented.

Q. I'm not saying you do; I'm saying that in such affairs, maybe the *first* time, it's usually there. At a party, a . . .

A. No, see, I used to work for Burt. He was my boss, and the first day I worked there I made up my mind I was going to go out with him. So I guess I was the aggressor in that. Matter of fact, he was sitting there, he was afraid to ride me home from work, for cryinoutloud! He was not the aggressor. He did not chase after me by any means.

Q. Had he done this before?

A. Oh, yes. He was going out with a girl when he was going out with me.

Q. Would you say this was a kind of way of life, a style of life, for him?

A. Yes. He's basically a one-woman man. He had been going out with this other woman who was about his age.

Q. And even in such things a man a can still be a one-woman man, even if he has a household and he has—Look, you just spoke about . . .

A. All right, look, all right. First of all, what I just said, when I met Burt, I did not know he was going out with this other woman. He had been going out with her for several years, before his son was born, and at that time his son was twenty-four. She had gone to his bar mitzvah. So you figure from thirteen. When I finally broke that up . . .

Q. Broke what up?

A. Well, you don't think I'm gonna let him—you can't split a man three ways. Two ways I can understand, but three ways, I . . .

Q. Yeah-yeah-yeah.

A. To this day, even though he spoke of leaving his wife, which I sincerely doubt, she is still afforded the style she's always had. You know, he's *never* begrudged her money, her way of life—although he does live his own way of life.

Q. Give me a brief appraisal of his way of life, that you spoke of.

A. All right, now: Burt comes here every night after work; he has his dinner; after dinner, we sit around and we watch TV, we may encounter sex or not. I guess it's like, like a married couple would be! He goes inside and watches the football game, I stay and watch mine on TV, and around II . . .

Q. You have two of them here?

A. Yes, that's the only way we can get over the football fight. So at 11:30 he leaves here, he goes back to Bayonne. I do not believe Burt is sleeping with his wife. I could be wrong, I'm not there. Gets up, goes to work, comes over here at night, has his dinner.

Q. So he's a sports-loving guy, a perfectly normal man as far as . . .

A. We just live like any normal person would live that was married. We go out for dinner once a week. I clean. I do his underwear, do his shirts—I send them to the Laundromat. Believe me, just like anybody else.

Q. You talked about the household you have here, which is perfectly normal, satisfying for both of you, you answer each other's needs, et cetera. Right?

A. Correct.

Q. What about marriage? Now this is the capital-M marriage, as an institution, as opposed to sexual freedom. I read an article quoting a man who is married but pretends that his wife is his woman, in company . . .

A. I can understand that.

Q. All right. As saying that, quote, it isn't, just isn't, *in* to be married these days. This same article tells of a group of executives discussing a guy for promotion. And they turn him down because he's happily married and, quote, hasn't got the guts to play around.

A. That's stupid.

Q. Then it mentions people that enter into marriage contracts. He'll pay his bills, she'll pay hers, how many kids they'll have, who'll take care of the housework. And it said that people do sign these things. Like leases. What do you think of that?

A. Well, the guy who introduces his wife as his mistress is just afraid—he just wants to go along. He's got to be part of the group. He's just—he doesn't have the balls to say, "This is my wife and I'm happy with her." You talk about the group of executives that sit there and, uh, discuss this gentleman for a thing, but say he doesn't have the balls to do it because he's happily married; they're fulla shit because *they* ain't. They're just jealous of the fact that this poor man . . .

Q. Yeah, but they *think* it's the thing to do. They're afraid . . .

A. Too many people think . . .

Q. Of course they're afraid of each other—right?

A. So many people think it's the thing to do that they ruin it for everybody else. There's nothing wrong with—I believe in marriage, believe me. I believe in marriage. I myself don't know if I could live with marriage 'cause I've been single too long. This may be why I am not . . .

Q. But you are, you *are* married.

A. No, no, listen to me for a second. I am, but I'm not. I get away with more than any married woman could ever get away with. If I want to go down to the bar for a couple of drinks, I go. If he comes home and doesn't have his dinner, tough shit, baby! You want it? There's a diner up the road. What's he gonna do? Walk out on me? Pack his clothes? I've thrown Burt out of here so many times we used to have the key on a latch on the side. The only thing, I throw him out, I throw his clothes out after him. I have more freedom than a married woman. Being married sort of—at my age to get married now would mean I'd have to cut out everything I'm used to doing. Getting up when I damn well please, going to bed when I have to.

Q. You mean if you had children?

A. Children, you know damn well, would stifle me completely. I'd never be able to do what I've been doing for—what? Since I'm nineteen? Eighteen? Since I'm eighteen I've been on my own virtually. My old man taught me to stand on my own two feet, and I did.

Q. But you said the Polish ethic was sternness.

A. That's right. I wasn't allowed to wear lipstick, nylon stock— I wasn't allowed to shave my legs till I was seventeen and my mother made me because I'm so dark-skinned. My father told me if I ever wanted anything in life I'd have to work my ass off for it. So maybe I'm working my ass right now, these five years.

Q. Let's shift gears here. Your first sex experience was when you were what? Eighteen? Nineteen? Sixteen?

A. Hold on. I was so damn skinny nobody wanted to touch me when I was younger. I guess seventeen. [laughter] That was a fit. He had an asthma attack; he had to call his mother. How the hell do you get your clothes on, the guy has an asthma attack and get his mother at the same time?

Q. This was someone from around here?

A. Locally, yes. A high school boy I was going with. And after that there was nothing there for a while until I got pregnant. Anyway, I cannot get married. I would ruin the life of some man. If he wanted to marry me for the legal institution . . .

Q. I really doubt that.

A. How the hell do you explain to a guy that "I'm sorry dinner isn't made, honey, but I felt like going out to have a couple of drinks with the boys?"

Q. How do you know you would say that?

A. I don't. I'd be afraid that I might. Oh, I almost got married.

Q. When?

A. Right after the baby was born.

Q. Which was—what year?

A. Oh, Good Lord! Hold on. The kid is twelve—no, not twelve, ten. That would make it, what? 1962!

Q. '64.

A. All right, '64. When the old man found out . . .

Q. The old man being your father?

A. Oh, yeah. Look, I didn't have my old man pay for *that;* matter of fact I couldn't. He threw me out of the house. But I went to a home for unwed mothers. And when I got big enough, and I needed money . . .

Q. Again, a Catholic institution? No.

A. Don't talk to me about Catholic. Believe me, I'll tell you one thing, Fred. They let me go to my own church, which of course I only went to because I wanted to get the heck out of there. Believe me, it's no fun with a whole bunch of pregnant broads. What I did, I went to confession. This was one thing that they allowed me to do. There was a church right around the corner. As long as we went in a group of threes. Don't ask me why. It's almost hypocritical. But for some reason I had to. And then I called up the baby's father and told him if he didn't come across with some cash I was gonna come back and let myself be shown all over town as big as a balloon.

Q. Who was the father?

A. One of my bosses. I seem to run that streak.

Q. Yeah, well, that's the atmosphere that breeds it, of course. I mean, it's . . .

A. There is no possible happiness out of it, there is no way out of it and there's no—the only way out of it is you're going to break up. Everybody might believe they're getting married, but it just doesn't work that way. [pause] All right, so Sam found out I had a boy . . .

Q. Who's Sam?

A. The father. After he found out it was a boy, he had never had a boy. He never had any children, his wife couldn't produce. She had something wrong with her, I don't know what the heck it was. Then he wanted to get married because he wanted the baby. The next thing I know we wound up in Maryland. We got the license, we went on up to the little chapel. I excused myself to go to the bathroom. I called my father, I told him to send some goddam money 'cause I wanted to come home! The very thought of getting married it—I just seemed too young. I mean, Christ! I got everything—it's a long thing to do. So I came home. Never got married.

Q. That first male in your life, who was that? Did that end with the asthma attack, and that was the end of that?

A. Oh, that was *it!* After that we were afraid to try it again. I thought he'd die sure as hell! He was going to [laughter] . . .

Q. I know it's not funny; it's terrible.

A. It was terrible then. Besides, trying to get your clothes on while he's choking to death isn't easy, either.

Q. No. Now, on the negative side, possibly, of your arrangement with Burt: Men like him would necessarily be members of the World War II or Korean War generation, and their upbringing tended to separate all womankind into Nice Girls and Bad Girls. They might believe, for instance, that while sex education and experience are important for a young man—this is while they're seventeen, eighteen, nineteen—the teacher is never a Nice Girl. Now maybe they don't consciously believe this any *more,* but we are all products of our upbringing and . . .

A. Well, see, Burt has—he was brought up in a different way. Myself being brought up as a Catholic and himself being brought up as a Jew. The Jewish men are different than, uh, let's not say Catholic, say Christian—basically most of the men were brought up to be the men of their families, like they were the rulers. And in the Jewish religion they're brought up to worship the mama and the baby sister and . . .

Q. The matriarch.

A. Right. So with Burt, he's still living on that. The by-product, where, as much as I do wrong, he only gets pissed off once a month.

Q. Well, what do you do wrong? For instance, neglecting the dinner?

A. Yeah, or I don't come home on time, or I forget something, like a suit that has to be picked up, which is more often than not. Uh, pissing away money. God forbid I should sit at the bar and buy a round. See, Fred . . .

Q. Well, would it be any different, however, with someone younger?

A. Oh, I don't think he might give as much of a damn, because I don't think a younger man would be able to support me in the style to which he would worry that much. In other words, if he's not paying my rent and he's not helping pay my bills, why in hell should he give a darn if I'm not home, if dinner isn't up? Now here's a man that helps pay my bills, he is paying the rent. You *do* owe him a small —I *do* owe him a small amount of respect. Maybe a lot, but don't let *him* know that. A younger man, he could not afford—now hold on. We figured out my bills the other day. They come to, just bills to date, $174, just for the month, and not counting rent, and that's another two hundred.

Q. Not bad.

A. Now my two days a week averages out around $90, those two days I work there.

Q. Now let me interpose this—and don't forget your train of thought: Do you work there because you *want* to have something to do?

A. No.

Q. You work there to get *away* from here? Do you . . .

A. No.

Q. —work there possibly because you would rather be a productive, useful person in some way?

A. No, I enjoyed staying home. I had to go to work because Burt moved, changed jobs, and he couldn't afford to give me enough money. So at that time he needed help. He wanted to buy into this company and he just didn't have the money right then.

Q. What is his work?

A. He is in the garment business.

Q. Anyway, the question was much more, er, cultural. Do you ever feel a separation between you because of this? Do you ever feel a kind of generation gap? Do you ever feel a divergence of interests, maybe?

A. Oh, Christ, yes! Look, do you know when the hardest part is, Fred? The holidays. New Years, Thanksgiving, Christmas, Easter.

Q. He's got to be with his . . .

A. —family. Right. Who knows? Hey, look, this was part of the rules when we started.

Q. Oh, you *did* set up rules?

A. Not spoken rules. But they were just . . .

Q. They formed themselves.

A. Right. His Rosh Hashanah, his Yom Kippur—these are things we never made up rules about, but are unspoken, unwritten rules. I don't know how else to term them. This is the way it has to be.

Q. So on those occasions . . .

A. I don't see him.

Q. And you miss him.

A. Look. He's part of my family, though he's not really part of my family, but—if you're gonna be with your family during Thanksgiving or if I'm gonna be with my brother or my nieces or my Mom or my other brother, well—it gets lonely then. I think that's the hardest part.

Q. Isn't it possibly the hardest part for *anybody* in your position?

A. I think it's hard for anybody in my position that has none—that has an extra-marital affair. A holiday is, is really a *bitch*. It's lonelier then than I think it is at any other time of the year. 'Cause if he doesn't come out early Sunday I know he's not coming *out* on Sunday. But if he's gonna—if I'm not gonna see him all day on Thanksgiving, I won't see him all day Christmas. I won't see him— Now my birthday this year is falling on a Sunday. He won't come out for my birthday this year. He goes out to see his grandchildren. It's—it's not a Sunday kind of love. [long pause]

Q. He has grandchildren?

A. Three. A boy and two girls.

Q. Have you ever expressed your unhappiness about this to him?

A. Believe me, I become an absolute *bitch* two days before and two days after. And I try not to be, and it doesn't work.

Q. Now, if that's true, and there's all this misery for you, couldn't this be cured by entering into a real, let us say, legal, arrangement? With a man?

A. That means I'd have to start all over again. Burt is not going to leave his wife.

Q. Why are you afraid of it?

A. What—that he's going to leave his wife?

Q. No, no, no, no! Of marriage itself. I mean, when I asked you this question earlier, I detected a real distinct fear of it. You in fact said so. You're afraid.

A. I am. I'm—you know what it is? I'm afraid of making a mistake. I've seen so much of it. Half of my girlfriends that got married after school, for Chrissake, nine-tenths of them are sitting home with three kids, big bellies, dirty laundry, and the old man is down the block, for Chrissake, having a couple of beers while she's sitting around in a housecoat. I just—I couldn't *live* that way! The hell! Get up in the morning, *do* the wash, *change* the baby, *send* the old man out to work, *send* the kids to school. I can't *live* like that, Fred. And I wouldn't want anybody else to—I wouldn't want to take out on anyone else something that I wasn't sure *I* could do.

Q. Are you sure this is not just because you haven't found a partner with whom you were really—with whom you might be compatible? Look, I'm not knocking it. I don't take that position that this is really *wrong.* What is unbecoming is what you *consider* unbecoming. Beauty is in the eye of the beholder, right?

A. I do not think that way, that you take it. And I'm not taking it wrong by any means. I have yet to meet a married man, damn few of them, that has left his wife to marry the woman he's supposedly escorting around. It's one thing to bed your honey, it's another thing to marry her. And this has nothing to do with that damn thing—if you can get the milk, why buy the cow? That has nothing to do with that. I *hate* that damn stupid saying!

Q. So your life now is working two days a week, and the rest of the week spending in householding, spending . . .

A. Oh, householding. The evening is dinner. Just like anybody else, we do. When the old man comes home I do dinner. He goes inside, watches TV. I do the dishes.

Q. Do you feel there is a lack in your life?

A. No, I think 'cause this is the closest I feel to marriage, without being it. In other words, even if I get ticked off in the middle of the night and I walk out, he's not gonna lock the door on me. He can't. This is mine. This is my . . .

Q. This happens in marriages, too.

A. This [her apartment] is sort of my refuge.

Q. Your fortress.

A. Something like that. When I close that door, this is mine. Nobody else's. And I can shut out the *world* if I wish.

Q. It's been said that mistresses in such cases are often in such categories as father-seekers, career girls and so on. Do you think you were ever a father-seeker? Are you one now?

A. I might be. Burt is so much like my father in every respect. Even though he's Jewish, he's of Polish descent. Uh, he has the sternness that my father had. When he puts his foot down I know he's putting his foot down. That's why I get away with so much and then I don't get away with it anymore, which my father allowed me to. He doesn't—which is . . .

Q. He lets you get away with less than your father did?

A. Oh, he lets me get away with more than my old man did. But in a way, when he's had it, uh—that's *it!* He doesn't resemble him as far as, you know, facially or coloring, but I'd say there was a good part of father image in that. It'd be a lie if I said it wasn't. Burt is the first person I found like this. The other gentlemen I went out with, the other *men* I went out with, or went any length of time with, nine-tenths of them were weaklings.

Q. Expand.

A. Expand. Okay. One guy I went out with for three years, Al, he wouldn't *move* unless his old lady told him. Chrissamighty, if his mother didn't tell him where the hell to go, that poor kid would be lost.

Q. How old was he?

A. Oh, thirty-seven, thirty-eight.

Q. Uh-huh. There's a theory that this kind of thing that causes men to go off the track happens about then, thirty-eight to forty-eight or so.

A. Yeah, that's how they went off the track and married somebody else! [laughs] No, Burt is the only person I've gone out with that had enough guts to tell me to stand up—you know, shit or get off the pot. Ben would never think of it. Sam would never think of it. Chrissamighty, Harry, he wouldn't open up his mouth if I *screamed!* Nine times out of ten I had the upper hand, and enjoyed every minute of it. This is the first person that won't let me have it. And maybe that's it, too. It's a change.

Q. Or maybe you're seeking what a lot of shrinks call the normal man-woman relationship.

A. Yeah, but . . .

Q. The boss . . .

A. He's the domineering person in the relationship, and believe it there ain't too many men around like that. I've never seen so many men pussy-whipped in my life.

Q. Pussy-whipped?

A. Don't tell me you never heard that expression? Pussy-whipped is, if you don't do what I say, you ain't gonna get any. [Phone rings. Interruption.]

Q. That was Burt?

A. He calls me every morning. Pissed off he couldn't find me last night.

Q. What do you think of wives who, a lot of people say, drive men into affairs by rejecting their husbands' advances at a time of pre-menopause, during menopause? The great weapon, menstruation. We know that doesn't preclude intercourse . . .

A. Baloney! Don't believe it!

Q. I know, I know. Let me finish. The man may look for an excuse. The rejection—even the rejection of one advance—can drive him out of his home into some other woman's arms. The reason they do it is they think they're getting old. How do you—what do you think of that theory?

A. Very simple. There's three sides to every story: his, hers, and what happens behind the door. Uh, I don't always believe that. I've heard so much bullshit about that. "My wife don't let me." Nine times out of ten she's sitting there with her tongue hanging out!

Q. Something else there—while this guy may have gone through all kinds of courtship rigamarole when he was younger . . .

A. He just wants his little piece *right now.*

Q. —when he was courting, now he'll go up to her and say, "Lie down, let's fuck." Right? And the woman doesn't like that. Right?

A. No, no, hold on . . .

Q. And again, psychologically, being part of the mechanism by which the man causes the excuse himself. Is that right?

A. A small—all right—a small, quick thing, one-two-three: Burt is a poor match-up with me. There was no caressing, there was no intimacy beforehand, there was just a matter of, "We're gonna *screw!*" Until one day I got so pissed off I told him if he doesn't start necking with me, that it, it's over. I cut him off for two weeks. "Until you start to learn to court me again." Yes, *it is* important, in every part. Even if you just say hello to me, "How do you feel?"

Q. Excuse me, I've always thought that *social* intercourse was a hell of a lot more important than . . .

A. Oh, good Lord! Just—I don't say it, because I can't stand people holding hands. There's nothing more disgusting than watching a couple swinging arm in arm down the lane, or . . .

Q. In love.

A. I don't know. I couldn't imagine myself swinging arm in arm down the lane. An occasional touch. A pat on the ass, a kiss on the cheek. Or just tell me I look nice tonight.

Q. Makes your whole day.

A. Look. Then I've got a reason to get up in the morning. I got a reason to maybe think of making love with you. You give a damn about me. But most guys forget one thing after they've gone out with a broad for a while. They like to neck, just as they did a long time ago, before it got built up. This way they figure you've been out with me a couple of years, why the hell do I have to bother building it up?

Q. A doctor I talked to about this said it is because a boredom factor enters.

A. It's there, all right. Again, thank God for my—after five years, by all rights, you should be a little bored, looking for a little piece on the side. And don't think I haven't been tempted, 'cause I have been. I don't know if Burt has, but I've seen some nice-looking men walk in there with—I'd like to romp in the hay with. But I found out doing weird things turns Burt on. He'll come home one night and I'll be wearing an apron.

Q. What's that mean?

A. That's what I'm wearing. An apron. Period. That's all. By candlelight.

Q. Since you have this relationship with Burt do you find yourself kind of going, socially, toward other girls who have similar relationships?

A. No, no.

Q. The companionship of misery, perhaps, the companionship of problems?

A. I'll tell you, mine is the same as any other married woman's. He may be late coming home, now who do I call? His wife? Do I call his brother? I mean, how the hell do I—at least wives are better off. At least if the husband is lying in bed someplace, they can call the hospital, they can call the mother's, or the police will call them. No policeman is going to call me. He's going to call the wife first.

Q. The question was, do you find yourself . . .

A. Hanging around people that are in the same situation?

Q. Yes. Do you find yourself more comfortable in their company?

A. No, I don't. Nine-tenths of the time we are with married couples who have accepted our relationship.

Q. Do you expect your relationship to end negatively? This arrangement?

A. Yes, I do.

Q. When do you expect it to end?

A. When we both run dry. I'll tell you right now, Fred. You've been trying to ask me why I don't get married, and . . .

Q. No, I'm not saying that. I'm saying that society would decree that.

A. I don't think they do.

Q. No, come on. People are people. It's what makes horse races. They're all different horses, we're all different people. It takes all kinds.

A. I could get married to him. I know if he asked me I would say yes, but I don't know if it would be because I'm deeply in love with him.

Q. Have you ever considered marrying?

A. Well, yes, but it's a wet dream. I have thought—getting married—I'm the same as any other woman. Security is a very, very hard thing to beat in our system. Right now, I *have* security. As a matter of fact, Burt is now getting a life insurance policy out on himself, for me.

Q. Does he show any signs of fears of death through his growing old, through fear of impotence?

A. I hope not. I'm trying like hell to make sure he doesn't. As you know, he's not a young man, and we can't have sex every night. But I got news for you: they get better as they get older.

Q. That's what one of my questions was. Because they prolong the . . .

A. That may be their *last time,* dearie, and they put their heart and soul into it.

Q. Exactly what I call "midolescence"—the behavior is so much like adolescence, and this refers to the stumbling approach, the boorish approach to the woman whom he's been bedding for twenty, thirty years, and . . .

A. That's why you slap them in the ass and say, "Let's go to bed now!" Although I would say one thing: I've gone out with younger men who have been just as good, in fact. I don't know where the hell they got trained, but have done just as well in bed.

Q. But you are, you have been faithful to Burt?

A. I have been for the last four years.

Q. That's a marriage, you know.

A. As close to marriage as I want.

Miss B

Q. How old are you?

A. Twenty-seven.

Q. And in your immediate family there are how many?

A. Two boys, four girls. I'm the youngest.

Q. Were there any differences in family life? Was there disappointment?

A. No.

> **Q. Were there any differences?*
>
> *A. Yeah, I was a girl.*
>
> *Q. Was there disappointment?*
>
> *A. Yeah, every time I got spanked.*

Q. Did you want to go to college? Did you start going to college and then give it up for one reason or another?

A. No. Did I want to? Yes.

Q. What prevented you?

A. I don't think a degree and a higher education are basically synonymous, you know. Yes, I wanted a higher education. No, I didn't need a piece of paper to prove I was highly educated.

> *A. I changed my mind.*

Q. Do you still feel that way?

A. Yes.

Q. I'm told by people who know you that you are extremely hostile.

> *A. I'll leave that up to you to decide. I'm hostile, I'm happy, I'm jolly, I'm curt, I'm intolerant, I'm sympathetic.*

Q. Do most married men ask you out?

A. Yes. I have been asked out by ninety-nine per cent of the married men I know. Now why are they asking me out?

Q. And are they representative of all the . . .

A. The ones that I have fucked? Years ago, a man would not date another woman unless his wife was an alcoholic, or insane. Now you've got married women also going out. No one person is going to fill another's needs 100 per cent. And what's the matter with a little extracurricular fun? Sex is a myth.

---

*The italic indented matter was written into the transcript by Miss B after she stole it.

for the reason for the affair anyway. None of my married-men relation-
ships have been because of or based on sex. Shrinks will tell you the
married-man sex is ninety-eight per cent of the reason for "straying."

They want me to be an adjunct, and I'm not an adjunct. The Detroit
syndrome [the need for a new model at regular intervals] is another
myth about sex. Another myth: that a guy's got to be hung, and so
many guys are insecure because they're not hung. "It's not how long
you make it, it's how you make it long." I think that's a good part
of sex, though.

Q. What?

A. I think technique is. Sex myths: Some women like a long cock,
some women like the girth of a cock, some women don't give a shit.
Also: If you don't screw before you get married you are a terrific and
wonderful person, and if you do screw it's bad. And words. To me
there are no dirtier words than "kike" and "wop," et cetera. "Fuck"
and "suck" are not dirty. It's unfortunate that every word that's
"dirty" relates to some aspect of sex. And people think differently
about sex because they have been raised and brainwashed to think
sex is dirty, sex talk is dirty, sex organs are dirty. Trained to think
virgins are wonderful. I think virgins are *awful!*

Q. You sound like something out of the last century. You sound
to me like a Suffragette, talking out of 1910. You sound like Susan
B. Anthony!

A. Oh, I think I sound like someone talking out of 1985, maybe
1990.

Q. You smoke a great deal? [she chain-smokes]

A. I don't smoke a great deal. I smoke a *lot,* yes, if I'm reading.

Q. Well, reading is work.

A. More myths: How to get a man: If you don't like the restaurant
he takes you to, tell him you love it anyway. Women are not supposed to be taller than men; they're supposed to be shorter—All this
rot about being a "man," being a "woman"—Myths not bought—
that's my second category: Many people are not concerned about
anything unless it touches them. The veterans' pay that's coming up
now—if you don't have a son or a relative who's a vet, it doesn't
concern you. It's not your problem unless you're involved. The
homosexual-bisexual thing doesn't mean a thing unless your daughter or unless your boyfriend or someone you care for is one of those
people. You couldn't give a shit less about the gay liberation movement. So you stay uninvolved and isolated so the only thing left for

a mido to worry and concern himself about is pussy. That concerns him 'cause most guys have a cock. I don't think there is a dirty word unless *you* object to it. You can get euphemistic if you want, but I don't know. Why do they call old people "senior citizens" instead of aged? It's important not to buy the myths, not to feel insecure because you're not hung, not to screw your twenty-three-year-old secretary because your wife is over forty—Don't you get all this in this thing?

Q. Yes.

A. Then what are you sitting here for telling me I'm only giving you my opinions? Don't underestimate my intelligence.

Q. I don't. I don't underestimate it at all. It's that in your effort to tell me what these people [the midolescents] are suffering from, you keep giving me a picture of yourself.

A. I can only tell you what I feel!

Q. Of course. That's all any human can give.

A. All right. Maybe I'm telling you something obvious and you're telling me something obvious. Unfortunately, the men I have encountered have felt insecurity about their home life, about their children, about their jobs and the successes they're not at home. And their actions or their reactions are carried out because they have bought these myths. They go and they buy a house and they buy a car, they buy a boat—and what do they do? They're so accustomed to buying that they continue the pattern. And then they buy a girl and they buy a new job and—what is there left to purchase? A friend. So they buy a shrink.

The marginal note said: "One doesn't simply encounter. There would have to be a choosing, conscious or unconscious. Get her to comment." And her reply: "None of mine were pre-planned. All were accidents. I never go looking."

Q. Do you prefer married men?

A. Since high school my life has been spent in offices. I either work for the president of the company or I work for a head something-or-other. Or a lawyer. I prefer men who are thinkers, doers, leaders.

Q. Were all your affairs work-oriented? Did you get into them somehow in a work situation?

A. No. My history teacher in high school. We laid each other. This teacher was taking a risk. I was taking a risk—the fact that we did it in a classroom . . .

Q. You've been described to me as a phone-ringer, a wife-caller. I suppose if I knew you well enough I might discover what is called "viciousness" by other people.

A. The only—I'm "vicious" because they love me. Don't you get it? Everybody wants to be loved, I mean . . .

Q. I'm not asking about *them* now, I'm asking about you.

A. Obviously everybody wants to be loved, and I'm part of that.

Q. So the hostile reaction emanates from "bad" affairs?

A. No, I can feel hostile without it.

Q. I wonder, then, why people say that you—that you're vicious, hostile.

A. I *told* you. It's because they *love* me. They want to hurt me for rejecting them.

Q. One of your former lovers told me that his shrink told him that what he was doing [having the affair with Miss B] was jeopardizing his marriage, that he was punishing himself because of his guilts.

A. Shrinks, unfortunately, didn't take into consideration that he didn't have much feeling for marriage and therefore jeopardizing it didn't mean a damn thing to him. Another myth shrinks buy: "People *want* to stay married, people *want* to be young, people *want* to be bought, people *want* to be sold." I believe people change. I thought only three or four months ago that a good relationship need not be worked on. I really believed that if you have a good relationship, emotionally, physically, culturally, et cetera, that you did not have to worry every time you opened your mouth as to whether you would offend the other person. That you should be honest in all cases, even though it may hurt this person. And now I have changed my mind.

Q. Total honesty? How could there be any diplomacy?

A. No, my point in saying that was that I don't think people *should* be totally honest. I think they should be ninety-nine and nine-tenths honest, because I think honesty is a very good trait. However, one has to take into consideration the result of their saying, "You know, dear, you really haven't satisfied me in sex for the past forty years," or "You know, I just can't stand your breath." I certainly wouldn't want someone to tell me after forty years that I'm a terrible person, that I'm a nag, that I'm—that I don't respond, either intellectually or sexually, or that I don't satisfy somebody's intellect. If he's found somebody more exciting overall than me, I would like it to be either told to me twenty years before or hinted to me for twenty years if I'm thick and haven't caught on. You see, in some instances, one practices moderation. Some people think cancer is the best, er, remedy . . .

Q. Cancer?

A. Cancer. Dragging it out. Other people, I think, need a heart attack. They need to be blasted and to be told, "Look, I don't like the way your breath smells and if you don't buy Scope tomorrow I'm leaving. And I don't like your mother-in-law who's interfering with us, because if she comes here and wants the window open I'm going to keep it closed, because I live in this house." Or whatever the hell grieves people, that they keep in, to the point where they're so bottled up and they have so many knots in their bodies they're very apt to come at their mother-in-law with an axe.

Q. Do you think you have made enemies, lost friends, hurt yourself? Do you think your passion for speaking out has cost you a lot of money?

A. Money? Financially? I think I have lost acquaintances, not friends. I think I have gained enemies. I think a lot of the enemies I have gained—oh, I don't think a "lot" of them, I think *some* of the enemies I've—gotten—have been warranted. Most of the enemies I have is through sheer jealousy or other things; somebody didn't like the way I look, and that's unfortunate. Most people think, "If you're not selling, don't advertise." Does this son of a bitch think I'm selling because I'm wearing what's comfortable or what looks good? Some medical organization a few years back came up with— that women who wiggle their ass— that there was no reason why your pelvis had to swing. I do not think I wiggle my ass the way I carry myself. But there are a couple of things I am very well aware of. I may walk to bounce my hair back. Sometimes I feel so good that I want to do that.

Q. Are you self-conscious about your dress?

A. I am self-conscious in that I dress as I please. I dress to be comfortable and because I think these kinds of clothes look good on me. But some people don't like somebody because they remind them of their fuckin' Uncle Charlie. Therefore they can't stand you because you remind them of that person. Broads have gotten pregnant and have been dumped by their boyfriends, have dropped their little baby in a garbage can, because it reminds them of the father who rejected them.

Q. Do you feel any regrets for ever having hurt anybody who was in love with you? Did they deserve it?

A. No. See, your question was, did I hurt them? If they hurt *themselves* is more applicable. But that's neither here nor there. The important fact was, two people were involved in a situation and one may have done something to prevent something from happening and the other could also have done this.

Q. Did you ever feel, during one of these relationships, that you might have been doing something—not wrong as you might have seen it, but wrong in society's eyes, in the context of the way we have to live, the things that keep us from getting arrested? "Thou shalt not fuck a married man?"

A. Well, let's not talk about judicial laws. I'll talk about societal laws. I think I've broken a lot of society's laws. And I think that's probably why a lot of people do in fact dislike me, because I am brazen enough to do it.

Q. Do you think you are brazen—really?

A. Oh, I think I have gumption like—that, er—is so rare, makes me smile . . .

Q. "You're so fuckin' smart, why ain't you rich?"

A. They're not synonymous.

I am rich. Contentment of the heart I prefer to contentment of the pocket-book. So I am rich.

I'll mention spirit. I love to laugh. That's one of the things about me. I love to laugh and I don't spend my time with people who don't smile.

Q. Do you want to get married?

A. If I wanted to get married, unfortunately—and I hate to sound narcissistic throughout a fuckin' interview—but if I wanted to get married, I could get married. No, I don't want to get married. At present. But come back next week and ask and maybe I'll have changed my mind. My mind's always ready for changes.

Q. What do you want out of life right now?

A. A dignified life.

Q. You said you like to laugh, you like to enjoy. What do you want out of life? What are you going to do all this week [interview conducted on a Tuesday]? Suppose I told you you were going to be hit by a safe a week from Thursday and you had all this time to live your whole life; how would you do that?

A. I would not go anyplace that had a safe nearby.

Q. Oh, *thank you!* I suppose the question deserved the answer.

A. See, I told you . . .

Q. But you're not helping.

A. I don't hope there'll be no tomorrow.

Q. Do you suppose you're young enough to be unable to imagine dying?

A. No. I don't think it's got anything to do with age. That's another myth. [She points to a list she has drawn up, in preparation for the interview, of the types of men she has had affairs with.] Do you want to ask me about any of these specific men?

Q. Yes, I want to find out why you chose them. Did they have anything in common, all of them?

A. Yes! Yes! Yes! They had something in common: I didn't choose *them*—we chose *each other.* That's the one thing I had in common with all eight of my—er, categories. Cop? I don't know why I put that down—of all the *seven* types that I remember. I don't know any middle-aged men who I carried on a relationship with who weren't married. Er—there may have been one or two who were divorced who I spent about three seconds with. However, the most interesting ones, and possibly the fact that they were successful in their business and unsuccessful in their personal life was one of the attractions. That, I also think, is a common ground. I like people who work hard, and I tend to think people who work hard are usually—end up successful. This, I think, is another myth that you're taught. For some people it works; for others, it doesn't. Some people get their jobs because their brother owns the company. But these guys of mine were all sort of self-made. However, I love attorneys because I love the law. My best friend is an attorney, the father of my kid is an attorney.

Q. Were these men successful in their work and were they, do you think, unsuccessful at home, or they would not have had anything to do with you?

A. I may have said it was unsuccessful as the antonym to successful to make it succinct, but I can elaborate on that. No, I don't necessarily think they were unsuccessful at home. I've already told you that I don't believe anyone can fulfill someone's needs 100 per cent. However, they were unsuccessful enough in their gratification, in their needs department, and maybe in their sexual department, to look elsewhere, and that's where I filled in. And I was delighted that I reached that hole to fill. A lot of people go on with each other for years, not going anywhere into someone else's needs cavity. The stockbroker. I tend to stay away from people who are salesmen. A stockbroker has to sell people things they may not want to buy. He is a prostitute; he is selling something that he may not believe in, and I don't like unprincipled people. That was a very short affair,

Possibly because he was an unprincipled, boring, selfish chauvinist.

Q. Short?

A. Three months.

Q. That's short?

A. The average affair is three months.

Q. Oh—is there an average?

A. Yeah. They can break down anything into averages. They just —it's a statistic I read somewhere that Dr. Brothers or her team may have—I don't remember where I heard or read it. I can believe it, because it seems to be true to my pattern and to my girl friends' patterns also. I don't care whether the average affair is three months, ten months! It doesn't make me feel more mature knowing that bit of information. In any case, I don't like people who sell.

Q. Do you think this affair led to this conviction?

A. No, he's not the first salesman I encountered. I like salespeople who don't *have* to sell you something. [The phone rings and, when the interview resumes, it drifts into a discussion of one of her older sisters.] She used to be my god—my goddess. That was the reason to require—for my having to have a two-bedroom apartment. She being my god, when I got pregnant for the second time, she said to me: "Keep this one. It'll be fun." And I believed, I believed her. She was my god—anything. And it has [said with a sharp tone of sarcasm] been fun! Why was she my god, or goddess? I think most people grow up with an idol or—she told me a few things that have remained, that I like to think I have retained. One of them was that you should walk straight, your stomach in, your feet out, not duck-walk, like you had a stick up your ass. I should clothe this body that I'm going to hold upright with fashionable clothes, fashionable not being "Is the mini in?" or "Is the mini out?" What I mean by that word is that if you see a beautiful piece of cloth which does nothing for you, but you love the cloth because it embodies pink and purple —anyway, this is what she told me. I'm pretty good in the sewing area and I am an expert on fabrics, so I put the two together and I think I'm a pretty well-dressed broad. She was my goddess in other areas. About men, and life in general. But in '68, when Robert

Kennedy got shot, she split for Europe; she wanted to be in a country, or with a people, or whatever the fuck she was looking for, that was not a dog-eat-dog land. Two years later she returned. I was then secretary to the president of [deleted]. In those two years I flowered like—like the beanstalk that Jack climbed. And in those two years she regressed. When she left, she was very—she taught me about opera and literature and the Saturday Review of Literature and all that. She is not reading any more because that is part of her new life style. So now you have the combination of two people who are totally different and—obviously she's not my goddess now, because I have become something totally different and she has regressed, in my feeling. And it's been very difficult for her to adjust to my blooming. Whereas I would admit that I was impressed by her, she would never admit that she was impressed by little sister. She's not a realist. She's a romanticist. She loves guys buying her dinner and all these things that show that you've become successful. We had a fight the other night because she said she had no ambition and I told her that even if she did, she didn't have the brains.

Q. Why would that turn you off from her? Any of that?

A. From the fact [shouting] that it was the second time in two months that I had confronted the fact that she resented me. Well, maybe an opinion that she resented me, I guess not a fact. Because of my being more successful and my having more interesting people surrounding me and then the—I think the crowning touch was that she said she was crazy about [she names a public figure in the intellectual world with whom she is having an affair]. But you know this is a repetition of a previous boyfriend two years ago, this [she names the president of a large company] because she knew I was having an affair with him, she used to live with me and answer the phone when he called. And about a year later she had screwed him. And so it seemed to me that all the guys I would pick, she would know.

Q. It's been said that a lot of midolescents whine a lot, they're very self-conscious, too, to the detriment of what they have with other people—secretaries, business associates, other girlfriends. Do you think that's correct?

A. I think the reason that people do get into this age, if it is, in fact, let's say, the beginning of their extracurricular affairs, it's not something they've done regularly before and it may be their first time at it. I think they feel that they're at the end of their rope, and whether it's the seven-year itch or the twenty-year itch, the marriage is not gratifying to them, it's not fulfilling for them, and they want to trade it in for a new model. They probably expected more and got less. They apparently have not given any consideration to how to fulfill their needs with their present partners. They may feel that they're impressing their peers by doing the same thing they are— "cheating." Certainly the whining—I think the question comes in from the fact that they are not *needed*. And they've got to find somebody new, now, to need them, and it took them all this long to find out that they needed to be needed. Which is saying a little something for them also.

The marginal note said: "Did she feel that all the married men with whom she had affairs were in need of being needed? If so, what evidence for this does she have? What did the men tell her, directly in words or indirectly in actions?" Her written reply was: "My feelings: (1) All humans are in need of being needed (and not just married men). (2) Evidence: After survival, I think this (need) is 2nd (in importance) human instinct. (3) In speech and action most people have told or shown their needs. (4) If you've never felt un-needed, that's your misfortune. You're missing one of the world's shittiest feelings that if you'd have felt you may be much more thankful for being needed."

Q. Or *against* them.

A. Yeah. One of the other myths, unfortunately, that society has to discard is that you can't have a friend of the opposite sex unless you are screwing them. Most married men will not want to be your friend unless you screw them. I think that's unfortunate. I have several married friends whom I don't screw, but they're always hinting about it. Or they're always trying to attempt it, or they just outright say, "I will not see you unless we screw, because you frustrate me and you are not a man and therefore you don't know how it hurts to have blue balls." And then they go into a sixteen-minute dissertation on how much blue balls hurt. This is the whole bit. Getting you into their guilt. You know if you feel terrible about what you're doing to them, here you are, making them miserable. Other people try to make you the guilty party if you're not screwing because you're *supposed* to screw people in the office. And if they can't make you feel guilty, and then they try to make themselves feel guilty, and they whine. Whatever it is that makes people run away from women who won't screw them.

Q. Does it hurt you when a man stops seeing you?

A. It hurts me to lose a friend.

Q. Getting back to your list. Are they all ten, twenty years older than you are?

A. Oh, yeah, I think they're all thirty-nine or over, that's one of my hard-and-fast rules. I should give a voice to the young men, whom I don't consider any more, though I have tried a few times to. A few times—more than one young man—every couple of years I decide that, "Well, it's time to try it again." And they just don't have the . . .

Q. Poise?

A. Tact—style, and they try to impress you, which irritates the shit out of me, which a man who has made it—as opposed to a man who is still climbing—doesn't have to do. They also have many more problems than the older guy, who's *supposed* to be the fucked-up one. They have their parental pressures. They have their—they're probably still going to church regularly, and they have other things that they feel they *have* to do, and they always do them. Things for everyone else other than themselves, and I think that by the time a guy gets into midolescence he begins to do things for himself. Now, my sex pattern, my feelings for sex have changed, so therefore, in that these men [on the list] encompass ten years—the poor guys up in the first five years didn't have it as good as the lucky last-five-year guys.

Q. Have what?

A. Have it as *good,* dear! Sex. Fucking.

Passion. Compassion

You know the ancillary things that—er, very briefly, my attitudes of sex were, "You should be a good girl and not screw until you're married and if you do, as long as you have a ring on your finger or a pin, that's a license to screw." A lot of people in my day, the early sixties, I think, got engaged just to have that license to screw, and had no intention of getting married. Then my attitude became, "Well, you can screw as long as you profess to him that you're a virgin." And I think the first five guys

The marginal note read: "How many—total now?" And her reply was: "12,048, going on 49."

I screwed, I told them I was a virgin. But in point of fact, since these guys were married, they couldn't give a shit whether I was a virgin or not. But it made me feel "decent," which is my point, that my sex things were totally my own head-conditioning. And once I got that straightened out, that's why the last-five-year guys were much more fortunate.

I was rid of my hangups.

Then I went into a sexual, ambisexual opinion—this is still in the first five years—"Well, it's okay to do it, more than one, and not profess you're a virgin, as long as you're drunk, and pretend you don't know you're screwing." I mean, here's a man infiltrating your body; you're supposed to pretend you don't realize it. And then I went into my laughing scene, where I would just laugh doing it because then you're not "bad." And then, in the next five years, I got into screwing with the window blinds open and the lights on. I thought, "The body is beautiful and you ought not to be ashamed of it," so I decided *that,* at some period in my sexual development, which I will call it because, I think it *is* a development. Now, once I opened the lights, then I could talk about sex. When I had my last two affairs, with these middle-aged guys, I had been able to talk about it, which made me feel very comfortable. It loosened, I think, my muscles. It made me . . .

Q. Vaginal muscles?

A. All my muscles. My arms weren't stiff. They're weren't tense. My neck could move. It was no longer "dirty" that the woman should also enjoy it. And that has a lot to do with what the sexual revolution is. So once I was able to accept the fact that it wasn't dirty, I of course, (A) performed better

was more loose, comfortable

(B) was willing to try different positions (C) was the aggressor in starting sex. Whereas before I used to be a dead fish. It was always the men who would begin. My God, if you'd show them that you wanted it in now, or you wanted more foreplay, you got no vote in the matter. So sex has become better or I have placed more importance on it than, you know, just getting plugged up.

Q. You really enjoy it?

A. Yeah. I enjoy it if I enjoy the man . . .

Q. There are very few broads who do it just to enjoy a prick.

A. What about all these broads who go to bars just to get laid? What about the broads who are picking up cab drivers?

Q. But don't they select?

A. A cab driver is hardly a selection.

Q. Do you have a favorite position?

A. Depends on the man I'm with. I mean, with [she names one of her lovers] our bodies fit perfectly so we can almost do any position. Some guys unfortunately can't do it in certain positions just because of the way they're built. A guy with a smaller cock, usually, with back entrance—and I don't mean in the ass; I mean back entrance in the cunt—it slips out if you move a bit too far.

Q. Do you find these guys preferable, in all ways, in the physical act of sex, to younger men?

A. I take a relationship into all categories. Were they preferable in sex?

Q. Yes.

A. Were they better studs? I don't know. You see, I if I liked them well enough I probably thought they were. And I if I didn't like them —they slurped their soup or they crunched their crackers, which irritates me—I probably thought they were lousy in bed.

Marginal note read: "Question was probably an error. This kind of thing may not be what girls her age or men her age think about at all." Her reply: "Yes, we talk about who's better, best. I, me, don't categorize people in that dept. or at least divulge it. I probably don't remember last nite's stale fuck, like yesterday's stale news."

My type of man, which is, you know, the married executive, the married business person is . . .

Q. Is "married" most important, or is "established" the word? A man who has achieved something.

A. My affairs unfortunately have been with marrieds, so I can't speak for the—I told you the divorced men . . .

Q. Is that only because most men of that age are married?

A. Well, it's a set of circumstances. I happened to run into these guys in the office. I worked with them and they were all married, practically. But I will say this, that the type of person I dated, I slept with, is aggressive in business, is a very hard worker, is teeming with energy, and he'll show it in bed also, whereas the younger guys feels his youth and all his other charm is almost enough.

Q. When you speak of charm, are you speaking of going through the ritual dance of sex, which the older man might be more willing to do?

A. No.

Q. Considerate?

A. Considerate, right. Considerate, with the female.

Q. A lot of guys are very stupid about it. I mean, he's hardly in her and off he goes.

A. Oh, that's okay too. I don't have anything against what kind of sex a person results in as long as he is utilizing his brain, as long as he's trying, you know. I don't mean really physical energy. I think if a guy is aware of my needs, that's an intellectual energy that he is using, to know that maybe I like foreplay too, God damn it. And after my fellatio, maybe he just doesn't stick it in. Maybe he'll touch my tit, God bless me I should be so lucky. And the married guy— the older guy seems to understand this. Whereas the younger guy thinks, probably, more selfishly. He's out, probably, to make a conquest. And he's out to relieve himself. So I have enjoyed sex with these guys, as long as it wasn't overdone. I'm not the type who requires sex every night, and, frankly, if a guy wants to do it three times a night, it repulses me. Spilling over his hangups on me, he wants to prove his virility, whatever he has to do. Some of the men I've dated insist on that. That's a kind of married's guilt routine. Try to make up for the months he wasn't seeing me. Well, I wasn't complaining.

Q. Did you find it painful?

A. No, I found it redundant, you see. No, I've never found sex painful, because then I probably wouldn't carry on the relationship. Because, although sex is an important part of it, as some people believe, I think it's important enough to consider if it's hurting you with this guy. I don't think there's too many cases of an over-hung guy. I've only run into one, and he was single. He probably didn't use it enough or it would shrivel up like the rest of them. To make one addendum about sex: the man who only wants a woman for a sexual relationship, I've never spent time with. These eight or ten men [the categories on her list] however many there are, have needed me for certain reasons other than sex. There are other needs that a married guy loves. Prove me wrong if I am. To have a girl buy him a present. How many wives do? They couldn't *imagine* his wife buying him a Dunhill lighter! And when a guy feels that a woman cares enough to pay for his cab fare, to buy him dinner, to share— to give him equal rights, and not to treat him just like a fucking sugar daddy—you know, the broad who goes to the dentist and says, "Give me the best work, sweetheart, my boyfriend's paying for it." You know, guys don't want that, and I certainly don't want a guy who only wants me for sex as well as guys don't want a girl who only wants them for money. And I'm very selective in my married affairs, and I don't think I have run into a guy who has only wanted me or needed me for sex. If, in fact, they did only want me for sex, why would they call me when their wife's taking a shower? You know, go take a walk, take the dog for a walk, and call me. If they only wanted me for sex, they wouldn't show me their needs, they wouldn't show me their cares, and they wouldn't show me all the things that they have shown me, which I think is healthy in a relationship, even though it's temporary. And I think every relationship is temporary, if you're married or not. Now I'd like to ask *you* a question, if I may. Do you feel in the next—oh, not the next generation, but the next five years, with societal changes—do you feel that in the next five years people who reach forty-five will not be so depressed about it? Will not need a million ancillary interests, so that they come home to their wives debilitated—do you feel there'll be a better relationship? That women are going to start understanding that it does take education, that it does take another interest, an outside—er—that it does take growth to keep . . .

Here she crossed out the words "does take education, that it does take another interest, an outside—" and wrote over them: "require an interesting conversationalist, an unsmothering party, a non-nag" and she added, after the ellipses: "together in a comfortable-feeling partnership."

Q. You're not asking me are people really going to change, you're asking are we going to breed better people. Yes, but I think that the impulses, the basic needs that must be satisfied—I think that the disturbances will take centuries to eradicate, not five years.

A. Well, you see, because in the past five years I've seen things, and read things—A woman who is unhappy and decides to leave her husband, you didn't see this five years ago. I think that with the divorce rate skyrocketing, you can . . .

Q. You may not hear it five years from now.

A. Reading about it and hearing about it and knowing that everybody's depressed and distressed because of the divorce rate rising—I think people will have to swallow the fact that they're going to have other—they're going to have different requirements, that they are not fulfilling. And they are going to have to smarten up a bit. Broads are going to have to be less emotional, they're going to have to be—more interesting.

Q. Ridiculous! People have to have something to be afraid of or they won't achieve . . .

A. They have that—animals and children. Why must they hate someone whom they have to fuck? The person that they have chosen? Not somebody that's relegated to them, not somebody they're stuck with, like a mother, or a child, but the person they chose.

[End of first interview. Second interview begins.]

A. I want to go over this [the transcript of the first interview].

Q. All right, let's fill in the blanks. Tell me about your father. To begin with, how much older is he than you?

A. I don't know.

Q. Guess.

A. I think he was fifty when he had me. He was born in 1897 and I was born in '46.

Q. What kind of relationship did you have with your father?

A. I don't know.

Q. If you don't know, who does?

A. I guess he did. If he—if he's analytical he knows. I certainly was not analytical from the ages of five to ten or . . .

Q. I'm not asking you to analyze, I'm asking you . . .

A. I don't *remember* from the ages of when he was around. I don't *remember* what kind of relationship we had. I . . .

Q. —to tell me your feelings about your father.

A. —I didn't analyze things. I don't remember. You don't understand.

Q. That's estoppel.

A. [laughing] Okay. [pause] My feelings about him were conditioned feelings. I'm not going to sit here and go on and tell you what my mother said and what my sisters felt about him. You asked me what I felt about him. Well, I - DON'T - KNOW! What do I feel about him now? In the present tense?

Q. All right. What do you feel about him now?

A. I think he's a hot shot. I think he's brilliant and I think he's paranoid and I think he's obsessed with sex. What does this have to do with the fact that I date middle-aged men? I don't have father images of men.

Q. Why *do* you date middle-aged men?

A. They—they're much more together. Safe.

Q. In what sense?

A. 'cause most of 'em are married. They're responsible to someone else's dictates.

Q. And you don't want to get married.

A. Right. I don't want to be bothered.

Q. Bothered in what way?

A. Phone calls. Sex all the time.

Q. Middle-aged men don't bother you with phone calls or with sex?

A. I said *all the time.*

Q. So they have family obligations that keep them away from you.

A. No, they don't—I don't know if that's what keeps them away from me. I think *me telling them* keeps them away from me. I don't think they have family obligations. I think they go to see other girls when they're not with me.

Q. You're telling them *what* keeps them away?

A. "Keep away and don't *bother* me all the time!" [She turns to the transcript and reads from a marginal notation: "If not hostility, then why does she pursue men under circumstances she knows may be emotionally destructive to the men and/or their marriages?"] Don't *I* get a vote in this? What about emotionally destructive to *me?*

Q. All right. Let's get into that, since you brought it up. Do you pursue married men because it's destructive to you? You were in love how many times? Were they middle-aged men?

A. My history teacher was ten years older than I was.

Q. And how old were you at the time?

A. Fifteen or sixteen.

Q. So he was twenty-six or twenty-seven. Hardly middle-aged.

A. All right.

Q. You were a young girl.

A. No, no, no. He was twelve or fifteen years—like thirty-two. Young girl?? My *dear,* you didn't know me then. Where do you come off labeling me.?

Q. You were how old? Fifteen? Sixteen? That's a young . . .

A. Chronologically, dear.

Q. And?

A. And I knew more then than I know now.

Q. About what?

A. I've regressed. About *everything.* About lies, about . . .

Q. That's a very broad subject. How did you know so much?

A. 'cause I lived, you see.

Q. Meaning what? We all live. What does that mean?

A. Live! Live! Live! As opposed to survive. Live! as to being aware.

Q. Aware of what?

A. Being aware of what's going on. Not being an isolationist. I was also a realist. I accepted things that happened. I didn't get hot and toddy because some girl tried to touch me or I didn't get hot and upset because I saw two boys together or whatever-have-you the way a lot of people did. I was living in a little Peyton Place. I was way ahead of my time.

Q. So you knew about sex?

A. No, I didn't. That's got nothing to do with being ahead of your time, knowing about sex. I mean, really—do you equate knowing what's going on with sex?

Q. That's what *you* just said. I asked you what you knew about, and the areas you answered were about sex.

A. No, the area was about different things. Because I picked homosexuals and lesbianism I didn't connote them screwing. I said touching. That was—when they—if two homosexuals held hands walking down the street I didn't say anything about screwing. Touching is not screwing. Whoever said that was synonymous? My God! I was just thinking of perverted—of things which I don't consider perversions but which society does. Things that are outrageous, which I accepted as being a part of life.

Q. Like?

A. Like people who want to like another—women who want to like another woman. Like people who want to—you know, everything that society says is terrible.

Q. So when you fell in love with your history teacher you were not a little girl even though you were only fifteen or sixteen. You knew all about life.

A. No, I didn't know all about life. I said I was ahead of my time. That doesn't mean I—if I ever said I know all about life I might as well die. I mean, if I have nothing more to learn about life, God have pity on me. [She turns back to the transcript and its notations. ". . . her feelings about her father."] Okay.

Q. I've asked you about that and you said you don't remember. So let's go on then, from there.

A. That's my past feelings about my father. My present feelings over the past few years . . .

Q. Do you feel close to your father now?

A. Well, if you can deduce somebody who's lived with their father for a big eight or nine years, who doesn't remember how one felt about her father, who remembers him only as a stranger, only being attacked by other members of her family and her mother and then, twenty years later he visits her maybe six months out of one year and five months out of another year, must you ask that question? Would you feel close to that type of person? I've got to love—I've got to feel close to somebody because I'm part of their *sperm?* That's a stupid question! Would you feel close to someone you—does the fact that he is your father qualify you for feeling close? He's got a label on him: he's your father. That's going to make you feel closer?

Q. Then I'll turn the question around. Did you miss the fact that you never had a father?

A. Feeling close to my father and missing him is a new question.

Q. Other people have fathers who are around, for advice, for comfort, for . . .

A. That's other people. You're asking me; I don't care what other people feel.

Q. Did you . . .

A. No, I never missed him. I got on. I didn't have time to miss him.

Q. Why didn't you have time to?

A. Because I was going to school, I was a little girl who was going to school every day and that was the only thing I did every day, five days a week. And I cleaned house on Saturdays and I went to church on Sundays. I didn't have time to know whether I missed somebody.

Q. You didn't have a father to talk to, to bring your troubles to, to go out with, to . . .

A. I didn't have a mother, either! To do that to.

Q. In what sense?

A. She worked all day too.

Q. Who brought you up?

A. The world!

Q. Who'd you talk to when you were a kid?

A. Myself.

Q. How about your sisters?

A. They used to torture me. They used to tie me up.

Q. And your brothers? You fought with them?

A. No. I didn't fight with anybody. I'm not belligerent. Can't you tell [laughing] by this tape? I'm not belligerent.

Q. Did you ever cry as a little girl?

A. I don't remember unimportant things. I've sort of put them out of my mind.

Q. What's unimportant?

A. Unimportant is what I did twenty years ago or what I did yesterday. I don't talk about last night's fuck. I don't talk about last year's relationships if I've cared to put them out of my mind. I do talk about things that were important to me, like last year's job, or last year's business acquaintance, or last year's book, or what have you. Those things are important to me.

Q. You still didn't answer the question. Did you ever cry as a little girl? Did you ever cry because you were unhappy?

A. No, I don't recall being unhappy.

Q. Ever?

A. Only when I got tied up.

Q. It was your sisters who tied you up?

A. Yeah.

Q. As a carry-over, do you feel resentment toward women?

A. [a long pause] Well, that's sort of a blank statement. I feel resentment towards women not because my sisters tied me up; I feel resentment toward women because they bore me. Do I feel resentment toward men because my brother told me I should carry his paper route for him when he couldn't? See—that's the fallacy in shrinks. They don't come at the problem as of what you're feeling now. They go into your childhood and say, "Well, since you were feeling this then, obviously you must feel it now." I mean, there's no change in your feelings. There's no growth in yourself as a person. They blame it all on your parents, or all on your siblings, or all on your bloody aunt. This is what I have against psychiatry. I can't blame my problems on my mother and I can't blame them on my brothers and sisters—as far as I'm concerned they did the best they could.

Q. That leaves only one person.

A. How could I blame me for getting tied up? You just don't seem to understand. Why was there a need for blame? I didn't blame anybody.

Q. Why did you bring up blame?

A. It was a part of life—don't you understand that these things are a part of life?

Q. New subject. How much schooling did you have?

A. Formal schooling? I probably got ten years of education. I didn't get very much education, if you want to talk about formal education. I educated myself. I pursued what interested me—not what was shoved down my throat.

Q. Did anybody ever provide any kind of guidance to you?

A. Yeah.

Q. What sort of guidance did they provide?

A. Me! *I* provided it!

Q. On the basis of what?

A. My thoughts and feelings. And my—my requirements.

Q. And that's the way you still live?

A. Exactly.

Q. How old were you when you had your first sexual experience?

A. I don't remember.

Q. Boy, have you got a memory!

A. I have a wonderful memory. The things that are not import— it is not important for me to remember when I first got plugged up, because when I first really got plugged up it was with a Tampax. I was fifteen and a half. That I remember. That was a new thing in my life. Sex I had read about, I had heard about, I had snickered about, it wasn't new that I got involved in it.

Q. Well, then what's the first involvement that you remember?

A. I don't remember. It was either my teacher or some football player.

Q. In high school?

A. Yeah. I hope so. I mean I hope I wasn't a virgin until seventeen. I think anybody who's a virgin to seventeen's got something wrong with her. I just think everybody should experience sex when they feel like experiencing it.

Q. So let's get into the heart of the matter—middle-aged men. Why do you prefer them?

A. I prefer any man who's mature.

Q. Whether he's middle-aged or not? Well, what do you think constitutes maturity?

A. Somebody who's not obvious; somebody who's not redundant; somebody who's not stupid; somebody who doesn't bother you every minute of the day; somebody who doesn't treat you like you're an adjunct to them; somebody who respects your rights.

Q. Who fits that bill?

A. I don't know anybody who does. And furthermore, somebody who doesn't worship you. You know, I had a guy the other day saying to me he wants to write a book with me; he respects my thinking. I can understand if he respected a thought of mine. But the schmuck said outright he respects my thinking. Means that everything I say is obviously going to impress him? And if it doesn't, he's going to be afraid to say it . . .

Q. Who comes close to filling the bill about a mature man?

A. [She names the public figure with whom she is currently having an affair.] Because I can talk to him about politics. I would really like to have a relationship where my guy can have ten magazine subscriptions and I can have ten newspaper, magazine subscriptions, newsletters, and we can—since we don't have time to read 'em all —sort of discuss it. That's my whole thing with [deleted]. We just discuss what the hell is happening in this world. I love it. To me it's better than sex.

Q. Tell me about the man who is the father of your child. How did you meet him?

A. Through his brother.

Q. The brother introduced you?

A. No, I introduced myself. The brother introduced me via phone —told the brother I was a nice girl and I needed a place to stay in California. It was an introduction of sorts but, you know, not face to face. You can say tête à tête there—it makes me sound [laughing] more dignified.

Q. You needed a place to stay in California and he supplied it.

A. Yeah, he said, "Come, come. Nothing will happen."

Q. How long did you stay there?

A. Oh, I don't know. Eight or ten days.

Q. And then?

A. I left!!

Q. With him?

A. *With* him? He's a lawyer, man, he's only allowed to prac— he's a member of the bar in California. What's he going to do? Take up with a broad in another state?

Q. And sometime within those eight or ten days, that's when your child was conceived?

A. Yeah. Probably sometime in one or two days.

Q. When you realized you were pregnant, what did you do about it?

A. I told him I was pregnant.

Q. Why didn't you have an abortion?

A. Cause my sister said it would be fun. My sister was my goddess.

Q. Did you expect that because you were pregnant this relationship with the father would continue?

A. No way!! I told you I don't like people who put labels on me. We never discussed it. You know, that was the greatest part about our relationship. We both knew we didn't want to be married. I mean, can you imagine an eighteen-year-old broad being knocked up not even discussing a shotgun wedding? That's where I was when I was eighteen; I knew that shotgun weddings were awful.

Q. Are you self-destructive? Do you do things that—wreak havoc with your life?

A. I do things that enable me to move on. People—some people —say I'm vicious. But I could have done a million things if I were vicious, you see. But I do let my anger out. You see, that's why I'm called self-destructive. Because I get all my feelings out.

Q. Do you provide a source of meeting needs for some men who can't get all their needs met at home?

A. I don't know. They provide me with a source of my needs, for meeting *my* needs.

Q. Who picks whom?

A. We pick each other. I said that—you know—we pick each other. But for my vote, I pick them to fill my needs, not for me to fill theirs.

Q. What needs are you looking to fill?

A. The ones that an ordinary person has to fill. I mean, you've got emotionally, intellectually—all the needs. The obvious needs.

Q. Well, oddly enough, most of the men who fill these needs for you turn out to be married men, and married men in their middle years.

A. Yeah? What's odd about that? They're together! Why do people that are the same age have to go out? That's another conditioned reflex which I—I—*resent!* Why does a man have to be taller than a woman? Why does a man have to be older than a woman? What is this shit? It just so happens that those men are more together. Now maybe in ten years it'll so happen that twenty-seven-year-old men will be more together when I'll be thirty-seven, and I'll like *them.* It hasn't happened yet.

Q. How did you get your last job?

A. That's irrelevant. What *is* relevant is—about how a woman of my age got into the position I got in and how other people felt she got into the position, because it's been said that . . .

Q. That you fucked your way to the top.

A. Yeah. And nobody fucks his or her way to the top; they always fuck their way down. I don't believe in fucking where you eat. I don't want to have a sexual relationship with my *boss.*

Q. Do you think you can go to bed with anyone you want to?

A. Anyone *in the world.* I mean, I can go to bed with—with—Aleksei Kosygin.

Q. Why stop there? How about a priest?

A. Yeah. I've been fucked by a priest. I know how Catholics operate. No—no, I haven't been fucked by a priest—it was, er—an attempted fuck.

Q. Who attempted? You or the priest?

A. The priest. See—that's another thing about me: I don't have a desire for sex. I never approached anybody to say, "Let's fuck." I approach some people to say, "Let's talk." I approach people to talk about sex; I approach people to—all kinds of things. I never had an—I don't have a need for sex. It may change. I mean, I *hope* it will change. People tell me that when I'm thirty-five I will be at my sexual capacity. At this point I don't have a need for sex. I don't get an itch to get laid. I've got pickles and bananas in the frig, if I want, and Tampaxes.

Q. Why do you fuck?

A. Because I like the person. I love the person.

Q. But you've said you've fucked with people you don't love. Let me push that point a bit. Have you loved everyone you've ever had sex with?

A. No. Certainly not the two guys I've fucked to try to purge myself of [she names two previous lovers.]. Most everybody else, yes.

Q. There are certain criteria that enter into your appraisal of a situation, whether you want to fuck or not. Do you like the person? Do you love the person? Those are the criteria that . . .

A. No—they're *not!* Love is only a very minute part of it. It's what he can *do* for me.

Q. In what way?

A. Intellectually, emotionally. Why do you have to ask that question? It's what he can do for me—whether he's there when I need him, I guess, is the most important part.

Q. If you could pick someone to have around most of the time, who would it be? Describe him.

A. What I said to you earlier. Someone who's not obvious, redundant . . .

Q. Don't tell me what he's *not;* tell me what he *is.*

A. Well if he ain't all these things, then most of the things that he is have got to be good.

Q. That's a cop-out.

A. It's a cop-out for me to say he's warm, sensitive and all that crap, because that's obvious. It's exactly what everybody wants, whether it's male or female, whether it's child or adult.

Q. You want someone who cares about you . . .

A. No. I don't particularly place much importance on caring about me.

Q. You don't give a damn whether the person cares about you?

A. I don't place any importance on it. I want him to need me more than to care about me, to think that I supplement his life in some way.

Q. That you should be an addendum to his life?

A. No. I don't ever want to be an addendum to anybody. You supplement his life when he needs somebody to talk to.

Q. You want someone who has a reasonably fulfilled life, but who needs you—for what?

A. Who needs me for the times that he needs me. I want somebody who has a full life in his career, in his joys with other women or with other business endeavors, but to need me when there comes a point of needing. Somebody to talk to, somebody to hold, somebody to . . .

Q. You're describing a mature man.

A. Well, I hope so.

Miss C

Q. Where and when were you born?

A. In New York in 1939.

Q. The purpose of this interview is to get the feelings, the responses, the reasonings, if you will, of a younger woman who has had affairs with older men. Do you fall into this category?

A. Yes.

Q. How many affairs with older men have you had?

A. That I would count, I would say I had—one affair with an older heterosexual and was quite in love for a long time with an older homosexual.

Q. Let's get some other basics down now. Where did you go to school? What was some of your background. Tell me, briefly, about your family—are you an only child?

A. No, I have a younger brother, two and a half years younger, who was born about the beginning of the second World War. Presumably—now when he was born, I—my father was sent into the Navy, uh, when I was about two. When I was about two and a half my brother was born. So—I don't want to psychologize on myself, but presumably that was not a good thing to happen—I was sent away for six months when my brother was being born.

Q. What does your father do for a living?

A. He is now—he teaches. He's technically retired but he teaches. He was in merchandising for a long time.

Q. Did you have a typical kind of father-daughter relationship? Was your father around—aside from the fact that he was in the Navy for a while—was your father around when you were a child?

A. He came back from the Navy when I was, say, um, six. He was —he physically was there. He is a very angry man, however, and was alternately extraordinarily charming and seductive and bizarrely angry and annoyed.

Q. So that he was, in a sense, very demanding.

A. He is—my psychiatrist likes to call him bizarre.

Q. It's an odd word for a psychiatrist to use.

A. Well, I will tell you a story about my father. This is from adulthood rather than from childhood. But at one point oh—maybe five years ago—I was playing tennis, and I don't play tennis very well —I was playing mixed doubles with some friends. And I was serving when my father came by. the court and saw me serving and began screaming at me from the sidelines that I was foot-faulting, which I may or may not have been. He screamed at me that I was foot-faulting, came galloping across the tennis courts and—y'know, right in front of my friends—grabbed the tennis racket from my hands and said, "I will show you how to serve so you don't foot-fault."

Q. The reason I ask about your father is I'm looking, of course, for common denominators, threads, in trying to find out why some young women are attracted to older men, and the first thing that jumps to mind, naturally, is that these women would be looking for a missing father, for a relationship they never had. Sometimes the evidence seems to bear this out and sometimes it doesn't. But, go on.

A. Well, in my case that may or may not be true. I have managed to get myself rejected in the same way that my father may have rejected me.

Q. Now let's have something about your schooling.

A. [laughs] My schooling—all right, my early schooling was rather unsettling, although I don't remember being unhappy in school as a young kid. Because of the war, and because my father moved, changed jobs right after the war, I figure that by the time I had been in fifth grade I had been in four schools, a combination of public schools and day schools. In fact my first great love was an older man. I was in first grade and he was in third grade—I don't think that counts. After that I was in public schools until I was in the tenth grade and then I went away to a girl's boarding school. And then I went to a woman's college. And then I worked for a while and then I went to graduate school.

Q. And your job is now what?

A. Teacher and would-be freelance writer.

Q. But your principal means of livelihood is teaching.

A. At this moment, yes.

Q. When you said you had one long affair—one affair and one a long affair—had you had any—dalliances?

A. Oh sure, I mean, I've had—someone once asked me, someone I met, asked me, you know, what sort of sexual background I had, and I said, "Oh, the usual." This was when I was in my early thirties, and he responded, "Oh, you mean"—I want to get this right— "thirty-six one-night stands." And I heard him to say—he may or may not have said it, "thirty-six-night stands." In other words, affairs of, say, three months, something like that. But with sort of the emotional climate of one-night stands even though it went on for thirty-six nights.

Q. Getting back to that question—you have had a number of, shall we call them, dalliances . . .

A. A lovely word.

Q. Were they frequently, usually, always, with older men?

A. [pause] They have almost always been with men who were somewhat older than I am.

Q. Meaning what?

A. Well, say, between five and ten years.

Q. But you never, let us say, as a girl of twenty-five, you did not have affairs with, or dalliances with, men in their forties?

A. Not in their forties, no, only in their thirties.

Q. Well, we'll have to rule those out.

A. Now there's—I suppose this also has got to be ruled out—at some point in my late twenties, I had [long sigh] a kind of perverse dalliance with a really older man, I mean someone in his sixties. And I think that—that's too bizarre to . . .

Q. No, no—it's the same sort of thinking involved here. What is it that you were looking for? What kind of dalliance was it? To begin with, was there a sexual relationship?

A. There was a sexual relationship of sorts, although it was not fornication.

Q. But sex was there?

A. Well, that's really all there was—that was there.

Q. What did you get out of it?

A. I don't know. Titillation, I think.

Q. In what sense?

A. Sexual titillation—I sometimes fancy that. There was absolutely no emotional content at all as far as I can tell.

Q. How long did it last?

A. Well, on and off, maybe a couple of months and then I would occasion—I guess I would see him once or twice a year after that.

Q. Was he married?

A. No.

Q. Bachelor? Divorced?

A. Divorced. He was a refugee. He was —it was bizarre. I don't think it fits into the pattern of things I have usually done. I think that and one other sexual experience with a man who was, say, ten years younger than I am, black, who I let me, who I really let pick me up, are I think more sort of experiments with what it feels like to be promiscuous than another sort of . . .

Q. How old were you when you had your first sexual experience?

A. Twenty-five.

Q. And was it with someone of . . .

A. Uh—I was twenty-five, he was—I guess I [pause]—he was sort of in his mid-thirties, maybe thirty-three.

Q. Was this a love affair or just a sexual encounter?

A. It was a prolonged sexual encounter. I was very—this was someone whom I had seen a couple of years before and he had wanted to go to bed with me and I had thought, well, I was a virgin and didn't want—to . . .

Q. Do you cherish the ideal of virginity?

A. Noooh. Not now. When I think—I think I was scared stiff in my early twenties. I had a mother who told me that if I was not a virgin I would either become promiscuous or have a nervous breakdown. In fact it—at least in part I forced myself to have my first affair . . .

Q. To rid yourself of this . . .

A. Yes. Encumbrance. I was a lot more attracted to him emotionally than he to me. He was very much in love with another woman he wanted to marry, and he told me about her, and I became really very attached to him. Jack Kennedy managed to get himself shot in the midst of all this, and I managed to get myself raped in the middle of all this. So, I—depended upon his tenderness.

Q. You were raped before or after your first . . .

A. I was raped a week afterwards. It was very funny [laughter]. The police were a little, ah—oh God! I had had intercourse once and then managed to get myself raped, but even the rape didn't take. It wasn't a rape, it was sodomy. He became impotent. And the police asked me with some blushingness whether I, since I was twenty-five and living in New York by myself—they presumed that I was not, er, a virgin, and I said with great casualness "Oh, no." And then they took me into the hospital for an examination, and the gynecologist blushingly told me that I was in fact still technically a virgin, so that the whole thing got very complicated.

Q. All right. Let's pass to the crux of the matter, when you—actually—an affair or a dalliance, as the case may be, 'cause I want to go to those involving men, let us say, between thirty-eight and fifty-five. They are the heart of this book.

A. Okay. The longest and most prolonged atachment to any man I've ever had was a ten-year involvement with an older man, a teacher, who was in fact homosexual, and we were in fact very in love and at one point we almost got to bed—he was, say, forty-two, and —no, I have to say we loved each other, and as, around the time he was forty, it all got very desperate and we would sit about and sort of hopelessly neck, and . . .

Q. Well, he was homosexual . . .

A. —he started going to a psychiatrist when he was, say forty-two . . .

Q. To rid himself of his unwanted—the current expression is "sexual orientation?"

A. I have always presumed so.

Q. In other words, you never consummated this affair?

A. But it was the most intense emotional involvement I ever had.

Q. Had he had many male lovers?

A. He had had some. He'd also been engaged for a while.

Q. To a . . .

A. To a woman [pause] who may or may not have turned to be have been a lesbian. She had also been married once before, but—they had been engaged, oh, four or five years before I started going out with him. She had had a nervous breakdown. So there was always a sort of perhaps naïve hope that, gosh, if he'd been engaged once before, perhaps he wasn't hopelessly homosexual.

Q. How did you meet him?

A. He was my teacher.

Q. How did your teacher-student relationship drift into a love relationship?

A. Uh—persistence.

Q. On whose part?

A. Mine.

Q. You pursued him?

A. I pursued . . .

Q. Knowing that he was a homosexual?

A. [Gesture of affirmation]

Q. That is a whole other book.

A. [laughter]

Q. You knew that there would be incredible frustration here? You wanted to be frustrated?

A. That's why—yeah.

Q. Were you . . .

A. Well, I—I don't know what I wanted. And to get back to this —he was one of the first men I—he was the only man I had ever known who—seemed to take me seriously. He was also a very, very tender man.

Q. Do you look for tenderness in people?

A. Yes.

Q. You enjoy tenderness? It gives you a feeling of—what? Your father was never tender, was he?

A. [pause] No. My father yelled a lot.

Q. Between yellings, was he tender?

A. He was flirtatious, but not tender.

Q. So that you wanted something that you didn't have elsewhere. And from what better source, on two levels, than an older man, who can be a father image, and a homosexual to boot, so that you don't have the frustrations and worries of sex. I'm reading in now, just tell me if I'm way off the beam.

A. I think, to say, the frustrations—that I was frightened of the frustrations and worries of sex—is a simplification. I'm not sure that that's—that that's true. I was having dalliances with other men in this period.

Q. Including fornication?

A. Including fornication. I love those Biblical words. Copulation. I copulated. [long pause] I—I think, rather than any sexual fear [speaking haltingly here]—it was a choice of someone who eventually had to reject me. In a perverse way, it was, let us say, safe. [pause] I told a close friend, about a year ago, that I had decided I probably would have made a better mistress than a wife. I don't think that's just self-defense. I mean, since I'm thirty-five now, that I—the chances of getting married are somewhat—slight.

Q. How old were you, incidentally, when you began this love relationship with your teacher?

A. Say, my early twenties, for about ten years.

Q. And, say, twenty-two to thirty-two. Did you at any time that you were seeing this man—at the same time—did you have any intense kind of relationship with any other older men? Whether sexual, or social . . .

A. Oh, God! [sigh] Yeah—all right. There, there was the man in his late thirties, who was a colleague of mine at the school I was teaching at, who—had been divorced three times and was in the process of leaving his third wife, and I for two years became his great confidante. We would have these conversations, y'know, we couldn't possibly go to bed together because then it would ruin our friendship. And it was really—I—really let myself be used. But I liked being close to him, and for at least a year I saw a lot more of him than his wife did.

Q. But you never did get to bed?

A. No.

Q. You had a tender—was he tender to you?

A. He was very tender to me.

Q. So you were searching for warmth. To use a cliché that fits—human kindness, understanding, and you found that you could get this from older men. Did you ever get this from younger men?

A. [long pause] Not that I can think of. If anything, they—if anything, the [pause]—the reverse.

Q. Younger men came on too strong?

A. No.—[pause] Not came on too strong, but younger men were —how'll I put it? I may have managed to get myself rejected by both older men and younger men. The older men did it, at least, while exuding tenderness. So I got something out of it. The younger men tended to be really sadistic. I remember once—oh Jesus!—I remember once having a [young] lover oh, maybe for about six months— I would see him once or twice a week with some regularity. And one weekend he had come and spent Friday night, and on Saturday morning would I please phone his dentist, and that he—he just didn't want to get out of bed, didn't want to go to the dentist and would I call up and pretend—this was someone essentially my own age— would I call his dentist? And so I pretended I was his secretary and he was unable to keep his dentist appointment and I hung up the phone, and he said "Ah, fine, and thank you very much, and now I've gotta go and see, y'know, Jane." And he got up and got dressed and left.

Q. Which was a blow to you.

A. Which was a blow to me. I mean, there was little fake tenderness involved. He was—he was good company, but there was no sense that he was, uh, tender.

Q. Then older men are more understanding, more likely to be sympathetic, to offer you companionship? Do you look to them for guidance in the affairs of your life?

A. Well, the long, the long, really love, for the teacher, really I looked tremendously for guidance, in—in a way that I have never looked, really, from anyone before except my psychiatrist.

Q. Did you ever feel a sense of sexual frustration with him because he was a homosexual, because you never got to—copulate?

A. [sigh] He—I—you know what I think—happened? Is, I think that—before, I said, as a kind of joke, about my first love was an older man when I was in first grade and he was in third grade, and the kids in first grade were supposed to go to the third-grade cafeteria once a year as a big treat instead of eating in their dining room. And, third grade consisted of four boys and twenty-two girls, and I was sick the day the class went, so I got to go by myself. I got asked whether I wanted to sit with the boys or the girls and I said "Aaahh, the boys!" And I got taken to lunch by the three older men. And I became so excited that the teacher had to come over and say, "Stop exciting her or she's not gonna eat any lunch." With this man, I am not conscious of my feelings of frustration as being sexual. He made me feel very excited, like a little excited girl. The feeling was the same. I would feel very revved up with him even though it wasn't —it wasn't ending in copulation. But he made me feel very excited. Other than not sexual. And I was [pause] frustrated, but not horny.

Q. Did you take out your sexual frustration—you said you had, you were at, during this time . . .

A. I had dalliances with other people.

Q. So that if there was sexual frustration you had other outlets for it. [pause] Tell me something about your teacher. You said he was engaged once and that it broke off. He had some male lovers.

A. He ended up with a male lover. For the last couple of years of his life . . .

Q. Last couple of years? Is he . . .

A. He was killed in an air crash. [pause] For the last couple of years of his life he lived with another man. In a sense, married to another man. The . . .

Q. How old was he when he got married, so to speak?

A. Let's see. He was sixteen years older than I am. And so he was killed when he was, maybe—forty five.

Q. And he had been living with this other man for . . .

A. Well, in a very discreet way because they were teachers, you know, they could not sort of set up housekeeping.

Q. But, in essence for how long?

A. A year.

Q. Who broke off the relationship? How did it end?

A. It never did end. It never did end. The night he was killed his lover called me up to weep. I just became—less central. And we stopped—we—it became less intense.

Q. How long . . .

A. And I—I will admit that I was. Y'know, I used to stay in the house with him and I would fantasize that he was getting up in the middle of the night . . .

Q. Did you sleep with him?

A. No. I mean, I slept in the house but not in the same bed.

[pause]. Um, and I would fantasize about—maybe he was getting out of his bed to go to his friend or something like that, and I would be jealous of that, and once he brought a young, very elegant, faggy English guy around to call, with me, which—uh—I got really angry at.

Q. You necked, you said.

A. Yes, lot's of—very, sort of teenage groping.

Q. With very little sex?

A. Very little sex. One night, uh, while this was going on, I said to him "There's something I want to ask you." And what I wanted to ask him is "What are you getting out of this?" That's what I wanted to ask him.

Q. Sexually? Or in toto?

A. In toto. And he said, "Let me tell you a funny story. During the war my brother said to me, 'Uh, there's something I must ask you.' He was somewhat more liberal politically than his brother. 'Do you, er, er . . . are you . . . uh, uh, a—a—Communist?' " And I knew exactly what he meant. What he thought I wanted to ask him. And so I said without ever asking him, "No, that's not what I meant." And I left the house and had a car accident.

Q. Let's go on to the second affair with a middle-aged man.

A. Okay.

Q. When? How old was he? The circumstances—how did you meet? Was he married?

A. All right. He was married, he was married, he was—fifty [pause]-one.

Q. And you were . . . ?

A. Thirty-three. He was married, both living in my town. He was wildly, physically attractive. I mean, unbearably good-looking. And came on very strong. And we met at a party where there was lots of dancing. And one whole summer we—we would swim a lot and we would have long, very titillating conversations. He used to talk dirty a lot, he likes to talk dirty.

Q. As a sexual stimulant?

A. Yes. And I had just lost a good deal of weight and, y'know, feeling pretty sexy. And, it was just that it was very, very—it was very, very charged. And then he took me out to a sort of romantic lunch, and during all this, by the way, he made it absolutely clear —first of all, his big come-on was to tell me about his past affairs. Now whether he did that as a sexual stimulation, or whether he was

so obsessed by his past affairs—all with younger women, always—
that he couldn't help but talk about them, or whether it was a way
to establish a sort of instant intimacy, I don't know. But I heard all
about his past affairs, one woman in particular whom he had left his
wife for. And then a whole series of sexual dalliances he had had.
God! I heard those fucking stories for two months.

Q. At any rate he was married when you were having this affair
with . . .

A. Yes, that is correct.

Q. And you were aware of it?

A. Oh, I was very aware of it. His wife was right there. We used
to—I used to—they used to invite me for dinner.

Q. Was his wife aware?

A. I don't know. I really do not know. In retrospect, he has since
left his wife, and I have talked to his wife. In retrospect, I do not
think she was aware. Although he would play the game that ah! yes,
maybe she was aware.

Q. Does she know now that you had an affair with him?

A. No! No, she does not. No one knows this.

Q. All right. You knew that he was married. How did you feel
about the possibility that your having an affair with him might
disrupt his marriage?

A. I never really considered that it would. The thing that I think
I am angriest about—although I certainly don't want him, I could
have had him. And it was I who would say things like, y'know—it
was I who was very casual and nonchalant about it. He was longing
to fall in love instead of having dalliances. I essentially protected his
marriage.

Q. By refusing to allow him to fall in love?

A. That's correct.

Q. You were not in love with him?

A. I longed for him—it—it took a lot of self-control—on my part.
Part of me would've adored to fall hopelessly in love.

Q. This was a full-fledged affair. I mean, this was—you were
going out together, you were spending time together, you screwed.

A. We screwed. And we spent a lot time in the country together.
We screwed once a week.

Q. And you felt—first of all, let's get this—what did you see in
him? What did you want? You—you longed for him. What did you
see in him? What was it about him that appealed to you? You were

then about thirty-three and he was fifty-one. That's eighteen years difference. What did you see in him? What did he represent to you? Or haven't you ever thought about it?

A. I find it difficult, because there's a whole part of him that I really don't like. And it really—uh—bored me and angered me.

Q. Was he a businessman type? An intellectual type?

A. No, no, he was a kind of failed architect.

Q. A brain worker.

A. He liked to think so. That's not vindictive. That, unfortunately, is accurate. That is going to be very sad for him. Part—while this was going on, younger architect friends of his were making tremendous successes. Younger male friends. I think—I can't answer what I saw—he was very glamorous.

Q. In what way?

A. He was very physically glamorous. The situation was very charged. I had never had an affair with a married man.

Q. Did that appeal to you?

A. It gave me—the secrecy of it gave me a charge. Also I may have been competing with some of my women friends, my married women friends, who were all having affairs.

Q. There was a sense of adventure, of excitement.

A. Yeah, there was a sense of adventure and excitement. Of secrecy, of [pause] . . .

Q. Let me, let me add another thing.

A. Yeah.

Q. In this case, I wonder, does that—adjective—apply: "safe"? Was it safe? You knew he . . .

A. Oh, yes. Very much like my first lover, who even told me that he was trying to get another woman to marry him. This man told me, on one hand that he would never leave his wife and that he loved her very much and in fact the first time we went to bed what the fuck did he talk about but (A) his wife and, secondly, the woman he'd run off with before. Which made me feel like *shhiiitt!*

Q. This was his third wife.

A. His—let's see—the wife he had when I saw him was his second wife. He has since shed her.

Q. I'm a little mixed up. Are we talking about the fifty-one-year-old man?

A. The fifty-one-year-old was on wife number two. The man who I'd had my first sexual experience with told me at that—was unmarried at the time, was in his sort of early thirties, I guess, thirty-five, maybe, and unmarried—and told me that he was desperately in love with another woman who didn't want to marry him.

Q. So you have, in a sense, this pattern. You have pursued men that—who gave you a feeling of safety. That you would never have to marry them. Are you avoiding marriage? Do you want to get married? Are you afraid of . . .

A. I—I don't know.

Q. Do you feel . . .

A. I really—I really don't know.

Q. Well, let me try to focus this. Do you feel that marriage would impinge upon your personal freedom?

A. [pause] It—it seems, not that I'm aware of. It seems unreal to me.

Q. Marriage does?

A. Yes.

Q. For you, or for others?

A. For me.

Q. That gives me a feeling—the way you put it, it gives me a feeling that you're saying "it can't happen to me."

A. Yeah, okay. That is—that is the feeling that I have.

Q. Because you don't *want it* to happen to you or do you don't think it *can* happen to you?

A. Because I don't think it *can* happen to me.

Q. That's a feeling of self-worth involved here. Or is it? Are you —do you think you are deficient in feelings of self-worth?

A. Thank you, doctor. Yes, something—something . . .

Q. You feel you're not worthy of—that's a funny way to put it because it's—it's a chauvinistic way to put it. Marriage is not a question of worthiness, but—what I'm trying to get at is—do you feel you wouldn't be a good wife? In any sense whatsoever? Therefore you don't want to test yourself? You don't want to . . .

A. Look, I feel that it is out of my hands. That's what I feel. That it is out of my hands, and that—it—it also is chauvinistic on my part, but that women are somehow chosen, and I have been found lacking.

Q. All right. Let's get back to your fifty-one-year-old lover, who was, for you, safe. Was he tender?

A. [long pause] He was alternately tender and remarkably cruel.

A. To you?

A. Yeah. As witness: it seems to me the first time you bed someone is not the ideal moment to start talking about your old mistress.

Q. That's an understatement. Well, we still haven't arrived at—aside from the fact that he was physically glamorous and attractive, you—we still haven't arrived at why you—who chose whom, by the way?

A. Oh, we both chose each other.

Q. All right, let's pursue this somewhat. We're trying to find out what it was that you saw in him other than that he was physically glamorous and attractive. Was there something else and, if so, what was it? What did you feel then, what do you feel now, in retrospect?

A. Okay. It—I have spoken before about this *charged* feeling, this kind of . . .

Q. Excitement.

A. —excitement, yeah. He made me feel like that. Which is kind of girlish.

Q. You have no way of analyzing. You can't say what elements went into this—electric feeling—between you? Was it between you, or was it all on your side?

A. Oh, no. It was between us. Let me just think for a second. [thirty-two seconds of silence] I—I'm sorry, that's not very helpful, to blank out. [shorter pause] I think I must have known, since he did not want to, uh—I wonder if I get a kind of horrible charge in, essentially, helping marriages stay together. My long, my two-year friendship with my colleague when I talked, for instance. It was a year when I was helping, keeping his marriage together.

Q. By . . . ?

A. By allowing him, not in—in that case it wasn't a matter of sexual frustration, but allowing, giving him someone to talk to so that it made what he considered to be the emptiness of his life, more bearable. I did somewhat the same thing with this man, who kept insisting that his wife didn't like sex very much. Whether that was true or not I don't know. I certainly was willing to believe it. And so by, by allowing him to get rid of some of his sexual tensions it really made his marriage much better.

Q. And you felt good about this? You felt—there's a Jewish word for this. A mitzvah.

A. A mitzvah?

Q. This is a good deed that helps. They add up the mitzvahs when your time comes and if you've got the right number of mitzvahs you go through the Pearly Gates. You felt that this . . .

A. Yeah, Okay. I—one really unpleasant part of me is that I like being a mitzvah and at some point I think "Oh, screw it. When do I get mine?" I set things up so I become—the confidante. In the case of this fifty-one-year-old man it was, the sexual partner I became, rather than the confidante. But it was the same role, really.

Q. So that contrary to what one might expect, rather than enjoying the thrill of being in the position to break up someone's marriage and to play the femme fatale, you enjoyed the feeling of helping to cement the marriage. Did the possibility occur to you that, despite everything you thought or felt, you might indeed be breaking up a marriage and, if so, how did you feel about that? That you were the catalyst to a divorce?

A. I think that, uh—I was seeing a psychiatrist at this time and, one of the things I was very blind about was how unreliable he was. Not my psychiatrist, but the man. And, there would be moments where I would get really panicked because he would be acting in such a way that I thought "God, he could go home and tell his wife in a moment of anger!" It—I suspect that part of him really wanted his wife to find out. And that really did frighten me.

Q. It didn't excite you—it frightened you?

A. No, it did frighten me.

Q. When you did things with him like, spending a day at the beach—did you enjoy his companionship?

A. A lot of his companion—well, first of all, as I say, companionship was very sexually charged, in the wildest way. It was, you know, exchange of titillating jokes, or . . .

Q. You said he liked to talk dirty.

A. Yes, he liked to talk dirty. So it was charged. I also enjoyed, because—swimming also was a sport that I had been very good at as a kid—taught by my father—and there was the kind of thrill of being thought good at this. I was in fact a better water sportsman than he was—this man, not my father—and so there was this kind of—and he was very flattering about that, you know, and I used to even give him some instruction. And that made me feel very good, it made me feel competent. [pause] There were long times when we'd spend times together without swimming, where at least some of the time I felt almost acute panic because I realized there was so much of him that I didn't like. And he used to compulsively repeat it—himself, for instance—he used to compulsively tell, uh, stories about what he was doing in his work. And it was just, almost *unbearably* superficial, and I would feel somewhat panicked. I didn't ever want to recognize how much of him I didn't like, how much of him I found boring.

Q. Did you ever on these beach excurisions have sex? Or that was confined to one night a week?

A. Uh—we would have sex once a week in New York, and his wife would come down from the country on Sunday night and we'd sleep together Sunday night. We never had sex more than once a week.

Q. You never had sex on these excursions?

A. No, you can't—once a week . . .

Q. The fun and games part of it never led to sex.

A. Ah—it would have been highly dangerous. Have you ever tried to find a really secluded spot in the dunes?

Q. You could [laughing] put up a tent, you know.

A. We fantasized about this once or twice, but we didn't. Now as to fun and games. He is a man who loves fun and games. One of the things that sort of upset him, I think, was that he used this—I—as far as I know, while I was sleeping with him he was only sleeping with me and his wife. After we stopped sleeping together I know that he had a very short, very intense affair with another woman in our town. That I know of. And I am willing to believe that he had other affairs there. I don't think ever more than one at a time. Seriatum, I suspect.

Q. What led to the breakup?

A. He said—he broke it up, and he said that, quote, affairs are very, very painful for me, said he. And all my affairs, said he, have always ended unhappily, and so I want to end this one, y'know, before it does—end unhappily.

Q. He suddenly made this speech at you one day?

A. Yes, he took me out to lunch.

Q. And what was your reaction?

A. My reaction was really great, uh, a great feeling of letdown.

Q. That this was all going to be over.

A. Yes.

Q. No more excitement.

A. Yes.

Q. No more secrecy. No more surreptitious nights in New York. No more possibility . . .

A. No more—nor more being wanted, really.

Q. There was no one at the time to replace him?

A. No. That's—I, I think, if I have to say what I felt like when we, when we broke up, is that, the gut feeling had no longer anything to do with secrecy or chargedness or—or anything, but was just a feeling of, ah—not wanted. Again.

Q. Another rejection.

A. Yeah. And, and some anger at this insistence that we would still remain marvelous friends, which I even then knew was a cop-out, a con job.

Q. You haven't seen him since . . .

A. Oh, yes, I see him. But I have not seen a lot of him since he left his wife. And the year before, after I stopped seeing him, I did see a good deal of him and there was one summer when I saw a good deal of him. It was on one hand plushly titillating and on the other hand it was very frustrating.

Q. If you had choice in the matter, would you pick an older man over a younger man to have an affair with?

A. [pause] The problem now, being thirty-five, is [pause] unmarried thirty-five-year-olds are full of —are usually full of sex-hangups. In a way that I don't think thirty-five-year-old women—I may be full of emotional hangups, as has come out, but I don't think I'm full of sexual hangups.

Q. And you're saying that . . .

A. And I'm saying that if I pick—the problem is, I mean if I sat down and said, well I want to have an affair with, y'know, X, I would rather have an affair with an older married man than I would with a man with my own age who's never been married.

Q. Because you feel that an older married man has—his fear of . . .

A. No, no. I think that for the moment I'm not talking about age, since I at this moment am almost old enough to qualify as midolescent. I think I would rather have an affair with a married man than a man who'd never been married.

Q. But I would like to pursue the "why" of this. Why—what is it about an older married man that makes an affair with him more either satisfying, or exciting, or stimulating, or worthwhile, than an affair with a younger man or an unmarried man? What element is it in an older married man that makes an affair with him a more desirable thing? And we'll rule out immediately the fact that there are vicious or vindictive traits in you that make you want to break

up marriages because you yourself have never been married. This—
then there has to be some sort of rationale whether—see if you can
dredge it up. Maybe it's . . .

A. Then I'm just—I'm trying to think the—I think what I was
trying to say—this is coming out horrible—that if I don't want to
pick a man with extreme sexual hangups, I've pretty much got to—
to choose a man who's married, no matter what his age is. I like to
think that I'm getting healthier.

Q. Growing.

A. Yes. And there's—there's some evidence that that is—true. I
would like to think that I might choose someone possible rather than
someone impossible.

Q. Well, let me—this isn't really a digression. Let me say this:
Most of us were brought up, whether consciously or unconsciously,
in ways that gave us hangups. But marriage is a sacrosanct thing, and
having an affair outside of a marriage is courting disaster. Emotional
disaster, social disaster—Does this . . .

A. When—when you started to say that, I thought "Shiittt!"
What I think I am coming to the point of, and I don't want to break
up anybody's marriage—is that what my fant—in other words I was
being practical before when I said, well, you know, thirty-five-year-
old men who've never been married have hangups. This may be true,
but the real point is that I think I'm getting to the point where I want
to look out for me.

Q. Well: How does this . . .

A. And so I don't want to have an affair with an older man who
will yet reject me again.

Q. So—the fact that . . .

A. Y'know—*I've had it!*

Q. The fact that he's married means there's no possibility that he
can reject you because he has already rejected you even in accepting
you because he's married. Here comes that element of safety again.
Only in this case it's your personal safety. You don't want to subject
yourself to another rejection.

A. It is, well—let me doc . . .

Q. I don't want to explain it *for* you. You . . .

A. It—one of my patterns is to avoid anxiety. Y'know, the chance
that—what if I were to fall in love with a man who's, say, married
and I really did want him? To avoid the pain of anxiety, I just skip
over the anxiety and get myself into a situation that, of course it's

going to fail. The rejection, painful as it is, is easier to face than anxiety. [long pause]

Q. So you can enjoy the relationship then, as long as it lasts, knowing, with this safety factor built in, that you're not going to get to the point where you want to marry the guy and are going to be rejected, because you don't want to break up the marriage—he's already married—therefore the situation cannot arise.

A. The situation cannot arise so I get rejected, which is easier than, uh . . .

Q. Worrying about whether you're going to get rejected.

A. Yes. Since I know that I am . . .

Q. It's a foregone concluison.

A. Yeah.

Q. So you can enjoy it, free and clear, of all tensions and anxieties. Just have a good time and know that eventually it's going to stop.

A. You're making it obviously seem more idyllic than it is. There was, of course, tension, and there was anxiety and there was longing. But there was also, this—this dead certain sense that it was going to —to come to nothing.

Q. It's like not . . .

A. Which is easier than having to face really wanting something and trying to get it.

Q. It's like not taking an exam because you're afraid of failing. If you don't take it there's no possibility of your failing.

A. Right. Not marking—not marking my own, uh—that's not really true. [pause] You know, this happens in other areas, when I was teaching before, not now, but in another school, I would have —I was convinced I was going to fail as a teacher, so I would not mark my papers. Which may be anxieties. Part of me wanted very much to be a good teacher, but—to think that, God! I might really get promoted and I might really stay there, was so anxiety-producing that I would just not mark my papers and then *of course* I would fail.

Q. It's a good system. [pause] In retrospect, what would you have done differently? Either with the long affair with the homo . . .

A. The thing I cry about—and I really do cry—is that I feel that I have wasted a lot of my life. [pause] You know, I've wasted, between one thing and another, between either sort of casual dalliances, love of a man who couldn't possibly return it, or an affair with a married man—I wasted such a bloody chunk of my life. I've accumulated experience but I sometimes feel very sad that I am—

that I have just wasted—I feel jealous of my younger colleagues, for instance.

Q. You don't regret the affairs themselves?

A. Regret them?[pause]

Q. Was the book worth the candle?

A. No, the book is not worth the candle, but that's different than regret. I am sad at a kind of wasted life, but that doesn't mean that I regret them.

Q. It's a funny thing from someone who's thirty-five years old to talk about a wasted life.

A. I don't always feel this way.[pause] Well, it—it is, [long pause] I've spent a lot of time sort of treading water, and it is that I regret. Or if not—that I feel sorry for myself about . . .

Q. Let me—I think we're going to wrap it all up now. Let me just pose a hypothetical question to which you can give me any hypothetical answer. If, today, or tonight or tomorrow, a man of fifty . . .

A. He will have to have gray hair, by the way, I realize.

Q. What does that mean?

A. It occurs to me that the men I find most attractive have gray hair.

Q. What does gray hair mean to you? Did your father have gray hair?

A. It—yes my father has—I like gray, curly hair. I mean, I like hair like mine. My father has hair like mine. But it's gray. It was prematurely gray. It's been gray ever since after the war.

Q. The navy did it to him?

A. Yes. A torpedo almost hit his destroyer. Turned it white in a single night. I—I didn't mean to interrupt. Go on with your question.

Q. If, if you were to meet a man—all right, let's say he *has* gray curly hair, and he's fifty years old and he's married . . .

A. And—uh . . . shhh. . . .

Q. —and there's some kind of spark . . .

A. —yeah, and that I feel sorry for him . . .

Q. Would you have an affair with such a man tomorrow?

A. If I were attracted to him and he could make me feel needed? Yes.

Miss D

Q. Your name was given to me by one of your friends. Obviously a rather close friend, who told me that as a young woman you'd led quite a—quite a wild life.

A. Well, that's all in the point of view. One person's wild life is another's calm existence.

Q. And you're now married?

A. For the fourth and—who knows?—maybe the final time.

Q. You're now married and in your fifties; you seemed to be a good subject for this because you had many affairs, when you were younger, with men who were at the time much older than you. Is that right?

A. Yes.

Q. For the record, where were you born, and when, where were you raised—that kind of thing.

A. I was born in Cincinnati in 1920.

Q. And your background?

A. I would say lower middle class. My father was a picture-framer, a toy salesman, a crockery salesman, a traveling salesman. My mother was a housewife, seamstress, with no schooling. My father had gone to college.

Q. How many children in the family?

A. Four. Two boys and two girls; an older brother and sister, both of whom are dead, and a younger brother who's practicing now in Arizona.

Q. A doctor?

A. Yes. I went to school in Cincinnati. I had about a year of college in [deleted] Normal Junior College, I had a year's apprenticeship at the University of [deleted] Medical School in laboratory technique, I went to cooking school, business college, various extension schools. An accumulation, altogether, of about three years of formal college, I guess.

Q. And you had a career?

A. Well, I went to work. I did many different things. The only thing that paid was working as an actress. But I worked for three or four years for almost nothing and then, finally, the union came, and we were paid, whether we were sponsored or not. I got married at nineteen the first time and married more or less to get out of the house because by that time I was—although I was in love, I realize it wasn't a good marriage—but, uh, my family found out I was sleeping with this gentleman and it was marry him or get out. So I married him.

Q. How old was he?

A. He was twenty, I guess. And then I went into a road show and he left for Philadelphia, and he was an actor, producer, director in radio. And I joined him there and—he was an alcoholic and he got fired for being drunk on the job and there was a lot of fighting—physical fighting. And one morning he just disappeared. I didn't see him again for ten years.

Q. How long were you married?

A. About six years, I guess, but we lived together only about six months. Then I married again in 1946 and got divorced in 1949, married again in '51, got divorced in '53 and married my present husband. I can't [laughing] remember all those things.

Q. From the time of your first marriage until, let's say, the time that you married your present husband, you from time to time had affairs with older men. How many such affairs would you say you had?

A. Oh, I don't think I could count them. Thirty, forty, fifty maybe. Very brief. Some of them lasted—I was alone for about six years and was not going with anyone with the idea of getting married and, uh, most of this occurred in Chicago, I guess, and they were men who were in their forties and they'd ship their wives away for the summer or see them just weekends. And it was a very nice arrangement because I never felt particularly alone and I had certain appetites and it was better getting them satisfied regularly by the same person than living with a bunch of one-night stands. It made my emotional balance clear and free to do whatever—to devote myself to my work. There was no involvement ever . . .

Q. You never got heavily entangled emotionally with any of these men?

A. Once or twice, and as soon as that started you could—I would bow out. Because I didn't want to get involved with something involving children or a divorce or breaking up a home.

Q. These were your own moral scruples at work?

A. Yeah, that's the way I felt.

Q. And you felt . . .

A. I was getting what I asked for. I didn't ask for anything in a monetary way.

Q. Well, what was the—aside from the satisfaction of your appetite, and by that you mean your sexual appetite—was there anything else that this fulfilled? Was there any need? Was it a question of companionship, of . . .

Q. Oh, yeah, I'm sure. Although it was a very limited companionship. It consisted of going out in the evenings and coming home alone.

Q. The men never came home with you?

A. No, no. I usually had a roommate.

Q. You went with them to their houses?

A. To a hotel, usually. A suite.

Q. You would see—how many times would you see one man?

A. Well, one man I saw for a year, another for about a year. There . . .

Q. Simultaneously? You had any number of simultaneous . . .

A. No, not two at the same time. There were a lot of one-night stands and those didn't work out.

Q. How did you feel about one-night stands?

A. Well, I was kinda screwed-up sexually. I had to be made to be laid, and I think that gets kind of dull. And after it was over I'd never want to see that person again, in that way.

Q. Could you amplify on that a bit? How would it affect the relationship?

A. Well, I couldn't meet somebody and say, "Let's go to bed." I had to be wined and dined and made over, and then we got to bed, and then—that is the end of that. I mean, if they wanted more than that, I didn't want any more than that. If they wanted it to be an involved relationship, I didn't want—I didn't want to be involved unless I saw there was marriage at the end of it.

Q. Since most of these were married men . . .

A. Yeah, it was out of the question.

Q. Well, why, then, did you select married men, men that . . .

A. *They* selected *me*. I can't ever remember in my life approaching anyone or picking anyone up except the guy I'm married to now.

Q. Why was . . .

A. I was always sought after, which was a big surprise to me.

Q. And you were never sought after by younger men?

A. Oh, yeah. Lots of 'em. That doesn't mean I went to bed with them.

Q. But you went to bed with the older men.

A. Yeah. I guess I knew I was safe.

Q. Safe from what?

A. Because I was—uh, this is complicated isn't it? I would have liked to have a long relationship with a young man if I thought it was—but they weren't interested in marriage. I wanted to get married. I believe that's the only way to live. Because if your sexual appetites are taken care of you can get on to other things. The young guys wanted one-night stands here or there with no idea of getting married. So I concluded, well, I'll take this other and I'll, in a way it is being married without being married. [laughter] I can go ahead and do what I want to do and my appetites are taken care of until the time comes when I can get a young man and get married.

Q. So you felt a certain safety in the older men?

A. Yes. And I'm sure there was a lot of father image there too. Because they were all very kind to me. Some of them advised me in my career, helped me with legal advice. They were mostly business-men.

Q. Did they all more or less conform to certain physical types, that you're aware of?

A. No. They had to have something in the head. They had to be someone I could talk to. I think I went out with one or two Charles Atlases and that was enough of that. I never did that again. And there was—there were a lot of people—Realize, this was a time when everyone was broke. And we didn't have any money. And people casually went to bed with each other just out of need, out of friend-ship.

Q. In your circle, or . . .

A. Yes. Realize I had a very limited circle. I only knew people in my business.

Q. Show business?

A. Yes, or people related to that. I didn't know housewives or carpenters or bricklayers or doctors.

Q. These were businessmen?

A. Yeah. Well, they would maybe be at the sponsor end of a radio show.

Q. Did you feel that these men were giving you fair return for yourself? Or that they were extracting from you something for which there wasn't adequate payment, in some way?

A. No. What did I have to give that they weren't giving me? As I say, I never felt very female. I mean, the business of virginity or I've-given-you-my-body, or the-best-year-of-my-life or something like that. No. I got what I asked for, and that's all I wanted.

Q. Let me get a little background. When was—how old were you when you had your first sexual experience?

A. Seventeen. I think. Really, completely—yeah. And I had — I had been laid by a lesbian and it startled me. She was a friend of a vaudeville entertainer. And their family and my family had been friends for years. And she came to Cincinnati and invited me to a hotel room and got me very drunk and made me take a bath and dressed me in a beautiful nightgown and went to bed and made love to me. And I passed out and woke up the next morning covered in hickies from my fingertips to my earlobes and down to my feet. And it was very hot. I remember going home—uh, I've always been one for no scenes, if possible. Nothing was said. I just said goodbye to her nicely, I'd see her again, and I went home and put on a high-neck sweater with long sleeves, and hoped to God my mother wouldn't notice. My younger brother was about ten then and the older kids were away at school. And I had been going to the movies—again, with an older man; he was about forty, a friend of the family. And he lived in a hotel, and I called him up and said, "I'm coming right down to see you." And he said okay. And I got dressed in a, a formal—I just figured that's what I'd better wear to this thing [laughter]. And I went down to the hotel room and I had —I asked him for three or four drinks, and I whipped off all my clothes and got in bed, and I said, "Now you do to me what men are supposed to do to women. Now!" And he was—"Oh, my God!" he said. "How'd I get into *this*?" But he did it. It was painful, and the second time around not so painful. And of course I got pregnant, and had an abortion. And I'd had infectious mononucleosis the year before, and when I went to medical school I'd got a positive Wasserman, so it looked like I had syphilis. But it didn't turn me off men, it just turned me on men. And that relationship kept up until the family found out about it. And then soon after that I left home.

Q. Well, then, interestingly enough, your first sexual experience —and you were then seventeen—was already with a middle-aged man.

A. Yeah, but all the men I married were my own age. But I think the next one will be younger.

Q. Got that in mind already?

A. Well, I never [she laughs heartily] get married until I have the one picked out, y'know. I haven't picked one out yet, so my husband is safe for a while.

Q. I'd like to explore this whole area of your relationship to middle-aged men when you were younger. These men . . .

A. Well, there was—it was absolutely cut and dried. I never attempted to find out who their wives—I saw their children's pictures, I heard about the children, I got the my-wife-doesn't-really-understand-me routine. I got all that. "But-I'll-never-divorce-her." These men were, uh, all Jewish, and—I don't know. I might have been doing something to get back at my mother. She was a very strong woman who taught me to hate Catholics, hate Jews, cigarettes. I tried to, but—I don't think you can generalize, because every person is different, every need is different. I had been told that Jewish men don't divorce their wives; they may horse around, but they don't get divorced. So maybe I felt a, a safety. As I said, I didn't get divorced the first time till I was ready to get married. I got divorced a week before I got married, although I was separated for six years.

Q. One of the other women who was interviewed said that she likes older men because their heads are more together. Did that play a role in your affairs?

A. Well, perhaps. [pause] I feel a great, uh, a great deal of sadness about my daughter because she's going through all this terrible heartbreak of, "He said something, then I said something, and how terrible, and I think I'll go jump off the bridge." 'Cause I can remember having terrible, terrible scenes over a word said wrong or something. And when you become older and more mature, we hope, that doesn't set everyone off.

Q. An older man can handle himself in such a situation with more aplomb.

A. Yes, if he's adult. A lot of men are not adult. They're older, but they're not adult. And I don't know what I mean by that.

Q. Well, I don't either, and in view of the ethics of our society—and we do live, for better or worse, in a . . .

A. Yes, we have been brainwashed and trained into a very strict code of ethics.

Q. Then wouldn't it occur to you to say that a man who is married and has a family and responsibilities, that such a man who carries on an affair with a younger woman is somehow putting his marriage into jeopardy? Because the possibility always exists that the wife may find out, that the wife may react in a violent way, that it may rupture their marriage. Can . . .

A. Yeah, I might have gotten *shot!* [laughter]

Q. Can such a man be said to be adult? In view of the fact that he's abrogating his responsibility, or at least threatening to?

A. Well [long pause] now, in a lot of cases the wives were out of town, that's all. They didn't have a partner at home in bed when they came home at night. A lot of men can take that abstinence. Other men feel, why should they?

Q. This isn't a question of physical presence; it's a question of moral presence. There is at all times, somewhere in the scene, whether physically present or not, the wife and family. And the affair with the younger woman represents a potential threat to that marriage. If you, as the younger woman, are looking for a man who's mature, responsible, and whose head is together, and you have a liaison with an older man who's married—aren't you then overlooking the fact that this indeed is not a responsible, mature man whose head is all together? There's something wrong somewhere in his emotional makeup that lets him carry on such an affair.

A. Well, I never considered morality at all. I've had eleven abortions and it never occurred to me that I killed a human being. Just that—that something interfered with my life at that moment and I had it taken care of. That's all. I don't know that I was amoral. I don't think I put that much into the relationship.

Q. You never permitted the relationship to develop to the point where . . .

A. One man, at Christmas, gave me some piece of minor costume jewelry, some necklace or something. And I fell in love with a younger man. None of these people [the older men] could I say I was in love with. To me, falling in love is total commitment. Everything else is of no importance. And when that is cemented, then I feel you should go on to living. I fell in love and we decided to get married. So I told the young man there was someone I had to break off with, and he didn't question it at all. So I went to this gentleman and told him, and he was *livid!* He was FURIOUS! And for the first time, I realized he loved me. I didn't really love him. I enjoyed his companionship. We played golf together, went swimming, went to the beach, went sailing, went out to clubs, bars, theaters. I realized he was very upset that I was going to interrupt what he had figured out was his-cake-and-eat-it-too.

Q. He had you . . .

A. And his wife and children, yeah. And I was breaking that up. And that was the last such relationship. Now, I never had any relationship after I got married in 1940. All of these other things occurred between my first and second marriages. I was married, but I didn't live with my husband or see him. So I was safe. That may have been another reason I got so many offers. Everyone knew I was married. It would have taken a bit of doing to undo that. They knew they weren't getting involved.

Q. Did any of these older men with whom you had affairs . . .

A. You make it sound like there were thousands.

Q. Well, you gave me a figure—thirty, forty, fifty.

A. Yeah, well, there were only three or four that I—I can remember the names of only two that were long-term affairs.

Q. Did any of them want to marry you?

A. No, it was never discussed. We always avoided such a thing.

Q. Because—why did you avoid it? Because it was a painful subject? Because there were technical, legal difficulties?

A. No. Everything was fun and games. We were coming out of the Depression. I often discussed their particular—aspects of their work. One gentleman was with a big food firm and they decided to put out some new product and we discussed advertising campaigns and ways of laying it out. It was just completely separate. I suppose it would be like going to the club, doing what you did at the club, and then go back home. And you certainly didn't want to talk to your wife about how well you played handball any more than you'd talk to your handball partner about your problems at home. You were more concerned with what you were doing right then at the moment. Occasionally, I thought, "Oh, my God! I'm not doing the right thing here."

Q. Who broke up these affairs? You, or . . .

A. I did.

Q. Why?

A. The one where the man got angry with me, because I was— I thought I was in love with somebody else. I saw these gentlemen only in the evening; the young people I saw in the daytime or weekends.

Q. Were you ever aware, even in a peripheral way, of looking for something beyond the man? Of looking for some sort of image, of looking for something that was lacking in your life and that you thought you could find through an older man? Whether it was security, or chasing a father image, or . . .

A. I think, ideally, I always hoped to marry a man who was as wonderful as I thought my father was. My mother tried to tear my father down and tell me he wasn't so wonderful. But what could be more wonderful than having a father who's a toy salesman? Who brought you everything every day? And any time one of us said, "Oh, I have to have a present for my teacher," my father would go up in the attic and come down with a gift. He—he knew everything about camping, about the outdoors, about cameras, fishing, decorating. In the last years of my association with him, before I left home, I discovered he could tap-dance. I discovered he could speak deaf-and-dumb language, and I thought, "My God! There must be so many more things about him!" My husband is an unending delight because there are many things I still don't know about him. He hasn't proven to be a father image come to life—he's too erratic. But I also had a —an Elsie Dinsmore, Pollyanna—this is what I thought my household was like. Meeting my brother again last fall, I realized, "God, it was *never* like that. How did I actually think it was?" A wonderful home, where everybody did everything together. I really thought that's what it was like. And I wanted that, and when I found out it wasn't that, it was about the time I left home, and then I look back and recall all the things my mother did. That I wanted that kind of—a home life—and I've always liked gray-haired men, bald-headed men, men who wore glasses. My father wore glasses as long as I remember. Uh, fireplaces. I was never—I never went out and played tennis. I went skiing one whole year. My God, what a bore! I mean, I liked the skiing, but, uh—I wanted to talk, and be—be quiet.

Q. You liked the quiet things in life?

A. Yeah, I was not—God! I can't think of anything I can do well, physically [laughing]. And I *do* mean it.

Q. The older men—we haven't really . . .

A. I haven't answered your question, have I?

Q. Yeah, that's what I'm trying to get back to. Whether you were ever aware, either then or now, either during the affair or after the affair, whether this man represented to you something that was lacking in your life, probably your father.

A. Security. They were all established men, financially.

Q. Men who had made their mark.

A. They had already gotten there. They all had cars. If they weren't driving them they had chauffered cars. I was constantly picked up in limousines. I mean here I was; as a lab technician I had a limousine pick me up after work while all the other girls stood on the corner and waited for the bus. And they knew it wasn't just Daddy Longlegs coming to get me. Uh—I want—you know, I guess it is a terrible wrench to have your home broken up. Because there's no money, and the mortgage is foreclosed, and your parents are going to separate. If there weren't solidity—I wanted the solidity, although I knew I—maybe I thought, euphemistically, the wife might miraculously might drop out of sight and the children with her and they'd take me.

Q. Ah, now we're really getting down to it. So there was . . .

A. Maybe I really—that's what I really thought could happen. Because I am practical but I'm also terribly romantic.

Q. So there was this picture somewhere in your mind or off in the distance . . .

A. They all had homes. And I used to think before I ever bought one that when you owned a home you owned it. You went to the store, paid ten dollars and got a home back. I didn't know that we didn't own our home. Years later, I found out my father never—he believed only in renting. He didn't believe in owning anything.

Q. Did you ever want to own a man—for yourself? To have him for yourself and yourself alone?

A. An older man?

Q. Yeah.

A. [long pause] Now there are many times I've tried not to think too much. Because the—I—even in my work, I used to fantasize and daydream in my work that I would come to New York and all the actresses would retire. And after a while I realized that wasn't even possible. Even if I were that great or anything. And I always put a —a barrier on my romantic fantasies.

Q. Did you have problems with feelings of self-worth? You said you never . . .

A. No, no. I had a fantastically reverse thing. Through a lot of religious training and my mother, I thought I was as great as any human being that ever was. I thought I was so great that if somebody else were less great than I or did something embarrassing that I should do something to take the embarrasment away from them because I was a much bigger person and I could handle it better without getting hurt.

Q. How did this reflect itself in your relationships with these men? Did you find it difficult . . .

A. I—this one man, I thought, well I'm not gonna let him get involved. I'm not gonna let him get in too deeply. When I found out he was—when he got so upset—I also thought I was so great and there was so much of me it was all right to spread it out a little. If I could be nice to someone, not knowing then that, uh, men can have many, many, many relationships without involving the heart at all.

Q. And you? Was your heart involved?

A. Not a lot of times. My heart's only been involved about twice or three times in my life.

Q. And the rest? Almost as a sex . . .

A. Clinically.

Q. —a friendship thing? Was it hard for you to become involved with a man whom you thought much inferior to you, say . . .

A. Oooohhh! Only in the head.

Q. That's what I mean.

A. Yeah, I remember one boy dragged up from nowhere who was trying to be an opera singer, and he spoke dese-dem-dose. You could imagine how *that* went with the kind of thing *I* was in. And I met him in cellars, in bars, and he ran with a group I realize now were kind of a bunch of hippies, and we would have big feasts of maybe four pretzels apiece and a bottle of beer. But I couldn't take it very long. I always wanted to be with someone who was smarter than I was.

Q. Could you have a sexual relationship with someone who was not as smart as you?

A. Yeah, I think so. I think I did. Because it was all wrapped up in the sex angle. Only. I had, I'm sure, several affairs for just that, and then got away as quickly as possible.[pause] Well, uh, maybe I was mixed up. But I just let things occur. There were many people I didn't go to bed with that wanted to. For instance, I would not go to bed with anyone that involved giving me a job. Saying, "Well, you could have so-and-so, you know, but in the meantime . . ." Oh, no! Forget the job. If I liked him, I would.

Q. So the criterion was . . .

A. Whether I liked him or not.

Q. Not what was in it for you.

A. No, no. Except for the sexual satisfaction. I had a guy tuck a fifty-dollar bill in my blouse. And I was starving. I couldn't pay my rent or anything. And I was drunk, too. And I simply took it out and gave it to him and had hysterics. I said, "I only do it for nothing." [laughter]

Q. Let me change direction here. Did you ever have—not counting the time you were separated and not married in fact although you were married legally—did you ever have an affair while you were married?

A. Yes, when I was married to my last husband—my third—I had several. And I never had an affair after I met my present husband, or rather after I married him, because my ex-husband raped me a couple of times and—uh, let's see—I was living with someone at the time I met my present husband, so I had to break that off. Yes, when I was married to my first husband, I tried to have an affair . . .

Q. Deliberately? You set out to . . .

A. Yes, I deliberately allowed—someone was after me, and I said, "Ooookay, oookaay. Maybe this will make me feel better." And it didn't.

Q. In what way did you think it might make you feel better?

A. Oh, revenge, uh, getting back. And, you know, you can't revenge anything like that. You're just hurting yourself.

Q. This was not a question of reinforcing your own diminishing feelings of attractiveness? It was just a question of getting back.

A. I guess so. No, I don't think I'm attractive. If anybody's in love with me [laughing] he's gotta be somewhat—peculiar. My first husband had his—the first affair I knew about was a very widely used assistant madam of one of the biggest establishments in town, and she told him that he was the best lay she'd ever had, or I had. I said, "Well, she would know." And then I said, "I hoped you told her where you learned everything you know." Y'know, the thing about —well, that's another story. Yeah, I had several affairs when I was married to my last husband, but it was running away, that's all.

Q. These weren't affairs you were seeking for positive reasons; they were affairs you were seeking for negative reasons.

A. I guess so, uh-huh.

Q. So they couldn't possibly have been good, or enjoyable.

A. No, at the time, no. I have had very little sex that wasn't enjoyable.

Q. You mean physically enjoyable—sex is an enjoyable thing.

A. Yeah, yeah.

Q. I'm talking about emotionally enjoyable.

A. I think the most unenjoyable sex I ever had was with my last husband.

Q. It was emotionally . . .

A. It was emotionally *disastrous.* Because I felt I had to submit and give in, and I hated it. And I don't think he enjoyed it, either. But he said, "You're my wife and this is what you're going to do." And that's enough to turn anyone off. I mean, why would you do that to a woman? What would you get out of it?

Q. That's the mentality of the rapist, and that's beyond the scope of this book.

A. I don't know if I helped you at all, if I've said anything of any value to you.

Q. Well, you certainly provided some insights into the thinking of a younger woman who has affairs with older men. [pause] Uh, let's turn . . .

A. I'll tell you something. I used to go into the ladies room at places like the Copa and Sardi's and Chez Paree, and hear these girls talk as they'd replenish their makeup, and one would say, "Well, what are you getting out of him? Are you getting anything?" And, "Yeah, I've got it all figured. If he doesn't do this, I'm gonna write a letter to his wife . . ." Now, in a sense, I'm one of them. But how *could* I be? I guess I forgave myself for what I was doing which was not morally correct by figuring as long as I wasn't getting anything material out of it it couldn't be all that wrong.

Q. One question remains—well, lots of questions remain unanswered, but one crops up right now: If you were having affairs because you enjoyed sex, you enjoyed the company, you enjoyed the relationship, you were not out to ruin anyone's marriage, you were not a destructive or immoral person in that sense at all—it was the farthest thing from your mind—why was it almost invariably an older man? What not a younger man who had, let us say . . .

A. Well, maybe the young guy couldn't afford it.

Q. Afford what?

A. Uh—usually when I went out with a younger man I paid the bill or split the bill. We didn't make that much money in those days. You had to get—if you wanted a decent meal you had to go out with someone older and established.

Q. It was a question of practicality.

A. Yeah, in a sense, it was.

Q. Well, try to project now . . .

A. Well, suppose it were right now.

Q. No, suppose it was back then and it was a younger man with means.

A. Welllll, now! That's funny, because I went with two or three younger men with means. I went with one guy in Ohio, they named a hill after his family. And he was the dullest son of a bitch [laughter] that ever [trails off into wild laughter]—And I don't think he was a very good lay, either, and I tried it. For a little while, 'cause I—this kid's father chased me around the house and tried to get his hands on me, for God's sake! Then I went with another young man I liked who was very funny and I thought maybe it would be nice if we got married, and he said, of course, "I wouldn't think of marrying you because I want to get ahead and I've got my eye on such and such a job and I'll have to go after one of the girls in the family." And that, of course, was the end of him. [pause] I think I—I practically talked marriage to the boys who carried my books home from school. And I—don't think that all these one-night stands that I dropped them; I'm sure they dropped me. As soon as they saw the wedding rings in my eyes—both eyes. Because that's the only thing I wanted to be, was married and have a family, and . . .

Q. Obviously, then, you . . .

A. I really clobbered up the whole idea of why I went with older men, didn't I? That was a set of circumstances. I don't think these men were going through any midolescence at all. I think they still probably are having their younger girls on the side. This was a way of life. I'm not sure I ever met anybody who was going through unusual or fantastic departures from his scheme of things. That was just part of the trappings of the makeup of the middle-class, moderately successful businessman. I don't remember any of them breaking up their families.

Q. Did any of them ever indicate that he might or would or could?

A. Well, I knew a nympho, and she went with one guy and literally wore him out. He picked up his family and moved, severed his relationships with his business associates and moved to another state to get away from her.

Q. That's the other side of the coin. The cases we've looked at, it's been a severing of the relationship on the other side, the man divorced, leaving his wife, leaving his children . . .

A. Yeah, well, in this case he left his girlfriend. I don't think men or the group of men you're concerned with, I don't think—no, I'll use another generality. I think they have been conditioned and brainwashed into believing what it's all about, which it isn't, and when they arrive at a certain age group, when they get there and find out that isn't what they really wanted, that life is shorter than they thought, how much was good that they had, how much was really great, and what do they really want to do, then they think about a complete change. We raise men to believe that they must be responsible. Why should they have to be responsible for something all the charm has gone out of?

Q. You're talking about the marriage.

A. Yeah. Because there's such a hassle of making it every day. And these men who haven't been imbued with this tremendous sense of responsibility, well, they figure that, well, they have to take care of their crabby old drunken mother, they have to take care of their father who is in some—one of my cousins had to take care of his father and pick him up from bars and get him out of jail and so on and so on, and then when his father died and he got established and everything, then he got rid of his wife. He got a girlfriend, too. He felt all his responsibilities that he'd been conditioned to believe he must handle, he'd taken care of all of them.

Q. How old was he when he did this—threw off the marriage and . . .

A. Oh, forty-six, forty-seven.

Q. Well, that seems to be the kind of thing I've been looking at, or for. But you haven't run across that. It seems . . .

A. I never met a man who was about to leave his—I don't think so, unless I put it out of my mind.

Q. Is it possible you misread some of these men? Is it possible some of them were willing to break up their homes for you and you just didn't see it?

A. Well, I think I've trained myself or taught myself to try to understand the other guy's point of view. When I helped form the union they used to send me out to get converts and I'd come back converted to the other side and they'd say, "Oh, you stay in the office and add up the figures." I'd say, "Well, they *do* have a point, you know." I don't think I misread anything, or didn't read enough into something. [pause] I think that being in love is loving someone more than yourself. There isn't anything you wouldn't do or help, and yet you might get down to the nitty gritty. Would you turn your husband in if he killed somebody and no one knew about it but you? You'd have to figure that out morally. Or would you help him escape? Or is that love? Or is it just protecting yourself? Some people don't know how to give. My husband, for instance: I don't think he knows how to give too well. So his love is a very moral love. He could not have an affair, I think, with a woman without falling in love with her. That way, it's all right.

V.
History, Literature and Headlines

Is midolescence, like jet lag, an affliction sired by technology, a child of the twentieth century? Certainly the literature of this century, literary creations from Charles Strickland to Herzog, express quite explicity the anguish felt at the second moment of truth in life, when youth ends and the door to aging swings ajar. But how far back does recognition of the crisis extend?

"The Middle Ages," says Dr. Van Den Haag, the psychiatrist-sociologist who offered his views in Chapter II, "called acedia what we today call alienation. And this was well known; it was known to the monks in the desert. As a matter of fact, antiquity knew about this already. It [a crisis] did occur in adolescence, and it did occur again when one was in middle age. Remedies were prescribed: prayer, work, keeping yourself busy. Not very different from the remedies that you prescribe today."

In looking for the antecedents of the middle-age crisis, or for the crisis itself, we can go as far back as the third century B.C., to the opening chapter of Plato's Republic. Nowhere is middle age mentioned, per se; life expectancy then was greatly abbreviated compared with life expectancies today. The Greeks, their span of intellect notwithstanding, thought of life as divided between youth and age. They did not know and did not use the modern term. But read

311

"middle" for "old" age in the following excerpt from Book I of the Republic and you may find parallels between these antique dialogues and some of the taped interviews in this book:

> This is a question which I should like to ask of you who have arrived at that time which the poets call the "threshold of old age"—is life harder towards the end, or what report do you give of it?
>
> I will tell you, Socrates, he said, what my own feeling is. Men of my age flock together; we are birds of a feather, as the old proverb says; and at our meetings the tale of my acquaintance commonly is—I cannot eat, I cannot drink; the pleasures of youth and love are fled away; there was a good time once, but now that is gone . . . Some complain of the slights which are put upon them by relations, and they will tell you sadly of how many evils their old age is the cause. But to me, Socrates, these complainers seem to blame that which is not really in fault. For if old age were the cause, I too being old, and every other man, would have felt as they do. But this is not my experience, nor that of others whom I have known. How well I remember the aged poet Sophocles, when in answer to the question, How does love suit with age, Sophocles,—are you still the man you were? Peace, he replied; most gladly have I escaped the thing of which you speak; I feel as if I had escaped from a mad and furious master.

Yes, that fragment of those majestic dialogues is plucked out of context. Socrates and his friends only touched upon aging in passing, in warming up to what the Republic is really all about, politics. But touch upon it they did. This chapter takes a rather peripatetic trip from ancient to contemporary literature and history, touching a few bases between the far-off past and the recent past in an attempt to show that midolescence is not all that modern. It is there in *some* form throughout the journey, by suggestion and implication in the distant past and, as we near our own time, more and more by explication. Toward the end of this chapter, as we enter the present, the hydra rears its most dangerous head. Not for nothing do disturbed middle-aged men feel sudden urges to press their Gillettes against their throats. Most midolescents of modern fiction feel the suicide urge; some real-life men, like two you will encounter here, obeyed it.

Life expectancy did not grow between Plato's time and the period of history sometimes still called the Dark Ages. Youth and Age were still the two great periods of life; there was no middle age in the Middle Ages. But there were midolescents, or their Medieval equivalents, as this passage from *Sex and the Mature Man,* by Louise P. Saxe and Noel Gerson, makes clear:

The relatively few records that have survived from the period after the fall of the Roman Empire . . . are as enlightening as the clinical reports of the most efficient twentieth-century hospital. During that long twilight, before the rebirth of civilization, a man was in his prime from seventeen to twenty. Between the ages of twenty and twenty-five, he was believed to be in his middle years. By our standards, he had just reached the threshold of manhood, but he *believed* [authors' italics] he had reached the top of the hill and was declining. As a consequence, he *did* slide down. The same story is repeated again and again in the faded manuscripts of monks and priests, the only people who could write. Great lords, merchants and peasants suffered alike from the same affliction during their early twenties: they frequently became melancholy, silent and seemed to withdraw into themselves; they often became agitated, anxious and restless. They complained of insomnia and constipation and bewildered their familes and friends by displaying irritability for no apparent reason. Then suddenly, inexplicably, their mood would change, and they would become lively and gay, even capricious for a time before the next cloud of gloom settled on their bowed shoulders.

Reading into the lives of people long dead is at best a shaky business, though a lot of writers earn rather stable incomes by doing it. The easy conclusions reached by historical novelists seem far too easy to really educated people. Dr. Van Den Haag made this comment as he and I were discussing some modern interpretations of the life of Leonardo da Vinci: "I have a great reluctance to pronounce myself on people that are not actually in treatment with me. It is fairly easy to find a theoretical framework into which their symptoms fit, and then to say they suffered from this, they suffered from that. But there may be another theoretical framework just as good."

I have done my best to avoid any such theoretical framework in looking back. That way lies absurdity. Was it midolescence that made Martin Luther nail the ninety-five theses to the door of All Saints Church in Wittenberg in 1517? (And he changed his career, right? Hell, he became a Lutheran!) And was it the Commencement of the Call or midolescence when Mohammed, aged about forty-three, began to preach and promulgate the religion of Islam, after so many placid years as a Mecca businessman? And why not drag in poor old Methuselah; when was *he* middle-aged, at four hundred and forty-four?

Trying to pin midolescence to such long-ago lives would be presumptuous at best and, at worst, ludicrous. My point—the only point I can make—is that if there is no explicit *proof* of middle-aged self-confrontation in the great lives of the past, there are still *signs*.

And whatever their motives, some expressed the confrontation in writing.

These lines were put down more than two thousand years ago by Quintius Horace Flaccus, as students of Latin call Horace. How vitally different are the feelings of the ancient Roman from those of George in Chapter I of this book?

It Will Soon Be Too Late

o crudelis adhuc

> Vain of thy charms, and cruel still,
> When winter's unexpected chill
> Thy pride shall humble; when the hair,
> Now floating on thy shoulders fair,
> Shall fall; and the bright flush that glows
> With tint surpassing damask rose
> On thy soft cheek, by sure decay
> Shall roughen, fade, and die away.
> How oft before thy glass thou cry,
> As the sad change appals thine eye:
> "Why, when in early youth I shone,
> Wore not my mind its present tone?
> Or why, since now such tone is mine
> Wear not my cheeks their youthful shine?"

Again, just why Horace expressed those thoughts is something long lost in the erosion of time, though the thoughts do seem to speak for themselves. Let us take a long, long jump, now, to a century whose chronicles are still matters of public record, the nineteenth, and look at three real lives.

Charles Dickens was a product of the most frightening poverty. In his formative years, his father, a naval clerk, became so helplessly mired in debt that the family was put in Marshallsea, a debtors' prison, until he could straighten himself out. Young Charles Dickens was put to work in a shoe-blacking plant before he was a teenager. When the family's fortune picked up somewhat, there was a chance for him to go to school, and the prospect of losing his miserable income shocked his mother: Give up the job? Unheard of! But he did manage ultimately to get to school, and while there, as an adolescent, he took part eagerly in student theatricals. A seed was planted that was to bloom much later in his life. Like Mr. E, in "The Men Speak," Dickens was bitten by the acting bug.

In his fifties, toward the end, Dickens had made countless lecture tours; he was in demand everywhere, on his continent and this one. It was not a great step to quit the lectern and take the stage; he had always wanted to be an actor, and now he saw nothing stopping him. He was welcomed to Drury Lane and he became a star. He also fell in love with a young actress, renounced his long-time marriage and set the girl up in rather expensive housekeeping. At Dickens's death, according to the apocrypha of his life, a newspaper reporter is said to have asked his daughter for a statement and to have gotten one that packed the chill finality of a coffin lid being slammed down: "My father was the meanest man who ever lived."

Like Edmund Van Deusen in Chapter III, Heinrich Schliemann was the son of a professionally religious father. But while Mr. Van Deusen's parents were strait-laced missionaries, Schliemann's father was a drunken, dissolute pastor, a man assessed by some Schliemann biographers as little more than an embarrassment to the little village in Germany where Schliemann was born in 1822. Like Dickens, Schliemann was assigned to grinding, thankless work when he was still a boy. He was a grocer's apprentice. But early on he became determined to do better than that. He became a cabin boy on a ship (which was wrecked, incidentally), then an office attendant and a bookkeeper.

Schliemann went on to several business fields and gradually amassed several fortunes, in his native land, in Russia and in the United States. And then, in his mid-forties, spurred by a passion for the Iliad that dated from his youth, when he learned Greek to savor the lines as the poet might have sung them, Schliemann 1) left his wife and married a girl young enough to be a daughter, 2) devoted the balance of his life to what some considered a ridiculous, Quixotic quest: He began looking for the city of Troy.

He expanded his financial holdings in digging up great stretches of Greek Isles and of the coast of what was then Asia Minor (now Turkey). It was there, on the Troad, the wide plain north of Lebanon, that Troy was understood to have been situated. There he found what he and many other scholars of the time proclaimed as Troy itself, including a wall of Priam's castle; it was determined, long after his death in 1890, that he had actually unearthed traces of the middle pre-Mycenaean period, something far pre-dating the generation of Homer's Achaeans. This perhaps mad, midolescent quest brought Heinrich Schliemann a place in history, which otherwise would have passed him over as little more than a money-grubber. This man, whose motives were wildly romantic, whose methods were primitive, is generally considered the father of modern archaeology.

Common soldiers die in wars; generals can be made, and unmade, by them. By 1864, it seemed to Abraham Lincoln that the Civil War would never end unless somebody did something. The Commander-in-Chief had grown bone-weary of such generals as George McClellan, a sincere but basically a parade-ground soldier, of Henry Halleck, basically a military politician. McClellan responded to Confederate thrusts with indecision and miscalculation, Halleck with forms in triplicate to Washington. Lee's army had been pushed back from Gettysburg the summer before, yes, but it was still very much in business in northern Virginia, and Lincoln needed a man who could make decisions and would fight.

Hiram Ulysses Simpson Grant was forty-two years old when Lincoln handed him the Army of the Potomac. Decide? "One of Meade's staff officers," Bruce Catton writes in *A Stillness at Appomattox*, "commented that Grant's habitual expression was that of a man who had made up his mind to drive his head through a stone wall." But there were misgivings.

Grant was a West Point graduate whose military reputation suffered terribly in his thirties from allegations of heavy drinking. He was a good soldier but at the same time a man who despised military rote and pompousness. In 1854, after having participated in the Mexican campaigns, he resigned his commission and tried farming, dealing in real estate and storekeeping, at no time with success. At one point it was said that he was making less than $800 a year; he was considered a broken and disappointed man. After Fort Sumter, he responded promptly to the national call for qualified military men, and a new reputation began to emerge. He took the Mississippi away from the Confederates and brought the South's forces to their knees at Vicksburg. Then came supreme command, victory in the east over Robert E. Lee, and later a Presidency for a man once considered a hopeless, brooding drunk. He was a midolescent saved from himself by his response to a national disaster.

Let me point out once more that no one in the nineteenth century thought of a problem like Grant's as the expression of a middle-age crisis. Today, a man's alcoholism is taken as a symptom of a deeper, larger disturbance, rather than as an isolated, self-contained disorder. But men like Grant were not too long dead and this century was quite young when cries of middle-aged frustration and despair began to increase in volume. This paragraph appeared in a book published in 1919:

> You know, I'm not sure that your husband is quite responsible for his actions. I do not think he is himself. He seems to me possessed by some power which is using him for its own ends, and in whose hold he is as helpless as a fly in a spider's web. It's as though someone had cast a spell over him. I'm reminded of those strange stories one sometimes hears of another personality entering into a man and driving out the old one. The soul lives unstably in the body, and is capable of mysterious transformations.

This, in summary, is the view of midolescence in Edwardian England. The quote is taken out of the context of *The Moon and Sixpence,* beside *Of Human Bondage* perhaps W. Somerset Maugham's most famous novel. Charles Strickland, the protagonist of *The Moon and Sixpence* and one of the great sons of bitches of literature, was a character suggested by the life of Paul Gaugin; in almost any lay discussion of middle-age rebellion, Gaugin is mentioned. In the passage quoted, the amorphous narrator of "The Moon" is offering his upper-middle-class diagnosis of Strickland's abandonment of his wife and children. There must be a woman, Mrs. Strickland and her friends insist; yes, the narrator says, he thought so, too, at first, but he has seen Strickland and has been told, bewilderingly, that "I've just got to paint, that's all."

The author, who was a medical doctor before he turned full-time to writing, insisted through his life that Strickland should not be taken as a direct fictional counterpart of Gaugin; that he used the *implications* of Gaugin's life for the fictional creation, not the actual events so much. Paul Gaugin did give up a successful career as a stockbroker to become an artist and so does Strickland. And they both died in the tropics; the author can be forgiven for not trying to improve on that ending.

But in fact, Paul Gaugin did not suddenly, summarily desert his wife and children, as Strickland does. The real man pleaded with the strait-laced, Dutch-born Mme. Gaugin to join him in the tropics with the children, but she would have no part of it; Strickland leaves a note saying little more than goodbye. Paul Gaugin had been an amateur painter for years before he stepped out of his old life and into the new one; Charles Strickland starts from scratch.

No one in those days talked about a middle-age crisis as such. It is in that landmark novel only by implication, the gentlest implication. Maugham, though he did flesh out the creatures of his imagination, hewed to the discipline of the story-teller, emphasizing the facts and letting them, not himself, letting the reader, not himself, make conclusions.

I don't remember how old I was when I first encountered George F. Babbitt. I can't have been more than a boy, I remember it as a depressing encounter. A movie had been made of the great Sinclair Lewis novel; it was hardly children's fare, but in the 1930's in the Connecticut town where I spent my early years, a weekly movie, any movie, was a family occasion. Here was bald old Guy Kibbee apologizing to the world for his brief moment of rebellion against it. I think I remember throwing up, as I often did when I was taken to movies that depressed me.

I have since read and re-read the novel many times, but never with the interest, the sense of discovery, that I felt when I read it in my search for literary midolescents. This book of mine opens with a composite person called George waking up; *this* is from the second page of *Babbitt:*

> There was nothing of the giant in the aspect of the man who was beginning to awaken on the sleeping-porch of a Dutch Colonial house in that residential district of Zenith known as Floral Heights. His name was George F. Babbitt. He was forty-six years old now, in April, 1920, and he made nothing in particular, neither butter nor shoes nor poetry, but he was nimble in the calling of selling houses for more than people could afford to pay . . . He seemed prosperous, extremely married and unromantic; and altogether unromantically appeared this sleeping-porch, which looked on one sizable elm, two respectable grass-plots, a cement driveway, and a corrugated iron garage. Yet Babbitt was again dreaming of the fairy child, a dream more romantic than scarlet pagodas by a silver sea.

Lewis's target, of course, was society, not an age group. A current of indictment of society runs through the body of the man's work. But, consciously or unconsciously (and he was that good a writer that I have to opt for consciously), he also chose a middle-aged man for his protagonist. In a 1961 afterword to a Signet Classics reprint of *Babbitt,* Mark Schorer of the University of California has this to say about the book:

> Babbitt moves through all of [the chapters of the book] in the course of his rising discontent—his rebellion, his retreat and resignation. Each of these moods, in turn, centers in a more or less separate narrative. The

first develops after Babbitt's one real friend, Paul Riesling, shoots his wife and is given a three-year prison sentence. It is this event that suddenly makes Babbitt feel that his life is empty and that all his bustling activities are meaningless . . . Now Babbitt meets a new friend, Mrs. Tanis Judique, an adventuress with whom, in the absence of Mrs. Babbitt, he begins a love affair. [After that affair ends], perfectly safe again, he recognizes at the end of the book that he has never in his life really done anything that he wanted to, and he hopes for a fuller, more independent life for his not very promising son . . . But he cannot define for himself anything real that he ever did want to do, except what in fact he had always done.

It was an unpleasant book about an unpleasant creature. What was its long-term, lasting effect? Today, people who may or may not know the name of Sinclair Lewis refer to neighbors they look down upon as babbitts. Old George F. has joined the lower-case immortals of literature, perhaps the highest accolade that posterity could bestow upon his round shoulders.

From the nineteen-twenties forward, more and more of this appears in literature. The writers' sights seem to shift gradually from society in general to middle age in particular.

Hermann Hesse fits here because his work mirrors the struggles that raged within himself. In 1916, at the age of thirty-nine, those struggles drew him into psychoanalysis; two years later, the fires of discontent banked but still smoldering, he went off to a remote mountain village in Switzerland. For four years he lived like a hermit, trying to sort out the bits and pieces of his life, trying to find meaning in a jumble of ideas, events and values. He emerged, briefly, in 1924, married, unsuccessfully, and returned to seclusion. His work showed reawakened freshness and vigor.

Out of those later years came the most controversial of his novels, *Steppenwolf,* which, like *Babbitt,* was an indictment of society and its false values and which, like Lewis's novel, employs the vehicle of a middle-aged life. But while George F. Babbitt was a "self-satisfied person who conforms readily to conventional middle-class ideas and ideals,"* Harry Heller is a man out of step with his world and time. Heller calls himself the Steppenwolf. A wolf of the steppes. A solitary, introverted creature. As midolescents through the bathrooms of history seem to be fond of doing, Harry Heller confronts himself

*From the definition of Babbitt in *The Random House Dictionary of the English Language.* © 1966 by Random House, Inc.

in the mirror and wonders "whether it isn't time to . . . have an accident while shaving."

The thoughts that beset Heller's-Steppenwolf's mind could have issued from the depths of any midolescent's anguish (or, indeed, the bewildered, ignorant anger of any adolescent):

> In desperation I have to escape and throw myself on the road to pleasure or, if that cannot be, on the road to pain . . . A wild longing for strong emotions and sensations seethes in me, a rage against this toneless, flat, normal and sterile life. I have a mad impulse to smash something, a warehouse, perhaps, or a cathedral, or myself, to commit outrages, to pull off the wigs of a few revered idols . . . to stand one or two representatives of the established order on their heads.

Like a man in quest of his vanished youth, Steppenwolf "sought out the little ancient tavern where nothing had altered since my first visit to this town a good twenty-five years before," a place to which a married man goes "to recover the atmosphere of his bachelor days, the old official to recall his student years." Steppenwolf lets his thoughts wander to the time when, as a young man, he spent nights in animated talk with friends, "but this too time had taken away. Withered years lay between those days and now."

And suicide. Steppenwolf, outlandish, ingenious, melancholy Steppenwolf, reaches an arrangement with himself that will let him live through the hideous years of desperation buoyed by a vision of death:

> Finally, at the age of forty-seven or thereabouts, a happy and not unhumorous idea came to him from which he often derived some amusement. He appointed his fiftieth birthday as the day on which he might allow himself to take his own life . . . Let happen to him what might, illness, poverty, suffering and bitterness, there was a time limit. It could not extend beyond these few years, months, days whose number daily diminished . . . When for any reason it went particularly badly with him, when peculiar pains and penalities were added to the desolateness and loneliness and savagery of his life, he could say to his tormentors: "Only wait, two years and I am your master."

For Ernest Hemingway, death and the prospect of death were not merely themes, they were obsessions; indeed, at the end, the writer, like Steppenwolf, appointed a day on which he allowed himself to take his own life. *Death in the Afternoon* and *The Green Hills of Africa* are about killing animals; the war novels are about killing men. And though midolescence does not go by that name in his work, there are few short stories that examine middle-aged despair as closely as does *The Snows of Kilimanjaro.* ("Close to the western summit there is the dried and frozen carcass of a leopard. No one has explained what the leopard was seeking at that altitude.") In *Across the River and Into the Trees,* a late-period novel that was rather badly received, Hemingway tells of an aging military man's attempt to relive his youth with a young woman in Italy, where the protagonist had been a young officer in a fondly remembered war more than a generation past.

F. Scott Fitzgerald, had he lived longer, might have outdone his *Babylon Revisited,* the short story in which a widower is confronted with a terrible reflection of himself in the eyes of his child and her guardians; whatever his problems are, they're just not interested.

And this list of mine could go on, through the popular literature of the 1930's, '40's and '50's, but one purpose of this chapter is to show parallels between creatures of fiction and real people, certainly including the real people I have interviewed. To the 1960's, then, with that in mind.

The midolescent Mr. B in "The Men Speak" is an academician who tells of being a compulsive writer of notes, letters and diaries, some of which fall into the hands of the wrong people, almost as though he had meant them to. Saul Bellow's *Herzog,* the hero of his 1964 novel, is an academician who pours out the blood of his wounded heart in scribbled notes, little fragments of agony, meant as letters. They are addressed to colleagues, to women who have loved him and women who have rejected him, to presidents and philosophers, and they are never mailed: The true addressee is the world. On planes, trains and on the trackless expanses of his imagination, Herzog re-travels the forbidding country of his life, his broken marriages, his smashed career, his grievously unhappy childhood.

But the fortyish, midolescent Herzog emerges a whole man. His notes to himself say that the blows of life do not knock out its ideals, that the way is still open to survival, that if man is to continue progressing he cannot dodge the dangers along the way. And while Moses Herzog does feel pain and self-pity, he does not lose sight of the possibility that the fault may lie within himself:

> Considering his entire life, he realized that he had mismanaged every-thing—everything. His life was, as the phrase goes, ruined. But since it had not been much to begin with, there was not much to grieve about.

If Moses Herzog is obsessed by anything, it is life, not death.

The leading man in Paddy Chayevsky's 1971 movie "The Hospital" is racked by just about all the symptoms of midolescent depression-mania ever squeezed from the collective findings of head-shrinkers. He is about to kill himself when a lovely young woman offers him her body as a receptacle for a purging of the demons that possess him. After this pleasurable exorcism, when he is much more relaxed and in charge of himself, he tells her that what has happened to his work as head of "The Hospital" bothers him more than his shattered family life and his just-cured and obviously imagined impotence. Work, he says, is a far more primal force than sex.

At the end of the film, with the hospital's disordered system crashing about his ears, aggravated by an invasion of black militants trying to take over the building, the doctor declines the young woman's offer of a total escape. She wants him to go away with her to a place far from civilization, where they will live on love and organic food. (I saw the film twice, and that scene twice reminded me of the wedding party of a playboy friend, then in his early fifties, who was about to head off into the Caribbean with his bride, two decades his junior; "She's gonna eat fish," my friend said, "and I'm gonna eat *her*.") Someone, the doctor says, gesturing at the pandemonium around him, has to be responsible for all this.

And so the doctor will try to face up to the problems he helped to create; Herzog will continue to seek answers; Babbitt will go on, with some hope of the future. But all this is interpreted, pre-digested reality, all this is the work of intelligent writers who know they have to give their readers something positive or their messages will not be delivered. Raw reality, real life, doesn't have to do that.

The midolescents I interviewed are trying to survive. Others surrender. For the most part, their stories do not find their way into books. But you will often find them in daily newspapers, told in short and simple style, in the tiny one-paragraph items that report deaths under subway trains, deaths by falls from hotel windows. The item may say that the victim "jumped or fell" to his death, and that he left a note. It will almost always include the victim's age, and quite often that age is between thirty-five and fifty-five. And the suicide is usually a male.

Statistical tables show that more men than women commit suicide; that the rate rises sharply in the middle years; that in the industrialized nations, except for the United States, it then dips again at the end of the middle years. Figures for the United States show a steep increase with the coming of middle age, and then the *rate* of rise slackens somewhat, but the line continues in a gentle ascent.

In 1970 Dr. Michael M. Baden, then Deputy Chief Medical Examiner of New York City, wrote that suicide there among male business executives was considerably higher than among women executives. Dr. Eugene S. Paykel, a psychiatrist and director of Yale University's Depression Research Unit, said in a 1971 interview that "much more than anything else psychiatrists see, depression runs the risk of a fatal outcome—suicide. And more suicide occurs in men than it does in women. So when men say they are depressed, it should be taken seriously."

But is it? On the NBC Television quiz show "Hollywood Squares," comedian Jan Murray, offering a joshing response to a question, got a big laugh from the studio audience when he said, "I called the suicide prevention center and they put me on 'hold.' "

What is behind suicides? It seems safe to say that in many cases these things are explosions of what Thoreau called "quiet desperation." In two 1973 cases that I know of, the victims were men who had apparently tried to tough out their growing despair quietly for a long time. Much too long.

On Dec. 4, 1973, Robert A. Morse, forty-five years old, the United States Attorney for the Eastern District of New York, submitted his resignation less than a week after he had been mentioned for a federal judgeship. He handed it to Jacob Mishler, the administrative judge of the court.

I do not know how much the judge knew about the prosecutor's private life; other members of the New York legal community whom I questioned about this case either pleaded ignorance or politely sidestepped my inquiry. But it is known that the judge was shocked and concerned by Morse's resignation; gently, he rejected it, asking Morse to think it over. Morse had been a valuable prosecutor. His racket-busting achievements had put many of his colleagues in mind of the young Thomas E. Dewey.

From the judge's chambers, Morse went to his apartment in Brooklyn Heights, and locked himself in. He wrote out a note, saying that he had long been considering suicide. Neatly, as he might have arranged the papers of a brief on a courtroom table, he laid out the contents of his wallet, including insurance documents, on a table in the apartment.

As he was doing this, apparently, Judge Mishler told several associates about the resignation offer. They rushed to Morse's apartment house—too late. Morse had already removed his shoes, had mounted the sill of a casement window in his stocking feet and had dived five floors to his death on the sidewalk of Pierrepont Street.

When policemen and journalists started looking for the underside of that thrown-away life, a pitiful picture began to take shape. The police investigators reported that the note Morse had left had suggested—their word—that he had been undergoing psychiatric treatment. Morse's friends denied this. No, no, they insisted, he had been undergoing a drastic crash diet, had lost forty pounds, and it was that that brought on his severe depression. Reporters who questioned the medical examiner's office were told among other things that dramatic loss of weight can bring on dramatic mental depression.

Was it a marital problem? Was there a woman in the picture? Only dimly. Morse had divorced his wife of sixteen years in 1966. They had a daughter. His suicide note expressed concern about the girl's right to inherit her maternal grandfather's estate. And Morse had recently been seen in the company of a woman. "I saw him about a month ago," a male friend of Morse's told a reporter. "He seemed very happy. He was escorting a charming woman and he looked like a guy who was madly in love." The woman's name was in Morse's note; it has never been disclosed.

The roots of Robert Morse's disturbance could have been far back in his youth and then again the trouble could have been much nearer to the time of his death. I don't know. If he had been nobody, his suicide might have been reported in one-paragraph items in the New York papers, if at all. Because he was prominent, he was on Page One. So it goes.

I began working on this book in the Christmas season of 1973. Among my neighbors are a couple who hold open-house parties every Christmas and New Year's Day, from 2 in the afternoon till the last guest leaves. For the guests, friends, neighbors and the children and grandchildren of Martin and June Mott, the 1973 Christmas party seemed a cheery, frenetic success, but the host seemed somehow out of it: Pensive, morose, distant, perhaps even disturbed. I managed to get his ear and asked what might be bothering him.

Martin Mott is a courtroom laywer. Quickly, he put on a happier face. "Oh, we've just got one less guest than we counted on," he said.

"It's still early. Maybe he'll still make it."

Martin finished his drink and gave the empty glass to one of his several married daughters to be refilled. "Not likely, Fred," he said. "He's dead."

"Jesus. Anybody I know?"

"I wouldn't think so. More a business associate than a social acquaintance."

I was ready to drop the matter; I didn't know the person. People do die. But Martin, who is the kind of man who would rather die himself than bore or depress anybody, looked at me with his eyebrows slightly raised, as though inquiring whether he should go on. I nodded.

"He was a client," Martin said. "I'd advise him on legal things. You know how that phone rings all the time?"

"Oh, yes," I said. It had rung several times during the party, and some of the calls were not just wishes for a merry Christmas. A lawyer's life is not his own. Martin's home phone has three extensions and a "hold" button.

"Well," Martin said, "a few weeks ago he started calling me again and again, here and at my office. He—" his daughter handed him the drink. "Thank you, dear," Martin said. The young woman kissed her father on the cheek; he waited until she had gone to join her mother in hostess duties before continuing.

"He'd ask me the damndest, most childish questions," Martin said. "He'd call in the morning and say that he was going to wear a gray suit and ask me if he should wear a blue tie or a red tie with it. He'd call on a Saturday and say his kid was driving a golf cart on the course and could he, the father, be sued if anything happened because the boy was too young for a motor vehicle license. Things like that.

"Last week he called and said, 'Look—I've been acting very strangely. I can't seem to decide the simplest things any more. It's very hard on my family; I realize it's having a bad effect on them.' Then he said, 'Do you think it would be feasible that I commit myself to a sanitarium for observation and rest?'

"I told him that that might be a good idea, that doing that is certainly nothing to be ashamed of, that people do it all the time and it helps them. Last Friday, he did commit himself to one of those places.

"On Saturday they found him hanged there in his room by the sash of his bathrobe. He was fifty-two years old."

"Martin," I said, "surely you're not blaming yourself for this?

Because you told him it might be a good idea to commit himself?"

"Oh, no, no, no," Martin said. "It's just that one month, here's this man, apparently a perfectly normal, happy man, good job, big home, nice family, apparently everything to live for, and then this thing takes hold of him and two months later he's gone. That's all. Not a very Christmasy conversation. You want another drink, Fred?"

"Please," I said.

VI.
Midolescence and Homosexuality

What a waste! It happens in gay life time after time! The fighting, the breakup, the grief—and then the awful grind of starting over with someone new. Gay life is saddest when it is condemned to a thousand beginnings. That is not the way it must be, but the way it is for so many.

—David Loovis, *GAY SPIRIT*

Male homosexuals, though they reject the traditions of maleness, though they retreat from women and parody the normal man-woman ritual dance in their sub-culture, are still in fact males to the ends of their days. And the male middle-age crisis allows them no exemption.

Fidelity is the cornerstone of normal, heterosexual, contractual married life; in homosexual pairing, mating and de facto marriages, friendship is the foundation but inconstancy is a constant risk that must be accepted. They are friends, they are lovers, but the door is always open. When one partner exercises his escape clause, the parting, for the other, is no less painful than it is on the straight side of the fence. With middle age, and the possibility of winning a new lover so much more remote, the loneliness felt by these men can be much more damaging, aliens, as they are, in a straight world.

327

The poet Hart Crane did not live to middle age. In that gifted homosexual's time there was no Gay Lib, no Mattachine Society, no campaign for détente between the gay and the straight world. Life among male homosexuals in the 1920's and '30's was furtive and usually totally closeted; their relationships with one another were necessarily much more transient than such relationships are today. Crane was thirty-two when he leapt from the deck of the steamer Orizaba, which was taking him back to New York from Mexico, where he had sought and failed to find peace of mind. From Crane's *The Broken Tower:*

> And so it was I entered the broken world
> To trace the visionary company of love, its voice
> An instant in the wind (I know not whither hurled)
> But not for long to hold each desperate choice.

How much different is midolescence for such men? Do they feel more or less despair, panic, frustration, than do heterosexual men? There are no simple answers to these or any other questions about them; in so many ways, they are not all that different from "normal people." It has been said of them that they are more promiscuous than heterosexuals because, among many things, they have more opportunities for promiscuity than do straights, and sexual flings for them are far less expensive. It has been said of them that, having no wives or children to invest pieces of their identities in, they put much, much more into their work, making their jobs, in effect, second homes, and when they lose jobs the impact is far more powerful.

And it can also be said of them that they are no less capable of affection, devotion or loyalty than their straight cousins. Their sense of humor, always tinged by self-deprecation, always evoking outrageousness, is perhaps sharper than straight humor. In one-night stands in his world, as an interviewee in this chapter says, it's not wham, bam, thank you, ma'am, it's wham, bam, thank you, sir.

To find out whether there are bridges between heterosexual and homosexual midolescence and to what special extent homosexuals suffer from the middle-age crisis, how they respond to it, I interviewed two men whose expertise in this area is difficult to question. Dr. Lawrence J. Hatterer is a New York psychiatrist who has dealt almost exclusively with analyses of male homosexual problems. Merle Miller is a writer and journalist who, in 1971, came out of the closet ("and I loathe the phrase; it's a dreadful phrase") with his declaration in a New York Times Magazine article that he was a homosexual. The doctor's clinical view of the problem and the writer's view, from the inside of the sub-culture, sometimes clash. Both men sometimes talk more about homosexuality itself than about homosexuality and middle age, but the insights they offered in doing that made the digressions worthwhile. First, the doctor.

Dr. Lawrence J. Hatterer

Q. Doctor, several prominent men have recently come out of the closet, declaring their sexual or cultural status and asserting their right to that status, and most seem to be middle-aged men. Now, I assume that this is one way in which they cope with the middle-age crisis.

A. It can be one. I think, however, to take any simplistic singular act and say that about it is a kind of naïveté, because a person does that kind of thing, particularly when it becomes a public declaration. If I were given the privilege to interview them in depth I would consider that it would be multi-dimensional.

Q. I'm sure it is.

A. We could guess at any number of the other dimensions, not the least of which, I'm sure, is that this is a conceivable, predominant one. I think that sometimes, with these men, it was important for them to make a mark; some of them would be doing this as a way of making a mark.

Q. The ones I'm talking about have already made their marks in life.

A. Certainly, but when people reach a certain point they may feel that they're not going to make another mark.

Q. Which would be middle-aged thinking.

A. Yes.

Q. Doctor, if a homosexual man is settled into a long-term relationship with another man, is it possible that under the pressures of the crisis as it applies to "normal men"—fear of impotence, fear of death or signs of approaching death, et cetera—will the homosexual man try to break out of that relationship as the heterosexual man will sometimes try to break out of his marriage?

A. I don't think you can draw the parallels here as closely. The homosexual life-style allows for polygamous activity on a very high level, for transciencies, for the acceptance of periodic relationships that can go anywhere from six weeks to six months to six years to twenty years. And the moving in and out of these relationships, because of no legal or economic or social bonds of any sort, make the parallels fall apart. I've done some homosexual-marriage counseling, you might euphemistically call it that—in which the fifty-year-old man that I saw was sort of over the hill sexually, and quite satisfied to settle out in a small Long Island town with his lover, the man he lived with. And the man he lived with had all his life been periodically interested in various other machismo types. His affair, at his middle-life period, was with a bisexual man who was slightly older than himself, and, really, he was just looking for another older man. The man that he was with had gotten a little too old.

Q. And was the original other partner older?

A. In fact fifteen years older. I don't think there is a need to "break out." The problems of the middle-life homosexual have much more to do with the ethos of homosexual life-style, which is youth, and virility, and up-front masculinity of a particular order. More often, my guess would be for a vigorous turning to career and other kinds of accomplishment.

Q. Were you alluding just then to the alienation that all middle-aged men might feel toward the youth culture?

A. I think the homosexual would feel even more oppressed. The priorities for physical attractiveness and the availability of polygamous activity are no longer so great for them. Many of these people go underground; there is less opportunity for the psychiatrist to see a large sampling. And the histories that the psychiatrist gets of his disturbed patients, or even those who aren't disturbed, are that they sort of retire, a lot of them, to a kind of quiet, conservative existence in which those early patterns—promiscuous, transient or flamboyant patterns—are no longer part of their life. They almost blend into the scenery.

Q. Do those homosexuals who do not have permanent arrangements tend to settle into them in their middle years?

A. I would say that a higher percentage do, yes. Those better-adapted homosexuals, those who commit themselves not only to the sexual but to the social aspects of homosexual living, and who settle into these relationships, have far fewer erotic symptoms. If anything, that later-life period, where the sexual obsessiveness and all the rest is not so pre-eminent, becomes a more comfortable time.

Q. Doctor, I talked to a gynecologist friend of yours, Dr. Paul Metzger, about this middle-age thing.

A. Oh, yes. Used to have an office . . .

Q. Nearby, yes. Let me read you part of the transcript of that interview. We were talking about homosexuality rather generally:

"An unanswered question for me is the fact that heterosexual beings are not, twenty-four hours a day, like the fish in my kid's fish tank; they are not forever moving, looking for food, their twenty-four-hour occupation. I get the impression that the homosexual male is always thinking, talking, looking sex! They try to say that this is a normal variation, and that it's only society that makes it seem abnormal. The American Psychiatric Association recently threw them a bone, saying, 'This is not an emotional disorder,' under great pressure from the Mattachine and other gay-liberation groups.

"Now, I think it's wise that they not be discriminated against in terms of being called nuts. But they threw that bone out, and Larry Hatterer said, 'That's nonsense! We must *not* accept as fact that this is a normal variation; we must *not* give in to that. Let's accept the fact that it may be a psychologic aberrancy and that there's a neurosis involved.'

"That doesn't put them down. A person may be far more successful as a human being than many heterosexuals in many other levels of measure. Let's not fail to understand that the homosexual who completely accepts his homosexuality is probably never going to give a psychiatrist any money, but the homosexual who fights it and has problems developing from it can be a problem."

That's the end of Dr. Metzger's quote. First, Dr. Hatterer, to the "promiscuity" of these men.

A. I think both facts are valid. One, which you have in general, is a higher degree of preoccupation with sexuality. The language is often highly sexualized in the sub-culture of homosexuals. It is just a clinical fact that, assuming an identity which one puts up front, their sexuality is going to make them in general more sexualized in their orientation to life. The point is, heterosexual people do not walk into a room and *declare* themselves as heterosexual! The fact that such a person has to make that distinction as a predominant part of his identity produces a great deal. Now, that's one factor. The other is the environmental factor, which is that the choice and the opportunity and the availability of sexual partnering is enormous by comparison.

Q. Comparison: For a homosexual?

A. For a homosexual. A simple example: Between my office here on 79th Street and 53d Street in New York City, if a young man is capable of it, he can have three orgasms for the price of nothing. Homosexually. If he were to choose to have similar experiences with three women it would have to cost him $60 at the minimum, if he could manage to solicit that many. You could go up to three subway urinals and be fellated, if you stood at any of them long enough, by three men, and do this all in the period of time it took you to come to orgasm. This cannot be done, in any shape, form or manner, heterosexually. You have six to seven to eight homosexual baths in New York, you have in the neighborhood of 140 bars, in which availability is present, and you have about seven homosexual movie houses. Plus the hundreds of urinals. I'm not saying there isn't a large percentage of homosexual people who do not avail themselves of any of this, and have their three orgasms a week with their mates, no differently than the average Kinseyan heterosexual. So I think that it is very dangerous to come to some blanket conclusions that "all homosexuals are sexually obsessed" any more than you can say that all heterosexuals are. What was the second part of the question?

Q. The fact that you challenged the finding of the American Psychiatric Association.

A. Yes. The guy who interviewed me, he didn't really present the whole picture . . .

Q. Somebody interviewed you?

A. Somebody interviewed me for Medical World News. Dr. Metzger is referring to my quote in Medical World News. My current view is that the major flaw in society's attempt to de-criminalize homosexuality is that they did not codify, they did not break down the whole subject into what one could call "normal" forms of homosexual behavior and quasi-normal forms and aberrant forms. In other words, by saying that it is not an illness and that only those homosexuals who are disturbed by their dysfunction are ill. Until the psychiatric profession makes it very clear to the public that these are not all the same things, and you can't umbrella them under the term "homosexuality" any more than you could umbrella, say, masochistic heterosexual sex with love relations, crushes, fetishism, bestiality, whatever—well, they threw the baby out with the bath water.

Q. How different is the "closet" homosexual today from what he was a generation ago?

A. Well, in the profession we have couples coming in where men have chosen to leave their wives to live with men; couples coming in where the male had [once] been homosexual, has taken on a homosexual lover, and they want to know how to handle the children. I mean, twenty, thirty years ago there were no such things. These were very unusual situations then.

Q. Those who leave their wives: Do they do that after twenty years of marriage, ten years of marriage?

A. Yes. I think there's a phenomenon now in which the men have had deteriorating relationships with their wives and in which they became homosexualized later in life, and we can no longer say it's completely the fault of the mother, the father, the early developmental problems. Those men had some vulnerabilities to homosexuality in the first place but they never went completely over the line. But maybe a life with a castrating wife for twenty years made them never want to go back to a woman; maybe they decided that, well, there are these new options today, you know. New York Magazine, whatever—the media has sent out the message: "Guess what, guys? You have a new option." And they get into these situations, and they forget that they're not nineteen years old and that they have spent twenty or thirty of their years in heterosexual life-style consciousness, and then they expect themselves to adapt to The New Scene. And it isn't easy.

Q. To a more specific area, Doctor, role-playing among male homosexuals, the dominant player, the submissive player: If a man has played the dominant role through his life, does that change in middle age? And, conversely, if he has tended to be submissive in the sex act or the whole relationship, does that change in middle age?

A. I think that's idiosyncratic. It is very much related to the particular man. Oh, they may find in their middle years that they have to become more aggressive with their partners than when they were younger, when they were young and beautiful and everybody wanted them. Or they may become even more passive, if they've been passive. And, whereas previously they got everything for nothing, now they have to go to hustlers and do a lot of things that are quite demeaning in their middle years because they are then less sexually desirable.

Q. Is it true that some homosexual men can play either role?

A. Oh, you might have a man who, socially, on the outside, is very dominant of his lover, and when he gets in bed he may be totally passive. In very good, in the best, homosexual relationships there seems to be an easy shift of role-playing. They—many don't play roles. They say to me, "I don't have to play a role. I enter him. He enters me. I'm in his mouth. He's in my mouth. We don't have any need for making male-female roles, dominance-submission roles, it's just unnecessary." And then again others say, "Listen, unless he rapes me, I'm unhappy."

Q. The "best homosexual relationships" being those where both partners are well adapted to this life-style?

A. Yes. The best-adapted ones are not concerned about roles. I think, on the other hand, that there can be distortions. I've noticed a pattern in which those males who want to maintain their male images very often may not want to be entered anally because they see that as too submissive a role. Or in the early years they may only want to be fellated. They may not want to allow the penis to enter them at all. I feel that in the early years, many of the more aggressive males feel they can maintain their aggressiveness by being the enterers rather than the entered. That is, in a sense, a parody of what happens between men and women. I think, as they become more committed and more involved, the shift then takes place; they allow both things to happen because they are not assigning any roles— whether they are being entered or entering themselves. And that happens at a later point in the evolution of their homosexual acts.

Q. Doctor, does experimentation increase or decrease in the middle-age period? Experimentation being a variation from a preference for rough trade, the more masculine partner, the truck driver, to the really homosexual partner.

A. No. My guess is that the guy who liked rough trade when he was seventeen will still like it when he is forty or fifty. But as they become more enmeshed in the homosexual sub-culture, I think there are greater attempts at multiple sexual partnering. But I think that has more to do with the evolution of their homosexual life-style than the fact that they are middle-aged and trying other things. If anything, I would almost answer that question in the negative: there may be some fears of experimentation at that point, fears of sexual potency and of low-level desirability, and because the axis of virility, youth and physicality has been diminished. I would suspect that there'd be more potency problems in this period than experimentation.

Q. In middle age, the heterosexual man faces challenges to his earning, or financial power. He faces the danger of being discarded, dumped, at a time when it might be supposed that all his experience was finally beginning to pay off for his company . . .

A. I would think homosexuals have the same problems.

Q. Is the effect on a homosexual of being dumped possibly more traumatic than for a heterosexual? Can we draw that line?

A. My guess would be that some men who have opted for homosexual life-styles, the better-adapted ones, are often more dedicated to their work because they don't have families and children. And their egos, their identities, become heavily invested in that area, and I would suspect that being divested of that would be much more of a blow to them.

Q. Such men, then, find their lives upset when that happens.

A. Yes. I see fewer and fewer homosexuals as they get older. I have a very small sample of homosexuals in their forties, fifties and sixties, because they are not as obsessed with their sexual orientation; they are not as troubled by it. Many have settled into careers or into living arrangements that are satisfactory. Or they have given up the chase, the promiscuous and rather traumatic life-style that some of them faced previously. It is even possible that they may have fewer problems during this period than heterosexuals. If not, why am I not seeing them?

Q. Do homosexuals possibly have less to lose, in terms of households?

A. Right. Essentially, they are living as bachelors. They do what they want, when they want. You listen to some guy talk about what he's gone through with his wife and children, and how he's feeling emasculated, and he can't handle this, he can't handle that. And then he talks about this other life of his, the homosexual part. He goes where he wants, he has sex where he wants, how he wants. He doesn't have to pay for it. He gets it at the snap of a finger, by going to a bath, perhaps. And maybe he goes all the way over.

Q. To full-time homosexuality.

A. Yes. And maybe this is because women are making it very difficult for men, and so a lot of them are turning to homosexuality.

It's easier than contending with the rough women around these days. Which of course is an oversimplification. What it is, I think, is where the roles are blending, the men are more challenged by women, where equities come up front, and the women are insisting on these equities. It takes more of a man's man to deal with that situation. Often, men default if they haven't been bred with enough strengths to cope. Competition, everything else that men are contending with today. A man is challenged in an enormous number of areas, in terms of meeting criteria of excellence, life standards, and so on. And many men are frightened by that.

Q. You mean heterosexual men are frightened.

A. Let's say men are *heterosexually* frightened. Now, we don't know if we're going to have a generation of men who, in their later life, decide that homosexual life is just easier. And hence you may find in the middle-age group those who may be lonely, may be isolated, may be having transient lives, and they don't feel that they have to contend with all the pressures of what it is to be a modern man, a successful one. Essentially, a homosexual can ignore the kinds of challenges that you and I have to face.

Q. What of the married men who cross over?

A. As I've said, some married men go through ten to fifteen to twenty years of being homosexualized by their wives. They become so emasculated by their wives that they find themselves more and more attracted to men. Whatever it is, for reasons of their inability to deal with women, they find it easier to conquer men, young men. Or maybe they want to revitalize their youth. That's another theory.

Q. One reason that a heterosexual male goes . . .

A. —for a young girl, yes. And we may have some bisexually oriented or latent-homosexually oriented men who never allowed their homosexuality to flower when they were in their youth, and they return to some homosexual pattern after many years of marriage, and children. I had a case recently, a pillar of the society, who got interested in boys. I met his wife, and I could understand. She was a Brunnhilde; she was a Mother Earth! I mean, one of the toughest women I've ever *seen.* And he probably had had a little too much of her. She was a good mother, she was even a good mother to *him,* but she wasn't a good *wife.* I'm sure that at some level, she de-sexualized him, as far as women were concerned, without his being aware of it.

Q. Do some women accept, tolerate, whatever, their husbands' turning to sex with men?

A. I was coming to that. There's a whole new thing in which a lot of the women are accepting, unconsciously, some form of homosexual behavior on the part of their men, just to get the men off their backs. That is, women who essentially think it's a good idea to keep their husbands just a *little* homosexual so that they, the women, can do what they want to do; they're not threatened by other women and they don't feel all that threatened by other men, because the husband knows he isn't going to be able to live openly as a homosexual. So they keep it quiet.

Q. What about the future, for the homosexual culture? Life-style?

A. I think that the hard-won tolerance and acceptance of adult homosexuality will settle out, as it has, ironically, in some way without all of the revolutions in countries where there's been a great deal of humanity toward the homosexual. But here—the chance is remote that a society that is currently still phobic about problems of sexual identity will in the *foreseeable* future assimilate and institutionalize forms of homosexual behavior as total options for *everybody.* I think that we will do much more of what the Scandinavian and English and a lot of other countries have done: allow people to live peaceably that way and not *discriminate* against them *legally,* job-wise, or in any other way.

Merle Miller

He says, in his 1971, New York Times Magazine article, "What It Means to Be a Homosexual":

> When I was a child in Marshalltown, Iowa, I hated Christmas almost as much as I do now, but I loved Halloween. I never wanted to take off the mask; I wanted to wear it everywhere, night and day, always . . . It took me almost fifty years to come out of the closet, to stop pretending to be something I was not, most of the time fooling nobody . . . I am still homosexual, and I have a writer's block every morning when I sit down at the typewriter. And it's too late now to change my nature. At fifty, give or take a year or so, I am afraid I will have to make do with me.

The wit and the personal charm of the man I interviewed for this book made it difficult to believe that business about writer's block. He certainly displayed no talker's block, if there is such a thing. He had just returned from a long "book-hustling" tour, as he called it, in connection with his *Plain Speaking,* which is among other things a collection of the more outspoken thoughts of a rather outspoken man, Harry Truman.

Q. Mr. Miller, most of the people in this book have been made anonymous, except for authorities. Now, you can be anonymous if you want. If you don't—and what did you say on the phone? You put it rather well.

A. I have no urge to be anonymous.

Q. Fine. Mr. Miller, how old are you now?

A. God, how old am I? Fifty-two.

Q. How long had you been considering that declaration of identity that you made in the Times article before you took the step?

A. Oh, about ten minutes.

Q. Was it an article suggested to you, or was it your idea?

A. It was my indignation which led the Times to suggest the article.

Q. Your indignation at what?

A. Oh, there had been a piece in Harper's by a guy named— Joshua—no, not Joshua, I forget his first name [the article, in the September, 1971 Harper's Magazine, was by Joseph Epstein]—which was a dreadful attack on homosexuals. I hated it. I had lunch the next day with two editors at the Times and expressed my indignation and said, "Well, for Christ's sake, this is ridiculous." I asked them what they thought of it, and they had both liked it.

Q. What exactly was the burden of that piece?

A. That if homosexuality were wiped off the face of the earth, we'd all be better off. Happier people. We could live our joyous straight lives and have no problems. I'm exaggerating.

Q. In a conversation with Dr. Lawrence Hatterer about all this, he mentioned that there seems to be a great deal of capitalizing on the controversy, the heat of the controversy. For commercial . . .

A. Well, I don't know what you mean by "capitalizing."

Q. He had been asked to take a position and get into a debate with people on TV and radio shows and he declined because, he said, "I know you're going to put words in my mouth and make me say things"—this is a doctor talking, and doctors do not generalize the way people like you and I might. Or I might, anyway. And he didn't like this at all. He said there is a tremendous attempt afoot today to upset the research of about twenty to thirty years on the subject.

A. There's *certainly* an attempt to upset the research of Dr. Hatterer, among others. I mean I—do you want me to talk about that, about Dr. Hatterer?

Q. Yes, of course.

A. I consider him a typical, old-fashioned Freudian, Jungian man who's—speaking of commercialization, who's made a great deal of money writing books about homosexuals and homosexual sickness, who claims to have cured a number of homosexuals. It's always very vague, you know, when you start to talk about cure. And if you talk about a cure you have to begin by saying there's a disease. May I say that he should be the *last* in the long line of people to talk about capitalization. That's his *business,* for Christ's sake! You know, these Socarideses and Hatterers remind me of blacksmiths in the '30's. They're in panic! They are losing their business. Because young homosexuals are refusing to say that they're sick. May I say that I have no—that I myself have been in therapy, analysis, Freudian, Jungian, of all kinds. And I bought all that crap. I mean, I thought there was something to be cured. Or that I would be led to lead the happy life through the likes of Socarides or Hatterer and their cohorts . . .

Q. Would you spell that name?

A. Socarides is spelled—I think—rather like Socrates, but that's the only resemblance. It's S-O-C—just the way it's pronounced. S-O-C-A-R-I-D-E-S, Socarides. Charles. And he is perhaps the outstanding spokesman of homosexuals-are-sick.

Q. Your position is that they are *not* sick? It is not an abnormality?

A. My feeling is that there are a great many people who are sexually attracted to members of their own sex, who have no interest in reproducing, which I suppose is a blessing at the moment—there seems to be little danger of the race dying out. And it's time for all these old Judaeo-Christian prejudices to be re-examined, and at the same time to re-examine all the things that traditional psychiatrists have been saying. Now there are a great number of untraditional psychiatrists these days. Some homosexual, some not; most not, who just don't go along with this nonsense . . .

Q. You mean themselves, or who deal with that sector of society?

A. Yeah, well—who say the—well as you know, the American Psychiatric Association has made its redefinition of what homosexuality is. Now, if homosexuals are sick, isn't it odd that these strange, disoriented, ill, uncreative people are able to create? I once wrote in a book [laughter]—I meant it as a joke but it happens to have an element of truth—that all good American pianists are homosexuals.

Q. [laughter] Really?

A. This is a coincidence. But quite a lovely one. I mean if one were to examine how many sick conductors of symphonic orchestras there are in America one might be very surprised at the statistic. I'm not singling music out, I mean, we can safely say, if all homosexuals came out of the closet—and I *loathe* the phrase; it's a *dreadful* phrase! There are some things you use because you can't think of anything better. Let us put it—a bit better . . .

Q. Isn't it horrible? You've got a deadline to meet and . . .

A. Closets. And we've got plenty of—if all American homosexuals, in the theater, in the professions, by which I mean doctors, lawyers, journalism, declared themselves, plus all the truckdrivers and the cops and the firemen who recently have been so active in protecting their virginity [laughter], my God! See, what most people say is, "Well, gee, I don't know any—except *you!*"

Q. I was very taken by a part of your first piece in the Times in which some friend says "I'd come up to visit you, but I don't want to bring my children," and you say, "Well, then why don't you not come at all?"

A. Well, there are some people who think it's catching. A virus.

Q. [laughter] It's not really smallpox, is it?

A. If you could just get an inoculation somehow! But what I started to say is that most people say, "I don't know any," which, of course, is perfectly ridiculous. They know *dozens.*

Q. They don't *want* to know.

A. Yes. The key is, "I don't want you to tell me." Now I think that's a complicated and interesting reaction. If you go back to the forties, there was a dramatization of André Gide's *The Immoralist,* which was indeed James Dean's first role on the stage. He played the Arab boy, and I think Louis Jourdan played the man. And at one point in the play he tells his wife, and she expresses great shock. He tells her he's really in love with this Arab boy, that he's really homosexual. And she expresses great shock, and he says, "But you already know." And she says, "Yeah, but I didn't want you to tell me." That is really the reaction more than any other. People don't want you to tell them. And I have no easy answer to why people feel this way.

Q. And that brings us back to you. Here it comes. Were you already, so to speak, quote, out of the closet, unquote, *then?* At the time you wrote the Times piece? As far as your social life was concerned, did all or most of your professional associates and your friends know of your sexual orientation *before* you made this declaration? And were you not married at one point?

A. Oh, yeah.

Q. Any progeny?

A. No, no. I was spared that. Did most of my friends know? Well, for Christ's sake, if they had any *sense* they did.

Q. The friends who said "We'd come up and bring the children, but"—were they reacting because you had made the move and they already knew this? Or did they not know it?

A. Well, I had homosexual friends, you see, and it wasn't so much *me.* I mean, hell, I'm not going to molest a child. But "God knows, Merle, who you might have there this weekend. And therefore I want to protect little George, age seventeen and a half." Incidentally, the difference between liberals and conservatives and reactionaries in this area—[pause]—in my opinion there's no difference between them. I mean the word faggot is as operative at a cocktail party of the New York Times or the New Republic as it is at a cocktail party of the National Review or the Des Moines Register.

Q. But so are four-letter words. I mean intellectuals who are fond of using four-letter words, pretending they're really—not gutter-types, but democrats, shall we say.

A. Yeah. There's been a great deal of talk about Mr. Truman and his language, but I don't think he ever used a sexual image.

Q. He didn't have to.

A. No.

Q. Mr. Miller, do you buy the concept of a male middle-age crisis?

A. There comes a period in all of our lives, surely, when we look back on what we wanted to have been and examine what we are. George Orwell said "All lives when viewed from within are a series of failures." A couple of years ago, Sam Behrman, God rest his soul, wrote a fascinating book, an autobiography, and he had known all the rich and famous—well, *almost* all of the rich and famous and creative people of his time. He said they all had one thing in common: they were discontent. And in that marvelous book of André Malraux, *Anti-Memoirs,* he's talking to a village priest and he says, in essence, "Father, you've been listening to confessions for more than thirty years. Well, what one thing have you learned?" And the priest said two things, really. He said, "There are no really grown-up people"—first. And number two, "Most people are more unhappy than you think." Well unhappiness, as you said lightly on the phone this morning, is a normal state of life, it seems to me. But there *does* comes a point, there *has* to come a point in everybody's life when you realize that—well, I read the obituary page of the Times first every day: I want to see if I'm there, for one thing. You know, maybe overnight I *went.* [laughter] And it's disconcerting, recently, that, er, some of my best friends are not only Jews, but *dead.* [laughter] Now my dear friend Anita Loos, age eighty-one, her new book has just been accepted by the Book-of-the-Month Club. Which is phenomenal! Marvelous! But you realize, if you have any sense, that it isn't really going to be much better.

Q. What's ahead.

A. What's ahead. And, you know, I always had the—well, the new book is number one on the best-seller lists and all that and money and all those things I had longed for so long. And [laughter] I thought they would change my life.

Q. We work for money.

A. Yes, not have to worry about next month's mortgage. But you aren't going to change that much.

Q. Did you go through, did you have such a confrontation with yourself? At the time you drafted the "out-of-the-closet" declaration?

A. No, no.

Q. Or did you have such a confrontation before this? Say in your forties, or thirties? Could you recall it for me? Reconstruct it? Was there any time, any one day, any one circumstance that made you look at yourself in the mirror and instead of shaving, say "Why don't I cut my throat?"

A. Oh, that's every morning. [laughing] Nothing at all unusual about that. I thought that's what everybody did.

Q. [laughing] Doesn't everybody?

A. Nooo. I think I am—by nature, by instinct, and by experience, and by training, a melancholy man.

Q. I don't get that impression at all.

A. Oh, that's just because I—you know, I've been doing the book-hustling.

Q. Barnstorming.

A. Oh, Christ, in sixty cities! And not only are they all the same city, but the guy on television is always the same guy. You wonder how they got him there before you got there.

Q. He's got one of these [an outline of questions] in front of him, right?

A. No-no-no! That's the difference. No, you see, you've done your homework. No, no. Their opening sentence is, "Well, I got your book last night and I've really only had a chance to thumb through it, but now let's spend the next forty-five minutes talking about it." I only walked out once.

Q. You did walk out? On the air?

A. I walked out. Yep. It was a woman. I arrived late. And the woman said, "Now by the way, what's the name of your book?"

Q. Oh, for Christ's sake!

A. And I said, "Madam, you are too stupid to talk to." And this was on the air. I got up and walked out. I didn't do that often. Well now, let me tell you about the Times piece. I was not prepared for the impact it would have or, whatever one wants to call it, the sensation it would create. I'd written for the Times, as you know, often, and I thought, "this is another piece for the Times, and there may be a little more reaction than most, but not a lot." As a matter of fact, on the day it appeared I didn't get one telephone call.

Q. It was on a Sunday. People are . . .

A. But beginning on Monday, I realized that a kind of revolution had occurred in my life and that I had created a revolution in the lives of a great number of other people. A thousand of them took the trouble to write letters.

Q. I think it did a hell of a lot of good, don't you?

A. Oh, no question. A number of people really thought they were the only ones in the world. In small towns, still, across this country, in this year of our lord 1974, or this year of our Nixon, or whatever, Henry Kissinger.

Q. This is your background, isn't it? You're from a small town.

A. Oh, yes. Only Jean Seberg and I ever got out. They built a big fence around it. [laughter] They ain't gonna let nobody *else* out! [laughter]. You know, "They wanna disgrace us." And the way we had disgraced them. Well, after the piece came out [pause] I—you know, I felt, my mother, thank God, is shielded from the New York Times. And we all know what *that* is. And [laughing] unfortunately it was widely syndicated and it appeared in the Des Moines Register.

Q. You must have realized what the impact would be.

A. I knew there'd be an impact, but anyway, my mother got it in the Des Moines Register and then I called her and told her I was going to be on the Dick Cavett Show. And she said, "What are you going to talk about?" And I told her, and she said "Oh, Merle, not *that!*" And I said "But you always told me to tell the truth." And she said, "But I don't like that kind of truth." And hung up and disinherited me. And it isn't as if Nelson Rockefeller were suddenly to find himself bereft of the family fortune. Someone said Sears Roebuck wouldn't even handle it, it's so small. Now, I'm not diminishing the pain it must have caused her. Because still, the traditional reaction when a homosexual tells his parents is, "My God, what did I do wrong?"

Q. Not what can *we* do for *him,* but . . .

A. Yeah. What did *I* do wrong.

Q. One of the worst problems of middle age is the confrontation over what *your* standards are, what *your* ideals are, and how you were raised. These are probably—since I'm forty-eight, these are nineteenth-century traditions handed to me by my parents. Now, for better or worse, I bought them. I bought them because it was the thing to do.

A. I—all this sex business aside—was never really part of the Establishment, or bought the values. I was always the oddball, and in all the movements. I was the guy who took the first Jewish boy to my fraternity . . .

Q. Where'd you go to school, by the way?

A. I went to the University of Iowa and London, the London School of Economics.

Q. What did you fancy you would be in life?

A. I fancied I'd be an economist.

Q. Another John Stuart Mill or . . .

A. Of course, or John Maynard Keynes. If I had known John Maynard Keynes was a homosexual—well, first of all, God alone knows . . .

Q. Now isn't that absurd? I mean what the *hell* is the difference?

A. If the Republicans had known in the '30's when Roosevelt was, by osmosis, but nevertheless, truly taking over a large number of

John Maynard Keynes's ideas, economic ideas, 'cause he was a great economist—If they had known he was a *queer,* you know, think of the uproar, the additional uproar!

Q. Five terms for Alf Landon. [laughter all around] Dr. Hatterer says that homosexual males, since they are, in fact, bachelors, suffer more in this period—thirty-five to fifty-five—when they lose jobs, because they seem to invest much more energy and interest in their careers than do heterosexual male men. Jobs, since homosexual males have no wives and children, become in a way a second home. Do you go along with this?

A. I should think in part that's true. But a large number of men, homosexual men I know, have lifelong partners. Hell, just last week I went to a—can you believe it?—a thirtieth wedding anniversary. Well, not "wedding;" they're not married. Two guys who have lived together thirty years. One, one of New York's most prominent lawyers and the best theatrical agent in New York. [pause] I've had two long relationships, one, which lasted ten years,and the other is now in its eleventh year. And I don't see a hell of a lot of difference between my relationship, in this case with these two guys, than most of my married friends. There are happy marriages, no doubt.

Q. Which leads us into this. It's been said that polygamy is something which homosexuals have to accept as part of their life-styles. The danger of it is there and if it happens they must be prepared for the shock of it. Now is this true?

A. What do you mean by polygamy?

Q. Well, promiscuity, straying from the partnership occasionally. How important is this in this period of life? Faithfulness?

A. [pause] I don't know of many husbands and wives who are totally faithful. I know *some.* The guys I just mentioned, so far as I know, for thirty years they've been totally faithful to each other. Which is fine. It isn't necessarily *my* life-style. Though at my age, sex, I like to say, is largely fond memory. I'm going round and round, but that maybe is how you get to the point.

Q. We're talking about the second home being a job, the investment of interest and energy in the career.

A. Well, perhaps. Perhaps that's the reason more homosexuals are in creative, rather than drudging jobs. Write our songs. I said all good American pianists, classical pianists, are homosexual, with a couple of exceptions. Well, in the same way, almost all our popular songs, these days, are written by homosexuals. Now if all those guys who wrote all those songs were suddenly to say that they were homosexual, I would think it would add tremendously—now you see, one of the things that really makes me not part of any movement is that it seems to me that if homosexuals want a fair shake, to use that expression, then they've got to declare themselves. They cannot continue to be hidden, and then complain about being oppressed.

Q. If they remain hidden then they're buying the values of what is to them the alien culture, and they want to be a part of that, and so you say, "stay out of our league?"

A. Exactly. I'm not interested. Oh, you know they would send money secretly to the Gay Activists Alliance or Mattachine Society. But as for open declaration, what we said earlier, a lot of people don't want to know. But once they *do* know, it doesn't make all that much difference. I don't figure my life-style in this small town in upstate New York has really changed at all. I do weekly get a letter from a madman in Brooklyn, who does not address me by name but who addresses the letter simply "To Brewster's Most Famous Homosexual." The letter is delivered deadpan by the mailman, put in the box with all the others, and—once you've talked about it, what else is there to say?

Q. Once you've talked about what?

A. Well, once you've said, "well, yeah, okay, so Merle Miller's a homosexual. And he wrote that piece in the Times, you remember." Now there are some people no doubt who chuckle and giggle, but once you chuckle and giggle a couple of times—so? And now, of course, there is the Truman book. Which is . . .

Q. Entirely apart from all this.

A. Entirely apart from all this. And everybody wants to read it. And of course, if possible, to be given a free copy.

Q. They want to find out if perhaps there is some homosexual propaganda in this? Christ!

A. [laughter]

Q. Sonsabitches!

A. A few [laughter].

Q. Your whole body of work before the piece doesn't mean anything, right? Or all your journalistic work, all your novels.

A. Nah! Forgotten all about that.

Q. Mr. Miller, our friend Hatterer says that there is a greater degree of . . .

A. I wish you would say "my."

Q. "My?"

A. You said "our friend."

Q. All right, my friend. He says that there is a greater degree of promiscuity among homosexual males than there is among heterosexual males because what he calls the sub-culture of homosexuality offers more opportunity for sexual activity; there is less courtship rigamarole to go through and it's expensive. Now how do you . . .

A. [hearty laughter]

Q. —feel about that? He said that between his office and 53d Street there are any number of men's rooms where a homosexual can go and have fun. But if you want to do that with women it will cost you money. Do you buy the promiscuity theory?

A. It's certainly easier for an unattached homosexual male to be promiscuous than it it is for an attached heterosexual male. No question about it. But you have to remember that there isn't any place *else* to go. You cannot carry on an office courtship. You cannot meet—oh, you can, with difficulty—someone with whom you work, for a cocktail, because then people start talking. There is a great— and I saw this only on television a few weeks ago on Channel 13— there is a great feeling that homosexuals by nature like the danger involved. Thus Oscar Wilde, the play about Oscar Wilde on Channel 13, was called "Feasting With Panthers."

Q. Yes, young men, rough trade.

A. Yeah. That's never been for me. Danger doesn't give me any great thrill. I'm a coward. I have no desire to be beaten up or get the S-and-M scene, or any of those things. It's just not for me. If I do meet somebody I usually spend most of the time listening to the story of his life. It's *much* more important than the sex.

Q. Well, Mr. Miller, you're a professional listener.

A. Yes.

Q. The journalist in you. You're naturally curious. [pause] You mean in a courtship?

A. No, no. I mean in a one-night stand, to use what I'm sure a lot of people say. A good large part of the night, if it happens, is listening to the guy's life story. And it always varies. I've heard it said, once you hear one you've heard them all. But it's *never* true, really.

Q. You'll pardon the expression, but I'm immediately reminded of the ten-dollar girl and "my wife-doesn't-understand-me." Why I should make that parallel I don't know, but I hear this and something clicks. Now does that offend you?

A. No, no, no. Perhaps there's one difference. It's usually all over in ten minutes, and no name is exchanged, very often; most of these guys, the picker-uppers, are married, or a large part of them are married. I'm doing a piece for a magazine about the married men. You know, what do you do when your wife finds out? What does one do? To which I have no answers yet, but it's certainly an interesting problem. Mostly, then, it's the hustler who's picked up by the guy. The guy is very likely to be a married guy, and I have no statistics on this except what these kids tell me. And it's wham, bam, thank you, ma'am, only in this case it's wham, bam, thank you, sir [laughter all around]. And then they, they *don't* want to talk. With me it's quite different. I am, as you say, I *am* a journalist and I'm *interested*.

Q. Do you have one-night stands now with people?

A. Sure. Not very often.

Q. Now, see, that's what I'm talking about. It would be technically illegal for me to do that, with a woman . . .

A. Well, sure.

Q. I could be sued and, in some states, arrested, for adultery.

A. Oh! You might get somebody pregnant?

Q. Yes. Right.

A. Which is also a danger. Of course, I don't know what would happen if you picked up a prostitute on 45th Street, where you might get a venereal disease.

Q. I sure would, and I wouldn't enjoy it, because first I'd get stabbed.

A. There's always that.

Q. What do you think is the greatest problem facing a homosexual male in middle age? And is it really different from what faces a heterosexual middle-aged male?

A. Oh, well, hell! Being middle-aged all by ourselves is an almost insurmountable problem. And I'm not sure it's any worse for a homosexual. Yeah, one of the things people say is, "Well, my God, what are you gonna do when you get old? Won't you live a lonely old age?" Well, the chances of *your* living a lonely old age are really not much different, are they? It's not much different for a homosexual. I mean, somebody dies, in a relationship, and then you go on alone. It's not easy. Being middle-aged and then *really* aged is a lonely, lonely thing. As it's often lonely when you're married, if you're heterosexual, and as it's often lonely if you're living with another man, because human relationships are almost impossible. Two people living the same lives, in the same house together, all the time. It may not even be what God had in mind. I'm inclined at times to think it's what Saint Paul had in mind. And it's not what *Jesus* had in mind . . .

Q. Do you think of yourself as a religious man?

A. No. No. But I'm certainly interested in who made it a different message than Jesus had in mind. And I think his message was fine. And then Saint Paul. Well, when he was running around the road to Damascus, something happened to him. I don't know what.

Q. He probably became middle-aged.

A. [laughter] He probably did. And then he made up all these rules. That we are supposed to live by, and hardly ever do, but pretend we do. Just *being* middle-aged is, oh Christ! it's difficult. It's almost impossible. I'm surprised there aren't more suicides.

Q. There are quite a few.

A. You're damned right there are.

Q. World War II did a lot to us, didn't it?

A. Yeah.

Q. It took up a little of our time.

A. It took up a few years.

Q. Set you back a few centuries.

A. Yeah. All those guys who missed it—well.

Q. Brand new show! World War II, the original cast!

A. [laughter] "All talking, all singing, all dancing!" Let me just say, I don't feel any deprivation, any great sorrow for myself. I speak, of course, in what you might call a banner year for me. The tour has been marvelous. But even last year, when I was working on the book and I was sure it would sell the usual fifteen or twenty thousand copies, I didn't feel any more unhappy than my heterosexual friends.

Q. Maybe you achieved that time of middle-aged confrontation six years ago . . .

A. Maybe.

Q. Seven years ago, five years ago, X number of—at thirty, perhaps.

A. Or maybe, though I'm inclined to dismiss it, I was meeting it when I wrote the piece for the Times.

Q. Maybe that was a catalyst.

A. I expect it was. As you know, I'm sure, I expanded the piece into a book, *On Being Different.* Some libraries—I have to tell you this—some libraries won't even handle the book.

Q. In those small towns?

A. Even in the town next door to mine, Danbury. It's not in the library. And when I—in Charleston, West Virginia, a couple of weeks ago, a bunch of homosexual kids, not maliciously, but as a prank, went around to the bookstores, saying "well, now, you're getting hundreds of copies of Mr. Miller's book *Plain Speaking,* aren't you going to order some copies of *On Being Different?* There are four bookstores in Charleston, West Virginia. All four said, "Oh, no. We don't handle that type of book."

Q. They probably have *Fanny Hill,* or Xaviera Hollander's stupidity, or Jacqueline Susann, or all this other pious pornography . . .

A. That's acceptable. When I was in college, about 1940, I was a malicious kid. I wrote a malicious column for the local newspaper, you know, saying, it shook the campus at least twice a week. And I was frequently called in by the Dean of Men, who was a marvelous man . . .

Q. In what way malicious, Mr. Miller?

A. Did I say he was malicious?

Q. No, you said the column was. What was it?

A. Oh, I just said things everybody else was saying, but I said them in print.

Q. By everybody.

A. By everybody. Faculty, students, everybody. The Dean would call me in twice a week and say "What is to be *done* with you?" [laughter] He'd say, "You'd be delighted if I kicked you out of school, wouldn't you?" And I said, "Sir, there's *nothing* you could do to please me more." And he said, "I'm not going to give you that satisfaction. The only hope is that you will grow older." Well, I always had a certain joy in kicking over the traces, and writing that Times piece may have been kicking over another trace.

Q. Were there any . . .

A. Bad things? If that was your question,—well, it wasn't very bad. The state troopers drove up one day, a couple of weeks after the piece. They drove up the driveway and said "Is this where Merle Miller lives?"

Q. They didn't know? It's their *business* to know those things.

A. They wanted to ask. They wanted me to *know* they were asking. I said, "Yeah." And they said, "That's all we wanted to know. Thanks." Well, that was all.

Q. That was enough, right?

A. I thought about it for a couple of days. My friend David thought crosses would be burned in the yard or that I would be stoned in the A & P. Well, I've been stoned in the A & P . . .

Q. With a six-pack in your hand.

A. Yeah, right.

Q. Mr. Miller, this concept of a cure for homosexuality, whether we buy it or not: Is there any time in life when such a cure is possible? And is there a period *past* any time for a cure?

A. Well, as I said earlier, you can only cure a *disease.* And I refuse to accept this, that I've got a disease. I am told, as one always is, that there's this wonderful new doctor in Los Angeles, or San Francisco, and he's cured a famous young actor and now the actor can marry this nice young actress or model or whatever she is, and they have a child, and they're ecstatically happy. And I don't doubt that that is true. I'm always suspicious of the New Messiah, particularly in California.

Q. Any new Messiah?

A. Any new Messiah. I agree with "Let's-wait-a-few years." And particularly in California, where you know there is one on every street corner and sometimes two or three in between. I mean you can't cross the street without bumping into one.

Q. A state full of madmen.

A. And frequently wearing sandals. And that will make them Christ-like. Which it doesn't. [pause] There are, to be sure, some homosexuals who wish they weren't and one of the reasons they wish they weren't is because it would be a lot easier not to be. I mean, our society certainly isn't that liberal so that anybody is going to pat you on the shoulder and say, "Well, gee. Gee whiz, isn't that fine." Although I did just read about a man who works for Fortune, you know, not the magazine, but that society that works with ex-convicts. If they have problems the ex-convicts come to this Fortune Society and say "This is my problem." In any case, one of the men who works there decided to come out of the closet, to return to that dreadful phrase . . .

Q. Not an ex-con?

A. Yes, an ex-con. Who worked for this society. And he was ready to come out on, of all places, the David Susskind Show. And he announced this to his friend and they had dinner, and they were ordering dessert and—that's probably the proper time to do it if you're having dinner—and [laughter] he said to his friend, "I'm going to tell—I'm a homosexual and I'm going to say so on the David Susskind show." And his friend said, "Oh, are you? I think I'll have tortoni." And the man from the Fortune Society said, "My God, I have just revealed a great painful secret to you. Is that all you have to say?" And his friend said, "If I could think of anything to say I'd say it. But I really don't think there's anything much to say." I have to say that's mostly been the attitude I have found. Most people say, well—perhaps behind my back they say other things, but to my face they say, "Well, uh, what are you gonna do tomorrow?" Or "What's for dinner?"

Q. It's like saying, "I'm sorry, but I have a broken leg." What do you do—offer condolences?

A. Yeah. No, no, no. I have—no condolences. Mostly people have said to me, "Gee, what a brave, courageous thing you did." And it wasn't so brave and courageous, it just—I probably needed the money from the piece.

Q. Mr. Miller, since for so many years you apparently played the social role of a heterosexual, have all those years of doing that left any permanent scars? Meaning, while a much younger man, a militant Gay Lib, perhaps, might feel perfectly comfortable with his lot as a *declared* homosexual, do you ever feel uncomfortable about yourself now? Do you regret what you did? Do you feel any loss of kinship, association, with the straight world? Do you now feel alienated in any way from the straight world of which you were ostensibly a member?

A. None. I get frequently annoyed. One of my very best friends, when the Truman book came out, and turned out to be an enormous success, she said, "Thank God, Merle, people no longer think you're queer." And I said, "Judy, well, maybe I could say I was misquoted in the Times." [laughter]

Q. [laughter] In how many words? Six thousand?

A. Six thousand words of misquotation [laughter]. And she thought she was paying me a compliment.

Q. Is there anything else you want to tell me? That you think ought to be said? For your contribution to the chapter?

A. Well, what really upsets me most about some psychiatrists—I never question how a man makes his living; whatever he wants to do is okay by me, including burglary, if he's *good* at it. The trouble is they're usually so *bad*. I'm perfectly willing to let them go along making their living in this way, if they can find customers. I do object to the attempt to say that sex and the preoccupation with sex, at least in my life, in the life of most homosexuals I know, is any bigger a part of their existence than it is with a heterosexual. Sex is the one area when we all lie, really, and we all overestimate our capacities and our desires. Most people do. Well, I don't think homosexuals spend any more time doing it than anybody does.

VII.
The
Years
Ahead

Can a man prepare himself for the transition from youth to middle age? And once there, in those boat-rocking years, is there anything he can do to keep himself on an even keel, clear of the rocks and shoals? Can those closest to him help him?

The warning signs are there and can be as insistent as a lighthouse beacon slicing through the night. But men's inner eyes too often have gaping blind spots, or their view of reality can be distorted by a deceptive intimacy, as though they are seeing themselves through the wrong end of a telescope. By the time a man's vision clears it can be too late, as it was for Mrs. C's husband. "Why wouldn't I listen?" he asks the woman who by then was his *ex*-wife. "Why couldn't I listen?" Mrs. C herself had been deaf and blind to what was happening. She speaks of the suddenness and unexpectedness of her husband's midolescent upheaval, and only now, with the shock beginning to recede and with the perspective of time, is she starting to recognize the symptoms that had been there all along. It was not a sudden change; she only *thought* it was. It was not unexpected; she only had *refused* to acknowledge it. No man drops off to sleep happy and well-adjusted and gets out of bed the next morning rent by demonic forces; there is no dybbuk that crawls into his psyche to transform him overnight.

355

I have no *formulas* to stave off or soften the blows of middle age. Neither do the psychiatrists, sociologists and other experts whose brains I tried to pick, though some of them have bits and pieces of advice. Sometimes those bits and pieces seem to clash head-on: Do *this,* says one expert; do *that,* says another. On one thing, though, they all agree: The way a man deals with aging, with sex, with career and with the thousand-and-one other elements that make up his life will depend on and reflect the way he has dealt with them all along. Beneath the outer self that seems to change in middle age lies a man basically consistent with himself. The anguish of middle age is in large measure the collision of that new man and the old one beneath the surface.

Here is Dr. Van Den Haag on the subject of preparing for and dealing with middle age:

A. There are some people who are simply resigned.

Q. Is that the healthy remedy? The sensible resolution to this problem? Being resigned?

A. No. The trouble with that is, you see, that there is no general prescription. Everyone should deal with his crisis in his own way. You have to look at the particular person. It is like the fear of death. What is the remedy for the fear of death?

Q. Not to die?

A. It depends on why this particular person fears death. After all, to be dead is like not having been born. It's not an experience that you have, because you don't *experience* it. But you have the *fear* of it, and the fear of it is usually located in some dissatisfaction with the life that you have led. But what to *do* about this dissatisfaction? It depends on the person. I think you have to face it. You have to ask yourself what it is that you can do better, within your powers, that you want to do better. Let me remind you: The religious, in former ages, would say, "Memento mori"—"Remember that you will die"—as a way of admonishing people. "Live so that when you die you will be satisfied." And that is what you have to say about this middle-age crisis. Try to live so that you feel your life is the life you want to lead, and don't pretend that it is society, or the weather, or the System that prevents you!

Q. Try to live this way within those boundaries that are already around you?

A. Yes, but the boundaries aren't entirely harsh. It's really you who will have to—nobody is compelled to live in the suburbs. Live in Manhattan if you want. [The suburbs] tend to lead to certain isolation. You don't *have* to be in your occupation; it's your choice. I don't believe that people are compelled. Some are, particularly . . .

Q. Professionals?

A. Well, now, of course, if you have been a lawyer for twenty years, suddenly to give up and decide to be an actor isn't going to be an easy matter.

Q. And a doctor can't do it at all.

A. Right. So you have to make a wise choice at the beginning, and if you've made the wrong choice, it's very hard to get out of it.

Dr. Van Den Haag is a strikingly articulate man. Many of the tapes in this book—humans being the tangential, incoherent creatures that they are—have had to have some editorial help. But the transcript of Dr. Van Den Haag's interview, parts of which appear in three chapters, represents almost 100 per cent what he said into my microphone. He is also a very busy, strictly scheduled soul. I arrived ten minutes late for our interview and he had already squeezed me in between two other appointments. But in the limited time available he said more than many others. He also seems to think —and certainly speaks—in neat, declarative, impressively parsed sentences. The total effect he projects is that of a young person, though the frames of most of his literary references are classic, not contemporary. He projects a sense of immediacy, of doing, of trying to accomplish. Our dialogue at one point went this way:

Q. How old are you, doctor?

A. I'm fifty-nine.

Q. You're fifty-nine? Fantastic! And are you married?

A. No.

Q. No? Have you ever *been* married?

A. So far not. I feel I'm much too *young* for that.

Our discussion about handling the middle-age crisis ended on this note:

A. I do agree that if you handle it well, in the independent professions, the bite of that crisis is much less strong than in others. You can go on writing books, see, in my profession. If they tell me they don't want me to teach any more, so what? I can still go on lecturing.

Is there a formula to be extracted from Dr. Van Den Haag's words? A clue to the secret of working *with* life and time instead of *against* them? If there is, if a man's life can be boiled down to so simplistic a concept, it would be much too pat anyway, much too easy and fatuous, to perorate at someone: "Keep busy. Remain curious about the world around you. Fill your time. Exercise your mind and take care of your body." What works well for Ernest van den Haag may not work *at all* for someone else.

Dr. William Lee Curry, professor of English at Adelphi University, is fifty-six years old, just past the outer edge of the age span we have adopted for midolescence. Dr. Curry shows no signs of convalescing from a bout with the problem; it seems to have passed him by—or he passed *it* by. Here is Dr. Curry on middle age:

A. Most university professors seem to be younger than their years or, in any event, the toll doesn't appear perhaps as early as with an advertising man, who's been on a pogo stick so long and who is perhaps legitimately more tired and maybe more bored with the whole scene than the academic person, who tends to be rather generally a more placid creature. And perhaps also the contact with youth through all those years is involved. You know, you continually have people always the same age, and you forget that you, yourself, are creeping onward. So there's a kind of fountain-of-youth syndrome on a university campus. In effect, many people I know would probably happily go on teaching forever if they weren't pushed out at sixty-eight.

Q. How active are you right now?

A. Oh, I'm very active. I teach two days at Adelphi and I teach, for Adelphi, an ABLE course in New York to Pentecostal ministers on Monday nights . . .

Q. An ABLE course?

A. ABLE is an acronym for—I think it is Academic Baccalaureate Learning Experience. And these are underprivileged people who are given a break financially and in some other ways. Mine are professional men. They're all ministers of South American and Puerto Rican backgrounds. A fascinating class! But anyway, that's three days a week, and then I often teach a course for N.Y.U. That's in the summer. We go up to Stratford to see Shakespeare plays, and we have meetings on the N.Y.U. campus and discuss the plays. So I do have these various jobs, and I lecture around.

Q. This takes up five days a week?

A. No, it doesn't take up five days a week. This is one of the delights of teaching. It normally takes up about three days a week, and on Fridays I head for Montauk and stay there until Monday morning.

Q. Can a man in your age group feel as out of it today as a man in my business or in business generally might? Does a teacher—can a teacher feel as alienated by this kind of cultural pressure, this feeling of alienation which has ruined many men in middle age, or does he not feel it all since he is constantly with the young?

A. Well, I can answer for myself and I can speculate about my colleagues. I would think that for a majority of them there is no wildly hostile feeling about the popping-up of the young because, as I said, we've been dealing with the young so long that we—we're sort of *inoculated* against them.

Q. Better prepared to deal with them?

A. That's right. As for myself, I have a kind of Peter Pan attitude about age, and I feel no sense of old-fogyness compared to the young people. In fact, I frequently think that they are older in their sedateness and in their modesty, with the present exception of streaking, which I think is very healthy. Let them continue with it! It's a healthy thing and they're far too conservative. Most faculty members are much more radical, or at least liberal, than are students. [pause] In going back to the important—to the way we approached the subject—I don't think that these are threats or challenges overtaking me, "Alas, alas, here comes old age . . ." I'll give you my personal attitude, and I would think that the majority of my colleagues don't feel this either. There are some who become, oh, kind of *sodden* with age, and they think, "Oh, damn, here we have to go again, teaching the students!" but those are few and far between, at least in my discipline. English literature is different perhaps, from physics or mathematics. I don't know why it should be, but the discussions tend to be different with every group even though the students are the same age. Nevertheless, you get bored with them. Perhaps in communicating a fixed discipline, more or less fixed, which is not a matter of opinion, you get bored with the same damn thing. In other words, there's a closer tie between the adult and the youth in my profession than there would be in advertising, in newspaper work, in medicine, or whatever. And we rarely feel resentment. Now and then, when a very young professor comes into the department, I don't feel resentment; I think how lucky the students are because, of course, there's a quality to youth which they can appreciate and they *do* appreciate. You get perhaps more young old people in teaching than in any other profession. The only other profession I can think of where youth seems to prevail, the quality of youth, is among my artist friends. They seem to maintain, some of them even in their physical appearance, the quality of youth. Sculptors, painters, musicians, dancers. They keep—first of all they keep aware of what's going on, and they keep vitally concerned with current trends, and of course the dancers keep physically very fit. But even the others seem to have an appearance of youth that my lawyer friends don't have.

Drs. Van Den Haag and Curry are not plagued by feelings of inadequacy, or there is certainly nothing in their words to hint at such feelings. Perhaps they are just too busy, intellectually busy, to find time to think about aging or inadequacy. And perhaps that *is*, despite that earlier disclaimer, one of the clues.

In a little pamphlet called *Middle Age: A Test of Time,* the author, Chester A. Raber, quotes these words of Robert Louis Stevenson:

> There is a sort of dead-alive, hackneyed people about, who are scarcely conscious of living except in the exercise of some conventional occupation . . . [my elision] They have no curiosity; they cannot give themselves over to random provocations; they do not take pleasure in the exercise of their faculties for its own sake; and unless necessity lays about them with a stick, they will even stand still. It is no good speaking to such folk: they *cannot* be idle, their nature is not generous enough; and they pass those hours in a sort of coma, which are not dedicated to furious moiling in the gold-mill . . . [Raber's elision] As if a man's soul were not too small to begin with, they have dwarfed and narrowed theirs by a life of all work and no play; until here they are at forty, with a listless attention, a mind vacant of all material of amusement, and not one thought to rub against another, while they wait for the train. Before he was breeched he might have clambered on the boxes; when he was twenty, he would have stared at the girls; but now the pipe is smoked out, the snuff-box is empty, and my gentleman sits bolt upright upon the bench, with lamentable eyes. This does not appeal to me as being Success in Life.

"Middle-aged people," says the author of the pamphlet, "should develop new hobbies and activities or revitalize old ones to take the place of departing children, the more physical endeavors of earlier years, and the routine and monotonous schedule of life . . . To investigate questions asked all through life and to permit one's curiosity to discover some of the mysteries of life are additional joys and rewards of well-used leisure time. Pursuing questions about the nature of our world and universe, biography, literary and spiritual qualities, political interests, social and cultural concerns constitutes leisure-time possibilities."

Those "spiritual qualities"—perhaps I should have said so long before this, but I'm not religious. I know that priests, ministers, rabbis and other spiritual leaders can answer the psychological questions and satisfy the psychological problems of the religious as well as psychiatrists can help those who seek psychiatric help; I concede that the confessional box, for those who believe, offers as much help as does a psychoanalyst's couch. And let the matter lie there; let the religious help the religious.

Advice is easy to give, of course. "Don't worry" never stopped *anyone* from worrying. It is easy to say, as some writers have in books addressed to the middle-aged: "You're bored with your work? Change jobs." Several of the men in Chapter III *did* do that, and it seems to have worked well for them. But it isn't done that easily. It *wasn't* done that easily, even for Mr. E, the psychologist-turned-actor; he laid the groundwork carefully before cutting the cord that tied him to his pre-midolescent career. And, as Dr. Van Den Haag points out, for some professions it seems close to impossible.

There is merit, then, in this advice to look to leisure time as a source of renewed interest. If the challenge has gone out of the 9-to-5 hours, if the excitement, the interest has flagged or vanished, at least the 5-to-9 time of day can offer stimulation and an avenue along which to flee from deadening boredom. I don't think the limb I'm out on is about to crack under the weight of this: An agile, alert and inquiring mind ages far more slowly than one that has been allowed to drift into flabby disuse.

Well, then, what about people like Mr. B, the professor-freelance writer? His mind was alert. He was in a profession that, says Dr. Curry, provides a "fountain of youth." What happened to him?

The heart of Mr. B's midolescent difficulties seemed to be—the heart. Sex. True, he *did* change careers, going into one of the very areas cited by Dr. Curry as an accelerator of middle-aging. But for Mr. B the change produced an opposite effect; he found Academe no longer challenging, no longer rewarding. Indeed, he was rebelling at campus life. And in the mad, wheeling-dealing world of advertising, he has found a new, exciting, stimulating career. That he was propelled into his new career as a by-product of his midolescent "non-affair" is almost incidental; he would have left campus life in any event, he says. *His* problem was sex. And offering advice about sex is rather like opening a can of worms. I will avoid any findings—if such a dignified word can be bestowed upon them—of my own and will turn, instead, to more knowledgeable people. To start with, two men who have been extraordinarily helpful all along, Drs. Metzger and Van Den Haag. Here they are, each in turn answering the question:

Q. Doctor, what role can a wife play in this period? How can she help her husband over this period to protect the marriage and the houshold?

A. (Dr. Metzger) When two people are in their thirties, they take sex for granted. Some nights it's good, some nights it's not so good. Generally, they tend to have a fairly decent sex life; they have now reached middle age. We assume that they've got something to work with that has gotten them there still married. The man and the woman who have an equanimity between them probably have a good sex life. The man who had good sex that morning or last night, with endearments and words of love, feels pretty good about himself. A lot of minor irritations during the following day do not matter so much. A woman in this period should be a woman in the understanding sense. She should do what she should have been doing all her married life. If her man can't perform and becomes upset, she says, "It doesn't mean anything, sweetheart; I can enjoy sex without an orgasm." Which, indeed, a lot of women can say truthfully. Or, "I enjoy intercourse and can have an orgasm without you having a full erection." As for the man, he can give a woman an orgasm with his mouth, on her clitoris. It may be the only way she can easily achieve climax. This, incidentally, includes about fifty to sixty per cent of all the women who ever lived. Perfectly healthy. If a woman never knew what it was to try other sexual techniques, other than the so-called conventional techniques, she'd better start learning when her husband hits the middle years. We're supposed to improve constantly. Why can't people alter their sexual habits? If the man has a desire that she wear her stockings, she says, "Harry, you're married twenty-five years, all of a sudden you want me to wear my stockings!" Or if he wants her to parade around the bedroom naked; she's got a good figure at her age, why shouldn't she do it? Because they didn't do this before: "Where have you been that you want such things, Harry?" Obviously, if there hasn't been some alteration in their sexual habits, sudden change could be difficult. *Maybe people ought to try to get reacquainted sexually,* once the kids are grown and out of the house. The shorter work week in Europe during the energy crisis probably saved a lot of marriages as well as a lot of businesses. They got more productivity in those three or four days than in the old five because the men had mornings at home without the children, when they could have sex with their wives. A relative of mine in Chicago started meeting his wife in a motel, once a week, as if they weren't married at all. At the time I thought they were a little crazy, but I'm not so sure now. You know the great joke about the seventy-year-old man married to the twenty-five-year-old girl and the girl comes home to find her husband in this bed with a sixty-five-year-old lady and the wife screams bloody murder. She asks, "What does *she* have that *I* don't have?" He answers, "For one thing, dear, patience." Whatever happens, it's all in the programing. And what is middle age anyway? The definition by Mark Twain, if I'm not mistaken, is that a middle-aged person is someone who's ten years older than you are. And remember our friend the bumblebee. He can't fly, but he doesn't know that. So he does.

A. (Van Den Haag) [the question again: What role can a wife play in this period? How can she help her husband over this period to protect the marriage and the houshold?] Best, probably, by doing nothing. I think an understanding wife, who tells a husband how she understands, is a terrible nuisance. I think a wife who tells him if he looks at a girl once more she will divorce him, is not helping. I think the best thing a wife can do is to leave things alone. If it is a halfway-good marriage, he will appreciate the emotional bonds he has to her, and in time find them most rewarding. I don't think you can advertise it, and there's no point in her having discussions with him; I don't believe there's much point in doing anything but just ignoring it.

Q. Can such discussions with him, or with a marriage counselor, do more harm than good?

A. I think such discussions, unless it's an acute case, are more likely to be harmful than good. Sometimes they equip people with a new *terminology,* but they can't change the *experience.* Of course, if he feels torn about a divorce, and she is, and so on, sometimes it does make sense to see a marriage counselor. But I think you should really try to deal with your own problems unless it comes to a point where you feel incapable of doing something.

And then there is Dr. Wortis, the pupil of Freud whom you met in Chapter I and who said he felt the whole world was sex crazy:

A. If a man is ensconced in a stable and supportive family situation, bolstered by affection and loyalty, if his family and his income

are reasonably secure, if his social role is still productive and dignified, there is no crisis. He just moves on to middle life. Sex is,
traditionally, in cultivated middle-class society, a combination of
affectionate relations and physical satisfactions. If they are maintained and satisfaction is reduced, there should be no problems; if
they are supplanted by affection, the change in the sexual pattern
need not be a problem. But if the sex role of a person is played
without regard to affectionate relations, then reduction of sexual
powers will be a problem.

Bits and pieces of advice, as I said, sometimes collide.

Our Mr. B, in Chapter III: this excerpt from *Sex and the Mature
Man* may throw a little light on his case and provide some kind of
guidance on midolescent trauma.

> Shortly before his fortieth birthday, Franz R. began to brood, spending
> long hours staring silently into his living room fireplace and frequently
> becoming quarrelsome, finding faults in the behavior of his wife and sons.
> Mrs. R. gave a surprise birthday party for him, and he disgraced himself
> by drinking to excess, cursing wildly and, finally, becoming ill. For
> several weeks thereafter he continued to brood, then suddenly demanded
> a more active social life. The friends of Franz and Mrs. R. were startled
> by his abrupt transformation. He became the first to indulge in petting
> with the wives of other men, and soon made it clear to several women
> that he wanted to have affairs with them. Several couples began to avoid
> Franz R. and his wife. The climax came at a party when he became
> embroiled in a violent fistfight with a neighbor whose wife he had tried
> to seduce earlier in the evening. His reputation as a professional man at
> stake, Franz R. was persuaded by his wife and several friends to seek
> psychiatric assistance.

The authors go on to describe the treatment. Franz R. turned to
a psychiatrist for help, and the psychiatrist discovered that Mr. R.
felt cheated out of his inheritance of a youthful sex life. As a young
man, he had to work to help his family out and, an immigrant, he
had the additional burden of having to struggle to learn English.
Other boys had active social lives but he—because he had little time,
because he was clumsy in his new language and because he was shy
—had little contact with girls. Other boys' boasting of their sexual
adventures convinced him he was missing out. These feelings apparently remained dormant until his fortieth birthday approached.
Then, certain that life was slipping away too quickly, he tried to
make up for lost time and lost good times, and in his desperation to

do so he risked his profession, his marriage and his friendships. The psychiatrist convinced him that he had been deluding himself, that other boys had been no more successful in their sexual exploits than he had been and, further, that his fear of approaching impotency, because of age, was a phantasm. "Franz R.," the authors note, "like so many men with a similar problem, was able to make a relatively swift adjustment to reality."

Was it the deprivation of his adolescence—his real or imagined failure to acquit himself with honor in the youthful fields of sexual competition—that drove Mr. B into his almost-disastrous "non-affair?" Perhaps. And perhaps if he had been aware that he had suffered no such deprivation he would not have been taken with—by?—"Melina Prokopoulos." Who knows?

If I had to summarize, thus far, what could be said about avoiding the rocks and shoals of midolescence, I would say:

—Self-awareness is the first rule. Awareness of what you are, of what you have been, of where you are now in life and what your goals were and are. Without self-awareness nothing else will work. —Keep the mind alert, agile and inquiring. Exercise it. If the job is becoming tedious, a grind, a bore, change jobs if you can. And if you can't, work on making your non-job-time stimulating and rewarding. Young men may have strength, stamina, agility and unlined faces, but they lack the experience, the tact, the wisdom, the savoir-faire that only living can bring. They're no competition for *you*. —Keep your sex life vigorous. It's been said several times already and I'll say it again here: You can have an active sex life almost until rigor mortis sets in. *Experiment.* Not with many women, unless you're single or you're one of those men for whom a free-and-easy swinging life carries no burdens of guilt. Experiment with your wife. As Miss A says, your wife may be panting for a more vigorous sex life.

We've touched on—and I want to emphasize that "touched" is the right word—introspective activity, intellectual activity and sexual activity. Now how about the body? Is it going to cooperate? Doesn't it start giving us trouble? Isn't it true that a man of twenty can abuse his body, drive it up to and past safe limits, fill it full of booze or pot, keep it going twenty-four or more hours without rest and it will forgive him his transgressions? And a man of forty or fifty has to treat his body with deference if for no other reason than that it may tire of all the mistreatment and lie down and die? Doesn't his heart slow down, or became erratic? Doesn't his stomach start rebelling? Don't his muscles groan for a little rest? Doesn't he . . .

Yes, yes, yes and yes. And then again, no, no, no and no. The body *does* slow down. But it doesn't *stop.* The fortieth and fiftieth years are milestones, not tombstones. Yes, there are new pains, new aches, but they usually mean far less than the sufferer thinks they mean. At twenty a pain in the chest is no more than a pain in the neck; at forty that same pain becomes, in the distorted view of the midolescent, a prelude to heart attack and death.

Some of the ills that midolescent flesh is heir to are imagined, but that doesn't mean the body can be ignored. Just the opposite. Middle-aged men must care for their bodies. Not coddle them; *care* for them. They have to keep their bodies, like their minds, active. Even here, though, there seem to be some collisions of opinions. In *The Years After Fifty,* Dr. Wingate M. Johnson says that Chauncey Depew, who died eighteen days short of his ninety-fourth birthday, has been quoted as saying that the only exercise he got came from acting as a pallbearer for his friends who *did* exercise. But Chauncey Depew seems to be in a minority. Most modern medical authorities feel that exercise, at least *some* exercise, is good for us, even for men who have had *genuine* heart attacks. Regular physicals are essential, not because middle-aged men have to keep up with how fast they are coming apart at the seams, but to be reassured that they are *not* coming apart. The man who learns that those shooting pains in his side are not the screams of an anguished heart but only the groans of gastric indigestion feels better not only in his side, but *all* over.

The heart, the mind, the body. They can be kept working for you, or allowed to work against you. The choice, as Mrs. B says, is yours. Youth is behind you, fatherhood is behind you, the years of ascendant accomplishment are behind you and you are on the long, level road of middle age. Walk, do not run.